33

A HISTORY OF
CANADIAN EXTERNAL RELATIONS

A History of
Canadian External Relations

By

G. P. ᴅᴇT. GLAZEBROOK

OXFORD UNIVERSITY PRESS
LONDON   TORONTO   NEW YORK
1950

Issued under the auspices of the
Canadian Institute of International Affairs

Oxford University Press, Amen House, Toronto
LONDON GLASGOW NEW YORK MELBOURNE
WELLINGTON BOMBAY CALCUTTA MADRAS CAPE TOWN
Geoffrey Cumberlege, Publisher to the University

Printed in Canada
by
THE HUNTER ROSE COMPANY LIMITED

PREFACE

THE first part of this historical study was published in 1942, and is reprinted with no changes other than the correction of a few errors.

The second part is of a somewhat different character. Before 1919 there was no Canadian foreign policy in the accepted sense, though there had long been important relations with the rest of the world. It is the development of that policy which is the theme of the second part of the book. In the view of the author a definite pattern emerges from the record, and reaches the end of a cycle as the book goes to press. From a purely colonial position in the world Canada has now taken her place as a middle power in international affairs, equipped with a diplomatic service and exhibiting a vigorous policy. The last stage in that progress, significant as it is, is no more than sketched from a stand so close to the events. It is to be hoped that for this, as for other parts of the long story of Canadian external relations, more specialized studies will be added to an already impressive list.

The author wishes to thank those scholars who have been good enough to assist with helpful criticism. To the Canadian Institute of International Affairs, which has inspired so much of the research into the subject of this book, he is indebted for encouragement and assistance.

G. P. deT. G.

University of Toronto,
January 1949.

CONTENTS

PART I. EXTERNAL RELATIONS TO 1914

PART II. CANADIAN FOREIGN POLICY

CONTENTS

PART I

EXTERNAL RELATIONS TO 1914

CHAPTER I

ORIGINS OF THE CANADIAN SOCIETY

THE history of Canada, as of all the Americas, begins with its discovery by Europeans as an incident in the expansion of trade; and continues as a result of the allied ambitions of commerce, missions, imperial designs, and pure adventure. Six states of Europe planted their flags in the new world: Spain, Portugal, France, England, Russia, and Holland. By chance or by plan the original expeditions landed at different parts of the long coast. Claims to territory were modified by the rivalries of the powers, so that the influence of each came to be exerted in a particular area, the whole character of which was coloured by the imported culture of that nation. It was the peculiar fate of Canada to receive the stamp of two of the European great powers; while by the fortunes of international politics the inward drives of Spain and Russia were arrested. Thus, if the shadowy story of the early migration of eastern and northern peoples be left aside, the history of the external relations of Canada has a beginning that is definite both in time and nature.

Before the coming of the Europeans there were in the lands that now comprise Canada no organized states: only Indian tribes living under conditions of barbarism or semi-barbarism, knowing little of their neighbours and nothing of a world beyond the limited expanse over which each group ranged. To this primitive scene the French, and after them the English, brought a culture that was utterly new and capable of revolutionizing the whole life of the region. The scientific knowledge of centuries was suddenly put before a people who knew none of it: sails to supplement the hard labour of the paddle, horses and wheeled vehicles, flint and steel, muskets for hunting or war, steel axes and knives. To these and other instruments were added the message of Christianity, borne by devoted missionaries; and the means of education, backed by the learning and culture of

3

the most advanced society of Europe. The French brought above all a sympathetic attitude toward the savage, a readiness to teach, an aim not to destroy but to live in amity. It was the tragedy of the Indian tribes that they lacked the adaptability to take advantage of their opportunity. It was true that the European brought evil as well as good: diseases that decimated the tribes; greed that led the traders to use all means, fair or foul; brandy and rum that turned the Indians to madmen; and a stimulation rather than a check to the inter-tribal wars. To some extent the natives did make use of European arts; and muskets, tools, and improved agriculture eased the life of the forest. But on balance the red man gained little and lost much by the coming of the European, in spite of all the magic gifts spread before him. He took much of the worst and little of the best; and, failing to assimilate himself to European culture, gradually saw his hunting-grounds possessed by the invader, his heritage narrowed to the pitiful reserves saved by tolerance from the broad acres of a once limitless domain.

North America was to be the white man's heritage. While these great continents appeared at first only to block a trade route to the east, experience soon proved that there were compensations, both directly for commercial interests and for the purposes of church and state. The fisheries of the banks of Newfoundland and in the Gulf of St. Lawrence were exploited even before there were settlements, and the fur trade developed from a casual barter by seamen to an industry worthy of pursuit. The early settlements made by France at Port Royal and Quebec owed their origin to chartered companies to whom the obligation of bringing colonists was a liability accepted in exchange for grants of monopoly rights in trade. When it became evident that the great St. Lawrence led not to China but to the rapids of Lachine, commercial energy found an outlet in the trade with the Indians, just as the search for the north-west passage by English adventurers was diverted to the trade at the south of Hudson Bay. The configuration of North America encouraged penetration toward the centre from widely separated coasts. The northern approach was the least hospitable and was used only by the great English trading company as an access to factories on the bay, and thence gradually inland for the better conduct of the fur trade. The Russian advance from the north-west was handicapped by mountain barriers and had no direct effect on Canada. Spaniards, the pioneers in American exploration, drove up from the south-west, but were blocked before they reached the future Canadian west. The English settlements on the Atlantic coast grew by degrees until the advance guard crossed the Alleghanies and pointed toward the very area into which the French were sending traders and soldiers. Moving on converging lines, the nationals of the two European powers increasingly found that they competed for the same prizes; and in a series of wars each strove to drive the other back to the sea. The Anglo-French colonial rivalry thus found local causes in North America as in other parts of the world; and, combined with more purely European issues, forbade a peaceful division of the still only partially explored continent. When any division did come it was between two groups both of English origin. Thus Canada developed under the impact of three political entities, first in turn and later in conjunction.

France planted her colonies at two points accessible by sea: on the Annapolis Basin of Acadia and at the natural fortress of Quebec. Both survived in spite of severity of climate, Indian attacks, and the lukewarm support of companies that were zealous only for trade; and both spread, with natural increase and immigration, into the neighbouring areas. There was, however, a marked difference in the strength of the social and cultural groups that resulted. In both colonies French institutions were introduced, but the French of Acadia never became as firmly knit as did those in Canada. In the former the social organization was less established, nor did the Acadians ever display, in peace or in war, the energy and unity characteristic of the Canadians. The Atlantic colony, moreover, was early distracted by the successive changes between French and English sovereignty; and the process of weakening was all but completed by the expulsion of the Acadians in 1755. It was on the banks of the St. Lawrence that the heritage of France was cherished and preserved. The form of government was an adaptation of that of a French province, closely under the orders of the court, and with administrative officers similar to those in France. The laws were based on the Custom of Paris. The church, while more ultramontane than in France, was the sole one tolerated; and the bishop, like those in France, was appointed by the King. Education was in the hands of the church. The system of landholding was also modelled on that of France, though it lost in the new world most of what remained of feudalism in the old.

By the fortunes of war Canada followed Acadia into the British Empire in 1763; but if France no longer held political sway in North America the imprint which she had made stood fresh and strong. Happy under a tolerant rule, Canadians underwent hardly more change than in owing allegiance to another flag. And even the flag continued to wave symbolically over Canada—to wave long after it had been cut down at home. For the *fleur-de-lys,* emblem of the old régime, meant more in that once Bourbon province than the *tricolore* of the revolution and of nineteenth-century France. The speech of the eighteenth century, the church, and the laws were at times threatened but never seriously endangered. The society of the St. Lawrence remained as it had been before the conquest: primarily agrarian with little instinct for trade, conservative in outlook, attached to the church, introspective and self-sufficient, closely knit, and untouched by the North American pressure toward worldly progress. This orphaned France, cut off from its parent as much by ideas as by conquest, gave to central Canada its first population and an enduring element in the later whole. There could be no further additions to the population by migration from France; but the original stock from the provinces of the northwest, numbering no more than 65,000 at the time of the fall of Quebec, multiplied and spread far beyond the bounds of settlement at the height of the old régime.

The transfer of British people, ideas, and institutions to the lands that were to become the Dominion of Canada was both direct and indirect: either straight from the British Isles, or after passing through a process of modification in the other and older British colonies of the Atlantic seaboard. It is only after six or seven decades that the pattern alters, to show British and American peoples distinct politically, and to allow their influence to be labelled as entirely different. Even in that stage it is to be taken into account that the American revolution could not remove all traces of racial origin. Of the three countries contributing main threads to the Canadian fabric before the more diversified immigration of the nineteenth century, France and England had in common that they were both European, England and the United States that they were peopled by the same stock. The second relation showed more points of similarity than the first.

Nova Scotia affords grounds for an investigation of British and American influences both before and after those became politically two. The future of Nova Scotia was made of immediate urgency both to Britain and her colonies because of its strategic position in the Anglo-French struggle. When Louisburg was returned to France as part of the settlement of 1748 a new base was begun at Halifax in the following year, and was developed as a naval station and seat of government. The deportation of the Acadians on the eve of the Seven Years' War lessened the threat of attack from within; but the scanty British population—estimated at 5,000—offered little security for the peninsula from external aggression. In New England there was apprehension lest Nova Scotia once more fall into French hands and become a danger to fisheries and commerce. William Shirley, governor of Massachusetts, long urged also the positive importance of the colony, pointing to its value for naval power in the Atlantic, and its ability to provide masts for the royal navy. For a time opinion in Massachusetts favoured the annexation of Nova Scotia as a precautionary measure, but more consistently urged a policy of anglicization combined with increased military strength. The interests of the governments of both Great Britain and the American colonies continued to depend on the successive political situations in the continent. With the fall of French power both were able to feel a sense of security that lessened their concern for Nova Scotia; but when the picture again altered to place an international frontier between British colonies and the new United States, Halifax took on a new significance as a British naval base.

Meanwhile New England had made a mark on Nova Scotia that was to be more lasting than its shifting political policies. Toward the end of the Seven Years' War settlers began to move in from New England, encouraged by offers of land and promises of civil and religious liberty. The appeals through proclamations and associations were the more readily received since a congestion of population in parts of New England created an economic pressure. While settlements were made or attempted in several parts of Nova Scotia, the ones most favoured were the deserted lands of the Acadian farmers and the valley of the St. John River. With New Englanders forming an increasingly larger proportion of the population, their influence began to be shown in all aspects of the life of the province, from architecture to political institutions. In the latter their aims not infrequently ran counter to those of the officials and colonists who had come directly from England, and amongst whom there was a small but powerful conservative element. The establishment of an elected assembly introduced the province to democratic government; and when the assembly met it proved to be largely composed of New Englanders. An attempt was made to introduce the New England system of local government by the town (township) meeting, but without success; and the legal practice of England was also preserved against proposals for Americanization.[1]

Being longer under French rule, Canada was later in receiving English-speaking immigrants. The vanguard who followed on the heels of Wolfe's army, though few in number, soon made their presence felt. Quite frankly they had come for trade, and to the governors who looked coldly on these interlopers in an Eden of orderly French, they pointed to the Royal Proclamation and the scattered broadsheets which had urged them to take advantage of this new British domain. Coming in the main from the neighbouring colonies and Scotland, they were neither able nor willing to fit themselves to the agrarian economy and authoritarian government that they found in operation: government and laws must be re-moulded to the English pattern, affording an institutional basis for economic development and external trade. So long as their numbers remained small, the local officials were able to check the bustling reformers, even when supported by the sedate periods of the dispatches from the board of trade. But if they could lock the door of the house which they had so carefully built, not even the most vigorous governors could save it when the very foundations were swept away by the American revolution. Paradoxically enough, it was not the appeal of the radical general congress at Philadelphia that caused the upheaval in Quebec, but the coming of the defeated tories, themselves fugitives from radicalism.

It was at once obvious that the United Empire Loyalists would modify the character of the population. In Nova Scotia, already dominated by the English-speaking, the change was rather to

[1] For the influence of New England on Nova Scotia see J. B. Brebner, *New England's Outpost: Acadia Before the Conquest of Canada* (New York, 1927), and *The Neutral Yankees of Nova Scotia: A Marginal Colony during the Revolutionary Years* (New York, 1937); also M. L. Hansen, *The Mingling of the Canadian and American Peoples* (New Haven and Toronto, 1940), I.

reinforce ties with England that had become somewhat attenuated by early migrations from New England. New Brunswick, carved out of Nova Scotia, was a direct result of loyalist additions to the scanty population of the St. John Valley. In Canada the result was not a modification but a complete alteration of the balance of population. Instead of a small group of traders as sole representatives of British stock, there now appeared *émigrés* from persecution, loyal to the crown—men whose claims could not be disputed, and whose very presence spelt a new Canada. So much was obvious. But that these same men should become the allies of the traders in seeking democratic institutions was quite unexpected. "I have great Reason to believe", wrote the governor, "these unfortunate people have suffered too Much by Committees and Houses of Assembly, to have retained any prepossession in favor of that Mode of Government."[2] Haldimand, of course, was wrong—wrong because he saw the basis of division in the thirteen colonies as between radicals and tories instead of between those who would or would not take up arms against the King. As in the maritime provinces, the loyalists in Canada built a strong bulwark against any break in the British connection; but they were determined that the colony should be British in local institutions as well as in its imperial setting. Just as the migration from New England to Nova Scotia had hurried on the establishment of an elected assembly, so, a generation later, the movement for elected institutions in Canada received the necessary impetus from the loyalist refugees. Those who followed the loyalists from the United States to Canada were influenced more by economic than political motives; and, as it proved, were in some cases opposed to the British connection and advocated republicanism. Though no reliable figures are available, a contemporary, an immigrant of 1808, estimated in 1814 that six-tenths of the population of Upper Canada either were born in the United States or were children of American immigrants.[3]

In all the provinces the War of 1812 brought to an end the first period of immigration. During the period of hostilities

[2] W. P. M. Kennedy (ed.), *Statutes, Treaties and Documents of the Canadian Constitution, 1713-1929* (Toronto, 1930), 171.

[3] M. Smith, *A Geographical View of the British Possessions in North America* (Baltimore, 1814), 51.

Americans could not cross the border, and when hostilities were ended there was less desire to emigrate to the lands of a recent enemy. There was also a policy, arising out of disaffection during the war, to restrict immigrants who might further endanger the loyalty of the populations. Not only did positive encouragement come to an end, but land-grants to aliens were either refused or accompanied by conditions. What the provinces lost in settlers from the United States they hoped to gain by immigration from the British Isles. The times were propitious. The years after Waterloo brought increasing hardship, particularly to the poorest classes, who were led by propaganda and organized aid to turn to emigration as an escape. Of the flood of people who found their way from Britain and the continent to North America the British provinces received a share. For the most part the newcomers were poor, some of them destitute. There were British families with some little capital who brought furniture, books, and even pianos to the virgin forest of Upper Canada; Irish families who faced the miseries of the voyage and the uncertainty of a new land in flight from the horrors of famine; groups of Germans uprooted from their native soil by economic or political motives. Agriculture in Upper Canada attracted those who had the means to secure land and begin pioneer farming. For others there were possibilities of employment in lumbering, ship-building, or the construction of canals and railways.

Both for the newcomers and the older inhabitants the success of the venture turned principally on economic conditions. Whenever employment was available and markets receptive both groups were satisfied: in leaner years both had cause for regret. Opinion in every province oscillated between an anxiety for immigrants and an apprehension lest they should be too numerous or too great a burden on the community. Pauper immigration was particularly feared in an age when no adequate provision was made for the poor in the country either of origin or of settlement. In 1842 a fleet of ships landed immigrants in New Brunswick, where in principle they were wanted but where in practice they had to find employment or be a public expense. A St. Andrews paper reported that the poorhouse was already crowded with the wives and children of destitute immigrants, and in Saint John an editor "heard that several destitute blind persons, and even unfortunate maniacs, have arrived in this city in some of the emigrant vessels this Spring, who of course will at once add to our already heavy Parish Charges".[4] The crisis caused by the sudden coming of thousands of diseased and destitute Irish, driven by the famine of 1846, turned to a ghastly tragedy at Quebec, where cholera and typhus decimated their ranks, carried off doctors and priests who ministered to them, and spread fever throughout Canada.

In spite of such real drawbacks the advantages of securing large numbers of immigrants were seen as greater than the disadvantages, and the governments of the provinces endeavoured to secure a steady flow. In this they found themselves in unsuccessful competition with the United States, in spite of lower ocean rates and the efforts of agents and emigration societies. One particularly annoying phenomenon was that only the poorer immigrants were landed at Halifax, Saint John, or Quebec, while the more prosperous ones were carried on to American ports. Emigration, either of those who stayed but a few months in the British provinces or of the native-born, was a constant drain on the population, unrecorded but not unnoticed. It was an old story. The first chapter tells of the forcible removal of the French of Nova Scotia and Prince Edward Island to the colonies along the Atlantic seaboard. Later emigration was voluntary, and at times, from political motives, such as in the case of Americans who returned to their country during the War of 1812 or of the *émigrés* of 1837; but the largest and most persistent emigration was owing to economic causes. Opportunities, both in agriculture and industry in the United States, constantly drew the young men.[5] On rare occasions they came back, and there was also some compensating movement of Americans to the British provinces; but on balance the latter were losing people to their greater neighbour, as they were well aware. Lower Canada was most conscious of its losses, but it was not the only one. "An exchange paper", wrote a New Brunswick editor, "says there are 4,000 Nova Scotians in Boston and 200,000 Canadians in the United States. Can any person inform us how many New-Brunswickers are now residing in the neighbouring Republic?

4 *St. John New Brunswicker*, July 15, 1842.
5 For a full study of this subject see Hansen, *Mingling of the Canadian and American Peoples*, chap. VI.

There must be a goodly number there. We are rapidly *annexing* ourselves by emigration."[6] No answer to the editor's query could be found in provincial records, but the census of the United States for 1850 showed 100,000 persons born in the British provinces, and that for 1860 a quarter of a million.

A study of the flow of people to and from the provinces reveals that by the middle of the nineteenth century no major changes had resulted in the character of the population. Prince Edward Island, blocked in its development by absentee landlords, had had virtually no immigrants. The population of New Brunswick remained small and homogeneous except for French settlements in the northern part of the province. Nova Scotia and Lower Canada had undergone no basic ethnological changes; and only in Upper Canada can a comparatively rapid growth in population be attributed largely to immigration. British Columbia had a startling inrush of prospectors when gold was discovered, but the miners made but a shifting population which drifted in or out according to the prosperity of the gold fields. Assiniboia had a mixed population of Indians, half-breeds, active or retired servants of the Hudson's Bay Company, a few British and Canadians, and Americans whose increasing numbers and influence were the significant aspects of the colony's population. All in all, immigration before confederation wove no pattern of population as varied as that caused by the coming of Europeans and Asiatics in later years. But if there was less mixture of nations and races, the effects of the steady flow of people from all parts of the British Isles, and of the exchange of population between the United States and British North America, may be judged to have had results as great, if not greater.

II

The origins of the people and the constant intercourse with other countries were from the first strongly reflected in the cultural life of the provinces. The schools of New France, the first of which were established before the middle of the seventeenth century, were in conscious imitation of those of France itself. To the extent that they differed it was because the con-

---

[6] *The Gleaner* (Miramichi), Dec. 30, 1850.

ditions of the colony did not allow for an exact duplication of the schools of the older society. When a college was founded by the Jesuits at Quebec the course was made as similar as possible to that in the Jesuit colleges of France. The text-books used in both primary and secondary education were brought from France, as indeed they had to be, since no printing was done in Canada under the French régime. The change from French to British rule threatened for a time to bring with it the abolition of the French system of education in favour of that of England. The whole staff of the Jesuit College returned to France, and restrictions on the religious orders seriously reduced the numbers of school-teachers. Undoubtedly it was an aim of British policy to introduce protestant education into the newly-acquired colony, but it was an aim that was before long abandoned. While provision was made for protestant schools for the minority, the education of the French majority returned to a parochial basis. Education became an essential element in the cement of French-Canadian nationalism. One other danger from abroad was seen in the practice, said to be common, by which French Canadians sent their sons to the United States to learn English and study commerce and industry. Objections were raised both on religious grounds and because it was said that the boys came to compare Canada unfavourably to the United States.[7]

The early educational institutions of Nova Scotia showed their European origin as did those of New France. The legislature of the colony followed the contemporary rule that only protestants might teach; and for some years a struggle went on between those who sought to keep a restricted and denominational system and those who urged the common schools. Similarly in New Brunswick different, and sometimes conflicting, points of view of education were brought by the various groups of settlers. In the early grammar schools all teachers were members of the Church of England, whether in orders or not; and the Society for the Propagation of the Gospel sent teachers at a time when they were badly needed. In 1820 the Madras system of schools, under which the older pupils taught the younger, was imported from England. It was not until 1871 that a system of free and non-sectarian schools was set up by a pro-

[7] *La Minerve* (Montreal), Feb. 6, 1853.

vincial statute. In Upper Canada the school system was influenced from Europe and the United States. A few private schools were opened from time to time, following the English public school tradition; but more characteristic were the common schools provided for under the act drawn up by Egerton Ryerson. These undenominational and free schools were worked out mainly from American models, with certain elements drawn from Germany and Ireland. In Vancouver Island a system of district schools was inaugurated while the colony was still under the Hudson's Bay Company, and in 1865 all common schools were made undenominational and free. The Roman Catholic Church, however, established schools in 1858-9 and the Church of England one for boys and one for girls at about the same time.

Many external influences may likewise be seen in the universities founded in the eastern and central provinces. As in England, opinion was divided as to whether higher education should be for the few or the many, and whether it should be denominational and exclusive or non-sectarian. King's College in Nova Scotia was founded in the former tradition, while Dalhousie University was explicitly to have no political or religious tests. Similarly in Upper Canada came a tug-of-war over King's College at Toronto, in which the forces opposed to denominationalism proved to be the stronger. Those who would have the doors of the universities opened only to the few were impressed, perhaps, by the fear that such levelling would lead toward American republicanism; but while American ideas encouraged those who wished to extend higher education to the many, there was no indication of an accompaniment of political philosophy. Models for organization and curricula were found in the British Isles and, to a lesser extent, in the United States and Germany. Bishop's College at Lennoxville consciously followed Oxford and Cambridge. For Queen's University in Kingston, Edinburgh was taken as a model. King's College in Toronto drew on the experience of English, Scottish, Irish, and German universities. Acadia University alone, because of immigration from New England, was largely affected by American designs. The universities of all the provinces had this in common, that they recruited their teaching staffs largely from the British Isles, by which means a constant contact was maintained with British scholarship and pedagogy.[8]

Beyond the formal education in schools and universities was the less organized reading by the public. In this, as in the textbooks, the direct influence of the culture of other countries may readily be seen. To New France, where the absence of printing forbade the competition of any local productions, books of all kinds were imported from France, and apparently widely read. In the libraries of the citizens of Quebec and Montreal works on religion and the Latin classics rubbed shoulders with contemporary literature and the critical writings of the *philosophes*.[9] After New France was politically separated from its motherland the cultural tie remained, and French influence was felt both directly through imported books and indirectly in the writings of French Canadians. There was, however, before the conquest as after, a selective process adopted in the acceptance of French ideas. French Canada was strongly Catholic, conservative, and opposed to revolution. And, while rejecting that part of French culture which contravened those principles, a local theme was added in the emphasis on French-Canadian nationalism. The comment of a recent observer from France is valid for the Quebec of many generations.

Les Canadiens ayant gardé les qualités intellectuelles qui caractérisent notre race, on voit pour ainsi dire à chaque page dans leurs œuvres, la manifestation de cette clarté, de cette méthode et de cette logique qui sont si françaises. Leur littérature se rattache donc à la nôtre, non pas seulement parce qu'elle a été écrite dans la même langue, mais aussi parce que toutes les deux procèdent d'un tempérament identique et d'une formation intellectuelle dont les éléments essentiels sont les mêmes. Elle est forcément, en outre d'inspiration française, c'est-à-dire que les auteurs, d'une façon générale, y développent les mêmes idées et les mêmes sentiments que l'on trouve dans la nôtre. Mais, bien entendu, cela ne signife pas qu'ils adoptent toutes nos opinions. Certaines tendances de notre esprit leur répugnent absolument, et c'est pourquoi ni le

[8] Sir Robert Falconer, "Scottish Influence in the Higher Education of Canada" (*Proceedings and Transactions of the Royal Society of Canada*, (1927), "English Influence on the Higher Education of Canada" (*ibid.*, 1928), "American Influence on the Higher Education of Canada" (*ibid.*, 1930).

[9] R. M. Saunders, "The Cultural Development of New France Before 1760" (*Essays in Canadian History*, ed. by R. Flenley, Toronto, 1939), 329.

réalisme, ni le scepticisme, ni nos idées révolutionnaires n'apparaissent dans leurs ouvrages. . . . Les écrivains canadiens français, idéalistes conservateurs, profondément croyants, ne ressemblent, par conséquent, qu'à certains des nôtres.[10]

English Canada too leant heavily on its mother country for the provision of books. From the comfortable houses of Halifax merchants to the isolated huts of Hudson's Bay traders English classics and contemporary books were to be found. Advertisements by booksellers show a range of imported works, and some favourite authors, such as Dickens, were reprinted in the local newspapers. While the writers of English Canada were not influenced by an aim of racial survival, they were none the less followers of English models. An occasional case may be found of other sources, such as the effect of Mazzini's philosophy on F. G. Cameron; but more common was the rule of looking to standard Victorian writers for ideas and form.[11] Canadian writers in both languages sought to depict Canada and Canadian scenes, but their works had no more natural a ring than the diaries and commentaries of English immigrants or travellers. It was not until the end of the nineteenth century that a native character could be seen in Canadian literature, and even then it developed slowly and with hesitation.

In other arts there was even more borrowing from abroad. Music knows no national boundaries, and the culture of any land would be poor indeed without acceptance of the great European composers, whose works were performed in the British American provinces as elsewhere. The folk music of the Province of Quebec was almost the only instance of native growth. The drama in Canada was, at least until the twentieth century, derivative in origin and largely so in performance. Painting, too, was chiefly the work of foreign artists who had migrated to Canada. Of the artists of the confederation era Berthon was born and trained in France; Jacobi was a Prussian by origin and a recognized painter when he came to Canada; Daniel Fowler was an English artist who migrated to Canada for the sake of his health; and Krieghoff came from Rotterdam.[12] Architecture in

[10] Georges Vattier, *Essai sur la mentalité canadienne-française* (Paris, 1928), 133.

[11] Lorne Pierce, "English Canadian Literature" *(The Royal Society of Canada: Fifty Years Retrospect,* Toronto, 1932), 57.

[12] Newton MacTavish, *The Fine Arts in Canada* (Toronto, 1925), 9 ff.

Quebec showed interesting adaptations to local climatic conditions, but elsewhere developed no new characteristics.

From earliest days the colonists in North America had brought their churches with them, and links with the countries of origin were maintained not only by subsequent immigration, but also by integral connections in organization, relationship to governments, or the work of the missionary societies. Canada in the old régime was uncompromisingly Roman Catholic, and, aided by Jesuit influence, had become distinctly ultramontane. Severed from France before the revolution, Canada had never to endure the religious vicissitudes that afflicted the church in the mother country, and looked askance at the anti-clericalism that marked revolutionary France. In other provinces were found Scottish and Irish Roman Catholic majorities, who shared with those of Lower Canada the organization and doctrines of the church, with a common centre in Rome. The Church of England was carried to British America as naturally as the Roman Church to French America. In all provinces it was in a minority position, but as the church of the majority of the influential groups in government and business it held a place higher than the mere numbers of its members would have given, and in Nova Scotia and New Brunswick it was for a time legally established. With the support of the Hudson's Bay Company the church was extended into the prairies and across the Rockies.

The presbyterian churches in the British provinces reflected the divisions that had come in the Church of Scotland. Presbyterianism also came from Ireland and the United States. The methodist churches have special interest as an external influence, since they brought to North America the evangelicalism of the English middle class and of the United States. Although their double source strengthened the Canadian Methodists both in numbers and ideas, it led in time to the necessity of a choice between American and English connections. While the Church of England in Canada was one of the bulwarks of oligarchy and conservatism, the Methodists stood for nineteenth-century English liberalism combined with the frontier spirit of North America. The Methodist circuit rider fitted into a landscape of primitive roads and pioneer farms as did the Anglican bishop into the more esoteric atmosphere of Toronto toryism or of the Halifax Banking Company. Other and smaller denominations appeared in the provinces as groups of immigrants from the United States, the British Isles, or continental Europe planted their churches in the new soil, sometimes greatly modified under new conditions, sometimes little changed from the parent stock. Together they added richness and colour and variety to the culture of British North America.[13]

III

The relations of the provinces with the outside world were affected by the geography of North America as well as by national origin. Had there been a block of population advancing steadily from the seaboard inland the story might have been a very different one. But conditions forbade such a development. The Atlantic colonies of Prince Edward Island, Nova Scotia, and New Brunswick looked eastward on the ocean and maintained connections by sea with the United Kingdom, the West Indies, and the neighbouring New England states. Between them and Canada was a long stretch of largely unsettled country over which communication by means other than rail was difficult and at best seasonal. Though Canadians owed a heavy debt to the St. Lawrence, their route to Europe was past rather than through the maritime provinces; and in its lower reaches the river was only a link, for, unlike the people of the maritimes, the eyes of Canadians were turned toward the west. Another and a longer break in settlement, caused by the wild stretches to the north of Lake Superior, separated Canada from the little colony of Assiniboia, which, isolated on the west as it was on the east, felt an increasing pull to the American settlements on the upper Red River. Far to the west the colonies of Vancouver Island and British Columbia fronted on the Pacific, and the stern ranges of mountains set up behind them a barrier more formidable than the wide prairie. They also were maritime provinces, maintaining contact with the American states nearby; but the distance to England was longer by thousands of miles than from the provinces on the Atlantic coast of North America. Spaced across the wide continent were these foundations on which a single

---

[13] On the protestant churches see G. W. Brown, "The Early Methodist Church and the Canadian Point of View" (*Report of the Canadian Historical Association*, 1938), and "The Formative Period of the Canadian Protestant Churches" (*Essays in Canadian History*, ed. by R. Flenley).

British dominion was later to be built; all for a time having as close relations with other countries as they had with each other. And thus the external influences on the various colonies operated concurrently, and were accentuated by the comparative isolation of each colony from the other.

The political philosophy and institutions of the provinces came from beyond their own boundaries, though modified in response to local conditions and progressive stages of development. The oldest colonies, Nova Scotia and Canada, under the successive French and English administrations, were long governed by appointed officials; but the permanent gift of England to the political life of her northern as to her southern colonies was the elective representative system. It was this which replaced both the centralized French bureaucracy and the conciliar system of early British rule. It was applied both to local and central governments. In the former the municipal councils were set up to take over the functions of appointed officers, and in the provincial capitals parliaments were called to follow the ancient traditions of the mother of parliaments. More than one governor called his little parliament with all the pomp that he could command; and, even in the forests of Upper Canada, the representatives legislated for the peace, welfare, and good government of their fellow colonists as their forefathers had done in the stately surroundings of Westminster. Criminal and civil law, the form of the courts, and, more important, the spirit of English justice, were faithfully reproduced in the new world. Only in French Canada was there an exception, for there the French civil law, so long in practice, was allowed to remain.

Political ideas, as distinct from political forms, came through individuals rather than by official action. Perhaps nowhere else could have been found as great a variety of political views as in the British provinces, for there they were held not only by those of conservative or liberal or radical temperaments, but were borne by every ship that docked, over every road that led from the south. The sources of ideas corresponded to the origins of the main elements in population, with one outstanding exception: the political philosophy of French Canada showed little reflection of that of contemporary France. The policies adopted by individuals or groups in the provinces carried at times touches of continental Europe, but the major programmes may be traced in most cases to either the United Kingdom or the United States, or to both. Such imported ideas were seldom untouched by local conditions and traditions, but only an elaborate study would disclose the degree of transmutation. Some of the party leaders were native-born, others were recent immigrants; and each group had adherents of the right or the left. Robert Gourlay, John Beverley Robinson, and Robert Baldwin had all drunk deep of English political thought. Such diverse figures as Thomas Haliburton, William Lyon Mackenzie, and Louis Joseph Papineau drew both on England and the United States. Just as the countries of origin sent their rich and their poor, so they sent their conservatives and their liberals. Letters, newspapers, books, and travellers kept the links intact and added the most recent developments.

It was no accident that in the British provinces could be seen in the years after Waterloo the same fundamental cleavage between the forces of conservatism and the forces of change that was so evident in Britain, in Europe, and in the United States. In each the struggle took its particular form. Jacksonian democracy triumphed at Washington, the liberals of continental Europe fought for their cause on a hundred fields, and the English parliament was invaded by victorious reform. The provinces too had their "reformers", seeking to dispossess entrenched oligarchies in the name of liberalism. The right of majorities, rights of the people, the power of the purse, elected institutions, cabinet government—these cries were not first heard in British North America. The grievances attacked were local, but the line of attack and the cures proposed were coloured strongly by the thought of other lands. The provinces had their revolutionaries and their moderates. A Mackenzie or a Papineau manned the barricades like any Parisian of 1830 and 1848; a Baldwin or a Howe would have fitted readily into the left wing of the English whig party.

Newspapers were full of political news. No doubt their readers were interested in foreign events as such, but they consciously or unconsciously looked at them through the eyes of domestic politics. The French revolution of 1848 was a case in point. Local newspapers, following it with great attention, tried to draw from it arguments for their respective policies. At first *La Minerve* saw in the revolution the triumph of the liberal principles which it entertained itself, and began to coin phrases about the mother country.

Puissent les nobles enfants de la France que nous pouvons aimer comme des frères, sans manquer à nos devoirs envers la couronne d'Angleterre, remplir avec calme, avec dignité, cet acte de souveraineté nationale.[14]

A few weeks later the editor felt it necessary to explain why he gave so much space to the revolution.

En publiant une revue des évenements gigantesques qui se déroulent chaque jour en Europe; nous avons cru faire plaisir à nos lecteurs, tout en servant les intérêts du pays. Pouvons-nous rester étrangères au réveils des peuples, des nationalités? Pouvons-nous rester froids en présence du spectacle grandiose qui nous est offert sur tous les points du continent à la fois? Ne devons-nous pas, au contraire, en les suivant, d'un œil attentif; y puiser d'utiles leçons de sages avertissements, pour travailler avec persévérance, avec energie, avec prudence, à assurer les droits et les libertés de notre bien aimée patrie.[15]

As the revolution progressed, and socialism became a leading issue, *La Minerve* became worried, and was obliged to make pointed remarks about the difference between liberty and licence, lest the growing extremes of old France be followed in the new world. More conservative French papers, as well as the English papers, were even less tolerant and more suspicious. The Second Republic gave way to the Second Empire, and while the conservatives may have been soothed, the radicals were not. *Le Pays* could not admire Napoleon III because it held that individual liberty was more important than military glory. Some of its contemporaries differed. "*La Patrie*, bleu d'habitude, est devenu indigo de colère parce que certains membres Canadiens français ont cru que l'occasion de la naissance de Louis Napoléon Bonaparte n'intéressait pas assez le peuple Canadien pour authoriser la législature à se donner un congé sur un pareil prétexte. . . ."[16]

Two years later *Le Pays* saw possible trouble in Europe, and told its readers that they could not be disinterested, since America was bound by many ties to Europe.[17] Such an idea, however, was not characteristic. The English Canadians, and to some extent the

---

[14] *La Minerve*, March 30, 1848.
[15] *Ibid.*, May 18, 1848.
[16] *Le Pays* (Montreal), April 12, 1856.
[17] *Ibid.*, March 23, 1858.

French Canadians, had tangible interests in their connection with Great Britain: government, trade, defence, immigration. The French Canadians had nothing so solid on which to base a connection. They therefore looked for common ideas or for new ideas in the same way, and only in a greater degree, that Canadians studied Italy, Russia, Hungary, or any other continental power.

In the realm of political ideas the provinces were closely attached to the wider world. But a link more tangible bound them in the practice of government to a power beyond their shores; for colonial institutions operated within the framework of an imperial structure. The degree of control actually exercised in the colonies by the metropolitan government differed from decade to decade. The direction of change was toward greater provincial autonomy, and by the middle of the nineteenth century responsible government was recognized as in practice in all the eastern colonies. Responsible government, however, was intended to be limited to domestic affairs, and indeed no demand for its extension beyond that existed until a much later date. There remained the definition of "domestic". To Durham it seemed feasible to draw the line by an explicit division of powers, but the list of reserved subjects which he suggested would never have been generally acceptable in the colonies. To remove immigration and crown lands, which he rightly saw to have imperial phases, altogether from the control of the provinces was politically impossible. No definite division was made, and legal flexibility allowed the interpretation of domestic to be widened. Sometimes this was for the benefit and at the insistence of the provinces, notably in regulation of tariffs; sometimes it was against the will of the provinces, particularly in the case of defence. There was no doubt that the relations of the provinces with foreign states were to be conducted by the imperial government; and the only ground for variation was in the decisions on policy. Tariff and trade questions generally came increasingly within the control of the provincial legislatures, but the determination of "high policy" was indisputably in the imperial orbit.

If the imperial connection, in the sense of control, slackened in the nineteenth century, their position within the British Empire was still a real and ever-present factor for the people of the British provinces in North America; and they would have been dull of wit indeed if they had never stopped to assess the assets and the liabilities, the best form and the possible future of that connection. In the early years of the provinces, during and after the American revolution, there were elements in the provinces which were secretly or openly disloyal. Recent American immigrants to Nova Scotia would, had they been able, have joined the revolutionary cause; and in the War of 1812 similar groups in Upper Canada gave cause for apprehension, and from them individuals returned to the United States when the war broke out. After 1815, however, there is no evidence of similar disaffection except to a limited extent in Upper Canada during the period of rebellion; and there is little evidence of any direct relation between the origins of the people and views as to the future position of the provinces. Nor did the differences of opinion follow provincial boundaries: rather they cut across racial groups, in any one of which great diversity of attitude might be found. Three possible courses may be distinguished as considered in the second quarter of the nineteenth century: independence, annexation to the United States, or continuance of the imperial connection.

The first was mentioned from time to time but was never widely supported. Not a few observers concluded that it was quite impracticable and would only lead to annexation. William Lyon Mackenzie expressed this most pithily when he concluded that, "on Britain we must depend, or with America we must unite, for national purposes. There is no third course."[18] Annexation as a direct policy was more seriously advocated. The economic progress of the United States was an obvious argument for annexation, or at least for closer relations. One compromise proposal came from the Quebec board of trade, that the provinces should have in the United States a representative to look after their commercial interests, but the British government's reply was that they were better left in the hands of its ministers and consuls.[19] Apart from those with Great Britain, the closest relations of the British provinces were with the United States. In every aspect of their lives the colonists were influenced by their neighbours; and perhaps it was partly because of the strength of that influence that the majority of the people of the provinces

[18] *Mackenzie's Weekly Message* (Toronto), Oct. 22, 1859.
[19] Public Archives of Canada, *Series G,* vol. 148, p. 142.

Empire as one family, and by working out the prosperity of that family through its own internal relations independent of foreign interference.[26]

The closer integration of the empire, whether by informal understanding or constitutional change, would more readily be secured if England knew more of the colonies. Pained feelings were not infrequently expressed at the lack of interest shown by Englishmen in the affairs of British North America. The editor of a tory paper in Toronto was shocked to read a speech by Lord Stanley on the state of the world in which he completely ignored Canada.

We do not wish to misunderstand our position. We are Provincials. We are taught it daily; but still with all this sense of our shortcomings, judged by a cosmopolitan standard, we do not think that justice is done to us. Pained are we to think that we rank far higher at Washington than at St. James. . . . Would a minister of the Crown in Canada, in London be looked upon in any other light, than a person to whom something civil has to be said, and to be got rid of, so soon as official business is dispatched? Contrast his reception with some *Furst* of Schwarzburg Radolstadt. . . .[27]

To remove this ignorance or indifference writers in the maritime provinces set themselves to explain the colonies to the mother country. Others pleaded for closer integration. "We wish England to give up addressing her colonies as a separate or third party", wrote a Toronto editor, "We wish Colonial to be adopted as British interests, and we desire to argue for them only to the extent that they are British. Let British or foreign then be our simple question. Let England view Canada as part of herself, —and let Canada never forget her duty as a part of the Empire."[28] As positive machinery for closer co-operation two suggestions were made from time to time—a permanent representative of Canada in London, and colonial representatives in the house of commons. But these were not pressed, and those who most actively supported the continuance of the imperial connection

[26] *The Pilot*, quoted in *Quebec Gazette*, March 18, 1846.
[27] *British Colonist*, April 3, 1858.
[28] *Ibid.*, April 14, 1841.

devoted their efforts either to more general arguments or to proving that the provinces profited by their position within the empire. Neither they nor those who took a more critical view could for long neglect two subjects most concretely apparent as colonial interests—defence and external trade.

CHAPTER II

DIPLOMACY AND WAR

INTERNATIONAL rivalries and war were carried by Europeans to North America together with political institutions, economic structure, and culture. Not that warfare of a kind was strange to the aborigines: on the contrary, the tribes fought each other frequently and with a ferocity that made the name of Indian a by-word for cruelty and a terror to the settlers. Thanks in part to their own inept handling of the natives the white men were from the first subject to Indian attacks; but they did not stop at defence, or even at calculated intervention in inter-tribal quarrels. To the warfare which they found and could scarcely have ended they added that which sprang from the competition of distant states, fought with weapons vastly more destructive than the tomahawk. It was in the course of world wars that the north of the continent passed wholly under British sovereignty; and the process of delimitation of political boundaries continued with far-reaching diplomacy as its means and war as the final arbiter.

For the colonies which were to form the nucleus of the Canadian Dominion the causes, the course, and the results of war were placed in a mixed setting of local disputes and the colonial and foreign policies of European great powers. The very fact that they were colonies implied that the determination and conduct of policy were beyond their orbit, and that terms of peace were reached at negotiations in which they took no part. It equally followed that a responsibility for the results of policy rested on the imperial authorities. The royal army and navy were intended to bear the brunt of fighting, supported by such colonial forces as were from time to time available. The position, then, in respect of the wars fought on Canadian soil was that the colonials had no voice in their origination or conclusion but did have a subordinate place in the campaigns. The advantages and disadvantages of that position might be—and indeed long have been—debated. On the one hand the colonies enjoyed the prestige and experience of the British government, and on the other hand were made to suffer for its mistakes or the results of policies unrelated to their immediate interests. If they could have been regarded as unexposed to attack except as a result of imperial diplomacy the defence provided from England would have been unnecessary. It is, however, safe to conclude that when defence was needed—whatever the cause—the British armed forces were essential. How far those forces could effectively operate in or for the colonies depended in part on the demands of campaigns in other parts of the world and in part on the geography of North America.

The half century from the end of the Seven Years' War to the end of the Napoleonic wars is an unrivalled quarry for the study of diplomacy and war in relation to the British provinces. In the British Empire and in France, the two countries from which came the people of Canada and Nova Scotia, major revolutions broke out, leading to issues which might be expected to divide the people of the colonies, and to international complications of the most far-reaching character. The response of the populations of Nova Scotia and Canada to the appeals of revolutionary and anti-revolutionary parties throws not a little light on the character and points of view of the groups which successively came to the provinces. The two wars of the period demonstrate the changing degree and the nature of co-operation between imperial and colonial forces; while the European alignments illustrate the effect of the international balance on the making of war and peace in North America. The rôle of the people of Nova Scotia and Canada in the American revolution was almost entirely negative, but the provinces as such were not unimportant in its outbreak, in the strategy of the war, and in the settlement that followed. That the transfer of Quebec from the French to the British Empire would influence the attitude in the other colonies had long been predicted. The removal of French pressure from the north gave to the thirteen colonies greater freedom to press their claims against the mother country. But while the fall of New France thus eased the situation of the thirteen colonies it did not by any means preclude the possibility of a war on two fronts. Sir Guy Carleton, early discerning that he might inherit the military power of his French predecessors and use the fortress of Quebec and the trained militia of the colony if force should be needed, bent his efforts toward securing the loyalty and active aid of the French Canadians. That the Quebec Act of 1774 was the practical means to that end was hardly disguised by its supporters, and was recognized by its opponents, both in England and the thirteen colonies. It was bitterly denounced in both places as an instrument of oppression, designed not only to destroy liberty in the St. Lawrence Valley but in the Atlantic colonies as well.

On the eve of hostilities the party of revolt in the colonies had, perforce, to find what methods they could of scotching a danger which they clearly saw to exist, for if Carleton's schemes should succeed they would be in a most perilous position: threatened by a British fleet based on Halifax, by land forces of French Canadians and imperial regulars from Quebec, and by the hostile Indians of the west. Obviously the first move was to attempt to secure the adhesion of the people of the two provinces to the revolutionary cause. Opinion was divided everywhere—in England, in the thirteen colonies themselves, and in Nova Scotia and Canada—and there appeared to be no inherent reason why two should not be added to the thirteen already being bound together to resist British policy. As a field for propaganda Nova Scotia would at first appear to be most hopeful, dotted as it was with New England families and in tune with the doctrines of self-government. Yet whatever were the feelings of the inhabitants (and they were undoubtedly divided), they could hardly be translated into action, for the small British garrison at Halifax was in easy touch with the British fleet. It was literally impossible for the revolutionaries to effect a junction with their supporters in the province, or even to prevent Halifax from being used as a base of naval operations against them. In all probability, therefore, the people of Nova Scotia would be unable to support them. The aspect of Canada was very different. If a combination of regulars, militia, and Indians could be gathered they might advance into the heart of New York and play havoc with the embryonic armies of the colonies. But could that offensive not be stopped at source? Was the population of Canada ready to follow its governor? Was it even loyal in a negative sense? Amongst the small English-speaking group in the province individuals and committees had shown unmistakable sympathy with the revolutionary cause, while the French were a recently-conquered people who might well be persuaded to throw off the foreign yoke. Hence the strategy was clear: to persuade the people of Canada to throw in their lot with the revolutionaries, and to enable them to do so by sending armed forces to their relief. The troops at the disposal of the governor would be overwhelmed, the loyalists suppressed, and the tories in the thirteen colonies given a practical lesson. Canada could be reached by land, and with its intermittent communication with England be brought into the fold in a way that Nova Scotia never could be.[1]

Some months before the war began printed leaflets and agents were hurried to Canada to encourage the faithful, convert the uncertain, and intimidate opponents. The merchants of Montreal, disgusted with the French institutions of the supposedly British province, received both literature and delegates with more than interest. Some of them went over to the revolutionary side and others were suspected of passive disloyalty. On the whole, however, they were unready to join in a fight for independence of the Britain with which their business connections were vital, and chose to bear the known evils of the Quebec Act rather than abandon their commercial structure. French Canadians were invited to escape from the tyranny of British rule, with a strong hint that any other course would incur the enmity of the sons of liberty. For months the bulk of the French Canadians were undecided as to the course they should take. The American promises of self-government made little impression in themselves, but the Quebec Act had failed to conciliate the habitants. By the seigneurs and the clergy loyalty to the crown was unquestioned, and the influence of the latter especially helped to turn the tide. But if the habitant was unimpressed by assemblies and juries, he found the new act oppressive after the relaxation of the strict rule of the French régime. The Franco-American alliance of 1778 might have been used as another lever to move the French Canadians against their new government, but neither

---

[1] For Nova Scotia and Canada during the American revolution see, *inter alia*, J. B. Brebner, *The Neutral Yankees of Nova Scotia: A Marginal Colony during the Revolutionary Years* (New York, 1937); G. M. Wrong, *Canada and the American Revolution: The Disruption of the First British Empire* (New York, 1935); Justin H. Smith, *Our Struggle for the Fourteenth Colony: Canada during the American Revolution* (2 vols., New York, 1907).

signatory wanted to see the *fleur-de-lys* restored at Quebec, and the suggestion of a combined attack by a French fleet and an American army—which might have had a marked effect—was never adopted. A combination of factors—Carleton's firm administration, the influence of the church, resentment against incidents of oppression by the invaders, and finally the failure of the invasion—drew the French at least into passive obedience.

With a population so uncertain the military problem of defending Canada, far more of attempting an offensive from it, was no light one. The fact that Nova Scotia was never seriously threatened illustrates the importance of British sea-power, as does, obversely, the vulnerability of Canada. The main route through the Alleghanies was formed by the Richelieu River-Lake Champlain-Hudson River system, and, since it might be traversed by either belligerent, an American raiding party wisely secured the fortified posts at Ticonderoga and Crown Point in the spring of 1775. The real invasion of Canada was in the autumn of the same year, when one army, following that route, captured Montreal and joined with a second army that had come by the valley of the Kennebec to besiege Quebec. Here was the one strong defensive position in Canada. The garrison, it is true, was small, and more than a half consisted of untrained Canadians; but the American force was likewise small and was handicapped by long lines of communication and bad weather. In the spring the strong arm of the royal navy had at last a chance; and when three men-of-war sailed up to the rock the siege was raised—never to be resumed. Some few hundreds of Canadians had taken part in its defence (and others had fought with the enemy), but the war was essentially one between British and American forces, the former handicapped by the European alliance against them. It was no national spirit that saved the British provinces from absorption in the new union, and kept them the basis of a second British empire in America: a national spirit was yet to be born.

If the British provinces during the war were pawns in the great international chess game, it was even more true that they were so in the peace settlement.[2] It did not, however, follow that the minor rôle assigned to them was altogether a disadvantage, for to some degree they were protected by the moves and counter-moves of the major pieces. While the United States had leant on French assistance in the war and was prepared to follow the French lead in the negotiations for peace, the aims of the two countries conflicted on important points. Washington had frowned on Lafayette's proposal for a joint invasion of Canada, fearing that it might restore Bourbon rule at Quebec; and, though the Americans hoped at one time to secure the cession of both Nova Scotia and Canada, they sacrificed even the hope of widened domains for the sake of the balance of power. The French government seems to have had no ambition to regain its American possessions, neither did it wish to strengthen the United States by such a broad acquisition. Its general plan was for a division between British, American, and Spanish power on the continent; and its apparent support of Spain's claims to the east branch of the Mississippi so alarmed the American plenipotentiaries that they hastily swung to support Britain in Canada and Florida as a counter-weight against the threatened Spanish encroachment on the west. It has been said, and with some justice, that Great Britain made an inadequate diplomatic defence of her colonies in the negotiations, but it is evident that she had no thought of abandoning them, and that the fault lay in her insufficient appreciation of the importance of the boundaries. Whether it was due to war-weariness, indifference, ignorance, or depreciation of the value of North American soil, the British let go the Ohio Valley and the trading posts on the south and west of the great lakes—a result which was viewed with horror by the Montreal merchants who knew every inch of the terrain. On the Atlantic end of the boundary the selection of the line from the St. Croix River to the highlands, threatened land communications by an American wedge between New Brunswick and Canada. The treaty of Paris left British colonies along the north of the continent. That they would remain British was to many Ameri-

---

[2] Full accounts of the peace negotiations will be found in S. F. Bemis, "Canada and the Peace Settlement of 1782-3" (*Canadian Historical Review*, XIV, Sept. 1933), and *The Diplomacy of the American Revolution* (New York, 1935); A. L. Burt, *The United States, Great Britain and British North America from the Revolution to the Establishment of Peace after the War of 1812* (New Haven and Toronto, 1940).

cans no certainty: that they would be confined by the terms of 1783 was not yet accepted in London or in Montreal.

More than a generation was to pass before the issues raised by the American revolution were resolved. During that time there was a spell of peace, and in it intervals when the tension relaxed, but there could be little expectation of permanent peace until after a further resort to arms. Danger to the provinces came both from North American and European politics. In Britain and the United States it was believed that the boundary of 1783 was subject to change. The British government retained hold of several important posts on the then American side for more than ten years after the peace, and cherished some hope that centrifugal forces in the new federation—as exemplified by the secessionist movement in Vermont—would lead to its collapse. The United States, for their part, had not altogether abandoned earlier ambitions of bringing the whole continent within their control. To the general idea of political expansion were added suspicion of a British alliance with the western Indians, land hunger, and designs on the fur trade of the north-west. It is possible, however, that such local differences would not have led to war had it not been for the recurrence of European complications. At the very time when agreement over the posts was being negotiated the intrigues of French agents in the United States were causing alarm in the Canadas; and even when the Jay Treaty had been signed the promise of peace was darkened by the repercussions of the Anglo-French war. The parallel with 1775 was all too apparent: would the United States again secure French assistance in America? The event proved that they did not; but nevertheless the European war strongly influenced the situation in America. The British blockade seriously impaired American shipping and foreign trade, adding a new source of antagonism to those already existing; while the exigencies of the struggle against Napoleon limited the ability of Great Britain to defend her colonies.

The militia system of the British provinces, as it appeared in the first half of the nineteenth century, was modelled on those of both France and England and had already a history on the continent of North America. In Nova Scotia there was no break in continuity, and part of the provincial militia was embodied for garrison duty in the period of the American revolution. In Canada, however, the cession and the years of adjustment had necessitated a suspension of the militia system, and such inhabitants as served in 1775 were volunteers enrolled as the authorities could secure them. A year after the siege of Quebec was raised the militia system was again restored by a series of ordinances, which, with the acts of the various provincial legislatures, made up a coherent system of which the principles were common to all provinces.[3] Certain central ideas run through the laws from the French régime in Canada and early British rule in Nova Scotia to the organization in the provinces as it was just prior to the War of 1812. Liability to service, with specified exemptions, was universal and compulsory. All men of military age were registered by districts and records were periodically sent to headquarters. Musters were held on two to four days in the summer, and at times some slight provision was made for training. All or part of the militia might be embodied for a limited period in time of civil disturbance or war, and when only detachments were required they were chosen by ballot. No pay was provided, and in most cases the men were obliged to provide their own weapons and ammunition. Modifications were made during the tense years of the Napoleonic wars by provincial votes for training and by the introduction of volunteering. "Flank companies" were formed in each regiment from volunteers who still received no pay but were obligated to drill for six days a month, and to find their own uniforms and muskets. Taken by itself the militia would be judged as of little avail for war. But it was at no time intended to operate alone, but as an adjunct to regular troops. Led by trained officers and stiffened by regular regiments it could, and did, give a good account of itself. In spite of requirements in Europe, the British government increased its garrison in British North America from some 3,500 in 1804 to nearly 9,000 in 1808 and 1809. Of the total about one quarter was

---

[3] Texts of the ordinances are in the *Report of the Work of the Public Archives for the Years 1914 and 1915* (Ottawa, 1916). Correspondence relating to the ordinances is in *A History of the Organization, Development and Services of the Military and Naval Forces of Canada from the Peace of Paris in 1763, to the Present Time,* edited by the Historical Section of the General Staff (3 vols., n.p., n.d.). For the history of the militia see C. F. Hamilton, "The Canadian Militia" (*Canadian Defence Quarterly,* V, 1927-8); E. J. Chambers, *The Canadian Militia: A History of the Origin and Development of the Force* (Montreal, 1907); J. P. Edwards, "The Militia of Nova Scotia, 1749-1867" (*Collections of the Nova Scotia Historical Society,* XVII, 1913); Benjamin Sulte, *Histoire de la Milice canadienne-française, 1760-1897* (Montreal, 1897).

made up of regular fencible regiments raised in the provinces; and while these were carried on the British budget they eased the problem of man-power. Such were the land forces on the eve of the War of 1812. The royal navy, the provincial marine, and natural and artificial obstructions, complete the tale of the means available for offensive or defensive warfare.

II

The testing of the system of defence was neither unexpected nor long delayed. In many respects the War of 1812 was strikingly like that of 1775, both in its origins and its course. Both formed part of larger international struggles; both involved invasions of Canada; and both illustrate the importance of British sea and land forces as the basis of the defence of the British provinces. But, while in neither case did the provincial governments have any voice in the diplomacy leading to the outbreak, the Canadian militia and the civil population supported those governments in action in contrast to the slight response or even hostility of the earlier war. In 1812 revolutionary propaganda was no longer an element, but the revolution had an important result on the attitude of the provincial populations. Whether the war was primarily caused by maritime disputes incidental to the use of British sea-power against Napoleon or to the ambitions of American imperialism,[4] it took the form not of a dispute over colonial autonomy but of a contest between national states. The American invasion of the colonies which had remained British could not be represented as a crusade to save those colonies from tyranny. It was a blow against the nearest territory of the enemy, and if successful must have resulted in conquest and perhaps their annexation. Colonial opinion on that issue could not be represented as unanimous, for there were groups of recent American immigrants whose allegiance was to the country of their birth, and who either returned as the war came or created disloyal elements in the provinces. The assembly of Upper Canada

---

[4] Of two recent books containing discussions of the War of 1812 that by J. W. Pratt, *Expansionists of 1812* (New York, 1925), emphasizes American expansionism; while A. L. Burt, in *The United States, Great Britain and British North America* argues that the maritime disputes were the chief causes.

blocked emergency measures which the lieutenant-governor considered to be necessary, and on some occasions units of the militia showed signs of disaffection. The dominant element in the population, however, with the United Empire Loyalists as its core, gave unquestioning obedience and support. In Lower Canada too, where once both English and French Canadians had wavered in their loyalty, the position had changed, but not in this case because of an alteration in the character of the population. It was true that once again an attempt at a return to French sovereignty might be feared; but France played only a remote part in the American War, and a France still coloured with the red of revolution. *Les Canadiens* were finding their destiny. It was to be neither in a reversal of the decision of 1763 nor yet in unconditional absorption within the world-wide operations of British foreign policy. As yet the positive lines were hardly drawn, but the War of 1812 demonstrated that the French of Quebec would defend their province against an invader.

War and revolution on two continents had hammered out a pattern in which the provinces of British North America saw themselves as at bay against the aggression of a far more powerful neighbour. The odds, however, were not as uneven as might at first appear. While the morale of the colonials was relatively high, the United States were as much, if not more, divided than they had been in 1775. New England was cold, if not actually opposed, to the war; and the British were careful to nurse this advantage by attacking only on the central and southern coasts, and by allowing the trade of New England to be carried on. The colonies were dependent on sea-communication across the width of the Atlantic, but since the American and French navies were unable to break that communication, it was only the element of time that was a handicap. The long land frontier with the United States, from Atlantic to Pacific, was guarded by few troops, scanty forces on the lakes, and few fortified positions, but the section that was actually vulnerable was only the central portion of that great stretch. On the east the maritime provinces, with their ice-free ports, were easily held by small garrisons in touch with the British fleet, while on the other extremity American power was so negative that the fur-trading post of Astoria was handed over to the North West Company.

For the British the American war was not unlike that waged with Napoleon in that they made the fullest possible use of superior sea-power and were comparatively weak in land forces.[5] While American men of war were victorious in several separate engagements, the British fleet was able not only to maintain communications, but to blockade the American coast and make combined naval and land attacks on American cities. On the other hand, the United States was able to take the offensive against the central British provinces of Upper and Lower Canada, which could not be defended by the British fleet since the rapids of the St. Lawrence prevented navigation beyond Montreal. The importance of naval force on the great lakes was further accentuated by the difficult transport over the crude Canadian roads. Honours on the lakes were not unevenly divided. When the United States secured control of Lake Erie in 1813 the British land forces were obliged to retire eastward; and, on the other side of the ledger, British ships on Lake Ontario held up the American advance on the Niagara peninsula.

On paper the armies were far from equal. The British regulars (including those regiments raised in the North American provinces) were few in number, particularly in the early part of the war when they could with difficulty be spared from Europe; but they were highly trained, and the American army on active service was only a portion of its nominal roll. The Canadian militia included only a handful of companies with any serious training, but—with some exceptions—it was more successfully employed than the American both as an auxiliary to the regulars and as a separate force. The American weaknesses in training and organization were hardly more serious than were those in strategy. The chief objective of the American staff should have been to cut the thin line of British communications at Montreal or Kingston, and thus isolate all forces, both on land and water, to the west. Instead of this, however, they began by attacking on their left flank with the hope of neutralizing or securing as allies the powerful Indian tribes to the west. Though, after some reverses, they were able to invade and occupy the west of Upper

---

[5] There is a considerable literature on the War of 1812. A good general account is C. P. Lucas, *The Canadian War of 1812* (Oxford, 1906). A. T. Mahan's classic, *Sea Power in its Relation to the War of 1812* (2 vols., Boston, 1905), interprets the subject widely.

Canada, the result of the war was no more affected in that way than by their offensive in the centre over the Niagara peninsula. Three years of campaigns ended with no decisive victories by either side, and with each ready to make peace. For the United States the first abdication of Napoleon spelt more British forces in North America and on the Atlantic, but the British had no desire to continue a struggle which they had never wanted, which was purely defensive, and which dragged on at a time when they most wanted peace after the exhausting and protracted wars with France, and freedom to face the more important settlement in Europe.

The settlement in America was made up of several instruments, of which the Treaty of Ghent was only one.[6] In the negotiations both sides, according to custom, presented maximum terms, the final result having the appearance of a return to the *status quo*. The British plenipotentiaries at first pressed for measures designed to bring more security to their colonies: revision of the New Brunswick-Maine boundary, an Indian buffer state, minor adjustments elsewhere, and American disarmament on the lakes. The territorial demands were eventually dropped, and the boundary remained as in the treaty of 1783, subject to later settlement of certain sections. In 1818 the whole line from the Lake of the Woods to the Rockies was, by agreement, established at the forty-ninth parallel of latitude. The boundary of New Brunswick was destined to remain longer a subject of dispute. Unilateral was changed to bilateral disarmament in the Rush-Bagot agreement of 1817, under which armed vessels of both sides on the lakes were reduced to the size of police forces. A British attempt to include an article explicitly nullifying American fishing rights in British North American waters was successfully resisted, and replaced by a convention of 1818 under which limited rights were allowed.[7] In Canada there was some dissatisfaction that better terms had not been secured. The fur-traders had hoped that the mistake of 1783 would be corrected, but their protests were of little consequence in view of the imminent transfer of the trade from Montreal to Hudson Bay. A more significant note was struck by John Strachan, later Bishop of Toronto.

---

[6] For the negotiations and terms of settlement see Burt, *The United States, Great Britain and British North America*.

[7] For the later history of the fisheries disputes see below, 158-63.

Though a staunch tory and imperialist, he hinted that British control of diplomacy had its drawbacks—an idea that later was to be more commonly and more vigorously voiced.

. . . We have just heard that the conditions of peace have been signed at Ghent & ratified by the Prince Regent. Our Envoys were not I fear endowed with much sagacity & firmness. I dread to see the articles.

This country has certainly derived many advantages from the war and if a proper line of policy be adopted it will become a most valuable appendage to the British Empire.

In regard to the vast expence of the war it is most true that much more money has been spent in the country than the soil is worth but this is not the proper way of stating the question. These colonies are the relique of happier times the memorial of the power and success of the British Empire under the most brilliant of her administrations and could not be given up without disgrace.

They have also been a receptacle for the Loyalists during the American rebellion and have claims on the protection of the Mother country which to a magnanimous nation are irresistible. But the Inhabitants of the Canadas had nothing to do about the Origin of the War they were to become its victims but the causes were national questions of vital importance to the welfare & prosperity of the British Empire. The great expence of conducting the war ought not therefore to be charged upon the Canadas.[8]

Seen in a perspective wider than was possible for contemporaries, the settlement of 1814-18 becomes a milestone in the history of British North America. Though modified in detail and even threatened in its entirety, that settlement proved to be the end of a series of wars which covered more than a century. France, Spain, England, and the United States had, in various combinations, struggled for the control of North America. The treaties of 1763 and 1783, in spite of the hopeful language in which they were couched, were temporary, and were known even by contemporaries to be temporary. While the peace-makers at Vienna—kings, ministers, and generals—conscious of the prime importance of their task, were able to legislate for but a generation, those who were appointed to the more humble task of making peace in the new world were able to establish the lines on which two powers were to live peacefully in that great con-

---

[8] George W. Spragge (ed.), *The John Strachan Letter Book, 1812-1834* (Toronto, 1946), Strachan to Colonel Harvey, Feb., 1815.

tinent. Not, indeed, that the peoples of the provinces were able to discern the final outcome of the settlement, for there were to be many more rumours of war in the next fifty years, and the problem of security was by no means seen as solved. But if the peace could not be taken as permanent, the war had brought a new consciousness of nationality, a more assured sense of orientation. Canadians, both French and English, had been ready to fight for their lands, with not a little success; and if defects in the system of defence had become more apparent, they were not beyond remedy. Disloyal groups had been more clearly revealed, and steps were taken to remove such danger for the future by barriers against American and encouragement of British immigrants. The second British empire in North America was coming of age.

III

Peace on almost any basis would have induced, as it customarily does, a relaxation of concern for military effort and reorganization; and, while the settlement of 1814-18 left much to be desired both in terms and promise of permanence, it was obviously much more than a truce, and gave ground for hopes of peace at least for a time. The peoples and the legislatures of the province turned to the problems of immigration and material progress, and revived political disputes which only later proved to be wider than domestic quarrels. But if the public thought more of peace than of war, the sky of North America was not so clear that the responsible authorities could neglect altogether questions of defence. For the next quarter-century the strategy of the defence of the British provinces as seen by the British was consistent in principles and not materially changed by the threats to peace that occurred from time to time. All plans were based on the dual assumption that, while offensive warfare against the United States was not practicable, the provinces were defensible. It was believed that the War of 1812 had demonstrated both the feasibility of successful defence, even against the larger neighbour, and also that the organization of land forces was fundamentally sound. The improvements that were considered to be necessary were to meet weaknesses which were emphasized more than revealed by the war. In this last phase of the old colonial system it was taken for granted that responsibility for defence both in thought and action, rested on the imperial government. It followed, then, that the weight of attack would fall upon the royal navy and the British regulars; but these two professional arms, it was believed, could afford adequate protection if—and only if—the provinces continued to provide the additional man-power of the militia. The successful operation of the three branches of the defence force depended on a fortified naval base on the Atlantic, improved communication within the continent, and strengthened or additional fortifications at vulnerable points. Such was the attitude of the British government toward the problem of defending North America from the sea to the head of the great lakes.

The war had amply proved the ability of the royal navy to maintain uninterrupted communications across the Atlantic, and not even a combination of powers could challenge the sea-power that dated from the battle of Trafalgar. The fleet must, however, have a base that was safe against land attack or raids from the sea, and for that reason Sir James Carmichael-Smyth, the head of the commission sent to inspect the defences of the provinces in 1825, advised a new citadel for Halifax.[9] Minor works were recommended, for storing ammunition and as "alarm posts and rallying points" at Annapolis and Windsor. New Brunswick was "the connecting link between Canada and Nova Scotia", and the commission pointed to the military importance of a satisfactory boundary of New Brunswick with Maine. For part of the year troops and supplies could be sent by way of the St. Lawrence, but in the winter the overland route through New Brunswick was the only one, and it would be endangered by the jutting north of Maine. The Temiscouata Portage road was not only close to the border but could only by politeness be called a road at all. In order to provide a communication safer in time of war the Kempt road, further from the

---

[9] The report of the commission, with the exception of an article (52) on the vulnerable points of the United States, was lithographed under the title *Copy of a Report to His Grace the Duke of Wellington Master General of His Majesty's Ordnance etc. relative to His Majesty's North American Provinces by a Commission of which M. General Sir James Carmichael Smyth was President, Lieut. Colonel Sir George Hoste, Captain Harris members* (1825). A summary of the conclusions is in Sir James Carmichael-Smyth's *Précis of the Wars in Canada*, edited by his son, Sir James Carmichael (London, 1862).

boundary, was projected, and was open over some sections in the thirties. Since Canada was the only province that was considered likely to be attacked it was essential to provide communications through as well as up to it. Rapids on the Upper St. Lawrence barring navigation, the British government, at its own expense, built the Rideau Canal, which had the additional advantage of being well back from the frontier. At first the imperial experts frowned on the improvement of the St. Lawrence, as opening it to American attack; but later encouraged canals on that river as a necessary alternative to the Rideau route. The seizure of control of Lake Erie in the War of 1812 underlined the problem of reinforcing the defences of the western part of the province, and gave a military importance to the Welland Canal. While the inland waterways, like the lower St. Lawrence, were frozen in the winter, by a happy coincidence the roads of Canada were comparatively fit for use when the bottomless mud was decently covered with snow.

The same lakes which afforded a means of communication for His Majesty's forces would be useless for that purpose if commanded by enemy ships, and become instead a highway for an invader. The Rush-Bagot agreement of 1817 was intended to cancel out all armed vessels save a few patrol boats, but, like many another disarmament agreement, its implementation followed slowly. Being only required not to keep armed ships in commission, both sides were slow to scrap them altogether; and there were many stories of warships being secretly built. A further complication was that commercial vessels could be converted into warships without great difficulty, and as the American merchant vessels were far more numerous, particularly on Lake Erie, and had more ports, the British authorities had cause for worry. In 1838, at a time of strained relations, the British government maintained armed vessels in commission over the maximum, by consent of the American government; and the president was empowered, in case of danger, to take similar action. In the midst of the excitement caused by the McLeod case congress appropriated $100,000 for warships. In 1843 the British government decided it could safely reduce tonnage to the figure of the agreement, only to reconsider its decision at the time of the Oregon dispute. The admiralty sent a shipwright officer to Canada to direct the construction of merchant vessels capable of conversion into armed vessels, but the work was not carried out because of the more pacific attitude of congress.[10]

Study of the War of 1812 and of the topography of Canada satisfied Carmichael-Smyth's commission that invasion need be anticipated at only a limited number of places, all of which were in Canada. The stronghold of Quebec had never been captured, but its fortifications were neglected. Montreal had always been an object of attack by way of Lake Champlain, and, in Carmichael-Smyth's view there should be a fortress on the island itself together with lesser works on the south side of the river. The next strategic point, Kingston, was not only a port, naval station, and dockyard, but controlled the entrance to the St. Lawrence and the projected Rideau Canal. Kingston, too, must then be fortified. York was not regarded as of immediate importance, but a fort was recommended for the Niagara frontier. Finally, some minor works were advised for the south-west extremity of Upper Canada. The proposals of 1825 were moderate and logical, but little was done to carry them into effect.

Of the land forces, British regulars continued to be stationed in all the provinces, the numbers varying from time to time. In 1835 they were reduced to fewer than five thousand, but five years later had again been raised to over fifteen thousand. The importance of the militia was constantly stressed by the imperial government, with suggestions that improvements in the system were not unneeded. Writing on the problem of defence in the shadow of the Oregon dispute, the colonial secretary quoted Sir George Murray as being of the opinion that there must be "a numerous, well-organized, and well-disposed local Military Force, to co-operate with the Regular Army". The Duke of Wellington, he added, had stated that "with proper Naval and Ordnance preparations, Canada may be effectually defended by a force of 10,000 British Troops, if supported by a loyal and well-organized Militia to the extent of 35,000 men". The minimum requirements, according to Wellington, were that the militia should be embodied and organized, and perhaps given some

[10] Public Archives of Canada, *Series G*, vol. 109, p. 458; vol. 116, p. 139; vol. 121, pp. 210, 217, 295; vol. 122, p. 458. See also J. M. Callahan, *The Neutrality of the American Lakes and Anglo-American Relations* (Johns Hopkins Studies in Historical and Political Science, Series XVI, nos. 1-4, Baltimore, 1898).

training.[11] While the provinces accepted the principle that the militia must be maintained, they did little to improve its efficiency. The Province of Canada adopted the legislation of Upper and Lower Canada with little alteration except for a significant move in 1846 toward more emphasis on volunteer corps with some training.

Such were the plans and the forces for the defence of the provinces. In all discussions on the subject, whether official or unofficial, defensive warfare was visualized not only as sound strategically but as not improbable politically. Was there, in reality, a prospect of attack by the United States? As a possibility it could not be, and was not, dismissed. The memories of 1775 and 1812 were still too distinct, and there was no ground for certainty that British and Americans could amicably divide a continent. In addition to such general impressions held in varying degrees, were periodic crises whose menace could not be ignored. The first arose from a curious tangle of domestic and foreign affairs that in itself illustrates the effects of interchange of populations and ideas. The doctrines of the rebellions of 1837 were in part inspired directly by immigrants from the United States or indirectly by admiration of American institutions and conditions. The military problem of 1837 and the years immediately following was not the suppression of local and ill-organized revolts, but the prospect that international war might result from sympathy, from border incidents, or from aggression finding an opportunity. The escape of the leader of the Upper Canada revolt, William Lyon Mackenzie, to the United States raised the possibility of an invasion on behalf of his cause; but whether the support he received, and the meetings in American towns which passed resolutions of sympathy, raised funds and even volunteers —whether these were inspired wholly by devotion to democracy or in part by anti-British sentiment is not easy to decide. But whatever the motives, the preparations on Navy Island created a military problem in Canada. The reckless capture of the *Caroline* at an American wharf led to the arrest of Alexander McLeod, a Canadian, and his trial for the murder of an American killed in the scuffle. Of many awkward situations arising from border incidents the McLeod case was the most serious. The British

[11] *Series G*, vol. 122, p. 99, Stanley to Metcalfe, Sept. 16, 1845.

minister in Washington wrote to Palmerston that the conviction of McLeod must mean war,[12] and Stanley informed Sydenham that he might need to retain regiments in Halifax.[13] Meanwhile the Canadian border was disturbed by plans of invading Canada drawn up by American secret societies—plans which bore fruit in actual crossing of the frontier by armed forces. Late in 1838 the Hunters sent a force across the St. Lawrence, and a battle was fought at Windmill Point, near Prescott.[14]

Happily for the peace of America McLeod was acquitted, the British government expressed regret for the *Caroline* affair, and the Hunters' Lodges gradually subsided into threats. In response to the tenseness of five years, there was reorganization and increase of the military force, but no changes of principle were made in the Canadian militia. The 1837 affairs had not yet been smoothed out when the first of two major boundary disputes arose. The line between Maine and New Brunswick involved, as everyone knew, a military problem in that an unfavourable settlement would seriously endanger communications between Great Britain, the maritime provinces, and Canada. The "Aroostook War" of 1838 hardly merited the name; but there were actual movements of troops by both sides, and fighting was narrowly avoided. In this, as in the Caroline affair, international negotiation rested entirely with the British government. Their conclusion in the Webster-Ashburton Treaty of 1842 came to be traditionally regarded as an example of British willingness to sacrifice Canadian interests, but later examination has revealed the treaty as a reasonable diplomatic compromise. Whatever a legal judgment of the evidence may show—and there is reason to believe that the British case was not a strong one—the settlement ended a long dispute at a time when relations were badly strained. Finally the Pacific coast was added to the sum of Anglo-American controversies by the dispute over the boundary of Oregon, held jointly since 1818. The gravity of the situation may be seen from the fact that the successful candidate for the presidency had used the slogan of "Fifty-four forty or fight" as an election cry, while Peel told the house of lords in more measured but

[12] *Series G*, vol. 108, p. 108, Fox to Palmerston, Jan. 10, 1841.
[13] *Series G*, vol. 110, p. 451, Stanley to Sydenham, Sept. 10, 1841.
[14] A full account of these events is in A. B. Corey, *The Crisis of 1830-1842 in Canadian-American Relations* (New Haven and Toronto, 1941).

no less certain terms that, while the government would attempt an amicable settlement, it was ready to maintain British rights in Oregon. Although the United States failed to realize its full ambition in the settlement, Britain too accepted a compromise. Once again it was charged that the British government had been weak, but once again the peace had not been broken. The accumulation of crises on the borders of British North America, serious enough in itself, was overtaken by another group of Anglo-American disputes ranging over an even wider area.

IV

The position of the British provinces was governed not only by bilateral relations with their immediate neighbour but by the world politics of the era. The nation of shopkeepers, who had so long and so effectively wielded the sword, were struggling to re-build a world in which they could carry on business profitably and at peace. One major object was to keep in the Americas an open door, through which to buy essential raw materials and to sell manufactured goods. One attempt at outside interference by the European powers was blocked by calling in the new world; and if the Monroe Doctrine was not the co-operative action that Canning had intended, it served the immediate purpose. It was, however, far from the wish of the British government that the continents thus insulated from European, should be the object of American, imperialism. Not thus would the door be kept open. The first area which threatened to be absorbed by the United States was Texas, which sought to break away from Mexico and join the nation. Both England and France were opposed to such a change, which would put within a customs area what otherwise would be an excellent field for free trade, and—from the English point of view—would unduly strengthen the United States and expose the rest of Mexico to annexation. In part at least those fears were justified, for shortly after Texas was absorbed in 1845, New Mexico and California were added to the rapidly-expanding republic. Soon afterwards the United States sought to buy Cuba from Spain, and again the British and French governments made clear their objections.[15]

[15] See J. H. Latané, *A History of American Foreign Policy* (New York, 1934).

However differently these events may be interpreted by historians, many contemporaries saw them in the worst light. American opinion accused England of selfish interference in the affairs of continents closed by the Monroe Doctrine to Europeans; while Britain, anxious to maintain independent states, accused the United States of aggressive imperialism. For the British provinces the whole issue had a double significance: the disputes threatened war with the United States, and American expansionism might at any time be turned northward. Throughout the provinces Texas, California, and Cuba were held up as horrible examples of the operation of a manifest destiny which had been before, and might be again, directed against British North America. An editorial in the *Quebec Gazette* is characteristic of a view that constantly found expression.

The ambition of acquiring territory, without being very scrupulous as to the means, seems to be inherent in the people of the United States. They are living on land mostly wrested from the aboriginal inhabitants, who have been exterminated or driven back to countries now claimed by the United States, and to which they profess to have an "unquestionable title". They acquired Louisiana and Florida rather as troublesome neighbours than by fair negotiation. Their citizens overran Texas, declared it independent, and it is now to be added to the United States. They have twice failed in their attempts to conquer Canada, and subsequently, in an underhanded way, have endeavoured to favour attempts to withdraw it from the authority of the British Government. It would seem that in the view of many of them "might is right". . . .
What may be the result of the existing state of things it is impossible to foresee; but it is evident that no country can be safe in the vicinity of the United States, but by means of power sufficient for its protection, and if needful, the punishment of the aggressor.[16]

The people of the provinces saw boundary disputes on their own borders and American expansion beyond them all as signs of the onward march of a republic whose orators had not hesitated to announce that it was the destiny of their country to spread on every side to the ocean. As if American affairs were not bad enough, British North America found itself drawn into the results of a dispute in the Near East. On the Pacific coast there was talk of a Russian naval attack. Even in Canada a story

16 *Quebec Gazette,* April 28, 1845.

circulated that Russian agents in the United States were looking for recruits to man a vessel purchased by the Tsar, and that New Brunswick or Canada was to be attacked.[17] But—except for British Columbia—it was improbable that the provinces themselves would be attacked, and their more constant interest in the war was in the aid they could give to Britain. Another case which had a direct connection with British North America was the Indian Mutiny. Here there could be no question of defence of their own territory, but military aid was offered and accepted.

The existence of threats to the peace of British North America was an old story, as was the need of provision against war resulting from them. There were, however, in the forties and fifties, new factors in the situation which changed both the character of the forces and the purposes for which they might be used. The prime military interest for the people of North America was still the defence of their own soil, but the establishment of colonies on the Pacific coast and the expectation of settlement on the intervening prairies meant that British North America offered a greatly enlarged target. A second and fresh object of military effort was support of Britain in wars outside North America. While interest was shown in such wars as those against China in 1840 and Afghanistan in 1842, it was not until 1854 that Britain was again engaged in a war with a great power after the defeat of Napoleon. News of the Crimean War brought in the British provinces a widespread anxiety to aid the mother country in any way feasible, not that the British Empire was felt to be in danger, or that the colonies had any definable responsibility, but simply as a spontaneous wish to lend assistance. In Montreal a public meeting was called by the mayor and addressed by English- and French-speaking citizens, all of whom laid stress on the Anglo-French alliance. Applause greeted all references to the fight against the tyrannical Tsar and proposals that Canadians should help. An address to the king was drawn up, expressing the sympathy of the Canadian people and the determination to resist all aggression against Canada.[18] Numerous offers of volunteers were made, and legislatures and societies voted sums for the patriotic fund. The Indian Mutiny provoked further offers of men and money, and in that case the former was

17 *Mackenzie's Weekly Message* (Toronto), April 7, 1854.
18 *La Minerve* (Montreal), May 6, 1854.

accepted as well as the latter, for the imperial government raised at its own expense, the 100th Royal Canadian Regiment of Foot.

While in both wars the Canadian government placed no obstacle in the way of British recruiting in Canada, the actual offers of troops were made by volunteer corps rather than by the government. The latter was, indeed, wary of sending from Canada the existing organized forces in view of continued apprehension of American aggression. In case of an invasion British troops, needed elsewhere, might not be available for Canada: and in any event the British government was already engaged in the gradual withdrawal of the imperial regiments. This was another and a most important new factor in the military situation, for it meant that the old principle of defence by British regulars aided by provincial militia was being discarded. A number of influences combined toward making the decision to withdraw the garrisons. An immediate and practical difficulty was the size of the British army. In 1845 it totalled 118,000 men, of whom 53,000 were within the British Isles, 26,000 in India, and but 39,000 available for all the colonies—between 11,000 and 12,000 of the last being in British North America.[19] The inadequacy of such forces in time of war was pointedly shown in the Crimean War and the Indian Mutiny. Furthermore, the cost of the garrisons was increasingly unwelcome. For 1846-7 military expenditure was £474,789 for the Province of Canada and £170,464 for the maritime provinces and Newfoundland. To a generation which was fast losing imperial enthusiasm, and tended to interpret the growth of autonomy as steps toward independence, such a burden was not only irksome but illogical. In 1846—the year of the abolition of the corn laws, and of the British Possessions Act—the first withdrawals were made. Further withdrawals in 1851 reduced the forces in Canada to 4,960 men and in Nova Scotia to 2,026—the latter being chiefly the garrison at Halifax. By 1855, with the Crimean War in progress, there were only 1,887 imperial troops in Canada, at a cost of £150,000, and in the maritime provinces but 1,086 men. There were none at all in Prince Edward Island.

---

[19] *Series G,* vol. 122, p. 99, Stanley to Metcalfe, Sept. 16, 1845. On the withdrawal of troops see C. P. Stacey, *Canada and the British Army, 1846-1871; A Study in the Practice of Responsible Government* (London and Toronto, 1936), and C. F. Hamilton, "The Canadian Militia" *(Canadian Defence Quarterly,* VI, 1928-9).

Whatever may have been said at the time, there can be little doubt but that the people of the provinces regretted the decision to call back the imperial troops. Some comments, however, are interesting. While it was admitted that they had been sent solely for the defence of British North America, it was often pointed out that any war would arise out of Anglo-American disputes and not from local differences. On the other hand, it was also argued that the colonials had not been bearing their share of defence, and had been too ready to let it all fall on the English tax-payers. Lord Elgin, the governor general who was attempting to work out a new type of imperial structure that would allow for autonomy without independence, saw the withdrawal of troops as part of a larger issue. He constantly urged caution, pointing out that the argument that the colonies should assume a larger part of the cost of defence would

encrease, I fear, the uneasy feeling which the Free Trade policy of the Mother Country and the language respecting the Dependencies of the Empire in which British Statesmen have of late years indulged both in and out of Parliament have tended to produce in the Colonial mind.—It would confirm the opinion, which already obtains too widely, that Great Britain begins to feel her colonies a burden and a nuisance—that she desires to sever one by one the bonds that unite her to them—that the connexion therefore will be of but uncertain duration—and that annexation to the States must perforce be looked to as the inevitable goal, the only practicable mode of terminating a provisional and entering upon a definitive national existence.[20]

The opinion began to gain weight that the vacuum caused by the removal of British regiments must be filled by a reorganized militia. In the forties and early fifties the militia in every province was little different from what it had been at the beginning of the century. Its paper strength had little meaning. Such volunteer corps as existed were starved, and even those that struggled toward efficiency were too often objects of public scorn. To avoid ridicule one Toronto unit used to drill in the woods, the men going to the rendezvous by separate paths.[21] In Nova

[20] A. G. Doughty (ed.), *The Elgin-Grey Papers, 1846-1852* (Ottawa, 1937), I, 267.
[21] G. T. Denison, *Soldiering in Canada: Recollections and Experiences* (Toronto, 1900), 30.

Scotia an act was passed in 1844 cancelling all musters, drills, and training unless specifically ordered, and the militia remained entirely passive until 1859. Joseph Howe described the militia of Nova Scotia in his usual pungent style.

By the returns of 1855, the militia of Nova Scotia, on paper, includes 57,855 men, of whom 1435 are commissioned officers. How many of these can 'set a squadron in the field', it were vain to conjecture. None of these has had a squadron to set for 20 years. Some of them are 'old fogies', fighting the battle of life with rheumatism, gout, asthma, dropsy, and other such like enemies, they are worse than Sepoys or Caffirs, or Zouaves, or Yankee riflemen a good deal. . . . These old gentlemen, if they ever knew anything did not know much, and we fear that the little they were taught four and twenty years ago would hardly qualify them to counteract the deviltries of a Canrobert or a Nana Sahib, who have been made 'wondrous wise' in the modern schools of military science.

These elderly gentlemen, may, then for all purposes of active warfare, be marked 'unserviceable', and set aside like old stores.

Then there are, amongst the other 1435 'braves' who carry Her Majesty's commission in their pockets, we should suppose, at least a third who know nothing of the science they have bound themselves, by the acceptance of their commissions, to study, and which the honour of the Crown may require them at any moment to teach. . . . There may be half a dozen good drills among the whole 1435; but this we believe to be a very liberal calculation. . . .

The two Volunteer Artillery Companies of Halifax and Pictou . . . including perhaps 100 men in all, are the only really efficient corps in the Province, and they, we opine, might be much improved.

In material the militia is sadly deficient. The whole of the arms in their possession are reported 'totally unserviceable and inefficient'. . . .

There is no organization, no science, no *esprit de corps*, no discipline. The militia of Newfoundland, New Brunswick, Prince Edward Island, are, no doubt, in much the same condition. There ought to be in these provinces 80,000 men capable of bearing arms—available at least for self-defence—and that might with a little care and forethought, and without much waste of labour, be brought to a condition more in accordance with the general interests and policy of the Empire than they are now.[22]

22 *The Nova Scotian* (Halifax), June 14, 1858.

Reform came first in the Province of Canada. Following the recommendations of a commission, the legislature passed an act in 1855 (18 Vict., c. 77) which, while it introduced no principles wholly new, did in effect fundamentally alter the organization of the militia. The old rule that all men of military age were liable for service was retained, but this "sedentary militia", as it was not unfittingly called, was still not to be trained, and gradually became little more than a memory. The point of the act was in its provisions for the "active" or "volunteer" militia. A few such units had existed in some form for many years, but had received neither public nor official encouragement. Now the volunteer units were to be both trained and paid, and attention was given to the need of modern weapons. A maximum of 5,000 men was set in the act, but in a few years it had been allowed to go beyond that under authority of an amendment of 1856, providing for unpaid as well as paid units. Much the same developments followed in the other provinces; though in Nova Scotia the plan was somewhat different. There the old militia was retained as well as, and in preference to, the volunteers. The effect was to drill a far larger number of men, though for shorter periods. But everywhere there was a new zeal for military preparedness. The local legislatures voted not inconsiderable sums of money, and the British government sent large numbers of firearms to replace the ancient and condemned veterans.

Although the new life breathed into the militia was due to the greater responsibility it would have to bear, it was not the only source of the defence of the provinces. The British regulars were to be recalled only by degrees, and for the time being were in sufficient numbers to stiffen the militia, especially in the period of reorganization. As a more permanent source of aid it was taken for granted that imperial troops would be sent if actual need arose. "The facilities of steam communication", wrote the colonial secretary, "have greatly diminished the necessity for a military force, as a mere precautionary defence against a remote danger, and it must be borne in mind that, if the security of Canada should ever be threatened, troops could be forwarded for its assistance with the utmost speed."[23] Given the supremacy of the royal navy, no difficulty would exist in the transfer of such

---

[23] *Series G*, vol. 143, p. 200, Newcastle to Elgin, March 31, 1853.

troops. The navy, too, continued to act as a guard to both coasts of British North America. Halifax had long been a naval base, and experience had shown that the maritime provinces were rendered safe from attack by the near presence of the British warships. The younger colonies on the Pacific coast saw their first need of defence during the Crimean War. The governor, James Douglas, advocated arming all the able-bodied whites in the colony with an auxiliary force of Indians, but the council decided that the whites would be less a protection than armed Indians were a menace, and preferred to leave the defence of the colony to Great Britain.[24] Douglas's appeals for a naval force permanently stationed in the colony were at first received coldly in London, but in 1855 a naval base was established at Esquimalt, thus affording security to the Pacific as well as to the Atlantic coast.

In the middle of the century, then, the defences of British North America consisted of the royal navy for the colonies on both extremities, a militia in process of reorganization, and the residue of imperial troops. A few fortifications had been added after the War of 1812, but on too modest a scale to be a major factor. Because of the disarmament agreement of 1817 neither Canada nor the United States had available naval forces on the lakes, which thus remained open to the passage of troops. Transportation was greatly facilitated by the completion of the St. Lawrence canals at the end of the forties, which, together with the Welland Canal, allowed for uninterrupted navigation as far as Sault Ste. Marie. Railways, too, were fast being built, and had an important place in warfare both for the greater speed of transportation and because they could be used in winter. But if Canada was fast building railways, the United States was building even faster. American railways ran toward the Canadian border, making possible concentration of troops on a scale and at a speed heretofore impossible. Behind this new strategic factor lay the military menace of a population that was rapidly growing out of all proportion to that of British North America. It was questionable whether it could still be said that the provinces were defensible. If hopes still lingered, they were soon to be all but shattered by the advent of the first great modern armies, born of the Civil War.

[24] *Minutes of the Council of Vancouver Island, 1851-1861* (Archives of British Columbia, Memoir no. 2), July 12, 1854.

CHAPTER III

TRANSITION FROM MERCANTILISM

M ERCANTILISM was the accepted dogma and practice of all imperial states in the age when North America was opened to European expansion. In conformity with the prevailing principles France and Britain were intent on obtaining from America raw materials to supplement those available at home, and on securing at the same time markets for their manufactured products. Trade and the flag were inseparable, for unsupported individuals had little chance of conducting commerce beyond the seas while rival governments were closing preserves for the benefit of their subjects alone. Economic motives account for the exploration that revealed the new lands, the foundation of colonies, and readiness to expend blood and treasure upon defence and development. But if the motive was economic, it does not follow that no other elements entered into colonization, or that colonies necessarily suffered because of that prime purpose. In infant years a colony habitually required and obtained most paternal care; but even in adolescence the balance of aid and restriction was not wholly uneven, as witness the zeal with which both parties looked to retaining advantages and dropping liabilities. Political institutions, protection, and culture should not be forgotten as assets gained by a colony; but even in the economic field, which will here be treated as a separate theme, an attempt must be made to see the situation as a whole, and not only from the point of view of particular or temporary interests.

For more than two centuries the older provinces of the dominion were economically dominated by the related factors of local conditions and imperial policy; and to the extent that the two could be dovetailed friction was avoided and profit accrued to those in the new and the old worlds. In so far as these provinces were concerned the principles of mercantilism, under the French or the English régimes, were simple enough. Production was to be concentrated on those goods which were not to be found in the parent state, and consumption was to be of manufactured articles bought in exchange. Thus an external trade for the colonies was automatically called into being, as part of the very reason for their existence. The second principle was that the commerce so created was to be carried in the ships of the metropolitan state, so adding a profit and making possible an expansion in the volume of shipping, factors essential to a world power. Employment and markets were thus assured within limits, as was a supply of articles which, at least in the early stages, could not be produced in a new and undeveloped country. If the colonies were not free to buy in the open market they were able to sell in a, closed one. They need have no concern for the provision or protection of the ships which were to carry their trade, although they were limited in the choice of carriers more strictly than in the choice of customers.

The particular regulations by which the imperial economic policy was defined and the rigour with which it was carried out varied from time to time. In the French régime little difficulty was experienced in imposing the principles. Such initiative as existed for the foundation of native industries came from France itself, as a self-imposed breach in the mercantilist system. Colbert's encouragement of industries or the aid given to the iron works of St. Maurice in the eighteenth century were not typical and were frowned on by French producers; but the very slight effect that they had in Canada shows how little opposition there was to the rule of buying from France. Agriculture, while engaging perhaps three-quarters of the population of Canada, did little more than supply the local market. The commercial instincts of the colonists were concentrated almost wholly on the fur trade, an admirable choice from the point of view of the mother country since it created an export of goods not produced in France and an import of manufactured articles for the trade with the Indians.

Under British rule the position was never again so comparatively simple: partly because of the more diversified economic ambitions of the colonists, partly because British policy itself was undergoing modifications. The northern colonies came under British rule before the revolt of the southern thirteen, and thus into the old colonial system. In that system the control of shipping was the main governing factor. "It was clearly understood by contemporaries", wrote Mrs. Knowles, "that the colonial system and the Navigation Acts were part and parcel of the same thing. Colonies were regarded as estates to be managed for the benefit of the mother country, and the economic instrument of their control was transport, and to regulate shipping to and from the colonies was to regulate the colonial trade."[1] Trade between the mother country and the colonies or between two colonies was to be in British (including colonial) ships only. Shortly after they became independent the United States were permitted to deal directly with the West Indies and Canada. From 1822 on further relaxations in the navigation acts were made, allowing a limited trade between the colonies and foreign states. The second instrument of control was the tariff. By the middle of the nineteenth century the colonies had secured a measure of independence in setting tariffs against foreign states, but it remained to establish the principle of placing tariffs against British goods. Related to the control of colonial tariffs was the system under which Britain, by conceding preferential rates to certain colonial goods, could encourage certain industries and so indirectly discourage others. But it was also possible to use direct discouragement of enterprises that threatened competition with English industries. When a governor of Nova Scotia reported a project for a local colliery in 1752 he was warned that "It would be contrary to those Rules of Policy, which this Nation has wisely observed in relation to its colonies, to bring coals into use in America, as the use of them would naturally lead them into the Discovery of a variety of Manufactures, the raw materials of which we now receive from them, and afterwards return in Manufactures. . . ."[2] A few years later another administrator of Nova Scotia could not "omit observing to your Lordship, that this Government have at all times been extremely carefull not to give encouragement to any kind of manufactures which might interfere with those of Great Britain".[3]

[1] L. C. A. Knowles, *The Industrial and Commercial Revolutions in Great Britain during the Ninteenth Century* (London, 1933), 295.

[2] H. A. Innis (ed.), *Select Documents in Canadian Economic History, 1497-1783* (Toronto, 1929), 212.

[3] *Ibid.*, 210.

Such instances occurred, but they were not frequent. There was a growing desire in the colonies to diversify their economies, but it is worthy of note that protests against British restraints became vigorous only when changing policy in Britain itself altered the balance of advantages and disadvantages for the colonies. Meanwhile both parties were not ill satisfied with the exchange of raw materials from British North America for manufactured goods from England, which formed the mainstay of the commercial activity of the former. The products which the colonies were able readily to export were fish, furs, forest products, and wheat.[4] There were natural products which could be provided in apparently unlimited quantities in some or all of the colonies; but the governing factor was not the extent of the supply but the conditions of sale, which, in turn, depended on the commercial policy and local demand in Britain, and on the international situation. The fisheries of the Atlantic coast, which first created a European commercial interest in North America, were of particular concern to Nova Scotia; and that province was enabled greatly to extend her part in the industry in the period during which her rivals in New England and France were handicapped by the wars of the end of the eighteenth and the beginning of the nineteenth centuries. The colony on the St. Lawrence concentrated on the fur trade, after the conquest as before it. Goods and capital required for the trade were obtained from London firms associated with those in Montreal, and ocean transport was conducted by English ships. The business was carried on in active competition with concerns in New York and with the Hudson's Bay Company. The boundaries as settled in 1783 and confirmed in 1794 took from the Montreal traders main posts and routes; they were gradually edged out of the south-west trade by the Astor interests and American restrictions; and the more economical transportation secured to the English company by its possession of Hudson Bay finally led to the collapse of the Canadian trade in 1821.

[4] Mary Quayle Innis, *An Economic History of Canada* (Toronto, 1935); D. G. Creighton, *The Commercial Empire of the St. Lawrence, 1760-1850* (New Haven and Toronto, 1937); H. A. Innis, *The Cod Fisheries: The History of an International Economy* (New Haven and Toronto, 1940); H. A. Innis, *The Fur Trade in Canada: An Introduction to Canadian Economic History* (New Haven and Toronto, 1930); A. R. M. Lower, "The Trade in Square Timber" (*Contributions to Canadian Economics*, VI, 1933); D. A. MacGibbon, *The Canadian Grain Trade* (Toronto, 1932).

Other changes in the international picture brought alternative opportunities to both the maritime provinces and Canada. If the fisheries were encouraged by England as a nursery for seamen, the forest resources of the colonies were also needed for the spars and hulls of the wooden ships of the royal navy and the merchant marine. In the early eighteenth century bounties on the timber industry of the American colonies were begun, and extended to Nova Scotia when that colony finally became British. After the American revolution an alternative source of supply of masts was successfully sought in New Brunswick, Nova Scotia having by that time been denuded of suitable trees. Small exports of oak, wooden staves, and potash were also made from Canada in the second half of the eighteenth century, but any large increase was blocked by the grip on the English market held by Baltic timber. Some increases of preference in the early years of the Napoleonic wars helped to compensate for the longer voyage, but made no marked change in the volume of imports from the British colonies. It was only when the emperor's continental system closed the Baltic ports that the British government took rapid action. Heavy duties were placed against foreign lumber, contracts to cut timber were awarded, and British merchants persuaded to turn toward the colonies. Measures designed as a guard against a dangerous shortage in lumber were continued for a generation, introducing and continuing the timber industry as a main factor in the economic life of New Brunswick and Canada. Agriculture employed a large part of the population of all the colonies but export of its products was slower in developing than that of fish, furs or timber. The United Kingdom still grew a large portion of the food for her own population and her landowners were averse to competition. The early years of the wars with France stimulated some imports of grains from British America, but the volume dwindled to almost nothing in the later stages of the Napoleonic campaigns. After the close of the wars small preferences drew some Canadian grain to the British market, but it was not until the forties that more generous encouragement swelled the grain trade into a major export.

In changing proportions and combinations these were the staple products on which the export trade of the colonies was built, and for which they exchanged manufactured articles and such raw materials as were not found within British North America.

Given a situation created by the resources of their lands and the imperial economic structure in which they found themselves, the colonials attempted to make the best of it. The direct approach was by seeking larger preferences and greater purchases in the United Kingdom, and these the merchants of the provinces were not backward in doing. In both Nova Scotia and Canada, however, there were also devised plans for a wider external trade which should supplement the bilateral one with Britain, and arising from the position of the provinces within the British Empire. For the Nova Scotians the aim was to create an entrepôt trade with Canada and the United States on the one hand and the British West Indies on the other. West Indian products would be forwarded to Canada, for example, and Canadian products sent on in return to the West Indies. At the same time there would be built up a trade with the other neighbouring colonies which were also within the protected empire.[5] Two obstacles stood in the way—lack of shipping, and American competition in the West Indies. The first the Nova Scotians attempted to surmount by the encouragement of steamship services, but success was slight. The second was beyond their power to overcome, for it depended on British restrictions on American ships. These restrictions varied in a most alarming manner, and it was all too apparent that the new gospel of free trade was making converts in England. The design of the Canadians was similar: to develop trade with the West Indies, and to siphon the commerce of the nearby American states, especially those of the growing middle west, through the St. Lawrence Valley. The belief that this plan could be realized arose from two assumptions: that the St. Lawrence was the "natural" approach to the interior of North America, and that American goods could be fathered by Canada to enter British markets under the preference. As in Nova Scotia, Canadians were helpless to direct the course of British tariff policy, but they could make themselves responsible for adequate transportation, first by canalization of the waterway and later by the construction of railways. So imbued were the merchants with the importance of the plan for a great external trade that they staked everything on communications.

   5 Innis, *Cod Fisheries*, 267.

Whether or not these cherished projects for the exploitation of the mercantile system could ever have been realized, they were in fact doomed to failure, for the mercantile system itself was dying. Free trade began to have solid support in England from about 1820, and Huskisson's tariff reforms made breaches in the old citadel. In 1839 the Anti-Corn Law League was formed and rapidly found a wide response for a programme which promised cheaper bread for the masses. The writing on the wall was visible across the broad stretch of the Atlantic. But if the old economic empire was dying, it died slowly, and in a blaze of glory and profit for the colonies. The Canada Corn Act of 1843 admitted Canadian wheat at a fixed duty of one shilling a quarter, and wheat milled in Canada at a proportionate rate. There were misgivings in England as to the wisdom of such an arrangement, especially when it allowed American wheat to be entered as Canadian flour; and such objections were only partially met by the Canadian action in placing a duty on American wheat imported into the province. The timber trade, which was relatively more important in New Brunswick than in Canada, also continued to enjoy substantial preferences until the early forties. In 1846 the blow fell with the news that the corn laws were to be abolished by successive reductions over a period of three years. Already the duty on timber had been cut down and further reductions had the effect of cancelling the preference on that staple as well. In British North America it seemed as if the bottom had fallen out of the whole economic structure, and the outcry was loud and prolonged. Bitter things were said about the hollowness of imperial unity, and the tories of Montreal voted in disgust for peaceful annexation to the United States. The British parliament, satisfied with the virtues of free trade and faced with an immediate demand for cheap food, was immovable. It did, however, take steps to free the colonies from the restrictions of the old system. The British Possessions Act of 1846 enabled legislatures to remove the preferences on British goods, and the navigation laws ceased to operate in 1849, allowing foreign ships to trade with the colonies. So perished the old imperial economic system.

II

To many people in the British colonies it seemed as if the old empire itself was to go as well. The year 1846, in which the preferences began to be removed, saw also the first stage of the withdrawal of the British garrisons. The two imperial props were pulled away at the same time: would the structure remain, and if so in what form? There was pressing need that the colonies take stock of their own positions; of their relationships with each other, with the United Kingdom, and with foreign states. The future of their external trade was a foremost question for the colonists to consider, but it was impossible to conceive of tariffs in a vacuum, for they were both cause and effect of a maze of political and social factors. So, while the thought on tariff veered wildly in this direction and that, it went deep into the basic economic aims of the provinces themselves and deep into the problems of external relationships. British colonies in an age of imperial disillusionment, American provinces next to a restless giant, fellow colonists who hardly knew each other—well might they ask themselves where they stood and what oath they should take.

After the first revolt against the change in British policy had subsided, cooler second thoughts would reveal both that the provinces had attained a not unenviable position economically and that the links with the mother country had by no means been severed. The flow of capital, essential for the development of the new world, had come and continued to come from London. In the new west, becoming of interest to the Province of Canada, the Hudson's Bay Company had financed exploration, agriculture, and government. In 1843 the British government enabled Canada to secure capital by guaranteeing the interest on bonds up to £1,500,000, negotiated by the treasury. With such support the bonds sold at favourable prices, mounting to £112:10. The proceeds were used for public works, principally canals, and provided work both for old residents and newcomers. Railway construction in the fifties was also made possible by English capital. The intervention of the Brassey firm in the Canadian railway field gave the prestige of the famous contractors to the Grand Trunk, and further support was added by the banking firms of Barings and of Glyn, Mills. In days when railways almost anywhere were thought to be a profitable investment such encouragement was hardly needed to induce individuals to buy stock in Canadian companies. Besides capital the provinces drew on Great Britain for experience in determining the lines on which their banks should be organized. From the first the general principles of Scottish banking were followed, allowing for branch-banking conducted by comparatively large concerns. The heresy of "free banking", as practised in the United States, for a time had some support, with the idea that more banks would create more credit, and that local banks would be more sympathetic to community needs than large ones with distant head offices. In 1850 a concession was made to that opinion in Canada by the Act to Establish Free Banking in this Province, but little advantage was taken of it, and the "aberration from sound principles" was not more than a threat.[6] Early life insurance policies were issued by the agencies of British companies, and caused an estimated export of £10,000-£15,000 in premiums. The first company to be established in British North America was the Canada Life Assurance Company, organized in 1847.[7]

British capital, British engineers, and British contractors played essential rôles in the construction of the canals and railways of British North America. Both methods of transportation were designed for foreign as well as local traffic by improving the St. Lawrence entry to the Great Lakes or by running steel up to the American frontier. The maritime provinces and Canada laid plans for lines of transportation that would at once promote their own external trade and make of their ports points of entry to eastern and central America. The name of the European and North American Railway proclaimed that purpose to the world, and if the Great Western and Grand Trunk railways had less descriptive names their objects were no less exalted. Though in the fifties an impressive amount of construction was completed in the Province of Canada, totalling some 2,000 miles, and providing rail transport from Rivière du Loup to Windsor, it was soon apparent that American traffic came nowhere near to expectations. Montreal had been connected with the western part of the province, and a line of railway to Portland, Maine, gave access to an ice-free port. Thus Canada was assured of a channel for her external trade throughout the year, provided that no obstacles were placed in the way of communication through foreign territory.

[6] B. E. Walker, *A History of Banking in Canada* (Toronto, 1909), 41.

[7] H. C. Baker, *A Lecture on Life Assurance* (Hamilton, 1848); *Prospectus, and First and Second Annual Reports of the Canada Life Assurance Company* (Hamilton, 1849).

The projects for connecting the all-year ports of the maritime provinces with the interior of the continent still lagged, so that no through route on British soil existed, and no links were forged to connect the province on the St. Lawrence with those on the sea. Of the western colonies Assiniboia was more accessible from the United States than from Canada. For years goods were carried by the creaking Red River carts between Fort Garry and St. Paul, and when steamships began to operate on the Red River in 1857 transportation was markedly easier. Both British Columbia and Vancouver Island could be reached only by sea, except for the laborious and specialized land transport which the Hudson's Bay Company had built up for its own purposes. The sea voyage from England took four to five months, though it could be shortened by proceeding to New York and over the Isthmus of Panama.

The efficiency of the postal system depended very largely on the state of facilities for transportation; and to some extent the reverse was also true, since the post office provided revenue for railways and steamships, and encouraged the construction of roads. From 1851 Canada, Nova Scotia, and New Brunswick were all in charge of the post office within their boundaries, but the carriage of mails between the maritime provinces and Canada, especially in winter, was slow. For mail from Europe to Canada resort was had to American railways. The people of Assiniboia also made use of the American postal system, and an attempt to remove this cause of Americanization of the colony by a mail service from Canada started in 1858 was soon abandoned. By the middle of the century three of the provinces had telegraph lines connecting with the American systems. In Canada the Montreal Telegraph Company ran from Quebec to Buffalo, and the Montreal and Troy Company built south to the border. New Brunswick had lines from Calais, Maine, to Saint John, and thence to Amherst, at which point it met the Nova Scotian government's telegraph to Halifax.[8] These facilities made possible rapid communication with the United States, and constituted the fastest avenue of news from Europe. Direct cable connection with Britain was not established until 1866, though there was a local cable between New Brunswick and Prince Edward Island from 1852.

8 John Murray, *Story of the Telegraph* (Montreal, 1905).

In the fifties the British colonies in North America had obtained better communication with the outside world than they had with each other. To the advocates of a political union the position was unsatisfactory; but from the point of view of external trade there was less to regret, for more emphasis was laid on trade with Britain or the United States than between the colonies themselves. There are no means of obtaining even an estimate of the relation between the external trade of the colonies and their total national incomes, but it is clear that it formed a large part. Though Canada was making some advance in that direction, none of the provinces was industrialized, and all depended on the sale of staple products abroad as a means of securing manufactured goods or other articles which they lacked. External trade created the greater part of their money income, leaving maintenance agriculture or fishing, and small industries—such as mills of various kinds—producing for local consumption. An examination of the external trade of the various provinces in the period between the adoption of free trade by Great Britain and the signature of the reciprocity treaty indicates the extent, nature, and direction of the trade.

In 1852 the principal export of Nova Scotia was, as before, fish, sent to the West Indies, the United States, and elsewhere. Lumber came second in value, and was sold in the West Indies and the United States. Coal was a poor third, and was bought in the United States and the other provinces. Of total exports valued at £970,780 the largest buyers were the other British provinces (£352,185), the United States (£257,849), with the West Indies not far behind. Great Britain bought goods to the extent of only £62,675. Imports were somewhat higher than exports, amounting to £1,194,175. The largest portion came from Great Britain, the second from the United States, and the third from the other provinces. The largest single item was cotton goods, coming principally from Britain. Wheat flour from the United States and Canada was close in value. Other items of importance, though considerably less than these two, were tea from the United States and the United Kingdom, sugar and molasses, fishing-tackle, iron, and leather.[9] For the same year the exports of New Brunswick were valued at £796,335, this excluding ships sold abroad. The

---

[9] *Journals of the House of Assembly of Nova Scotia, 1853.*

order of importance of exports was the reverse from that of Nova Scotia, forest products making up much the largest item, and fish coming second. The first were sold principally to the United States, and fish sales were widely distributed. Of total imports of £1,110,601 rather more than a half came from the United Kingdom, the leading articles being haberdashery, cordage and rope, hardware and iron, tea, and leather. Wheat came almost altogether from the United States; flour from the United States and Canada; fruit, vegetables, and livestock from the other provinces.[10] Canada's exports of £3,513,993 were made up of wheat and flour to the United States, Great Britain, and the other provinces; timber, potash, and pearlash to Britain; and dried fish in limited quantities to foreign countries. Her imports, shown as £5,071,623, came chiefly from Great Britain and the United States, the principal items being as follows: from Great Britain—oil, cottons, woollens, silks, linen, haberdashery, fancy goods, iron and hardware, coal, railway rails, earthenware and glassware; from the United States—sugar, tea, tobacco, salt, leather, oil, cotton, iron and hardware, machinery, hides, tallow, and books.[11]

External trade had by no means been destroyed by the abandonment of the old imperial system: if it had been the whole economy of the provinces would have been shattered. But while the extreme pessimism of the late forties had been exaggerated, it by no means followed that the provinces were satisfied with the new order. They continued to believe in preferential markets as an objective, and were determined to find them wherever they could. Tariffs against imports must be retained in some degree for revenue purposes, and there was a growing belief in tariffs for protection, especially in the more industrialized Province of Canada. There had thus come to be a conflict between the fiscal policies of Great Britain and her North American colonies; the latter clinging to a régime under which they had grown up, and seeking to build anew, on any available design, the structure which had in such a disconcerting fashion been blown down.

The colonists did not cease to petition for a return, at least in part, to the old protective system; but even thinly-veiled threats that the new policy would bring the empire to an end did not shock English opinion. The empire, was the reply, was based

---

[10] *Journals of the House of Assembly of New Brunswick,* 1853.
[11] *Tables of Trade and Navigation for 1852.*

not only on trade, but in any case free trade was better for the colonies. Nothing could shake this new belief in free trade, to which the British government now clung with all the passionate zeal of converts. Some echoes of the doctrine were heard in the provinces, where it began to be argued that, since free trade was so advantageous, it should be adopted there as well. The Montreal *Economist* devoted itself to this cause and a free trade party was formed in Montreal. The Free Trade Association, however, admitted the necessity of tariffs for revenue purposes, as was made clear in its manifesto of 1846. On the whole, however, there was little support for this position, it being pointed out that England, with her manufactures and shipping established, was in an altogether different position. To the editor of the Halifax *Times* it appeared that such measure of free trade as already existed had already displaced the manufactures of Great Britain and made the people of the province into "hewers of wood and drawers of water". The further extension of free trade, perhaps, could not make things any worse.[12]

Free trade in itself was not a popular policy; though reduction of tariffs through reciprocal agreements was generally thought to be hopeful. On the other hand, opinion in favour of protection was significantly growing in Canada, but not as yet in the maritime provinces in which manufacturing had hardly begun. Discussions inevitably arose as to whether the economy of Canada was, or could be, suited to a protective system. The argument on one side was that Canada must remain agricultural, could not compete in manufacturing, and therefore should have a low tariff. A further objection was that protection was a tax on consumers for the benefit of a small minority.[13] Others held that the climate was too cold for extensive agriculture, while the existence of water-power was promising for manufacturing. So far the picture of manufacturing was not impressive. There were cotton-mills at Sherbrooke and Chambly; woollen mills at Sherbrooke and Cobourg; three manufacturers of rope at Montreal; paper-mills at Portneuf, Chambly, Stanstead, and in Upper Canada; iron at Long Point, Three Rivers, and St. Maurice; glass at St. Jean;

---

[12] Sept. 29, 1846, quoted in the *Quebec Gazette*, Oct. 14.
[13] *Le Pays* (Montreal), Feb. 26, 1856.

tanneries in Montreal; and axes and nails were also manufactured.[14] It was all on a small scale, though it was to increase rapidly in the fifties.

The Canadian tariff of 1847 was regarded by English exporters as protective, and a group in Glasgow petitioned that it be disallowed. Grey brought this to Elgin's attention, and, while admitting the right of the provincial legislature to adjust its own tariff for revenue purposes, he pointed out that the effect might be a decreased purchase of Canadian grain if the colonial market was closed against British exports in exchange. The British government refused to be persuaded of the virtues of another assault on the sacred citadel of free trade, and sternly resisted protective measures in New Brunswick which began with a bounty on hemp, accompanying the refusal with a lecture on the new economics. If the colonies, as the colonial secretary more than once pointed out, could not see the advantages of free trade over protection, they should at least steer clear of differential duties.[15] R. B. Sullivan made a protectionist speech in Hamilton, urging the promotion of manufacturing in the province as a means of increasing capital and population. He disavowed any hostility to British manufacturers, but suggested that they and Americans should establish plants in Canada.[16] There were more converts to protection in the next few years, and in 1852 and 1853 definitely protectionist motions were debated in the assembly. The movement gathered strength, and was implemented in the Cayley tariff of 1858 and the Galt tariff of 1859.

Generally speaking the free trade movement was defended by pointing to the success of that policy in England, and the protectionist movement by the example of the United States. When the latter policy gained the ascendancy in Canada English opinion was not only shocked by the unwisdom of the Canadians, but alarmed as to the effect on British trade. Further protests against the Galt tariff were forwarded to Head by Newcastle, who pointed sorrowfully to the inability of Canada to follow the best fiscal tradition. It was in reply to this and the enclosed memorial of the Sheffield Chamber of Commerce that Galt made his famous

---

[14] The *Economist*, quoted in *La Minerve* (Montreal), Sept. 24, 1846.

[15] *Journals of the Legislative Assembly of the Province of Canada*, 1856, appendix 28.

[16] Edward Porritt, *Sixty Years of Protection in Canada, 1846-1907* (London, 1908), 198 *ff.*

pronouncement.[17] He argued that his was a revenue tariff, made necessary by the conditions of Canadian public finance, and was unlikely to encourage any serious amount of manufacturing. But the most important part of Galt's report was the claim that the Canadian legislature had unlimited control of its tariff. "It is . . . the duty of the present Government distinctly to affirm the right of the Canadian legislature to adjust the taxation of the people in the way they deem best—even if it should unfortunately happen to meet the disapproval of the Imperial Ministry. Her Majesty cannot be advised to disallow such acts, unless Her advisers are prepared to assume the administration of the affairs of the Colony, irrespective of the views of its inhabitants." Nothing could have been more definite. It was a claim, and as it proved a successful claim, to the fiscal independence of a colony. The old imperial system was indeed passing.

Vancouver Island deliberately followed a policy of free trade, and proposals for a revenue tariff of 5 per cent. on all imports, made from 1852 on, were rejected by the legislature. The high tariff of the United States bore heavily on the colony, and when the attempts to have the reciprocity treaty of 1854 extended to cover Vancouver Island failed, Victoria was made a free port in 1860, with the object of making the island a centre of trade on the coast.[18] The mainland, on the other hand, imposed 10 per cent. duties on a large list of imports for purposes of revenue; and in the united colony of British Columbia tariffs were retained.

The movement for protection was severely limited in scope by the parallel attempts to secure reciprocal trade agreements both as between the provinces themselves and with the United States. That an agreement between the provinces met with the less enthusiastic and general support illustrates the lack of ties between them. In 1847 Nova Scotia, and in 1848 Canada, passed permissive acts allowing the executive at any time to admit, by proclamation, the products of any other province. The Canadian act, however, was never implemented. An agreement was reached between Nova Scotia and New Brunswick, which was actually carried into effect; but Prince Edward Island abstained altogether, seeing no advantage to herself in the plan. In 1859, after it had accepted confederation

17 *Province of Canada, Sessional Papers,* 1860, no. 38.

18 *Minutes of the Council of Vancouver Island, 1851-1861* (Archives of British Columbia, Memoir no. 2).

on principle, and after Galt had conducted his tariff argument with the British government, the Canadian government initiated a movement for closer trade relations between the provinces. Two alternative suggestions were offered: that existing arrangements for the exchange of produce or manufactures of the provinces should be extended; or that there should be complete freedom of trade between the provinces—a colonial zollverein. Galt's memorandum went to the board of trade, which returned a lengthy answer. In general the opinion was, as it had been before, that the plan was undesirable. Since the colonies used the tariff as a means of revenue, and since their products were highly varied, it seemed impossible to have a widespread agreement amongst all British colonies. The economies of the North American colonies, however, were sufficiently alike to allow of limited arrangements, but only under the condition that "any exemption from import duty, applied to the produce and manufactures of these provinces respectively, shall be equally extended to all similar produce and manufactures of all countries". To do otherwise would be to magnify the Canadian sin against free trade, the ark of the covenant. A zollverein would probably be based on the high Canadian tariff, and was, therefore, *ipso facto,* objectionable.[19] The British government was evidently prepared to disallow any acts intended to carry out such a plan, as it had already disallowed acts of New Brunswick and Prince Edward Island which would have raised differential duties against the United States. With this cold reception the plan for economic federation fell to the ground.

There also followed on the abolition of the imperial preference system various attempts to obtain access to the markets of the United States, particularly for the grain and lumber which had formerly enjoyed a protected position in Great Britain. There were two ways of doing this: by political union, or by trade treaties. The former was an extreme measure, but the commercial class, particularly of Canada and New Brunswick, saw ruin staring them in the face as a result of British free trade. Inclined to think in terms of black and white, their financial discomfort was added to a weakening imperial sentiment on both sides of the Atlantic. If the mother country ignored their interests they must find salvation elsewhere. Few people could think of Canada,

19 *Journals of the House of Assembly of Nova Scotia,* 1860.

or even of British North America, as an economic unit in itself: it must be attached to one or other great Power. And then there was the tradition that the United States prospered in contrast to the struggling colonies. To many people it seemed that the old ambition of developing the St. Lawrence valley as an economic avenue between North America and Europe had failed of realization. Fate was against it, and fate now pointed another way. In Canada the annexation movement was brought to a head by the test of responsible government in the Rebellion Losses Act. Tories shed loyalty when the world they had known and governed was turned upside down, and the Montreal manifesto of 1849, calling for annexation to the United States, was an outburst of economic and political grievances. The chief force of the movement was in Montreal, the centre of the commercial interests. In Upper Canada there was little sympathy and considerable resistance. In Nova Scotia and New Brunswick the same combination of political and economic events produced cries for annexation, particularly in Halifax and Saint John, and in the lumber districts of northern New Brunswick; also to some extent in Prince Edward Island.[20]

It is doubtful whether this annexation movement need be taken seriously as a political force. Much of it came from an angry opposition, and was of an emotional type that tended to fade with time. A revival of prosperity helped to cure the ills of which the annexationists complained, and the persistent efforts of Elgin's government to secure reciprocal tariff arrangements with the United States gave promise of a cure that was not so excitingly naughty but at least more palatable. The reciprocity treaty, long under discussion, was finally passed in 1854.[21] It provided for the free exchange of grains and flour, animals and meats, vegetables, dairy products, fish, coal, and lumber. Limited reciprocal rights were given to coastal fisheries, and American vessels were admitted to equal rights with Canadian on the St. Lawrence. The treaty did not cover any manufactured goods, since it was believed that the "budding efforts" of the provinces in that field would not stand against equal competition. "Open the floodgates of the United States to-day, and our thriving manufactures would

[20] C. D. Allin and G. M. Jones, *Annexation, Preferential Trade and Reciprocity* (Toronto, n.d.).

[21] On the negotiation and terms of the treaty see D. C. Masters, *The Reciprocity Treaty of 1854* (London and Toronto, n.d.).

be assuredly swamped."[22] The treaty included all the British provinces except those on the Pacific coast. The government of Vancouver Island attempted to arrange for the inclusion of that province, but without success.

The effects of the treaty on the provinces concerned, as shown by the statistics of the years just before the American Civil War created abnormal conditions, were less than the optimists had expected but still important. In Nova Scotia both imports and exports increased materially, and the United States became the largest seller and buyer. Sales to the United Kingdom were smaller absolutely as well as relatively.[23] A similar change occurred in New Brunswick. Whereas in 1852 that province exported goods valued at £603,295 to the United Kingdom and only £83,792 to the United States, in 1859 the figures were £716,436 and £236,014 respectively; and in imports the United States passed Great Britain.[24] In the same year (1859) Prince Edward Island bought from Nova Scotia, the United Kingdom, and the United States, in that order, and sold fish and farm products in the United States.[25] In Canada too the volume of trade had increased. Types of goods imported had changed little under the treaty, but while Great Britain had been slightly ahead in 1852, by 1859 the United States had taken a decisive lead. In exports the change was even more marked.[26] While a marked increase of external trade had taken place—during, and perhaps because of, the reciprocity treaty—the millenium once pictured had not arrived. The fisheries of the maritime provinces, which had been at a low ebb before the treaty, were now subjected to even greater competition from Americans, who continued to receive a bounty. The imposition of higher tariffs, especially by Canada, antagonized American manufacturers. Intercolonial reciprocity, frowned on in 1860, was accepted in principle in 1861. The desire to retain the treaty waned appreciably in the provinces and began to disappear altogether in the United States.

To facilitate trade relations with Canada a number of foreign countries appointed residents of Montreal as consuls, these receiving

22 British Colonist (Toronto), Dec. 20, 1855.
23 Journals of the House of Assembly of Nova Scotia, 1860.
24 Journals of the House of Assembly of New Brunswick, 1860.
25 Journals of the House of Assembly of Prince Edward Island, 1860.
26 Province of Canada, Sessional Papers, 1860, no. 23.

exequaturs from the British government. In 1850 Belgium, Portugal, and Denmark all took this action, and in 1851 the Hansa towns and Hanover followed suit. In 1856 the executive council recommended that France should appoint a consul-general in place of its consular agencies at Quebec and Montreal. The British government was willing for the change and approached the French ambassador, who however, reported that his government could not at the time take such action.[27] But at the very time that the reply was made a French mission under M. Belvèze, commander of a French man-of-war, was touring Canada with the object of establishing commercial relations. Great enthusiasm greeted the French party, and an elaborate survey of the conditions of the province was made.[28] As a result of the trip the French tariff was modified so as to admit Canadian wood and ships, and a consul-general was appointed in 1859 who came to live in Quebec.[29]

The external trade of the provinces of British North America not only survived the radical fiscal changes undertaken in England, but continued to grow. In tariff policy and arrangements significant alterations were made in the provinces, but on the whole they were alterations intended to preserve by other means the essential characteristics of the old régime. Budding industries complicated the situation by causing the introduction of protection for home products; but essentially the provinces looked to external trade, and to finding their main economic strength from the sale of the staples with which they had been richly endowed.

27 Public Archives of Canada, *Series G,* vol. 151, pp. 92, 196.
28 Belvèze's report is printed in *Le Pays,* Sept. 2, 4, 6, 9, 1856.
29 L. P. Turcotte, *Le Canada sous l'union, 1841-1867* (Quebec, 1871), 267-9.

CHAPTER IV

THE PATH TO CONFEDERATION

HARDLY had British North America begun to settle down to plan a new order to take the place of the old when the shock of the American Civil War threw out all calculations and forced a reconsideration of plans. It was not so much that the elements in the situation were new, for the provinces had long been accustomed to American influence in varying form and degree. Nor even was it that entirely fresh ideas were evolved to fit the changed circumstances. The moves open to the provinces in constructing their external policies were strictly limited in number: it was only in emphasis, combination, and speed that there was room for choice.

The Civil War caught the provinces in a stage of transition in every important aspect of their external relations. The old mercantilist empire had come to an end amidst cries of despair and bitterness. The imperial defence system, as it had been known, was doomed; and so faint was the imperial faith in Britain that many contemporaries on both sides of the Atlantic believed that it would not long outlast its traditional manifestations. The older colonies were at once seeking to repair the lines of trade and to adjust themselves to an age of iron and steam. Bold steps in the construction of railways had brought heavy commitments and uncertain results. The people of Canada were casting anxious looks towards Assiniboia, wondering how they could arrest its growing attachment to the neighbouring states of the union. Far to the west the colony of British Columbia was in gloomy convalescence after the hectic fever of the gold rush, looking for a sign as to the way it should take toward renewed strength. The problems of the sixties were, indeed, such as might challenge the wisest statesmanship.

Civil War in the United States, with military operations mounting in scale and tempers fraying, could not but affect in some degree those provinces bordering on the scene of action, accustomed to constant interchange of people and goods, hardly knowing whether they were more drawn by community of interests or repelled by fear of aggression.[1] The frequent crossing of the border, which had become an accepted condition, was curtailed even before the outbreak of hostilities by threatening conditions in the United States. For two periods, also, legal barriers were set up by the American government. In 1861 passports were required of Canadians embarking at American ports, a rule which seriously impeded winter travel between Canada and Europe. A few months later the regulation was withdrawn, but at the end of 1864 again passports had to be carried by all foreigners entering the United States. In spite of the inconveniences resulting from general and particular restrictions to travel, the people of the provinces might well have wished that the boundary could have been completely sealed, as the lesser evil compared with the danger of being involved in the war. On the issues of the war there were no general opinions. Had the North been fighting against slavery, as it first appeared to be, its cause would have met with wide approval, for slavery was generally condemned in all the provinces. But on the issue of states' rights there was no such settled conviction. The coercion of the southern states received some adverse comment, and was sometimes related to the disturbing process by which the United States had been absorbing its neighbours.

Judged in terms of practical aid it would seem that the cause of the North was the more popular one. In spite of the efforts of the authorities to enforce the Foreign Enlistment Act, Canadians enlisted in the federal armies, and offers were even made to raise regiments in Canada. By far the largest number came from French Canada—perhaps three-quarters of a total estimated by a contemporary at 40,000, of whom, it was said, 14,000 were killed.[2] While a portion of these enlisted because of conviction, and others for adventure or employment, many were persuaded by the recruiting agents sent to Canadian towns, or deluded into crossing

---

[1] For the relations of British North America with the United States during the Civil War see J. W. Holmes, "Border Relations between Canada and the United States during the American Civil War" (unpublished M.A. thesis, University of Toronto, 1933); L. B. Shippee, *Canadian-American Relations, 1849-1874* (New Haven and Toronto, 1939); M. L. Hansen, *The Mingling of the Canadian and American Peoples,* vol. I, *Historical* (New Haven and Toronto, 1940).

[2] *La Minerve* (Montreal), Nov. 16, 1865.

the boundary on some pretext. The bounty offered to recruits no doubt was often the inducement to enlist, and when that failed attempts were made to fill up the ranks by crimping. There are few indications of enlistment by Canadians in the southern armies, but that can, at least in part, be explained by the wide barrier that separated the provinces from the confederacy. To international complications arising out of Canadian enlistment— voluntary or forced—were added those created by the desertion of United States citizens from the federal armies to Canada. The presence of such deserters was unwelcome both because they added to unemployment, and more particularly because of the friction caused on the border. There were cases of their pursuit on Canadian soil by American forces, cases which could not be ignored by the Canadian authorities.

Any gratitude that might have been felt in the North toward the colonials serving in their armies was more than offset by a belief that the provinces, like the mother country, really favoured the South, both in thought and in deed. British recognition of the confederacy as a belligerent, the activities of the English-built privateer *Alabama,* and expressed sympathy for the South in Britain once more fanned into a flame old embers stirred by the seizure of confederate agents from the British ship *Trent.* To the Anglo-American disputes were added those that arose out of the plots of confederates, who swarmed in the provinces as did federal recruiting officers and federal detectives. Canada in particular was dangerously exposed to being forced into the position of territory added to the general conflict. In 1863 Lord Monck warned the British minister in Washington of an intended raid from Canada, and so enabled the federal authorities to guard against it. As the war went against it, the confederate government made desperate attempts to create a diversion by opening up a new front. In the spring of 1864 three commissioners were sent to represent the "Confederate Department in Canada", and—apparently supplied with ample funds—the unwelcome visitors assumed extraterritorial status. The largest design, for a northwestern confederacy within the United States, came to nothing. Two or three abortive raids involved violations of Canadian neutrality. The most futile of the plots was the one that caused the greatest repercussions. In October, 1864, a raid from Canada was organized against the town of St. Albans, in Vermont. Banks were robbed, a cashier was shot, and attempts were made to burn the town. The affair was condemned in Canada, but when the returning raiders, though arrested promptly, were at first discharged on the ground of exercising belligerent rights there was a bitter outcry in Northern papers. The number of actual armed outbreaks as a result of confederate plots was small, but there were frequent alarms which were almost as effective in maintaining international tension.

Threats to neutrality implicit in maritime disputes and border incidents were accompanied by a revival of the old issue of annexation. Amongst the American public and press were men, of whom the most vociferous was the editor of the New York *Herald*, who urged annexation of the provinces. With the close of the war the American government was left with a great army, and memories of quarrels with both Great Britain and Canada. The old opposition from the South, based on resistance to the addition of further free soil, was gone; nor was the South more friendly to either Britain or her colonies. Within the republican administration that took office in 1861 there were both anglophobes and expansionists, and the assassination of Lincoln left Seward a freer hand under Andrew Johnson, his imperialist zeal being curbed only by a congress hostile to Johnson and cautious about expenditure. The secretary of state's roving eye fell on the Caribbean, Alaska, the Hawaiian Islands, and Canada. He had visions of extending American power to the far east, to South America, and to the Arctic Ocean. Nor was Seward the only prophet of manifest destiny, for many a writer saw the blessings of American government extended to more than a continent.[3] The Fenian raids on New Brunswick and Canada in 1866 were greeted with scarcely concealed approval by the expansionists in the republican party; and a bill was introduced into the house of representatives "for the admission of the states of Nova Scotia, New Brunswick, Canada East, and Canada West, and for the organization of the Territories of Selkirk, Saskatchewan, and Columbia".

If the provinces exaggerated their own importance to a people preoccupied with war and post-war problems they were at least not without evidence of hostility or even of aggressive tendencies.

3 For contemporary American opinion see J. P. Smith, *The Republican Expansionists of the Early Reconstruction Era* (privately planographed, 1933).

They endeavoured to justify their claims to neutrality by enforcement of its obligations, but there was no escape from the conclusion that measures for military defence must accompany legal correctness. For the defence of the colonies three elements were to be considered: the militia, fortifications, and aid from England. At the outbreak of the Civil War there were slightly more than 4,000 imperial troops in all British North America; about 5,000 equipped and partly drilled volunteers in Canada; and the same in the maritime provinces together.[4] Steps were taken by the British government to send immediate reinforcements to the extent of three regiments and a field battery, and after the *Trent* affair, larger reinforcements still. These measures were designed to meet a temporary emergency, and did not alter the policy that the government had adopted in the forties: that permanent garrisons would gradually be withdrawn and imperial troops sent only to meet specific dangers; and that the defence of the provinces must primarily depend on an adequate number of trained volunteers. Two examinations of the situation, made on the eve of the Civil War, served to strengthen the adherence to that policy. Reporting in 1859, the majority of the three commissioners appointed to consider the expense of military defences in the colonies found that "a system of defence, based upon the presence of Imperial garrisons in every part of the empire, is as inefficient as it is burdensome; and that the right system would be one based on local efforts and local resources". To this they added that Canada was subject to attack only by the United States, and that the time required for that country to prepare an invading force would be more than enough to allow for British troops to be transported to the colony. A select committee of the house of commons on colonial military expediture reported in 1861 that, while some discretion should be left to the government in judging individual cases, "the responsibility and cost of the defence of such dependencies [the colonies] from perils not arising from the results of Imperial policy ought mainly to devolve upon themselves".[5]

That the willingness of the colonies to undertake military obligations should vary in direct ratio with the apparent danger

---

[4] C. P. Stacey, *Canada and the British Army, 1846-1871: A Study in the Practice of Responsible Government* (London, 1936), 118. The military position during the Civil War is analysed in this work.

[5] Both reports are printed in *Province of Canada, Sessional Papers*, 1862, no. 17.

of war was to be expected. The *Trent* affair produced a quick response. In Canada the existing volunteers drilled enthusiastically and offers of further corps were made. Joseph Howe offered every able-bodied man in Nova Scotia for military service.[6] A public meeting in Saint John drew a large and enthusiastic crowd. Enthusiasm soon cooled. At a second meeting in Saint John speakers expressed surprise that attendance was slim.[7] Howe ceased to see danger from the United States. Canada was, as it always had been, the most vulnerable of the colonies, and the apprehension of war led the government to appoint in 1862 a commission to consider military affairs. The report, presented to parliament in May in the form of an enabling bill, was an ambitious one, providing for an active force of 50,000 men with a reserve of the same size. Conscription by ballot might be resorted to if necessary. The annual cost was to be $1,100,000. The bill was bitterly attacked by members from both Upper and Lower Canada; was defeated; and the government, already weak, resigned. The succeeding ministry, that of Sandfield Macdonald and L. V. Sicotte, returned to a variant of the old system, at a cost of rather less than half of what had been proposed in J. A. Macdonald's bill.

The failure of the militia bill served to bring out a variety of opinions both in England and Canada. New arguments were offered to those in England who felt that Canada did not bear a fair share of her own defence. In the press and in parliament criticism, some of it bitter, was expressed. Writing to the governor general shortly after the session of parliament had closed, Newcastle hoped that "the general spirit of those debates will not have been misinterpreted", but admitted that "the rejection of the Militia Bill has produced a disadvantageous impression on the minds of the English people". Coming to the practical problem of how to provide for defence he stated he had "the opinions of the best military authorities, that no body of troops which England could send, would be able to make Canada safe without the efficient aid of the Canadian people. Not only is it impossible to send sufficient troops but if these were four times the number which we are maintaining in British North America, they could not secure the whole of the frontier. The main dependence of

[6] Public Archives of Canada, *Howe Papers*, Howe to Mulgrave, Nov. 30, 1861.

[7] *The Morning Freeman* (Saint John), July 3, 1862.

such a country must be upon its own people." The least number of men which the provincial government should look forward to drilling would be 50,000.[8]

In the provinces public opinion was divided on the fairness of the attitude of the British government. The case was never fully presented, for colonials seized almost entirely on the allocation of costs, concluding that they should or should not bear a larger share. Undoubtedly that argument was also the one most obviously influential in England; but there was also the strategic factor, brought out both in the commission of 1859 and the committee of 1861, that assistance could be given more effectively by an adequate force to be sent as occasion required than by permanent and necessarily small garrisons. The public in British North America did not, however, miss the point that the need for defence might result from imperial rather than local policy, and might be an imperial as well as a local interest. "It is something new", wrote a Saint John editor, "to see the statesmen of England look forward to shame and dishonour with such philosophical calmness, such cold, calculating indifference. . . . While we form part of the Empire England must and will do all she can to protect our soil—not indeed for our sake but her own."[9] The same theme was elaborated by a rival paper in the same city.

The Colonies should undoubtedly provide for their own internal security and peace, and they have already manifested a disposition to do this; but that they should provide means to defend their territories from enemies externally, when made so by Imperial policy in which the colonies have no voice, we unequivocally and decidedly dispute. When Great Britain sent her trained and trusted warriors to these Provinces, after the perpetration of the outrage on board the *Trent*, it was not to defend Provincial interests, for none were jeopardized by any provincial policy or likely to be so, but to maintain imperial interests, if an attempt had at that time been made to seriously imperil them, against all opposing forces.[10]

In Canada East the radical *Pays* burst out at the suggestion that England would not defend Canada.

[8] *Canada, Sessional Papers*, 1867-8, no. 63, Newcastle to Monck, August 21, 1862.
[9] *The Morning Freeman*, Aug. 7, 1862.
[10] *The Courier* (Saint John), April 12, 1862.

Situation singulière! Rester colons, pour le plaisir de s'appeler sujets britanniques, pour les beaux yeux de l'Angleterre, et cependant demeurer obligés de nous défendre contre les ennemis de la métropole comme si nous étions indépendants! . . .

Comment! S'il plaît aux Anglais et aux Américains de se quereller à propos de bottes, pour des questions qui ne nous intéressent pas plus que les affaires de Chine ou du Japon, nous serons tenus de verser notre sang et de nous ruiner parce que le Canada est une colonie Britannique . . .[11]

Other papers of Canada East took a less decided line, arguing that Canada and England should share the burden. In both parts of the province there were expressions of opinion more sympathetic to England, and the attitude of Le Pays could be set off against that of the right-wing tories who urged large expenditure for defence, and placed unlimited confidence in the British government. Each accused the other of sinister motives: the left holding that peace could be maintained were it not for the imperial connection and the misguided imperialism of the tories, and the right constantly hurling the epithet "annexationist".

The third factor to be considered in relation to the defence of the provinces was fortifications. In 1863 and 1864 Lieut.-Colonel W. F. D. Jervois was sent by the war office to Canada. In his first report he assumed that, failing naval superiority on the lakes, the whole province west of Montreal was indefensible. The second report, however, included works at Kingston, Toronto, and Hamilton, with an estimated total cost of £600,000. Naval force sufficient to maintain communications would also be required. Quebec and Montreal, sea-ports and more readily defensible, were to be fortified at a cost of £743,000.[12] Most of the plans were never implemented, though they did not cease to be discussed. Jervois's first opinion, unpopular as it was, that Canada West could not be defended, at least not without considerable naval power, was perhaps not far from the truth. A huge American army, once freed from the Civil War, and with railways at its disposal, was formidable out of all proportion to the army of 1812. For the maritime provinces the royal navy would always be a protection, but not even troops could reach Canada in

---

[11] Le Pays (Montreal), Oct. 11, 1864.

[12] The second report is in Journals of the House of Assembly of Nova Scotia, 1865, appendix 35.

winter except by the arduous land route followed by the imperial reinforcements in 1861. The problem of defence was clearly different in the several colonies both in the danger anticipated and the means of repelling it. They had in common, however, a continuing apprehension of American aggression and a realization that the military empire, as they had known it, was gone.

The economic problems of the provinces were partly accentuated, partly caused, by the Civil War. Factors beyond their control had been causing disturbing changes in the economy of the British North American provinces. Industrialism and free trade had together upset the old régime under which the natural products of the provinces had been carried to a protected market in ships built of North American lumber. The new age of steam, iron, and free trade had called for major adjustments. Coal and iron had now to be imported, and money borrowed for the railways that had become a necessity. For a brief period all seemed to be well: capital and equipment flowed from England, and the reciprocity treaty promised a new avenue of protected trade. But it was a delicate balance, all too easily upset by events abroad. Financial stringency in the United States and England automatically affected the provinces, and on the eve of the Civil War the provinces faced a partially-completed network of railways and a heavy debt. The war had a disturbing effect in many ways. An observer in Canada West found business depressed, prices low, the value of land down, the influx of British capital stopped, and money leaving the country. "We are as a people", he wrote, "affected most acutely by the abnormal conditions of our great neighbour. . . . Our currency is deranged, our exchanges affected, and, generally, the whole course of commercial transactions so governed and diverted that reciprocal trade has almost become an affair of gambling."[13] Even if difficult, the trade with the United States made up more than half of the total external trade of the British provinces, and during the period of the operation of the treaty the value of that trade had more than doubled. That this increase was only in part caused by the treaty itself was not fully realized at the time, and when abrogation became a possibility it seemed that a major catastrophe was impending. To some extent, no doubt, the political friction of the war years

13 *Whitby Chronicle*, March 16, 1865.

at least hurried on the American decision to terminate the arrangement. But only about six per cent. of the total foreign trade of the United States was with the British provinces, and the decision was not for them one of overwhelming moment. There had been growing resentment by American manufacturers against the increasing tariff protection adopted in Canada, and it was argued that the provinces had not lived up to the spirit of the agreement. By taking the southern free traders out of Congress the Civil War opened the way for a policy of protection.

While intercolonial trade came to be thought of as an alternative to that with the United States (which was expected greatly to diminish), it had also been investigated for its own merits. In 1861 the government of New Brunswick proposed a plan for free trade between the maritime provinces; and the British government not only withdrew its opposition, but gave its blessing to the inclusion of Canada as well. A difficulty which had stood in the way had always been the higher tariff of Canada, but by the end of the war reductions in Canada had brought the tariffs of the province sufficiently close to allow for a customs union of some type to be seriously considered. A collective effort was also made by the provinces to extend their trade with Mexico, the West Indies, and South America. In September, 1865, "The Confederate Council for Trade" met at Quebec "in reference to the Reciprocity Treaty with the United States and commercial matters generally", and agreed to recommend the opening of negotiations for more extensive trade. To this the colonial secretary gave his warm approval, and a commission was appointed by the governments of Canada, Nova Scotia, New Brunswick, and Prince Edward Island. Acting under instructions from their own governments, and with the necessary good offices of the British government in relations both with other colonies and foreign states, the commissioners left on their tour after a meeting in London. When their investigations were completed the commissioners made a report, with some definite suggestions: improvement of transportation and postal facilities; a reduction of duties, by reciprocal treaties or otherwise, levied in the West Indies, Brazil, and the Spanish colonies on the staples of British North America; and an assimilation of the tariffs of the British West Indies in respect of the same staples.[14] Four years later plans were being considered for the extension of trade with Portugal and Mediterranean countries. All these, however, were no more than plans, and no solid alternative had yet been found to replace the security of either the old imperial preference or the reciprocal agreement with the United States.

A combination of circumstances thus brought the people of the provinces consciously to consider their future. One possible course was to remain as they were, but to do so would simply be to accept present conditions that were far from satisfactory and future ones which might be a great deal worse. Inevitably there was revived the recourse of peaceful annexation to the United States, by which the problem of defence would automatically cease to exist and the ex-colonials would participate in the economic advantages enjoyed by the United States. It was toward this end that at least some of the campaign against the reciprocity treaty had been waged in the United States, and there were not lacking individuals in the provinces who were willing to join with the larger neighbour. In Canada East the conservative and liberal newspapers accused the radical party of a dangerous admiration for American institutions, and a tendency toward annexation. *L'Ordre* was said to favour annexation openly, *Le Pays* to be always praising the United States, and the *Witness* and the *Herald* to follow *Le Pays*. Their admiration for the republic's institutions was not shared by *La Minerve*, which saw corruption in its people from the customs officials up, and lamented the fate of those French Canadians who had emigrated to the United States.[15] The conservative *Courrier du Canada* used harsher words:

Le Pays, de Montréal, avec cette pertinacité maladive qui characterise le mal, ne cesse d'exalter les autres pays mais surtout les Etats-Unis aux dépens du Canada; pour ce faire ils soustraient, mutilent, et combattent la verité à outrance. Les malheureux lecteurs de ce malheureux journal n'apprennent pas un mot de la gangrène morale qui ronge la société américaine et qui se traduit heure par heure dans la presse de cette infortunée république.[16]

---

[14] *Report of the Commissioners from British North America Appointed to Inquire into the Trade of the West Indies, Mexico and Brazil* (Ottawa, 1866).

[15] *La Minerve*, June 22, 1865.

[16] *Le Courrier du Canada*, Sept. 4, 1865.

Such language was not unusual in days when editors were accustomed to express their views with unrestrained vigour, but the accusations of favouring annexation or independence were met with a revealing argument.

Il est faux qu'il y ait ici un parti annexationiste. . . . Il y a tout simplement des gens qui voient clair, qui consultent l'avenir et qui se demandent: si l'Angleterre nous abandonne, ou ne promet pas de nous défendre en cas d'attaque et n'en prend pas les moyens, que faudra-t-il faire? Il y a deux modes d'existence politique possible en dehors des arrangements actuels: l'indépendence ou l'annexion, lequel choisir?[17]

The idea of union with the United States was, in fact, based not on ideological principles but on specific interests. There was always a minority which supported annexation on general geographical or economic arguments, but it was not that minority which was influential. The position in the sixties was not unlike that which gave rise to the annexation manifesto of 1849, but the earlier movement had had more vitality and wider support than the later. Belief in the imperial connection was strong throughout all the provinces, but scepticism would inevitably increase if no advantages, or even positive disadvantages, appeared to be the only reward of loyalty. The provinces were still faced with the problem of their external relations in the future. Discouraged by the decline in foreign trade, alarmed by the imperialism of the United States, they wanted to be reassured that British connection spelt tangible aid and not merely risk of international friction. It was not only in Canada East that such ideas were being discussed. A supporter of the government, a journalist in Woodstock, Canada West, was alarmed by what he heard around him.

It is rumoured, that a desire for annexation to the United States is widely spread absorbing all other questions. This is not true, but it is true, that there is a strong feeling in favour of independence taking possession of the public mind created and fomented chiefly by the leading merchants, in this section, who are doubtless inspired by a desire to guard their own interests. The reasons the[y] adduce for the agitation are "that Canada is indefensible"—"that it is absurd to burden the country with an enormous debt as a condition of the Imperial grant for the fortification of Quebec" "that Canada has no need of expensive defences under the present friendly feeling which

17 *Le Pays*, May 18, 1865.

exists between Canada and the United States"— . . . it is my duty to inform you of the feeling, that prevails here that if we are left to ourselves or forced to incur a burden of debt for our defences the cry for independence I fear will be irresistible in this western peninsula.[18]

Peaceful annexation was being seriously discussed, though how much solid support it had is impossible to tell. The other positive course which the provinces might take was toward political union, either by regions or of all the provinces together. Long advocated by individuals, the idea of a union of some or all of the colonies had lacked the force to carry it over the objections raised. In the sixties a remarkable combination of circumstances occurred: the maritime provinces were seriously contemplating a regional union; the Province of Canada looked for a way out of its own hampering dualism; the colonies of the west seemed to be slipping toward the United States. The two countries which exercised most influence on British North America were, directly or indirectly, exerting pressure toward union. The United States supplied coercive force by the military and political threats that were read into the actions and speeches of her politicians and publicists. The British government, lately lukewarm toward union, came to use every means at its disposal to encourage it.[19] Pushed and pulled toward a decision, provincial governments and legislatures gazed down the untracked path that led to a new British North America and a new British Empire.

II

Responsible government, which its ardent supporters saw as a *deus ex machina* to solve the constitutional riddle of the old imperial system, set in bold relief the very problems which it was intended to remove. A local ministry in virtual control of the executive power was expected to draw a nice distinction between domestic and external affairs. It is not surprising that it sought to draw within its orbit those subjects which it could with advantage control, and to label as external equally controversial ground which could be held only with loss and worry. But the movement which

[18] Public Archives of Canada, *Macdonald Papers*, General Letters, J. McWhinnie to Macdonald, May 1, 1865.

[19] Chester Martin, "British Policy in Canadian Confederation" (*Canadian Historical Review*, XIII, March, 1932).

culminated in Galt's assertion of fiscal independence in 1859 was a Pyrrhic victory, for a British parliament and public could not follow a logic under which its soldiers but not its goods might be exported to the colonies. Out of the welter of conflicting opinions on both sides of the Atlantic a few themes may be isolated. In Great Britain there was little enthusiasm for the colonial connection, but a willingness to carry it on subject to a reasonable degree of compromise on the outstanding questions. In the colonies, which were much more vitally affected, large majorities were anxious to remain within the empire, but found the existing position ambiguous and unsatisfactory. Union of the provinces was welcome to both: to the mother country because it promised some solution of the defence question, and to the colonies because they believed that it would give them economic, military, and political strength. It is, however, the paradox of the confederation movement that the central issue of the control of external relations was left almost untouched.

The idea of a union of some or all of the provinces was not a new one, but—as in the case of the earlier union of the thirteen colonies—external pressure was required to bring them together. The collapse of the old economic empire in the forties had forced the colonies to reconstruct their scheme of external trade, which they had attempted to do by tariff agreements with each other and with the United States. The latter seemed to fail with the abrogation of reciprocity, and the former could be extended only by a joint improvement of transportation. The Civil War forced a more serious consideration of the defence question, and the British policy of withdrawal of troops at least suggested defence based on political union. Finally, belief in colonies had reached its nadir in the mother country, and the British government was ready to give its powerful support to the federation movement, with its eyes open to the possibility that it might be the forerunner of independence. Threats to territory, both that held by the colonies and that in the west to which they had some aspirations, combined with British coolness toward economic or political empire, drove on the union movement over the obstacles of provincial consciousness and minority fears. In the complexity of issues raised by the federation project no single aim—whether of internal or external application—can be said to have had a determining effect on any one province. The public, the press, and the legislatures weighed the arguments for and against, examining the proposed constitutional machinery, financial settlement, the possibilities of increased trade, effect on the imperial tie and on relations with foreign powers. External factors by no means constituted the sole considerations, but they did receive great attention at a time when the economic and military position of the provinces seemed so uncertain.

Trade played a leading part in the debates in all provinces.[20] A minority party in Prince Edward Island argued that the removal of customs barriers would reduce the price of imported goods, and that agricultural products could be sold in Saint John and Halifax, which was particularly necessary in view of the coming abrogation of reciprocity. The majority opinion, however, denied the validity of this argument, and held that Canada would furnish no market for the Island's staples in agriculture and fisheries, and that profitable markets already existed in Great Britain, the United States, and the West Indies. In Nova Scotia the proponents of confederation argued that the geographical position and the potential manufactures of the province could be exploited only in union with a larger territory, of which Nova Scotia would become the "Atlantic frontage". To this it was answered that free trade could be secured without political union, and that there was in any case some doubt as to whether the infant manufactures of the province should be exposed to the cold breeze of free competition. Very much the same arguments were used in New Brunswick. Neither in Nova Scotia nor New Brunswick did the trade issue bulk so large as other aspects of the project. For British Columbia the prospects of trade with eastern America were too visionary to have a popular appeal, but commercial dependence on the Pacific states was objectionable because of the high tariff against the province, and confederation—given effective transportation—might provide an alternative. There was, however, some fear that a tariff controlled by the dominion would possibly not be calculated in the interests of British Columbian industries and agriculture. No aspect of confederation was given more attention; and advocates of confederation were even driven to suggest that there might be a special tariff for the province. It was in Canada that the

---

20 The published debates of the legislatures of Prince Edward Island, Nova Scotia, New Brunswick, Canada, and British Columbia have been used for the following passages.

commercial aspect of confederation was debated most hotly, following a tradition of signal optimism or pessimism toward each successive plan for the improvement of trade. If the maritime provinces needed a hinterland, Canada, "shut up in prison for five months of the year in fields of ice", needed a sea-coast. There were hopes, too, of intercolonial trade, which, as Cartier pointed out, had been insignificant, but which might be considerable. Another defender of confederation spoke of exchanging Canadian grain and flour for fish, oil, and coal; but the opposition replied that there was little Canada could buy from the maritime provinces, and if there were a prospect of such trade it could be arranged by tariff agreement as readily as by political union. Other members of the legislature were concerned about the possibility of lowering the Canadian tariff, just as members in the lower provinces were concerned about raising theirs.

A constant argument in favour of confederation was that it would make possible the improvement of transportation. For Nova Scotia and New Brunswick this meant an intercolonial railway connecting their ports with the cities of Canada. To them it was a *sine qua non,* and perhaps the only undisputed advantage. Canada was less certain about the intercolonial railway. It would, it was true, give them access to winter ports, but it was generally recognized that it could not be profitable. There was talk of better canals coming as a result of confederation but the most important project after the intercolonial was that of a railway to the Pacific coast. In the maritime provinces expansion to the west was a distant objective, but at least to an important body of opinion in Canada it was essential, even if not pursued immediately. In British Columbia communication with Canada was even more the price of union than it was in the lower provinces, and the adhesion of the Pacific province was made contingent on the construction of a railway within a stated period.

The Fenian raids—actual or threatened—gave a background of realism to all discussions on union, as did the broken trade relations in the economic sphere. Defence, equally with trade, was dependent on adequate communications, though whether or not the intercolonial railway, close as it must be at points to the American border, was an effective instrument for the movement of troops and supplies was a moot point. At least it was more hopeful than the toilsome march overland which the imperial troops had been obliged to take during the Civil War. There was one point undisputed about defence: the British government was convinced that it could be effectively organized only by a single political unit, and for this reason more than any other urged on the confederation. The executive council of New Brunswick, while admitting that the wishes of Great Britain were "entitled to great weight", retained the right to settle the destiny of the province, without which right it claimed that the conferring of self-government would have been a mockery. The Fenian raid of 1866, ineffective as it was, partially removed the argument that defence was primarily a Canadian problem. In Prince Edward Island objections on other counts overrode the defence argument, and indeed the islanders had little consciousness of danger to their own territory. During the debate in the assembly of Nova Scotia Tupper, Archibald, and others agreed that the British view that the defence of the provinces could be effective only after confederation was a sound one. "If we are able to defend ourselves", said C. J. Campbell, "without the assistance of Great Britain, let us say so; but if we are not, let us concede what the mother country desires." Against this the opposition expressed a readiness to make a joint contribution to defence without confederation: and one member, McLelan, claimed that Nova Scotia was already "one vast drill-shed", and that England would certainly aid against "the danger she has brought upon us".

In Canada, the most exposed colony, the discussions of the defence question were most lengthy, but followed much the same lines as in other provinces. On the one hand it was said that the advice of the British government should be followed, in view of its place in the defence scheme of Canada, and having regard for the military power and possible aggression of the United States. Many members spoke on the general theme of unity being strength, but there was apparently little knowledge of what this meant in military organization. The strategic importance of Newfoundland was a more concrete consideration; but on the whole the government speakers left themselves open to the criticism that they could not show how added strength would be gained. On the other hand, said members of the opposition, confederation would increase territory to defend more than men and resources to defend it. The maritime provinces could hardly assist Canada, though Canada might be called upon to aid them. On the whole the best policy was to remain neutral and avoid the appearance of possible conflict with the United States. Military preparations might precipitate a preventive war waged by the Americans. For British Columbia the relation between confederation and defence seemed remote, and was little discussed. Some effort was made to represent the transcontinental railway as playing for British Columbia the same sort of rôle in defence as the intercolonial railway was expected to play for the eastern provinces. In point of fact it seemed difficult to believe that Canada could send of her scanty military resources to the Pacific. Britain was thought of as the real source of aid, and the naval station at Esquimalt bulked even larger than that at Halifax. But in any case there was less sense of danger in the west than the east. British Columbia had had no acute problems of neutrality during the Civil War, and there was only a threat of a Fenian raid. The menace of Russia, at one time in the picture, had been removed with the purchase of Alaska in 1867.

All discussions of defence in the provinces were surprisingly devoid of any real understanding of military affairs or of the broad strategy involved. Weakness on that side, however, was more than made up by the wealth of political controversy which tied defence to the imperial connection or to union with the United States. A shocked member of the Nova Scotian assembly stated that no man would openly advocate annexation, but, while there was certainly less talk of it in the maritime provinces than elsewhere, it could not be dismissed. In the assembly of Prince Edward Island Coles said that "I look upon this talk about the Mother Country casting us off from her apron strings, and this shaking of the stars and stripes in our face, as only stories intended to frighten the timid. Let us remain true to the Mother Country and she will stand by us." Gray, on the other hand, saw the issue squarely as a choice between federation and absorption by the United States. Almost the same words were used by Cartier in the Canadian assembly, who added that only by confederation could "the whole strength of the empire" be concentrated at the needed point in North America. In the opening speech of the debate Taché had spoken of the inevitability of Canada joining the United States, either by force or willingly, unless confederation were accepted. Macdonald hammered on the theme that the imperial connection must be maintained, and that with that "alliance" came protection. Member after member spoke of American aggression, and accepted the view that it could only be met by confederated provinces attached to Great Britain. The government supporters claimed, too, that confederation would not lead to independence; which, in any case, would be an untenable status. There were not lacking critics of these arguments who deduced that confederation would both weaken the bonds of empire and antagonize the United States. The tide in Canada, however, was running strongly toward confederation, and its sponsors refused to admit that it could be a step toward independence. Had it not the blessing of the British government?

In British Columbia the debate concentrated more directly on the three alternatives: to maintain the existing situation, accept annexation to the United States, or enter the dominion. In no other province did opinion appear to be so equally divided. The particularism which was strong in the maritime provinces was even more marked in British Columbia, separated as it was by thousands of miles from Canada. There was an active feeling for the imperial connection, based on tradition and constant, if difficult, intercourse. One opponent of union with Canada, speaking in the legislative council, balanced its advantages with that of empire membership:

The question has always appeared to me to be this:—Confederation with England, which we have; confederation in its truest sense; Confederation with all the security of protection, and all the pride of self-government, now or hereafter to be, when the colony shall have population and wealth sufficient: or Confederation—or, as it should be termed, "Incorporation"—with Canada. Incorporation with a country to which we are bound by no natural tie of affection or duty, and remote in geographical position, and opposed to us in material interests.

On the whole the mainland was in favour of confederation and Vancouver Island opposed. In both places—and especially in the island—there were minorities actively promoting annexation. Economic connection with the United States and geographical proximity were supplemented by the inrush of American prospectors to the Fraser in 1858 and the Cariboo in 1860. Frequent signs in the United States that British Columbia would be a welcome addition, and frequent signs in Great Britain that a break in the imperial tie would not be opposed, helped to strengthen the movement. It was touch and go for a time, but in the end the province declared for confederation with Canada. With the addition of British Columbia, the prairies, and Prince Edward Island the territorial unification of the British North American provinces was completed, and there the decisions on external relationships reached the end of a chapter. The old issues of the previous generation did not at once die; but, once the choice was made, provincial independence and annexation to the United States were relegated to the class of minority and unpatriotic opinions. As such they reappear, time after time, in new guises and under fresh circumstances, softened, reduced from the stark superlatives that make of the pre-confederation decades the frankest forum of British North American opinion on external relations.

Chapter V

THE OUTLOOK OF THE DOMINION

THE federation movement, completed in 1873, brought together as a political entity colonies and territories comprising the northern half of North America, an area of some three and one half million square miles, or nearly as much as the total area of Europe. The dominion reached from the Atlantic stronghold of Halifax to the Pacific ports of Vancouver and Victoria, and from the American border into the barren and uncharted waste within the Arctic circle. On the east the ports of the St. Lawrence and of the maritime provinces were established links with Europe; the western coast looked across the broad Pacific Ocean, on the far side of which Japan was beginning to emerge from its feudal isolation and China had recently and reluctantly admitted westerners to a footing on its ancient state. On the north-west corner of Canada lay Alaska, just purchased by the United States from Russia; and along the whole southern frontier ran the writ of the government at Washington. Such were the limits. Within the boundaries of the dominion were seven provinces. Prince Edward Island, Nova Scotia, and New Brunswick on the east occupied their present territory, as did British Columbia at the other extremity. Quebec and Ontario consisted then of only the southern portions of the present provinces, and Manitoba was but a tithe of what it was to become. Across the north of the central provinces and over the prairies ran the North-West Territories. For this sprawling new country a start had been made in the provision of means of transportation. Roads did well enough for local travel and canals for a limited time and place. Railways already served the most thickly settled areas, but there were still big gaps.

In the constitutional structure that had been designed to bind together provinces and territories the influence of other countries may readily be distinguished. Canada was not a sovereign state

94

but in a status that defied existing terminology. In the words of the British North America Act it was a "Dominion under the Crown of the United Kingdom of Great Britain and Ireland, with a constitution similar in principle to that of the United Kingdom". There was no necessity to refer in more detail to British parliamentary procedure and cabinet government, which, in varying degrees, had been followed in the provinces since the assembly of Nova Scotia had sat in 1758 and miniature parliaments were provided for the Canadas in 1791. By the sixties the process of development had assured local autonomy, through the cabinet system, over local affairs; and no demand as yet existed for the extension of control to foreign affairs. The constitutional history of the provinces had been so much a reflection of that of Great Britain that the partial turning to American institutions, caused by the struggles of the early part of the century, had been almost forgotten. When the federal principle was borrowed from the United States it was not wholly because of its intrinsic virtues, but because circumstances did not allow the unitary state that some of the fathers of confederation would have preferred. The expedient of federalism was little used in the world of that day, except in the United States, and that example was not altogether a happy one. The architects of the Canadian system never failed to point out that their federation would escape the dangers that were so manifest in the days of the Civil War. After all, there were Alexander Hamilton and the other federalists; and if their example had once been fatally ignored, it was still good for those who would escape the centrifugal effects of states' rights.

The constitution of Canada, then, was intended to combine the basic principles of the British parliamentary system with an improved form of federalism. Autonomy in local affairs was limited in law, if not always in practice, by the powers of the governor general and the right of disallowance vested in the British government. The British North America Act, being a statute, could be amended only by the imperial parliament, and its final interpretation lay with the judicial committee of the privy council. For external affairs the imperial authority in Canada was more than a shadow. Executive government was explicitly vested in the queen, and in foreign or imperial affairs her representative, the governor general, was subject to instructions from

London. Through him all dealings with foreign powers must be conducted, even between Ottawa and Washington. Lack of control over its own external affairs would have seemed to make the dominion a colony, just as complete control would have made it a sovereign state. Neither extreme was popular on either side of the Atlantic; for, while Canadians were not seldom critical of supposed British neglect of their interests abroad, they shied away from any suggestion of independence. In conformity with the British tradition of compromise this situation was met by progressive and practical changes in the methods by which Canada saw to her own affairs both in London and foreign capitals. The machinery creaked, but on the whole it served the purpose.

Resources were there in plenty: land for farming, fisheries, timber, furs in diminishing volume, gold and other mineral deposits hardly as yet touched. There was much to be done in this wide domain. Who were the men who would exploit the new state that they had called into existence, and govern its relation to the outside world? For this great land the population was absurdly small. The first census after confederation, that of 1871, gives the population (including Prince Edward Island) as 3,689,257 persons. All but a million lived in Ontario and Quebec, and west of the great lakes were but a bare hundred thousand. Statistics of racial origins are available only for the four original provinces. There were some two million persons of British origin, one million of French origin, and small minorities from elsewhere. Of these latter much the largest group was German, and that was only two hundred thousand, most of whom lived in Ontario. The British and French groups together made up 92 per cent. of the total. If these figures are compared with those showing place of birth a different picture appears. In the province of Quebec only eighteen persons are listed as born in France, while in Ontario more than a quarter of a million had been born in the British Isles. In Nova Scotia and New Brunswick the overwhelming majorities were native-born. The census of 1881 (which covers all provinces) shows little change in racial origin. Out of a total population of 4,324,810 persons, 2,548,514 were of British origin, 1,298,929 of French, and 254,319 of German. The British and French groups had declined slightly, to 89 per cent. of the whole.

Thus the population was not widely diversified, and immigration changed it little, for in the first ten years after confederation immigration from all sources varied between 25,000 and 50,000 a year. And in any case it is questionable how far an analysis of the origins or birthplaces of the people throws any light on their attitudes toward the outside world. Those of French origin were of Canadian birth. They retained French traits, habits, and methods of thought. They had a sentimental tie with France, but no love for the contemporary French state or its rationalistic outlook. No people in Canada were politically more North American. The people of Nova Scotia and New Brunswick, native-born like their compatriots in Quebec, had a deep interest in the affairs of Great Britain and the United States, from one or the other of which most of their ancestors had come. The number of recent immigrants in Ontario from the British Isles gives no ratio of attachment to their country of birth. Many of the Irish looked on the United Kingdom with unfriendly eyes, although they did not organize for hostile purposes as did some of the Irish in the United States. The German minorities in Ontario and Nova Scotia maintained some cultural traits, but on the whole they had little in common with the Germany of Bismarck, and caused no modification politically in the foreign relations of the dominion.

On the other hand, it does not follow that old and new comers alike had at once taken on a single Canadian nationality strong enough to cover the traces of origin and birth. The fathers of confederation were politicians, not alchemists, and to create a new political unit out of several smaller ones was not at once to transmute the whole. Confederation, indeed, had opened the way for new divisions without healing all those that already existed. Opposition had been least serious in the province of Canada, but in the other provinces—east and west—it had been strong enough to delay, and almost to prevent, the completion of the plan. In all the Atlantic provinces there were bitter protests against being sold to Canada, and that feeling did not die with the conversion of Joseph Howe. "Maritime grievances" became a tradition in the history of the dominion, and so familiar was the theme that its real significance was sometimes unduly discounted. Even a transcontinental railway could not overcome the divergencies that emerged between the outlook of the western and that of the central provinces. The failure to attain to a full national spirit must be put down to a variety of causes, a variety too complex to be examined seriously here. One or two comments, however, may be made in reference to the connection between regional division and external relations. The pressure of a common danger had been an important factor in driving the provinces together; but the Fenian raids and threatened raids, which had evoked some national spirit in the immediate era of confederation, became only a memory. Agreeable as was the decreasing tension in Canadian-American relations, it incidentally removed one of the most potent centripetal forces. Decision on, and conduct of, all external relations were made more difficult not only by conflicting opinions and interests in various parts of the dominion, but also by the competition for power between federal and provincial governments when "provincial rights" appeared as a barrier to the strong central government that had been envisaged by the fathers of confederation.

Provincialism and regionalism were not the only enemies of Canadian nationalism. The racial division which Durham had found so far advanced in his day did not disappear with union of the provinces, but continued in two forms. Centred in the province of Quebec was a self-conscious racial unit which found its inspiration not in contemporary France but in specially distilled traditions of the old régime both in Europe and America. The other distinctive racialism was that of groups in all the provinces who stressed attachment to the Britain of their own day. In the nineteenth century at least no force of comparable magnitude arose from the presence of other racial units in the dominion. It is perhaps fair to add that no large element in the Canadian population could be regarded, far less regarded itself, as hostile to a real Canadian unity; but cross-currents and conflicting priorities were none the less problems to the Canadian nationalists. Indeed, the very word "nationalist" is difficult to apply to Canada for it meant different things to different men; more especially was it suspect as seeming to imply a break in the imperial tie. That it proved possible to build Canadian political parties which embraced all provinces eased the pressure of centrifugal forces, but the caution with which those parties approached the formulation of external policy is in itself a reflection of conflicting opinions.

The confederation of the British North American provinces coincided with national movements on three continents. With blood and iron Bismarck and Moltke subdued the proud power of the Habsburgs and overthrew a Bonaparte at the head of the traditional military state of Europe. The North German Confederation, born in the same year as the original dominion, was broadened into the German Empire while Manitoba, British Columbia, and the prairies were being added to Canada. At the same time the unification of Italy triumphed dramatically as the armies of the king entered the city of the Caesars. In North America the United States had just survived its civil war, with the forces of separatism defeated. Far across the Pacific Ocean the Empire of Japan was taking the first steps in its startling march toward the status of a world power, with an economy, government, and defence forces modelled on those of European states. It was an age of nationalism, the bitter fruits of which were not to ripen for two generations. Both in Europe and Asia nationalism was an expansive, and frequently an aggressive, force. Not long after her revolution, Japan set out on the long road leading to domination of the mainland. The European states competed in the Balkans, and far beyond Europe into unexplored and undeveloped colonial areas. Economic imperialism could not be practised without annexation, and annexation by one power could not be ignored by its rivals. Neither in Europe, nor Asia, nor Africa could there be extension of territory or influence without a threat to the interests of other ambitious states and to the balance of power.

In North America in the same period nationalism manifested itself through the more peaceful exploitation of undeveloped territories, happily spacious enough not to arouse international competition. It was on this latter type of nationalism that Canada entered in the years immediately following political union. The decisions to explore the hinterland, control the Indian tribes, build railways from coast to coast, and people the unoccupied lands, were the counterpart of the western drive of the United States, and were typical of the North American conception of imperialism and national destiny. For Canada, with its small population and limited financial resources, the task of subduing half a continent to an economic and political system was formidable indeed. There was more than enough here to occupy all the energies and means available without looking toward the distant scene. And yet the country's activity could not stop at its own borders. True, there was no reason or desire for territorial expansion, beyond that implied in a series of boundary settlements; yet the dominion was, as the old provinces had been, not without essential external interests. The spread of agriculture to the western prairies and the pursuit of mining in the precambrian shield would but increase the need for foreign trade. Nor could the dominion do other than inherit such international political issues as had existed for the old provinces.

II

The immigration policy of the dominion, at least for some decades, was influenced more by the need of peopling and developing the country than by any plan of selection designed to create a well-knit nationality. In the newspapers and parliament frequent references were made to the need of more people, especially of workingmen. The competition from the United States, in taking men both from Europe and from Canada, was all too clearly realized; but Canadians comforted themselves with the idea that the United States was enjoying temporary prosperity and an exaggerated reputation. By the general act of 1869 (32 and 33 Vict., c. 10), consequently, few barriers were placed. Lunatics or physically incapacitated persons were excluded lest they become a public charge; and the governor was empowered to prohibit the landing of paupers. From time to time advantage was taken of this last enabling clause with the object of preventing unemployment. Foreigners coming to reside in Canada might receive naturalization, but by a curious and awkward arrangement they remained aliens in any other part of the British Empire. This situation, although frequently criticized, was not cleared up until 1914.[1] Equally anomalous, and much more inconvenient, was the absence of comprehensive provision for the extradition of criminals. Neither imperial nor Canadian legislation fully covered the field, and for many years the effective rules were those laid down in the narrow confines of the treaty of 1842 between Great Britain and the United States. At every step of every case, said Edward Blake, quoting the words of a judge, it was necessary "to decide how much of the Canadian law is consistent with so much of the imperial law as is consistent with the Treaty".[2] It was another nine years before a Canadian act, designed to cover all countries not having treaties with England and affecting Canada, received the royal assent.

[1] M. Hancock, "Naturalization in Canada" (*Papers and Proceedings of the Canadian Political Science Association*, VI, 1934).
[2] *Canada, House of Commons Debates*, 1880, p. 873.

Some analysis of the nature of education, of local writing, and of books in circulation in Canada, may provide an indication as to whether these revealed any national characteristics, and whether there was any attempt to influence the public mind toward a growing nationalism. If there had been any general purpose of adopting the ancient expedient of using education for political ends it would have been almost completely defeated by the clauses in the British North America Act which assigned control of education to the provinces. As in the period before confederation, the schools and universities drew heavily on the methods and the books in use in other countries, but there were occasional examples of attempts to provide Canadian material. In Ontario the *Ryerson Readers* were designed to replace the *McGuffey Readers;* but "the *Ryerson Readers* were more restrained in attempting to cultivate national feeling. They did not glorify Canada with the exuberance with which the *McGuffey Readers* glorified the United States. To have done so in the years after 1867 would have seemed to many in Ontario base disloyalty to the Imperial tie."[3] A cleric in the eastern townships, writing in 1870, was alarmed by the spread of American heresy to the Church of England in Canada. The latitudinarianism introduced from the United States, he said, had extended to extreme secularism in education, which "has insinuated itself into a large number of our High Schools in the Eastern Townships, which have been seed-plots for the propagandism of extreme American ideas hereafter to bring forth their fruits".[4] It was a parallel to the efforts of the Roman Catholic Church in the same province to protect the schools from French rationalism.

Printing and circulation of books in Canada were to a considerable extent governed by the eccentricities of the contemporary laws of copyright; and the objections raised in Canada to the operation of those laws gave rise to problems in imperial and foreign relations. The story is a long and complicated one, but the gist of the Canadian protests was that, while the lack of copyright restrictions allowed American publishers to reprint English

---

[3] H. F. Angus (ed.), *Canada and Her Great Neighbour* (Toronto, 1938), 89.

[4] I. Constantine, *On the Influence of American Ideas in the Anglican Church in the Diocese of Montreal* (Montreal, 1870).

works at will, the same freedom was not given to Canadians.[5] Reference to the correspondence on the subject reveals both the nature of the dispute and the sources from which Canadians received books. Writing to the colonial secretary in 1890, the Canadian minister of justice described the situation as he saw it.

The reading public of what is now the dominion of Canada has been principally supplied with British literature by American reprints. The high prices of British editions have made this unavoidable. In spite of the pointed and repeated warning to British publishers given by the colonial office for 40 years, very little has been done to change this state of things by providing cheap editions of British works. Even to this day the English editions cost from four to ten-fold the price of American reprints. The result is that the business of publishing British literature for the Canadian reading public is done almost exclusively in the United States. The American publisher, unrestrained by any international copyright law or treaty, is free to reprint any British work and to supply it, not only to the reading public of the United States, but to the reading public of Canada, while the Canadian publisher is not free to reprint any such work on any terms, unless he can obtain the permission of the holder of the copyright in Great Britain. In some noted instances this has actually led to the transfer of printing establishments from Canada to the United States. In other cases, English publishing houses have set up branches in New York or other American cities, with the view of reprinting for the United States and Canada the copyright works which they have issued in London.

Canadian publishers, the minister went on to say, cannot compete in offers to reprint English books, because American firms have not only their own great market but that of Canada as well. "Over-weighted, as we continually are, by reason of the vast competition of the United States in every branch of trade, industry and commerce, your lordship will not wonder at our being disposed to complain when, in regard to so important a matter as the furnishing of literature for our people, we are hindered by a monopoly; nominally in favour of the London publishers, but really and practically in favour of the publishers of the United States. . . ."[6] The government claimed that public opinion was strongly critical of the arrangements as to copyright,

[5] For a brief account of the development of the dispute see A. B. Keith, *Responsible Government in the Dominions* (3 vols., Oxford, 1912), 1216 ff.
[6] *Canada, Sessional Papers*, 1892, no. 81.

and comments in the newspapers support their claim. The editor of the Toronto *Mail*, for example, wrote that "it is idle to suppose that American reprints can be kept out of Canada, and Canadian publishers be prevented from supplying the void. Costly English editions are unsuited to Canada where everybody reads and every reader owns the books he reads. *Lothair* at £1.16 stg. may find its way into English circulating libraries and the mansions of the aristocracy; but a dollar edition is what is wanted for Canada." There was, he added, an American dollar edition which supplied the Canadian market.[7] Throughout the whole copyright controversy there was almost no reference to Canadian books or authors. Perhaps it was partly because of tact and the particular point at issue that the demand for British works was so constantly stressed, but it remains true that Canadian literature was not, apparently, a major consideration. Canadians read the books of Britain, France, and the United States; and the national aspect of literature was in the attempt to encourage printing and publishing. The Canadian author's point of view was urged on Sir John Macdonald by William Kirby, who argued that the way to "promote Canadian Literature and encourage Canadian Authors" was "by establishing a *Prosperous Publishing* business in Canada".[8]

The people of the dominion, like their ancestors in the old provinces, followed the affairs as well as the literature of other countries. Some events abroad were, of course, treated simply as news, with no particular significance to Canadians. By dint of copying from British or American papers, Canadian editors had always managed to eke out their own scanty sources of information. The telegraph and the cable brought more recent and more steady news than the "latest advices from Europe" which had once formed the basis of the periodic budgets in the newspapers of the provinces. Some events were regarded with detachment in one part of Canada and with more direct interest in another. For example, the Franco-Prussian War was to an Ontario editor "a pitched battle between sovereigns for kingly power and aggrandisement",[9] but at the news of an early French victory a Quebec paper announced that "Aujourd'hui, ce n'a été par toute la ville

    [7] *The Mail* (Toronto), May 4, 1872.
    [8] Lorne Pierce, *William Kirby: The Portrait of a Tory Loyalist* (Toronto, 1929), 378.
    [9] *Whitby Chronicle*, August 4, 1870.

qu'une joie, qu'un délire."[10] Whatever sympathy may have existed in Ontario for either belligerent was purely passive, and probably the *Globe's* approval of British neutrality represented general opinion, whether or not the editor would be followed in his desire for "the entire abstinence from participation in all European complications". When an emissary came from France to start a recruiting office in Montreal, offering free passages to France and a bounty on arrival, some Irishmen came forward, but French Canadians waited to see what position France would take on withdrawing troops from Rome.[11] Positive proofs of friendship took the form of subscriptions for the French wounded, and a message came through the consul-general from Jules Favre, thanking the subscribers and adding that "if the recollection of the mother country has remained green in their hearts, neither has France forgotten them."[12] The views of English Canada on the third republic were mixed, the only strong opinion being condemnation of the Paris commune. To French Canadians, however, the third republic threatened a radical and secular conquest of a mother land from which they still derived much of their culture.

If French Canadians hesitated to recruit for service in the French army because of the projected withdrawal from Rome, they had enthusiastically joined the Zouaves of the pope's own garrison. In response to an appeal from the pope, and encouraged by the bishop, a committee was formed in Montreal at the end of 1867 to organize a detachment and raise funds for its expenses. In February a group of 135 (all that could be accepted) sailed from New York, and six other detachments followed. While some never got beyond France, 328 men reached Rome and took part in its defence against the army of Italy.[13] These defenders of the temporal power symbolized the reality of the link between the papacy and the church in Canada. At home the clergy were holding the fort against the forces of liberalism. Since the days of the early Jesuit missionaries Quebec had always been strongly ultramontane, and had offered strong resistance against

[10] *L'Evénement*, quoted in Georges Vattier, *Essai sur la mentalité canadienne-française* (Paris, 1928), 252.

[11] *The Globe* (Toronto), July 25 and 27, 1870.

[12] *Ibid.*, Sept. 28, 1870.

[13] B. M. Corrigan, "Canadian Crusaders" (*Queen's Quarterly*, XLVII, spring, 1940).

any contrary philosophy. The general ultramontane revival of the sixties led in Canada, as it did in France and Germany, to threats of schism and to bitter controversy. The syllabus of 1864 and the dogma of papal infallibility were, of course, noted in English-speaking Canada, but had no important repercussions. In Toronto the editor of the *Globe* badly misjudged the situation when he decided that " the world will go on as usual".[14] The editor of the *Leader* was hostile toward the ultramontane policy, but did not dismiss it so airily. The chief protestant newspaper of Montreal, the *Gazette,* favoured resistance to the pope's actions. The real effect of the ultramontane policy, however, fell on the Roman Catholics of Quebec. For the church authorities to show displeasure of liberalism or gallicanism was not new; for many years they had labelled the *Institut Canadien* and the rouge party as undesirable. In the late sixties a strengthening of the ultramontane party amongst the Quebec clergy coincided with the corresponding ascendancy of that party at Rome, and was encouraged by it.[15] The *Institut* was pursued with increasing vigour, and Joseph Guibord, a member who had been one of the group that appealed to Rome against the condemnation of the society, was refused burial in consecrated ground. The "old catholics" of Quebec, like those of Germany, could make no headway against the ultramontanes, whose "Catholic programme" of 1871 launched a new excursion into politics, like that of the Centre party. No compromise with liberalism was to be tolerated in church, culture, or the state; and it was only the growing ascendancy of Laurier that curbed the movement.

While the influence of the papacy on Canada was continuous and important, that of France was—except in the cultural field—hardly more than sentimental. The two countries that most directly affected Canada were the United Kingdom and the United States. Even if there had been nothing more in common with the United States than a frontier the affairs of a powerful and expanding country must have been of immediate interest to the dominion. And the final delimitation of this particular frontier was still seen as open to question, not so much from legal disputes over boundaries as from the remaining force of "manifest destiny".

14 *The Globe,* May 16, 1870.

15 O. D. Skelton, *Life and Letters of Sir Wilfrid Laurier* (2 vols., London, 1922), I, 120 *ff.*

Annexation, peaceful or forced, was still discussed, and Canadians noted with ill-concealed alarm indications of expansionism in the republic with the not always unfavourable response in Canada. Fenian threats, the perennial argument over fisheries, and incidents in the use of border waterways added particular problems to the general one of maintaining friendly relations. But Canadians were not wholly occupied with defensive measures. There were many ties between the people of the two countries. Immigration from one to the other, similar environments, similar ways of life, and common reading brought the two peoples together. Canadians, too, never paused in the endeavour to establish favourable trade relations with the United States; and while they never reached the complete goal, they were not unconscious of the place in the Canadian economy of whatever trade did exist. Relations with the United Kingdom were in one sense more remote and in others less so. Distance was hardly more of a barrier than the divergence between European and North American social structures. On the other hand, the effective majority in Canada held a belief in the empire that was made up of a variety of components. Many Canadians came, or their parents had come, from the British Isles; and they, with others who had less blood relationship, were definitely, and sometimes aggressively, British. There was a general confidence in British institutions of government and law—a confidence which was only strengthened by comparison with parallel institutions in the United States.

While such ties of empire cannot be measured they were none the less real. There were also aspects of the relationship of the dominion with the mother country which could be, and were, analysed and weighed. In the first years of the dominion Canadian opinion was evoked by public expressions in England on imperial affairs, by the imperial policies of both English parties, and by English diplomacy affecting Canada. There were then seen to be two major schools of thought on colonial affairs; the one, generally held by liberals and particularly by the Manchester school, being that the future of Britain lay in free trade, that the colonies were moving toward independence, and that it was desirable that they should do so; the other, of which Disraeli came to be the spokesman, declared that the liberals had all but destroyed the empire, and that it must be rebuilt by the establishment of some form of centralized institutions. To most Canadians neither of these propositions made any appeal, for they wanted to maintain the empire without imposing on it centralized government. To occasional conferences in London little objection was raised, but a permanent council was not then, and never became, popular. There were minorities which were opposed even to the loose unity that existed, and others which advocated definite machinery of government for the whole; but the great mass of Canadians took the middle position, favouring continuance of the connection without central government. Beyond ties of tradition, blood, and sentiment, what positive advantages were seen? In trade the preferential system was gone, but there remained a substantial volume that might be jettisoned by a political break. The garrisons were almost gone, but aid in war was still assured. English diplomacy was frequently criticized, but Canadians—in spite of outbursts at times—still wished to retain the support of the great naval power. It was true that Britain might pursue objectives of no interest to Canada, but in reality there was no obligation to aid in them, and no prospect of England's strength being threatened. Amongst many examinations of the whole position, as it appeared in the age of confederation, that by the editor of the Montreal *Gazette* is as frank and as representative of any in an important English-language newspaper.

Our present relations with the Empire, if let alone by agitators, either upon this side of the water or the other, are satisfactory. What is required is that an understanding should be arrived at with the mother country that its policy is settled, and is not to be suddenly or capriciously altered. It is not for the sake of effecting any great legislative or constitutional changes that we think these London meetings of colonists are useful, or the proposed colonial conference desirable. It is in order that public opinion, in the mother country as well as in the colonies, may be aroused, and definite opinions of Imperial policy formed, where now all is confused and uncertain. It is greater security of tenure, not change, that is desirable.

The danger that we can ever become so entangled and involved in the network of Imperial interests that we cannot free ourselves is a mere chimera which can frighten nobody who is conversant with the facts. And if we should negotiate respecting tariffs or commercial intercourse with the mother country we should certainly not do so upon any less favourable terms with them than with our neighbours whom some are so eager to treat with now.

. . . but if it can be shown that its [the empire's] preservation will involve burthens which we cannot bear, or disadvantages which are in no wise balanced by advantages, the time will come to give it up.[16]

Canada was preoccupied with problems of internal growth, but by no means exclusively; nor were even those problems themselves dissociated from relations with other countries. The new federal government was developed, as it had originated, in the light of examples elsewhere. Organization of new departments and civil service reform, for example, followed the experience of other states. The railway to the Pacific, which bulked so large in Canadian politics for the first decades after confederation, brought experts, equipment, and capital from abroad. It required immigrants for its construction, to give it business, and to build up the west. It was seen as an imperial road to the east and listed as a contribution to empire defence. The wheat produced in Ontario and then in the prairies had to be carried to tidewater and sold abroad. The men who came to develop Canadian industries formed trade unions that either were modelled on or affiliated to those of Britain and the United States. The whole Canadian economy assumed foreign trade, and that in turn called for diplomatic action. Looking about in the age of confederation Canadians were seeking to broaden the scope of their commercial relations. The entrance of British Columbia into the dominion spelt a way to the trade of the far east. The West Indies, South America, and Australia were also new fields that had hardly been touched. The older channels—to Britain, France, and the United States—needed to be cleared if the best results were to be obtained.

Canadians, therefore, were increasingly concerned about their relations with the rest of the world. That Canada also formed part of a great imperial system accentuated that tendency more than it restricted it. There was, it is true, friction resulting from the process of pursuing Canadian aims through British means; but the friction was noticed more than the more remarkable adaptation of a colonial organization to a constantly changing need. In a generation after confederation a way had been found by which Canada could in effect conduct her own diplomacy, without disrupting the empire, and without sacrificing all the bargaining power held by *civis Britannicus*. By an unorthodox

[16] *Montreal Gazette*, Jan. 5, 1870.

process, and almost by the back door, Canadians entered the field of diplomacy, there to try at the lists the fortunes of their country. The first venture is of peculiar interest, since it involved almost every possible related issue: the imperial connection, defence, trade, and fisheries. And the setting was British-American-Canadian relations, the central avenue of Canadian external relations.

CHAPTER VI

A VENTURE IN DIPLOMACY

IN the years immediately succeeding confederation the external relationships of Canada fitted into the triangular pattern which had been, and was for long to be, dominating. With the neighbouring United States and the distant centre of the British Empire the dominion had its closest connections; and on a satisfactory series of arrangements with these two great powers depended her security and much of her strength. While many of the links which Canada had with these countries were constant, they varied in strength from time to time; and there were aspects of their policies at this particular time—both as directly affecting Canada and toward each other—that were beyond the ability of the dominion to influence, and yet of immediate concern to her. One worrying factor was the lack of imperial enthusiasm in Great Britain, resulting in what was felt to be distressingly mild concern for Canadian interests. Macdonald poured out his woes into the sympathetic ear of Lord Carnarvon:

. . . We are glad to know that we have in you a friend. I may almost say a friend in need, for we greatly distrust the men at the helm in England, who cannot, I fear, be considered as appreciating the importance of maintaining the empire as it is, intact.

We indulge the belief here, however, that Messers Bright, Lowe and Gladstone (shall I say Lord Granville?) are not true exponents of the people of England. We may perhaps be obliged to appeal from the government to the people of England.[1]

It was neither the first time nor the last that Canada and the United Kingdom saw the imperial relationship differently. English commerce was flourishing under the sun of free trade, and there was little inducement to make commitments for the sake of a colony which had ceased to have the virtues of a "plantation",

[1] Public Archives of Canada, *Macdonald Papers*, Letter Book 14, Private. April 14, 1870.

and whose imperial zeal must have seemed to rise with her troubles and fall with her progress. It was a phase of English policy which was to pass with the revived imperialism of the later seventies and eighties, but it came most inopportunely at a time when Canada needed diplomatic and perhaps even armed assistance in her relationships with the United States. There had emerged from the once-doubtful strife of the Civil War a united country, freed from the divisions of the slavery issue, and with a large army. Incidents of the war period had made for bad blood with Great Britain and—to only a lesser extent—with Canada. There was talk of a post-war settlement of disputes: not in this case between belligerents, but to discuss issues which the war had raised. In such a settlement the government of Canada wished to take part, having specific points to bring forward; but, as neither a strong nor a sovereign power, had to appear in some type of junior partnership with the British government. The matters of immediate concern to the dominion were defence, the fisheries, trade, and an indemnity for losses incurred in the Fenian raids.

The problem of defence was how to ensure protection against official or unofficial aggression from the United States. The old fear of annexation by force was not yet dead, kept alive both by memories of the past and by contemporary words and acts that seemed to spell trouble.[2] Senator Sumner, Senator Chandler, President Johnson, President Grant, and Hamilton Fish, the secretary of state, all spoke of the desirability of the peaceful annexation of Canada. These and similar opinions in portions of the press found their way to Canada. The situations in Manitoba and British Columbia were both such as to give anxiety. The close connection of the Red River colony with Minnesota, the rebellion there, and the fear of American expansion into the new Canadian west combined to make an awkward position. The acquisition of Alaska by the United States and the San Juan boundary dispute made the Pacific Coast another vulnerable area, especially as communication with it from Canada was slow. The Canadian government was acutely conscious of the possibilities.

It is of great importance [wrote Macdonald to Rose] that a part of the force [to the Red River] should be Regular Troops, as it will con-

---

[2] L. B. Shippee, *Canadian-American Relations, 1849-1874* (New Haven and Toronto, 1939), 200 ff.

vince the United States Government and people that His Majesty's
Government have no intention of abandoning this continent. It has
got to be a fixed idea in Washington that England wants to get rid
of her colonies, indeed Mr. Fish has not hesitated to say so. I may
mention to you, in entire confidence, that Fish had the impudence to
ask Thornton to ascertain whether His Majesty's Government would
offer any objection to a free vote being taken in Canada, or in any
portions of it, whether the people desire to join the United States or
not, and stated his conviction that if this vote were taken a large
majority, nine-tenths he said of the people, would vote for annexation. He went further and stated that the refusal of reciprocity
was a legitimate mode of coercion. . . . Council has made an indignant minute on the subject . . . we walked into Fish at the rate of
a hunt.[3]

There was indeed ground for apprehension on the part of a
weak country faced by a great power in which even the high
officials did not hesitate to talk of annexation. True, they always
called it peaceful annexation, but the line between persuasion and
force has not infrequently been a narrow one. Added to words
were deeds—or, to be more accurate, the absence of deeds. It
was a conviction in Canada that the failure of the United States
authorities to restrain or punish the Fenians demonstrated a lack
of goodwill that was little short of hostility. Taking words and
deeds together (and the two seemed to spring from the same
attitude) there was at least *prima facie* evidence for the belief that
military and naval forces in Canada must be calculated on the
basis of a possible invasion. The degree of that probability was
a subject of dispute, but there was at least agreement that defence
must not be neglected.

Just as Canada—in the eyes of many Canadians—was in need
of adequate defences, the imperial troops were being withdrawn.
The decision to reduce the garrisons in British North America
had been taken many years earlier, and had always been regretted
by the colonials.[4] The British government was determined to
reduce all colonial garrisons, partly for the sake of economy, and
partly because its available forces were too widely distributed.
In the case of Canada there was an additional reason arising out
of the belief that the dominion should accept the burdens as well

[3] *Macdonald Papers*, Letter Book 13, Private. Jan. 26, 1870.
[4] See above, 50-1.

as the advantages of greater autonomy, and to some extent an impression that Canada in any case was moving, if not toward complete independence, at least toward a status which could no longer be called colonial. The exigencies of the Civil War period caused temporary reinforcement of the imperial troops, and the danger from Fenianism further delayed reduction. The cost to the imperial treasury for the year 1867-8 was £1,243,423, a figure considerably higher than that for either the Civil War years or previously. In Canada it was hoped that circumstances would induce the British government to delay or modify its plan of withdrawing the troops. Both the Fenian menace and the threatening aspect of affairs in the Red River district were presented as arguments in favour of at least temporary delay; but the British government was inexorable, and toward the end of 1871 the last of the British garrisons (except that at the naval station of Halifax) marched out of Quebec, where they had been stationed since they had first stormed that fortress over a century earlier.

It was said and understood that the withdrawal of the troops did not absolve Great Britain from rendering assistance to Canada in case of need. It was obvious, however, that only naval forces could be rapidly brought to a North American scene of action; and in any case the British government, both directly and through its governors, had persistently urged the doctrine of colonial responsibility for the first line of defence. The fortifications that were agreed upon in 1865 were never created, except for additional works carried out by the imperial government at Quebec. The Canadian government provided itself with money to proceed with the works planned for various cities, but the fortifications were not built, and in 1872 the original plan was dropped. Beginning with the last years of the imperial garrisons a Canadian military organization was slowly built up. A statute of 1868 (31 Vict., c. 40) retained in principle the obligation to military service, but in practice provided only for a volunteer militia. Under the statute 40,000 men were to be paid and drilled, but only at first was this number actually reached. There was a department of militia, but at first no headquarters staff and no auxiliary services, such as commissariat. The first steps toward a regular army were taken in 1871 with the raising of two batteries, one at Quebec and the other at Kingston, to take over and preserve the works and arsenals at those places.

The Fenian movement was, as has been suggested, closely related to the whole military question; as it was, also, to the Canadian position in regard to the projected diplomatic settlement with the United States. The Fenian Brotherhood, which was formed in 1858, turned after the Civil War to a plan for putting pressure on the British government (by means of invasions of Canada) to make concessions to the Irish revolutionary party. There was more talk of invasion than actual crossing of the frontier, but actual operations were sufficient to justify apprehension. The public—especially near the border—was certainly alarmed, and there were constant rumours of further attacks. The danger made it necessary to spend more on the militia than would otherwise have been considered, and there was loss of life in repelling the invaders. What made the whole Fenian question bulk so large was two related considerations: that the Fenians might find reinforcements and do extensive harm; and that the American government, by failure to prevent the raids or adequately to punish the participants, exhibited an unfriendly attitude. The first apprehension proved to be ill-founded. The second was based on at least some real evidence. Without going into the details of the motives and acts of individual Americans or the government, it is only necessary here to understand the Canadian point of view. In summary this was: that the raids had cost Canada men and money, that the United States had not made proper efforts to prevent them, that an indemnity should be paid, and that the British government should press the dominion's claim. When Cartier and McDougall were in England they learnt of negotiations on the *Alabama* claims, and suggested to Granville that if a tribunal were set up on that subject individuals in Canada and the government should have an opportunity of presenting their claims about the Fenians.[5] In the spring of 1870 the Canadian government stated its intention of urging that the imperial government demand reparation, on the ground that the American government had information which would have enabled it to stop the raids. They pointed out that the Canadian government, though not being able to stop the St. Albans raid of 1864, because of lack of fore-knowledge, had made pecuniary compensation. Before this privy council report could reach England, Granville

⁵ *Canada, Sessional Papers,* 1869, no. 61. Cartier and McDougall to Governor General, May 20, 1869.

had written to the governor general, Sir John Young, saying that His Majesty's government would urge the American government to counteract any such movement in the future. The Canadian cabinet was furious, and wrote a bitter memorandum which Young refused to sign, but sent to Granville. In it the council expressed its "unfeigned regret" that no demand for reparation was being made. They belived that "there is no precedent in the history of civilized nations for a great power such as Great Britain submitting to such outrage on its loyal subjects without making a demand for adequate reparation". After further pressing, Kimberley, the new colonial secretary, suggested that the Canadian government draw up a full statement of facts and claims. The resultant memorandum, accepted by the council on January 25, 1871, went over the familiar arguments at some length, seeking to show by reference to particular cases that the United States government was well warned in advance and could have prevented the raids.[6] As a result of this correspondence the imperial government agreed to bring the claims before the joint high commission which was to meet at Washington.

Not the least important of the issues coming to a head in the early years after confederation was that of the trade and commerce of the dominion. In no field was the close dependence of Canada on satisfactory relations with Great Britain and the United States better illustrated. Of the total external trade of Canada in 1870 as much as 89.5 per cent. of the exports and 88.5 per cent. of the imports were accounted for by those powers together. Although Great Britain bought from Canada considerably less than she sold to her, the firmness with which free trade doctrines were held left little prospect of preferential duties. In the case of the United States, however, Canadians continued to cast longing glances at the reciprocity treaty of 1854, a renewal of which, in some form, would be especially advantageous in consideration of the growing height of the American tariff. The question was whether the United States could be induced to make a new treaty, it being borne in mind that she had renounced the previous one. It seemed probable that a case made solely on the virtues of tariff agreements would be insufficient to carry the day. As

6 The documents are printed in *Canada, Sessional Papers*, 1872, no. 26.

make-weights the Canadians had two inducements to offer: admission to their fisheries, and use of their canals.

The fisheries of Newfoundland and Canada, plentiful and accessible to American ships, constituted a real bargaining-point. The fisheries controversy was an old one, both as to the interpretation of the treaty rights of American citizens, and as part of the general negotiations on commercial relations. The concession in the Treaty of Paris of 1783 to Americans of the right to fish in colonial waters was considered by the British government as abrogated by the War of 1812. Americans, however, did not accept this interpretation and continued to fish after the war as before, until some twenty of their boats were seized by British cruisers. The convention of 1818 defined the position by allowing to American citizens fishing rights in parts of the shore of Newfoundland and Labrador, and the Magdalen Islands; the United States renouncing any claim to enter the three-mile limit elsewhere, except to obtain shelter, wood, and water, and to make repairs. The reciprocity treaty of 1854 greatly enlarged the freedom of American fishermen by providing for reciprocal and free access to the coastal fisheries, with some exceptions; but when that treaty lapsed in 1866, the convention of 1818—with its limited concessions—once more came into force. The provincial governments assumed that the privileges accorded to American fishermen automatically came. to an end, but at the solicitation of the British government agreed to retain them temporarily. The Canadian government professed that they had "no disposition to use the apprehension of national differences arising out of the fisheries, as a means of influencing the United States to replace their trade relations with British North America on a satisfactory footing",[7] but it is probable that they were not without belief that the fisheries could be used as a means of pressure toward restoration of reciprocity. They suggested that for the current year the provinces should allow American vessels to fish on payment of a licence fee, the proceeds from which should be used for "the maintenance of a joint marine police". The licence fee was duly instituted, consisting of 50 cents and later of $2 per ton of the vessel. In spite of the original intention the system was carried on from year to year—although there were constant complaints

[7] Canada, Sessional Papers, 1871, no. 12. Minutes of Canadian Government, March 23, 1866.

from Canada of widespread evasion—until 1870, when the dominion government decided to terminate it. There followed a period in which the convention of 1818 came into operation once more, accompanied by disputes as to what were Canadian waters.

Both before and after 1870 there was a necessity for naval policing, which was performed partly by the Canadian and partly by the British government. In each of the first three years after the abrogation of the reciprocity treaty there were four or five vessels of the royal navy protecting fisheries in the Gulf of St. Lawrence, and during the same time, one or two provincial boats. In 1870 there was one British vessel and eight Canadian—the latter officered as far as possible by retired naval officers. The division of responsibility and expense was in dispute between the two governments, and constant complaints were made in Canada that protection was insufficient. The abolition of the licensing system was received with outspoken criticisms in the United States, being described as unneighbourly; and a long argument went on as to exactly from what waters the American vessels were to be excluded.[8] In the summer of 1870 the dominion government, after reviewing the whole controversy, urged the British authorities to suggest to the American government a joint high commission to settle the dispute.[9] In the speech from the throne in 1871 it was stated that the fishery question would be submitted to a joint commission, which, however, would include it as only part of a large agenda.

The coasting trade, too, was to be a matter for reciprocal concessions. By a Canadian statute of 1870 (33 Vict., c. xiv) the coasting trade from one Canadian port to another was forbidden to foreign ships, with the exception that the governor in council might declare that this did not apply to ships of a country which admitted British ships to its coasting trade. The explanation of this move was made by the minister of marine and fisheries in his annual report for 1868-1869. The United States, he argued, had not reciprocated in a liberal policy in relation to the coasting trade, the use of canals, or fisheries.

[8] *Canada, Sessional Papers,* 1871, no. 12.

[9] *Canada, Sessional Papers,* 1885, no. 101a. Memo. of July 4, 1870, by the minister of marine and fisheries. This lengthy memo sets out the Canadian position, and the history of the fisheries question from that point of view.

I am of opinion that the true policy of the Canadian Government at present should be to retain all the privileges which it now possesses, until fresh negotiations take place for new trade relations between Canada and the United States, when the opening of the coasting trade of the Dominion to United States shipping can be included in any arrangements which may be made, if the Canadian government should then be of opinion that it would be advisable in the interests of Canada to do so.[10]

The second major Canadian asset suitable for bargaining was a waterway from the middle west to the sea. It was a less certain asset than the control of fisheries, since there were alternative transportation routes, while the best fisheries were in Canadian waters. Indeed, the diversion of traffic to the Erie Canal or to American railways at Buffalo was a constant nightmare to those Canadians who were directly or indirectly interested. There were, however, certain types of freight which could be carried most economically to tidewater by boat; and it was in the knowledge of this that Canadians had banked on extensive American use of the canal system which in the forties they had been completing at great expense. The reciprocity treaty for the first time admitted United States vessels to navigation of the St. Lawrence and the Canadian canals with the same tolls as those paid by British subjects. Used as a make-weight in the negotiation of that treaty, the navigation privilege automatically fell with its termination. The United States had a *quid pro quo* in the coasting trade, to which Canadians had not been admitted even under the reciprocity treaty, and in the bonding system. The latter enabled Canadian imports and exports to be carried to and from American all-year ports without paying duty, and its withdrawal was a bogey that was often displayed. But the United States had little to offer in water transport to set against the Canadian canals. The treaty of 1854 admitted British subjects to the free navigation of Lake Michigan. And until 1895, when a Canadian canal was opened at Sault Ste. Marie, Canadian vessels were dependent on the American one for entrance to Lake Superior.

Fisheries and canals were consistently brought forward as inducements to the United States to re-enact a reciprocity agreement. Added attractions were indeed needed. The United States was in itself a huge free-trade area, rich in most natural resources

---

[10] *Canada, Sessional Papers,* 1870, no. 11.

and well advanced in manufacturing. Canada, on the other hand, was in a comparatively early stage of manufacturing, with limited markets, and dependent on a relatively large volume of foreign trade. She was, moreover, attempting at the same time to build up a more mixed economy, and to sell her staples for imported goods (which must, to a large extent, be manufactures). American dissatisfaction with the treaty of 1854 was not due only to the political relations of the Civil War period. The Canadian protectionist tariffs of the fifties were thought by many Americans to be striking at the very roots of any permanent reciprocity between the two countries, and to violate the treaty in spirit if not in letter.

There was never any doubt that Canada wanted to reach an agreement with the United States, even if individuals tried to bolster national pride by statements that the United States must not think Canada dependent on her charity, and that Canada could get on very well without reciprocity. The plain truth was that all parties, and nearly all groups, were anxious to secure a successor to the treaty of 1854. The only disagreement was on the terms to be accepted. Before the treaty had even run out the provincial governments were struggling to secure its renewal or replacement. With confederation the aim did not change, though at times it seemed politic not to press it. Deputations to Washington and inquiries made through the British minister brought news that there was little hope at the time. It had not been easy to float the treaty of 1854—even on champagne—and subsequent events had made Washington even less receptive.

You know [wrote Macdonald] that I have always held that a renewal of those relations can only be effected by the pressure of American interests upon Congress. It is obvious that congress must look at the question from an American point of view entirely, and until convinced that it is for the advantage of the trade of the United States to negotiate a new reciprocity treaty no such treaty can be obtained.

In the state of feeling that now exists toward England in the minds of too many people in the United States, nothing like favor can be expected by her. This feeling has absurdly enough been extended to Canada, although during the whole of the Civil War we spared no pains to perform our duty as a friendly neighbour. Still, the feeling exists, and therefore any appearance of undue anxiety on the part of Canada would only tend to defeat the object in view.

Canada is quite ready, through the British Ambassador, to renew the negotiations at any time, and Mr. Fish is fully informed of that fact. We can do no more. It would be altogether indecorous and improper for the Canadian government to commence a system of lobbying for the purpose of securing the support of individual members of congress.

We have gone to considerable expense already in disseminating information on the subject of trade, and from time to time, as it may be necessary, will continue to do so.

The truth seems to be that, until your public men get out of their heads the ridiculous notion that by restricting mutual trade annexation will be secured, no earnest attempt will be made to secure reciprocity. Meanwhile Canada will not entertain for a moment the proposition[11] to give the freedom of the St. Lawrence for the sake of the reduction or abolition of the import duties on coal, lumber and salt.[12]

It was becoming increasingly evident that no progress could be made in tariff negotiations except in relation to other subjects of common interest, and probably not until the soreness still existing from the Civil War could be alleviated. In full-dress debates in the Canadian parliament in the spring of 1870 the opposition followed the obvious tactics of accusing the government of lack of enthusiasm for, and inefficiency in the pursuit of, a reciprocity agreement. The latter may, to some degree, have been true; but there is little doubt that government and opposition were one in their aims. The wisdom of the new regulations concerning the fisheries might be questioned in view of the need of conciliating American opinion, but the government believed that it had tried concession without any good result. Apart from the fisheries altogether, there were many groups represented at Washington opposed to tariff reductions on particular classes of goods—as there were always likely to be surrounding any legislature. To meet their attacks nothing was effective beyond a series of compromises. It was, however, possible to attempt to remove political bones of dissension, which acted as a barrier against agreement on any subject. The British government had for some time been moving toward a kind of peace conference with the United States. What

[11] A United States suggestion of February, 1870. See Shippee, *Canadian-American Relations*, 315.

[12] *Macdonald Papers*, Letter Book 14. To G. W. Brega, April 4, 1870.

form it should take, what subjects were to be included, and how Canada might be represented on it were all subjects of vital concern to the dominion. Out of a successful conference might come the twin benefits of better feeling between the British Empire and the United States and accord on the matters of particular interest to Canada, the discussion of which seemed to have reached a stalemate.

II

The holding of a conference at Washington was the result of a combination of circumstances. The British government, apprehensive of the state of affairs in Europe, and particularly of the denunciation by Russia of the Black Sea clauses of the Treaty of Paris, was anxious to avoid any possibility of a war on two continents. The tradition that peace with the United States was a *sine qua non* of foreign policy had not yet been established in London, but for the time at least there was a pressing reason for the settlement of disputes. The American government, recently freed from the encroachment of Napoleon III on North America as well as from its own Civil War, felt less necessity for immediate agreement, and there were not a few prominent Americans who talked almost lightly of a possible war with Great Britain. But with the replacement of Sumner by Hamilton Fish as secretary of state, there was more willingness for compromise. The position of Canada in this situation has been differently interpreted. To Ripon's biographer the Canadian issues were incidental and an embarrassment.[18] To Canadians they seemed at the time and since as of major importance. Whether the British government would have been eager for settlement had there been no European complication, is purely speculative. As it proved, the situation was advantageous to Canada in so far as it started the wheels of diplomacy; and disadvantageous in so far as it reduced the bargaining power of the British government, and made it too ready for concessions. Both British and American statesmen were inclined to believe that the status of Canada was a provisional one which could hardly last. The repeated prophecies in the United States that annexation was a question of time were based not, as once,

18 Lucien Wolf, *Life of the First Marquess of Ripon* (2 vols., London, 1921), I, 239.

on the assumption of military force, but on a doctrine of inevitability tempered by the peaceful persuasion of economic power. But, while nursing this comfortable expectation of the eventual acquisition of most of the rest of North America, Americans saw the need for settlement of immediate questions, particularly in regard to the fisheries, and, to a lesser extent, the unsettled boundaries with Manitoba and British Columbia. Absorbed in European affairs, anxious to promote world commerce by means of free trade, and unimpressed by the value of quasi colonies, British statesmen were tempted to accept the American suggestion that their bilateral differences would be more easily settled if Canada were no longer a part of the British Empire. But, while recognizing the possibility—even the probability—of peaceful separation in the future, they were for the time being ready to sponsor the Canadian case up to the point where it endangered the success of the settlement as a whole.

The form of the Anglo-American negotiations is explained by the course of the *Alabama* dispute. A treaty of arbitration for the *Alabama* claims had been rejected by the American senate, and the British government was therefore unwilling to risk indignity by pursuing the matter through ordinary diplomatic channels. It was, however, urgently necessary to remove the United States as a possibly hostile force in case of war with Russia. In the dilemma Lord Tenterden, the assistant under-secretary for foreign affairs, made the ingenious suggestion of a joint high commission.[14] It was to be first proposed for the discussion of affairs other than that of the *Alabama,* but with the private understanding that the American government should add the *Alabama* case, and that this be accepted. In conformity with the tried diplomatic procedure of private agreement before official correspondence, Sir John Rose (then resident in London) was sent in January 1871 to Washington, there, where he was *persona grata,* to discuss plans with the secretary of state. Fish was already looking toward a general settlement having, in the previous September, suggested to Thornton (the British minister) that all issues should be dealt with together. Despite the opposition of Sumner—who wildly demanded the withdrawal of Britain from the Americas—Fish found sufficient support before the month was out to accept the

14 *Ibid.*

proposition brought by Rose.[15] The official correspondence was then solemnly conducted on the agreed lines, and the decision that a joint commission was to meet in Washington duly recorded.[16]

The negotiations leading to the creation of the joint commission were apparently carried through without consulting the Canadian government and without any decision as to what part, if any, Canada was to play in the commission. It was, of course, clear that at least some of the subjects directly affecting the dominion would be on the agenda, but that alone would not satisfy Canada. While in England in 1869 Cartier and McDougall had represented to Granville that no steps toward reciprocity should be taken without consultation with their government;[17] similarly they had asked that the dominion government and individual citizens should be allowed to appear before any tribunal considering claims for damage by Fenian raids.[18] Macdonald had also told Rose, in writing on the fisheries question, that "should the question come up you must press on Her Majesty's Government that no negotiation should be entered upon or treaty concluded without reference to the Canadian government".[19] But by what means was Canada to take part in the Washington discussion? Obviously not by separate representation. The proposal that was hit upon in London was to include a Canadian in the British commission. Rose was thought of, as having carried on the preliminary discussions, but was unacceptable in Canada as not a Canadian by birth, a resident in England, and a partner in an American banking house.[20] Macdonald himself was suggested, and the governor general put the question before him at the beginning of February.

I have thought over Lord Kimberley's proposition [he wrote to Lisgar] that I should act on the Joint Commission with the United States on Fishery and other matters. I am a good deal embarrassed by not being able to communicate with my colleagues on the subject.

---

[15] Allan Nevins, Hamilton Fish: The Inner History of the Grant Administration (New York, 1936), 425, 441.

[16] The text is in Canada, Sessional Papers, 1872, no. 18.

[17] Canada, Sessional Papers, 1869, no. 59. Privy Council Report, June 11, 1869.

[18] Canada, Sessional Papers, 1869, no. 61. Cartier and McDougall to Governor General, May 20, 1869.

[19] Macdonald Papers, Letter Book 14. March 11, 1870.

[20] Macdonald Papers, Letter Book 15. Macdonald to Lisgar, Feb. 4, 1871.

My first impression was that it would be better for Canada not to be represented on such a Commission. But then one must consider that if Canada allowed the matter to go by default, and left its interests to be adjudicated upon and settled by a Commission composed exclusively of Americans having an adverse interest, and Englishmen having little or no interest in Canada, the Govt. here would be very much censured if the result was a sacrifice of the rights of the Dominion. England would at once say that the offer was made to Canada to be represented on the Commission and that it was declined.[21]

Macdonald agreed, however, that he would act, subject to his colleagues' consent (which was readily given), and after securing from Kimberley an admission of Canada's exclusive rights to fisheries within the three-mile limit. There was indeed no apparent alternative. It was obvious that a single Canadian would occupy an unenviable position, since he presumably might fail to sway his fellow-commissioners, yet must accept responsibility in Canada for the decisions. On the other hand, there was at least a better chance of furthering Canadian interests by this means than by official correspondence over the long route to Washington by way of London. During his stay in Washington Macdonald kept in touch with his cabinet by means of an exchange of letters and telegrams; but the course of the conference could by no means be plotted in advance, and to some extent he was obliged to act as best he could, with no time for consultation, as circumstances arose.

The British commission was headed by Earl de Grey and Ripon, and the other members were Sir Stafford Northcote, a member of the opposition in the house of commons, Sir Edward Thornton, the British minister to Washington, Montague Bernard, professor of international law at Oxford, and Sir John Macdonald. Macdonald was appointed a plenipotentiary under the great seal, and received his instructions[22] from the foreign office. At the first session de Grey "announced that his Commission—which he pointed out was not a British but an Imperial body, Canada being represented by Prime Minister Macdonald—was fully empowered to sign a treaty".[23] But when later de Grey explained that any

21 *Ibid.*
22 The text is in *Canada, Sessional Papers,* 1872, no. 18, pp. 5, 11.
23 Nevins, *Hamilton Fish,* 470.

fishery treaty must be ratified by the Canadian parliament, one of the American commissioners said "that they thought they were dealing with the British Empire and not with Canada".[24] It was the beginning of the long story of foreign uncertainty on the constitution of the empire. It was also a new departure that involved possible difficulties in the relations of Canada and Great Britain. E. B. Chandler of New Brunswick and Francis Hincks of the Province of Canada had accompanied Elgin to Washington in 1854, but only in an advisory capacity. The Webster-Ashburton Treaty of 1842 and the Oregon Treaty of 1846 had been negotiated by British plenipotentiaries. There were no precedents.

The high commission set to work on February 27, 1871, and the treaty was signed on May 6.[25] The subjects most discussed were the *Alabama* claims and the fisheries. In the former Canada had no direct interest, and the United Kingdom had none in the latter. To Macdonald the whole conference was a dual struggle, with his fellow-commissioners first and with the Americans second. To the British members, on the other hand, the pressure of Canadian demands complicated their task of securing a settlement. To the Americans it was a constant puzzle whether they were dealing with one country or two. That was the crux of the situation, and one not fully recognized by either Macdonald or de Grey. The British Empire commissioners composed a body which was neither national nor international. Canadians were hurt that their interests were not pursued with more zeal, and more than once Macdonald talked of withdrawing. There had been no previous agreement between United Kingdom and Canadian governments on the course to be pursued in respect of particular subjects. Macdonald, although appointed to the same status as the other commissioners, seems to have felt no responsibility in matters not touching Canada, and to have given little weight to the general attitude of the British toward a settlement with the United States. ". . . The British Commissioners [he wrote] seem to have only one idea in their minds, that is, to go home to England with a treaty in their pockets settling everything, no matter at what cost

[24] *Macdonald Papers*, Letter Book 15. Macdonald to Tupper, March 21, 1871.
[25] For detailed accounts of the conference see Nevins, *Hamilton Fish*, chap. xx; Shippee, *Canadian-American Relations*, chap. xv; Goldwin Smith, *The Treaty of Washington, 1871: A Study in Imperial History* (Ithaca, 1941).

to Canada."[26] Had he not been so harassed by his particular problems, Macdonald might have recognized more freely that the British were prepared to make concessions for the sake of peace and their European danger; and that an established peace would at the same time remove whatever menace there was to the security of Canada. To de Grey it seemed that the Canadians gave too little weight to the need of compromise for the sake of peace. "They are filled with a belief", he wrote to the foreign office, "that they can bully the Americans into giving way and seem indifferent to the risk they run by such a policy."[27] Yet it is not surprising that a prime minister responsible to the Canadian parliament and electorate should have envisaged with apprehension the reception of a treaty that would certainly be believed to be unfavourable to Canada. "I have taken strong ground with my colleagues [he wrote] that it would be exceedingly unwise to agree to any terms which it is not reasonably probable would be accepted by Canada as should any Treaty be made and afterwards rejected by our Parliament the feeling of irritation would be greatly increased."[28] He was also playing the dominion game with another object. Fish inquired whether a fisheries treaty would have to be ratified by Prince Edward Island and Newfoundland, and de Grey was uncertain of the constitutional position. "I did not choose to enlighten them upon the point as I think it well to keep the case of Canada separate. If we come to any satisfactory Treaty, I shall endeavour to have it limited to the Dominion of Canada, so that if Prince Edward Island and Newfoundland desire the advantages of the Treaty they must come into Confederation."[29] In the light of his own feelings and of the pressure from Canada, Macdonald was going far in the direction of sacrifices for the sake of imperial unity. When it was first proposed that a fisheries treaty must be ratified by the Canadian parliament Macdonald was put in an exceedingly difficult position.

If a majority of my colleagues should at any time conclude to accept terms which I do not approve of, I must of course, either pro-

[26] *Macdonald Papers,* Letter Book 15. Macdonald to Tupper, April 1, 1871.

[27] Quoted in Smith, *Treaty of Washington,* 70.

[28] *Macdonald Papers,* Letter Book 15. Macdonald to Tupper, March 21, 1871.

[29] *Ibid.*

test and withdraw, or remain on the commission and trust to the . . . ratification of the Treaty by Canada.

If I take the first course, it will disclose to the Americans the fact of a difference of opinion, a conflict in fact, between Canada and England. This the Americans are anxious to establish, in order to get up a sort of quarrel between the two, and strengthen that party in England who desire to get rid of the colonies as a burden.

If I continue to act on the Commission I will be attacked for making an unworthy sacrifice of Canada's right and may be compelled to vote in Parliament against a Treaty which I had a hand in making.[30]

Anxious as Macdonald was to secure a satisfactory settlement of the fisheries, his determination must not go to the point of incurring a major political disaster. A few days later, when de Grey said that Macdonald's insistence would bring the negotiations to an end, the latter felt it necessary to modify his position previously taken that parliament would not accept the projected treaty.

My reason for taking this line was it was evidently Lord de Grey's aim to make me and Canada responsible for a breach of the negotiations generally in case things went wrong. I was resolved not to let any blame be attachable to Canada in that respect, and thus strengthen the hands of the party in England who consider Canada a burden to be got rid of and an obstacle to friendly relations with the United States.[31]

Thus the Canadian government had, like the British, aims in the negotiations wider than the actual subjects discussed. Macdonald was a skilful negotiator and he fought a good fight, but the final terms were far from those which he, or any other Canadian, wanted. The San Juan boundary, being relatively unimportant, was little discussed, and was finally submitted to arbitration by the German Emperor (articles xxxiv-xlii).[32] The Fenian claims were, on the American insistence, ruled to be not within the agenda—a result which Macdonald regarded as fortunate, since it had been arranged that England would indemnify Canada if the United States refused. There remained reciprocity, communications, and fisheries, which the Canadians hoped to link together

[30] *Ibid.*

[31] *Ibid.* Macdonald to Tupper, March 29, 1871.

[32] The award, dated October 21, 1872, was in favour of the United States' claim.

in the traditional manner. In spite of Macdonald's effort, however, no tariff agreement could be reached. The articles on communications (xxvi-xxx) provided for the free navigation of the rivers St. Lawrence, Yukon, Porcupine and Stikene, and of Lake Michigan. The British agreed to urge the Canadian government to allow to Americans the use of Canadian canals on terms of equality with Canadians; and in return the American government opened to Canadians the St. Clair Flats Canal, and agreed to urge the state governments to allow the use of state canals connected with border waters. Bonding privilege was to be allowed to and from the ports of New York, Boston, and Portland, or other ports designated by the president (art. xxix). The ships of either Canada or the United States might carry goods from one port in the other country to another, provided that part of the transport was by land carriage in bond (art. xxx). The chief effort of Canada was toward an acceptable solution of the fisheries. It was their chief asset, and Macdonald made repeated efforts to put it against at least some degree of reciprocal trade. The Americans, however, were adamant; and the only free trade was to be in fish and fish-oil (art. xxi). The inshore fisheries of each country were thrown open to the citizens of the other (arts. xviii-xx), and the claim of a superior value of the concession made by Canada was to be examined by a special commission (arts. xxii-xxv).[33]

On May 8 the Washington Treaty was ready for signature. Fish and de Grey warmly congratulated each other—and it came to Macdonald's turn to sign. With the pen in his hand he turned to Fish and whispered "Well, here go the fisheries"; and, as he rose from the table, "They are gone".[34]

III

Macdonald was not without a sense of drama, and his gesture in signing the treaty, as well as the violent protests he made during its negotiation, must be discounted. Certainly he had failed to secure the terms which government and popular opinion sought; but that is not an uncommon result of any diplomatic

---

[33] This arrangement led to the Halifax Commission. See below, 158-9.
[34] Nevins, *Hamilton Fish*, 490.

compromise. The original Canadian aims had not been set low, and what had actually been attained was not contemptible. The fisheries had not brought their price, but there was still a chance of a dividend being voted by the commission to be set up. Reciprocity had been denied, but the door was not closed. Canadians had no real desire to exclude American shipping from their canals, or to forgo the canal tolls. The Fenian claims had not been considered, but Macdonald considered that he had a promise from de Grey of compensation from the British government. The San Juan boundary was to be arbitrated, and the decision might fall one way or the other. It remained to make out a good case in Canada, both to placate Canadian opinion, and to persuade parliament to pass a bill implementing those parts of the treaty which required legislative action.

As Macdonald now bent his energies to this task, he had, he found, rather overplayed his hand in his letters from Washington to the cabinet, and some of his own colleagues had to be converted. Parliament would not meet for nearly a year, and in the meantime he would say as little as possible, while preparing his defences. First, he must see what could be obtained on the Fenian account. Apparently the British government was willing to pay a modest compensation if all the other questions at dispute with the United States were settled—that is to say, if the Canadian parliament passed a fisheries act, or at least if the Canadian government used every means in its power to induce parliament to pass the act. Although Macdonald had talked of not supporting the treaty, it is most improbable that he ever intended to take such drastic action. At Washington he had tried to compensate for the disadvantages of his minority position by threats that he would not sign, or would sign only with reservations, or that he would not press legislation in parliament. And now his caution in committing himself was certainly done in part as a wish to confuse the opposition, and probably in part as a method of bargaining with the British government, as here used. But having extracted this conditional promise of a cash payment he and Hincks soon turned to the more attractive alternative of a guaranteed loan to be used for the building of railways and the improvement of canals. After a cabinet meeting, Macdonald wrote to Lisgar that the government would do everything in their power to carry the treaty if the guarantee was made, and that the popularity of the loan would "assure you of the moral certainty of their success in Parliament".[35] A surprising note of optimism was suddenly struck, which must have confirmed the British government in their suspicion that Macdonald could get the treaty through if he so desired. After a correspondence covering months a cable was received on March 18 which promised to guarantee a loan of £2,500,000 when the Canadian acts to implement the treaty had come into effect, and subject to Canada's abandoning all claims on Great Britain for losses from Fenians.[36]

No one knew better than Macdonald that there was real and widespread opposition to the treaty. As soon as the high commission was mooted, suspicions were voiced, in parliament and out, that Canada would be the loser, as, it was said, she always had been. Many Canadians regarded the United States as the traditional victor in all international disputes, and expressed the fear, too, that Britain would sacrifice Canada to an easy settlement with the American government. The important debates in parliament did not come until the treaty was discussed in the spring of 1872, but for the intervening period something of the temper of the country may be seen from the comments in newspapers. The importance of the subject of a settlement with the United States derived not only from the direct pecuniary interests of the country, but also from the fact that it related to the central themes of Canadian foreign relations. Nothing so bared the thoughts of Canadians as any issue which brought up their relations with the United Kingdom or the United States: and when both were involved (as was usually the case) the country began to take stock of its position. It was the signal for sweeping statements, hazardous prophecies, and verbal battles without quarter.

The San Juan dispute was distant to old Canada, and while there were various hopes expressed that the matter would be settled (and in the right way), it made little stir in the east. The Fenian question came nearer home and invoked the Canada-United Kingdom-United States triangle. The *Globe* refused to be frightened, but drew interesting conclusions: the Fenian scare was perhaps being magnified in order to get through the military

[35] *Macdonald Papers*, Letter Book 17. Macdonald to Lisgar, Jan. 22, 1872.
[36] Shippee, *Canadian-American Relations*, 399.

estimates.[37] Then it had the effect of stimulating Canadian nationalism. "Canadians have gained more in national character during the last six years than in any previous twenty and if we ask, what has caused this, we shall find that the outrageous proceedings of the Fenians and their abettors have been among the chief agencies."[38] A month later the same paper was more indignant with the American government for its "tacit consent" to the raids, but declared that Canada would not be driven into annexation by such tactics.[39] The chorus soon began of calls for an indemnity to cover raids and threats said to have cost Canada $4,000,000. The *Daily News* of Montreal argued that England should either put sufficient pressure on the United States, or else provide troops to protect the border.[40]

The coincidence of Fenian raids and the withdrawal of imperial troops was, to Canadians, a most unfortunate one. The *Globe* refused to visualize the possibility of a war with the United States, and took a firm line against a standing army. It was left to a small town paper to repeat the thought that had so often been uttered:

If English statesmen imagine that Canada is going to turn her youth into policemen and establish a cordon along the frontier, to keep back the Fenian invaders, they are very much mistaken. The Canadians are ready to do their share of the duty imposed, but they must not be expected to perform impossibilities. . . .

It should be borne in mind that Canada is at any time liable to be made the battleground for settling any dispute that may arise between Great Britain and the United States. . . . Why then are we asked to defend the country against these attacks occasioned through quarrels in which we have no concern?[41]

Reciprocity was very much in the public eye from the time of the abrogation of the treaty of 1854, and the newspapers reflected the general interest. There is no doubt that a renewal was desired, but there were many comments by the editors (as by members of parliament) to the effect that Canada must not be considered as dependent on it, but could stand on her own feet.

37 *The Globe* (Toronto), April 18, 1870.
38 *Ibid.*, April 25, 1870.
39 *Ibid.*, May 26, 1870.
40 Quoted in *Whitby Chronicle*, June 9, 1870.
41 *Barrie Examiner*, Jan. 21, 1869.

Even stronger were the objections raised against any suggestion that by withholding reciprocity Canada could be forced into annexation. The editor of the *Globe,* one of the most powerful organs of opinion, reacted violently to the American suggestion of a zollverein.

Canada, we are always proud to assert, is at present an integral part of the British Empire; and whoever, in the whole history of the past, heard of an instance of part of a Kingdom or Empire entering into a commercial arrangement with its great commercial and political rivals for the purpose, avowedly, of putting excessive differential taxes on the produce of the rest of that Kingdom or Empire? . . . Yes, the very same persons who have trotted out their Independence and Annexation hobbies, and found they would never do, now fancy they can gain the same end by this uniform customs plan. The only recommendation about it is that it is not so manly as the proposal for annexation, but has more of the sneak about it. . . .[42]

The tory *Leader* of Toronto followed much the same argument. Exclusion from a reciprocity treaty would not induce Canada to leave the British Empire. "Neither annexation nor independence has held any place in the Canadian mind."[43] On the fisheries the *Globe* steadfastly defended the Canadian policy of abandoning the licence system, and argued for the protection of the gulf fisheries as a major asset. At the very time that Macdonald was trying, in Washington, to get some *quid pro quo* for the admission to inshore fisheries, the *Globe* was announcing that an exchange of that privilege for reciprocity would be one-sided.

In the interval before parliament met the government did not define its stand on the Washington Treaty, but Macdonald, as a good strategist, sought to protect himself against a newspaper onslaught. He wrote to Alexander Morris from Washington to persuade the friendly newspapers to hold back until the *Globe* had committed itself against the treaty. He would then be free to criticize it himself without allowing George Brown to occupy the strategic position of imperial loyalty.[44] Brown obligingly attacked the treaty as one that had "no parallel in British history—with one exception, the Ashburton capitulation".[45] During

42 *The Globe,* March 25, 1870.
43 *Leader* (Toronto), Jan. 1, 1870.
44 *Macdonald Papers,* Letter Book 15. April 21, 1871.
45 *The Globe,* May 19, 1871.

the month of May, too, the *Globe* collected comments from other newspapers. *Le Pays* had condemned the treaty outright, and said that the only honourable course open to Canada was to reject it. *Le Nouveau Monde* remarked that "no doubt we have sacrificed more than we have obtained; but there is one important interest which has been protected—that of peace". *Le Constitutionnel* and the *Gazette de Hyacinthe* were both provisionally opposed. Turning to Ontario, the *Globe* reported the attitude of a number of newspapers there. The St. Thomas *Home Journal* called it not a treaty but a surrender. The Perth *Courier* believed that with the fisheries Canada lost her only bargaining point. The Belleville *Intelligencer* called it "a one-sided bargain". The Galt *Reformer* remarked that "we are anxious to have peace and harmony between Brother Jonathan and ourselves, but to secure this, we are not willing to sacrifice great interests and receive therefor comparatively nothing in return". The Collingwood *Bulletin* wrote that ". . . if the mother country imagines that she can arbitrarily dispose of our fisheries to meet her own private needs she is mistaken"; and the Ingersoll *News* made the deduction that "if this treaty, or that part of it which concerns us, had been negotiated by Canadians we could have obtained better terms". No doubt the *Globe* was to some extent choosing its papers, but it also quoted the Ottawa *Citizen's* survey of the field, and its conclusion that "judging from the general tone of the Canadian press, we should think that the Treaty will not prove acceptable unless it contains some qualifications not yet made known". The Halifax *Morning Chronicle* is quoted as calling it "a disastrous Treaty for this Province"; and the *Globe* claimed that "there is not a single paper of any note in the Maritime Provinces that recommends the adoption of the Treaty by the Canadian Parliament". On the other hand, the Whitby *Chronicle,* which itself condemned the treaty, reported the Halifax *Express* and *Times* as in favour, though it stated that New Brunswick was altogether hostile.[46] Throughout June and July Brown continued to attack the treaty, and to quote other hostile comments on it. Macdonald was defended by some editors as "doing his duty", and criticized by others for giving way. The British government was frequently accused of ignoring Canadian interests for the sake of its own

46 *Whitby Chronicle,* June 1, 1871.

selfish success. The attacks on the treaty, said Brown, were not of a partisan nature—even if he did show a particular pleasure in coining phrases about Macdonald.

That there was some opinion on the other side of the case may be seen from the editorial columns of the *Leader*. "The clauses affecting Canada are conceived in a reasonable spirit of equity and are well calculated to cement a lasting union between the United States and Canada."[47] The Halifax *Reporter* is quoted as saying that "what is wanted is a market [for fish]. That the treaty provides. As for 'ruin, etc.' the fishermen of the British provinces fished alongside the fishermen of the United States for twelve years and without finding themselves ruined by the near neighbourhood of their rivals." *La Minerve* defended the treaty on the ground that Canada would be the first to suffer from trouble between Great Britain and the United States, and that it was a protection against annexation.[48] A final quotation, suggestive for the future, may be noted. The editor of the Kingston *Whig*, surveying the Washington settlement, concluded that, "of course we have no wish to see Canada annexed to the United States, far on the contrary; but we desire to see Canada so far independent of the Home authorities, that she can make commercial treaties of her own, and so bring about the leading wish of all who desire to see Canada take her due place among the nations of the earth".[49]

Judging by the early editorial reactions to the treaty—even making allowance for exaggerated and unrepresentative statements—the prospect of carrying the treaty in parliament must have seemed doubtful. By the time that the session opened on April 11 the cabinet was united in its defence of the Washington settlement. A reference was made to it in the speech from the throne, and in the debate on the address Alexander Mackenzie made a brief criticism and Francis Hincks a brief defence.[50] The main debate began on May 3, when Macdonald introduced a bill to give validity to the treaty, in so far as it affected Canada.[51] His speech covered the whole question, both in the origin of the

47 *Leader*, May 13, 1871.
48 Quoted in Smith, *Treaty of Washington*, 140.
49 Quoted in *Whitby Chronicle*, June 8, 1871.
50 *Canada, House of Commons Debates*, 1872, 21, 24.
51 *Ibid.*, 294-345, 346 ff., 431 ff.

commission and the terms of the treaty. After pointing out that parliament was free to accept or reject the treaty, he argued that it was important for the security of Canada that Great Britain should have an *entente* with the United States, and that the circumstances of the time justified taking up Canadian commercial questions at the same time as the imperial matter. He explained his own appointment to the commission and why he had accepted, and then turned to a detailed defence of the clauses affecting Canada. Mackenzie and Edward Blake, leading for the opposition, denied both the necessity of the concessions made to the United States and the advantages said to have been gained by Canada. On May 16 a vote was taken on the second reading of the bill and it was passed with a majority of sixty-six. The bill returned from committee without amendment, and received the royal assent before parliament rose. The act (35 Vict., c. 2) provided for the admission of United States vessels to the eastern fisheries, for the importation without duty of fish and fish-oil, for the transit of goods through Canada in bond, and the carriage of goods in American vessels from one part of Canada to another.

Thus ended the dominion's first experience of diplomacy. The government had succeeded in getting support for its policy, and it survived the election of the summer of 1872, though with a reduced majority. Macdonald declared that to win the election he had worked harder than he had ever done before or would ever do again. "Had the result of the election", he told Dufferin, "shown that the people of Canada disapproved of the treaty and a new ministry been formed on that basis, the relations between Canada and the mother country would have been the reverse of pleasant and one cannot foresee what political consequences would have flowed from the change."[52] He claimed that he had endangered his own political future and sacrificed the interests of Canada for the sake of the empire. These lofty sentiments show only one side of the picture, but one that was prominent to Canadians. It was a tradition—later to be reinforced by the Alaska case—that British diplomacy too often threw Canada to the wolves. The high commission represented a compromise between abstention from, and full participation in, diplomatic negotiations. The results were palatable neither to those who were openly critical nor to

[52] *Macdonald Papers*, Letter Book 18. Sept. 2, 1872.

those who nominally supported the treaty. It remained to be seen by what other means this curious empire could carry on its affairs with foreign states.

In the meanwhile there was the settlement to be worked out. The value of the Canadian fisheries and the use of Canadian canals by Americans had still to be dealt with; and then there was the perennial question of reciprocity. Hope had not died: indeed there were signs in the United States of a move for lower tariffs, and an agreement might perhaps be secured even if the fisheries card had already been played. And now relations with the United States were presumably freed from any threat of war. This was indeed a relief and a change: apart from that the main themes in Canadian foreign relations—so fully played in 1869-1872—were still to be carried on in repetition and variation.

CHAPTER VII

TRADE, FISHERIES, AND DIPLOMACY

S INCE the Canadian economy was so largely dependent on foreign trade it followed that commercial conditions in other countries, and commercial relations with other countries, profoundly affected Canadian well-being. For the first few years after confederation prosperity in England, Europe, and the United States brought an increase in the external trade of Canada and a corresponding development in home industry, finance, and the construction of railways. The public revenue, arising almost entirely from customs receipts, was comfortably maintained so long as trade continued at a high level. Canadians could (and some did) view with comparative equanimity the collapse of their hopes of reciprocity in 1871, and tell themselves that they were not their neighbours' slaves. But with the good they needs must accept the bad. Late in 1873 came another swift descent of the business cycle. In Europe and America prosperity suddenly turned into depression, and Canada could no more escape the effects of the latter than welcome the more palatable fruits of the former. The effect, it is true, was delayed: for it has been characteristic of Canada's position that she has neither soared to the heights nor plumbed the depths known to some of her large customers. The total of external trade reached a new maximum in 1874, faltered badly in 1875, and was materially reduced in 1876. Such was the situation that forced itself on the Liberal administration which came into office in 1873. For this, and for the succeeding government, a primary task was to restore foreign trade at least to its previous position; and the weapons which lay to their hands were commercial agreements with foreign states and stimulation of trade by protection or low tariffs. Here was ample scope for decisions on policy and for Canadian diplomacy.

Alexander Mackenzie's government leant toward a low tariff and toward a restoration of reciprocity with the United States.

If the American government proved to be reluctant it might be persuaded by an offer to replace the proposed compensation for Canadian fisheries with a reciprocity agreement. Having ascertained that the British government would have no objection to the change, the Canadian government sent George Brown to Washington in February 1874 as a "confidential agent", where he "speedily succeeded in ascertaining that a general willingness existed on the part of the leading statesmen of the United States to enter into a new commercial treaty".[1] Whether Brown was misled by wishful thinking or by American hospitality, the report that he made to Ottawa was optimistic enough to start arrangements for a formal negotiation. Mackenzie applied for the appointment by the imperial government of Canadian commissioners— Brown and a member of the cabinet—to be associated with the minister at Washington, and to occupy a position not inferior to that of Macdonald in 1871.[2] Dufferin at once telegraphed the wishes of his ministers that negotiations should be begun, and Sir Edward Thornton, the British minister at Washington, was promptly told to undertake them. A few days later Brown was accepted as a commissioner (the proposal of a cabinet minister to serve with him having apparently been dropped), and plenipotentiary powers were forwarded to him. Mackenzie had urged from the first that the British minister, without the support of a Canadian with local knowledge, could not adequately handle negotiations which directly affected Canada alone. The British government for its part, made it clear that the responsibility for attempting to change the operation of the Treaty of Washington must rest on Canada.

As to the scope of the negotiations, Mackenzie was satisfied that the restoration of the free list in the treaty of 1854 (as was proposed by the British government) "could not now meet the requirements of the trade of the country nor be in itself a satisfactory exchange for the fishery compensation and other advantages expected from Canada by the United States under the implied terms of the Treaty of Washington".[3] He proposed to extend the list

---

[1] *Canada, Sessional Papers,* 1875, no. 51. Privy Council Report, March 26.

[2] Public Archives of Canada, *Alexander Mackenzie Letter Books,* III. Mackenzie to Dufferin, Feb. 24, 1874.

[3] *Mackenzie Letter Books,* II. Memo. by Mackenzie, March 9, 1874.

materially by adding manufactured articles. To this there were three objections: to the argument that it would injuriously affect British exporters he simply replied that they also would receive the advantages of any reduction of duties. He satisfied himself by consulting Canadian manufacturers that they would not make any protest. The third difficulty, and the one which worried him most, was the loss of revenue consequent on removal of duties on some exports; and he was thus torn between a desire for lower tariffs and a fear of increased taxation, already felt to be threatened by the cost of the Pacific railway.[4] The Canadian proposals were agreed on in April by corrrespondence between Brown, who was in Washington as agent or plenipotentiary from February to June, and Mackenzie, in consultation with Cartwright (the minister of finance). They finally took the form of a long memorandum signed by Thornton and Brown, and were read to Hamilton Fish, the secretary of state, on April 27. The tone of the memorandum[5] is set by the statement that "an impartial examination of the commercial relations between the United States and the British North American Provinces for the last fifty years, cannot fail to establish, we venture to think, beyond all doubt, that the trade between them has been exceedingly valuable to both countries, but that the United States have, from first to last, reaped the largest advantage from it". The "impartial examination" then shows that the United States had suffered more than Canada from abrogation of the treaty of 1854, and that the American tariff prevented enlarged trade with Canada. The British representatives (Brown and Thornton) had, on March 28, proposed to Fish a renewal of the treaty of 1854 as a substitute for the arbitration provision of the Washington Treaty. Fish then suggested an enlargement of the scope of the treaty, and, while leaving it to the other side to make a proposition, mentioned enlargement of the Canadian canals, and the addition of some manufactures to the free list.

The Canadian proposals in the memorandum were: (1) to add to the free list under the treaty of 1854 manufactures of iron, steel, or wood, agricultural implements, oils, and some items of

4 *Mackenzie Letter Books*, III. Mackenzie to Brown, March 28, 1874.

5 The text is printed, together with some official correspondence, in *Correspondence Relating to the Negotiations for a Reciprocity Treaty* (Cmd. 1060, 1874; North America, no. 4).

lesser importance; (2) that American fishermen should have access to the Canadian coast fisheries on the same terms as under the Treaty of Washington; (3) that the coasting trade of each country should be open to the vessels of the other; (4) that the canals of each country should be open to the vessels of the other, the Canadian canals be enlarged, Lake Michigan be open during the duration of the treaty to navigation by Canadian vessels, and that vessels of either country be open to registry in the other; (5) that joint commissions be formed for the improvement of the rivers St. Clair and Detroit and Lake St. Clair, for the erection of lighthouses, and for the preservation of fish in inland waters; (6) that citizens of either country might secure patents in the other; and (7) that a joint study be made of the prevention of illicit trade.

Fish received the memorandum without enthusiasm and carried on further negotiations in a manner hardly more satisfactory to Brown, who managed to retain, however, a restrained optimism.[6] A draft treaty was agreed on in the middle of June,[7] and Brown was almost frantic lest it be delayed too long for the senate's consideration. His fears proved to be well founded, for the senate declared that the last few days of the session did not allow time for proper consideration of the treaty; and when it did come before that body in the following February it was rejected.

So fell, once more, the Canadian hopes of reciprocity, and the liberal government was obliged to turn from diplomacy to face the growing demand for salvation by protective tariffs. In the session of 1876 both houses of parliament devoted long hours of debate to the causes and cure of the depression. The main thread of the argument was the effect on Canada of her commercial relations with Great Britain and the United States; and, following on that, whether the solution of the problem lay in more tariff protection. No pretence was made that there was not a depression: the difference of opinion consisted in various views as to how it should be met. David Mills, in moving for a select committee to inquire into the causes, said that he was of opinion "that we are suffering to a very considerable extent from commercial depression

---

[6] Some of his letters from Washington are in Alexander Mackenzie, *The Life and Speeches of Hon. Brown* (Toronto, 1882), 212 *ff.*

[7] The text is in *Correspondence Relating to Negotiations for a Reciprocity Treaty.*

in consequence of our intimate commercial relations with the trade of the adjoining republic. . . . It is not very easy for the merchant to remain prosperous while his customers are impoverished, and it is not very easy for the people of this country who are engaged in commercial pursuits to be in a highly prosperous condition while those with whom they are dealing are suffering from financial depression."[8] The accusation was frequently made that Canada was a "slaughter-market", either for Great Britain, or the United States, or both. One member of the house of commons revived the argument that the Americans were trying, by economic pressure, to drive Canada into annexation.[9]

And so the debate went on, for hour after hour, with lectures on the balance of trade, presentation of tables of figures, and numerous accounts of the hardships of this or that industry. The only practical focus of the discussion could be the tariff. To the supporters of free trade England stood as the example of success; the advocates of protection held up the United States as the leading case for their thesis. All this was ground that the legislatures of the old provinces and of the federation had gone over, again and again. Yet it seemed ever fresh to each generation. And perhaps the pressure of economic hardship was real enough to justify yet another re-examination of the Canadian policy. Certainly no better time could be found for the furthering of the protectionist creed. In both houses it found a number of convinced advocates as well as more cautious members who seemed to be on the verge of conversion. The ranks of the defenders of "the grand principles of free trade" were by no means broken, but no count was taken when the battle was over. The house of commons had the more specific task of passing a budget. In his budget speech R. J. Cartwright, the minister of finance, pointed to the decreased trade and the consequently reduced revenue. The government, he said, had "been importuned from many quarters to declare themselves in favour of a high tariff. Some of the gentlemen who have addressed us have done so as the advocates of protection, pure and simple; others . . . have contended, and not without force, that circumstanced as we are, in connection with the people of the United States, it becomes the duty of the Administration to meet the peculiar policy of that

---

[8] *Canada, House of Commons Debates,* 1876, 65.
[9] *Ibid.,* 129.

people with a reciprocal policy in the same direction." Cartwright was not prepared to take a free-trade stand, but he argued against the supposed advantages of high protection, and found that it had brought evils in its train in the United States. High protection, having failed in the United States, would not be introduced into Canada where it would increase taxation and enrich the few. So the tariff should remain at its existing level.[10] Resistance to tariff increases was maintained with difficulty, and was partly unexpected in view of increases already made. The drift toward higher protection, which in any case was becoming more marked, was further intensified by the continuance of depression. Evidence taken by select committees of the house of commons revealed the pressure by manufacturing interests towards higher protection. The committee of 1874, for example, on the basis of replies to a questionnaire from 215 manufacturers, reported a general complaint against the "unequal competition" with the United States, and a claim that higher rates would not necessarily raise prices to the consumer.[11] In 1877 the Toronto Board of Trade changed to a policy of protection, and in the following year the Manufacturers' Association of Ontario, which had formerly been divided on the issue, voted unanimously for a national policy.[12] Under the circumstances the liberal policy was hard to defend and the continual sniping of the opposition foreshadowed their adoption of a programme of protective duties. The conservatives, indeed, were not slow in taking advantage of the opportunity of offering a cure for an admitted complaint. Sir John Macdonald made a prolonged defence of protection in the house of commons. In the upper house Senator Read, a confessed believer in protection, moved for a "national policy" by which reciprocity of trade with the United States was obtained or a reciprocity of tariffs was established by Canada.[13]

In introducing the budget in 1877 Cartwright was obliged to report a deficit of nearly two million dollars for the previous year. There were, however, in his opinion, special reasons for this:

[10] Ibid., 253.
[11] Journals of the House of Commons of the Dominion of Canada, 1874, appendix 3.
[12] S. D. Clark, The Canadian Manufacturers' Association: A Study in Collective Bargaining and Political Pressure (University of Toronto Studies, History and Economics Series, vol. VII, Toronto, 1939), 6.
[13] Canada, Debates of the Senate, 1877, 248.

extraordinary expenditures, shrinkage of trade, and a bad harvest. Depression was universal, and the United States, with its protective system, had suffered more than had Canada. But the depth of the depression had, he believed, been reached; and while some modifications in the tariff were proposed, there was to be no material change. In the course of the long attack on the government's policy, Tupper concluded that there had been no improvement in economic conditions "nothing to justify the hon. gentleman in refusing to so readjust the tariff of Canada as to protect and preserve her credit". The government, he said, "have nailed their colours to the free-trade mast, and that sooner than yield, they will go down with the ship, and down they will go".[14] In the session of 1878 the same debate, with much the same arguments, was continued, and on March 7 Sir John Macdonald moved:

That the House is of the opinion that the welfare of Canada requires the adoption of a National Policy, which, by a judicious readjustment of the tariff, will benefit and foster the agricultural, the mining, the manufacturing and other interests of the Dominion; that such a policy will retain in Canada thousands of our fellow countrymen now obliged to expatriate themselves in search of the employment denied them at home, will restore prosperity to our struggling industries, now so sadly depressed, will prevent Canada from being made a sacrifice market, will encourage and develop an active interprovincial trade, and moving (as it ought to do) in the direction of a reciprocity of tariffs with our neighbour, so far as the varied interests of Canada may demand, will greatly tend to procure for this country, eventually, a reciprocity of trade.[15]

This guarded but all-embracing proposition was then defended. By sweeping references to history and to contemporary conditions, Macdonald sought to prove that no country had risen to prosperity on free trade, and that none had survived which was entirely agricultural. Examples were adduced, from Athens to modern Russia, to strengthen the case, and a sad picture was painted of the depressed state of industry in Canada and of the many Canadians who were forced to seek employment in the United States.

The election came in September, still in the midst of hard times, and the conservatives were returned to office with a majority of eighty-six. In March 1879 Sir Leonard Tilley, the new minister

[14] *Canada, House of Commons Debates*, 1877, 165.
[15] *Ibid.*, 1878, 854.

of finance, introduced the budget that was to give effect to the
national policy. The conservative party lived up to its pledge of
greater protection. The new tariff, as compared with the previous
one (that of 1874), was more complicated and considerably
higher. Where fully manufactured goods had formerly paid 17½
per cent. they were now to pay up to 30 per cent., and in some
cases the rate was as high as 40 per cent. A wide range of goods
were covered, and in general the tariff "represented a decision to
promote industrialization in terms of a Canadian rather than a
North American market".[16] For ten years thereafter further modifications in the tariff were all in an upward direction, until new
circumstances forced reductions once more.

II

The liberal and conservative parties differed on the height of
the tariff; and by an emphasis on the protection of home industries
the latter might have seemed to minimize the significance of
external trade. This, however, it was never intended to do. There
was a firm belief that Canadian industry and agriculture could
flourish only behind the shelter of a tariff wall, but no Canadian
government had ever failed to point to the value of foreign trade.
The Hansard of these years is studded with statistics, and the
deduction was constantly made that the woes of the dominion
were due in large part to a decline in the volume of trade. The
"national policy" was intended not as a brake but as a stimulant
to trade, and whether or not it was the cause, the event was
what had been desired. The picture began to look more cheerful,
as the following figures show.[17]

Year	Imports from U.K.	Imports from U.S.	Total
1879	$30,967,778	$42,170,306	$78,702,519
1880	33,764,439	28,193,783	69,900,542
1881	42,885,142	36,338,701	90,488,329

---

[16] W. A. Mackintosh, *The Economic Background of Dominion-Provincial
Relations* (Report of the Royal Commission on Dominion-Provincial Relations,
1939, Appendix 3), 19.

[17] *Canada Year Book*, 1939, 507.

More interest was centred on the figures for exports, which were distinctly encouraging.[18]

Year	Exports to U.K.	Exports to U.S.	Total
1879	$29,393,424	$25,491,356	$62,431,025
1880	35,208,031	29,566,211	72,899,697
1881	42,637,219	34,038,431	83,944,701

The balance of trade was still unfavourable, which disturbed some of the parliamentary economists, but the volume of exports was a respectable and an increasing one. Nearly half of Canada's external trade was with the United Kingdom, some forty per cent. with the United States, and only about ten per cent. with all other countries. The national policy explicitly left the door open for reciprocity, but it was improbable that the United States would accept the invitation. The free-trade policy of the United Kingdom offered no opportunity for extension by governmental action. There remained, however, the rest of the wide world with which to trade; and what was a relatively small volume might be increased by means of tariff bargaining as well as other means. The most hopeful direction in which to look seemed to be the British, French, and Spanish West Indies, trade with which was traditional, but had not grown as was hoped. At the same time were added, as possible customers, Brazil and Mexico; and (arising out of negotiations on colonies) Spain itself. The only great power with which direct trade negotiations were considered was France.

For the benefit of the house of commons detailed statistics were prepared on trade with the West Indies, Brazil, and Mexico since 1875.[19] Trade with Mexico proved to be insignificant. In 1874 and 1875 Canada had imported a large amount of sugar from Brazil, and in 1880 this was recommenced. Imports from British and foreign West Indian islands were scattered over a number of items, but were only in large volume in sugar, molasses, and salt. Lumber, fish, and manufactured articles were exported to Brazil in small amounts. Fish was much the largest export to the West Indies, with small quantities of agricultural and manufactured products. Parliament was distressed by the slow growth of West Indian trade; particularly—as some members argued—

18 *Ibid.*, 506.
19 *Canada, Sessional Papers*, 1884, no. 67.

on the ground that it was highly profitable, showing a favourable balance of trade, and offering opportunities for Canadian shipping. Long hours of debate were spent in attempts to analyse the reasons for the small amount of trade, and two main causes were put forward: that steam communication was inadequate; and that the Canadian tariff prevented the purchase of raw sugar, which would be the natural exchange for Canadian products. The second consideration became bogged in party discussions of the tariff. The first was met by the completion of an agreement with the government of Brazil, under which the two countries were to subsidize a line of steamships to Brazil and the West Indies. The arrangement came into operation in 1882, but later broke down. One of the chief competitors in West Indian trade was the United States, and when that country negotiated a flag treaty with Spain in 1885, allowing American ships the same privileges as Spanish in the Spanish West Indies, alarm was expressed in Canada. The only answer could be the conclusion of an equally satisfactory arrangement with Spain. The diplomats were also needed to encourage trade with France. The registry of Canadian ships in that country was found to be—because of the form of an Anglo-French treaty—on less favourable terms than the registry of British ships. To secure an equally advantageous position, the Canadian government was prepared to reduce the tariff on French wines, the bargain to be sealed in a commercial treaty. It was not enough to talk of the superior character of Canadian goods: not enough even to exhibit wares at international exhibitions, such as those at Sydney, Philadelphia, and Paris. Trading was bargaining; but international bargaining could be conducted only through traditional and recognized channels. By such logic were Canadians driven to study the complicated structure of the British Empire.

The position had to be examined from more than one point of view: the effect on Canada of existing British treaties, the extent to which Canada could conduct her own foreign relations, and the machinery—existing or to be created—by which Canadian affairs abroad could be conducted. Before confederation, and in the first decade after it, the practice was to include the colonies in British treaties of commerce. Many of these treaties obligated Canada to give most-favoured-nation treatment to the countries concerned; and two of them—that with Belgium of 1862, and that with the German Zollverein of 1865—extended to the relations between Canada and Great Britain, thus complicating the establishment of an imperial preferential tariff. In 1877 the British government proposed that the self-governing colonies should be notified of a pending commercial treaty, and given the option of adhering to it or being explicitly excluded. The adoption of this principle allowed the Canadian government a new freedom of action of which it took advantage.[20] In 1881, for example, the colonial secretary transmitted to the governor general a letter from the foreign office stating that

negotiations will probably be opened shortly with the Egyptian government, for the conclusion of a commercial treaty with Egypt; and I have to request that you will inform me, at your earliest convenience, whether there are any matters in respect of which your government desires to make any special proposals.

The colonial article referred to in the enclosed letter is the clause now adopted, exempting the colony under your government, and others of the more important colonies, from the operation of the treaty, but providing that its stipulations may be applied to any such colonies on notice to that effect being given within one year from the date of the exchange of the ratifications of the treaty.

In this case the Canadian government did not wish to be included; but in a convention of commerce between the United Kingdom and Morocco, which had limited obligations, the opposite decision was made. A third negotiation of the same year was with Ecuador. The colonial secretary sent to the governor general a copy of the treaty, already signed, together with a draft protocol which was to be signed before ratification of the treaty was executed. The draft read as follows:

The undersigned, in proceeding to the exchange of the ratifications of the treaty . . . between Her Majesty and the Republic of the Equator, have agreed to the present Protocol.

The stipulations of the aforesaid Treaty shall not be applicable to the Colonies and foreign possessions of Her Britannic Majesty hereinafter named, that is to say: —
The Dominion of Canada. . . .

Provided always that the stipulations of the aforesaid Treaty shall be made applicable to any or all of the above-mentioned colonies

[20] For the correspondence concerning treaties with Serbia, Roumania, Ecuador, Morocco, Egypt, and Montenegro, see *Canada, Sessional Papers,* 1883, no. 89.

or foreign possessions of Her Britannic Majesty, on whose behalf notice to that effect shall be given within one year from the date hereof, by Her Britannic Majesty's Minister at Quito to the Ecuadorian Minister for Foreign Affairs.

The colonial secretary's letter was dated July 8, 1881. On October 14, 1882, a request for an early reply followed, and it was not until November 16, 1882, that the governor general was able to reply that the privy council had reported against inclusion in the treaty. The wheels of Olympus ground slow. In 1880 the Canadian government asked to be excluded from a treaty with Roumania. In the same year a treaty was made with Serbia and, apparently inadvertently, Canada was included without being consulted. The colonial office then inquired if this was satisfactory, and on hearing from Ottawa that it was not, had to request the Serbian government to have Canada excluded by action of the national assembly.

Apart from such a slip, the technique in respect of new British treaties seemed to work smoothly; and problems arising out of treaties concluded earlier had to be met as they arose. All such treaties, whether or not they were advantageous to Canada, were not initiated with the object of meeting particular Canadian needs. Yet such needs existed, as, for example, the improvement of trade with the Spanish West Indies and the sale of wooden ships to France. Since Canada had no power to conclude commercial (or any other) treaties by her own authority, it became necessary to work out a system within the imperial framework as it then was. Like most such imperial problems, this one was met by experiments of practice rather than constitutional definition. From the Canadian point of view it was essential that Canadians, versed in the matter at hand, should play a major rôle in negotiations, whatever their legal status might be. There being no Canadian political representative abroad, Sir Alexander Galt was dispatched in the autumn of 1878 on a special mission to Madrid and Paris. Formal negotiations with the Spanish and French authorities were conducted by the British ambassadors at the capitals, it being left to them to consult with Galt and to arrange for him to discuss details with the governments in question. If a draft convention were concluded it would be sent to the British government and would have to be approved both by it and the Canadian government before its signature was authorized. As it proved, that stage was never reached, not apparently through the fault of the procedure or the negotiators, but from the complications caused by a third party in the French scene, and by a change of government in Madrid.

Galt's official reports to the government contain no hints as to the adequacy of the procedure, being for the most part accounts of interviews and correspondence with British and French officials.[21] His private letters to Macdonald, however, describe the early difficulties that arose in Paris. He arrived there in December, armed with letters from the foreign office; but Lord Lyons, who had had no experience of a dominion diplomat, acted with what Galt considered to be a discourtesy and deliberation that stood in the way of success.[22] After bearing it with impatience for a short time, Galt wrote to the foreign office. His appeal had "a wonderful effect. Next day I got an *affectionate* note from Lord Lyons . . . before I had time to answer it he called on me in person and made all proper amends, saying he had arranged an interview for to-day with the Minister of Commerce—apologized about not having asked us to dine and asked us to come to-day. . . ."[23] Galt then went ahead with direct negotiations, and considered that he was on the verge of success when the French drew back because of a complication caused by tariff relations with Austria-Hungary. In sending his report home, he again showed that he was not without a diplomatic sense, pointing out that, if negotiations failed for the time being, the Canadian terms should be kept secret against a later renewal of discussions.[24] Passing on to Madrid Galt found his relations with the ambassador there were smooth, and in dealing with the Spanish he adopted the usual bargaining device of maximum terms: "Our memorandum", he wrote to Macdonald, "covers concessions that if granted would go far to give Canada the whole carrying trade between the United States and Cuba—as well as exceptional advantages for our own productions. But you must not expect us to obtain all this. I shall be quite satisfied if we get a substantial rebate on the duties on our productions, with the privilege of the Spanish Flag—for the mail steamship line. . . ."[25]

21 *Canada, Sessional Papers,* 1880, no. 104.
22 Public Archives of Canada, *Macdonald Papers,* "Sir Alexander Galt". Galt to Macdonald, Dec. 18, 1878.
23 *Ibid.,* Dec. 20, 1878.
24 *Ibid.,* Jan. 1, 1879.
25 *Ibid.,* Jan. 20, 1879.

The Spanish, like the French, negotiations failed of success at the time, but—as in the case of the American negotiations—the advantages of participation in them of a man well-versed in Canadian affairs were fully demonstrated. Exactly what the status of the Canadian in such discussions should be was still an open question, but there was a growing feeling in Canada that it should be in some way diplomatic, and that the representative for the negotiation of trade treaties might well be also the holder of a new office proposed to be set up in London. The importance of having a Canadian representative in England had led first to the appointment of one with semi-official standing. Sir John Rose was, from 1869 to 1880, accredited to Her Majesty's Government "as a gentleman possessing the confidence of the Canadian Government with whom Her Majesty's Government may properly communicate on Canadian affairs".[26] The experiment was fully justified by results, for Rose was able to handle such questions as the transfer of the Hudson's Bay territory, the negotiations leading up to the joint high commission at Washington, and Canadian Pacific Railway finance. The Canadian government, however, was anxious to regularize this ill-defined position, and while in England in 1879 Macdonald, Tilley, and Tupper wrote a memorandum on the subject for the colonial secretary. In it they argued that the time had come when relations between the dominion and the home government could no longer be satisfactorily maintained purely by correspondence through the governor general, and that an officer should be stationed in London who would discuss directly the various matters of common concern, thus obviating the necessity of periodic visits of Canadian ministers. Such officer, they suggested, could be accredited, in association with the imperial representative, to a foreign court for particular negotiations. The suggested title for the new officer was "resident minister", and his status would be "quasi-diplomatic". In November the colonial secretary sent a copy of this memorandum to the governor general, with a covering letter. The British government approved of the general idea, but suggested two modifications: since Canada was an integral part of the empire, the Canadian representative could hardly be diplomatic; the foreign secretary would decide what

<hr>

26 M. H. Long, "Sir John Rose and the Informal Beginnings of the Canadian High Commissionership" (*Canadian Historical Review*, XII, March, 1931).

part he might play in foreign negotiations. In December the
Canadian privy council reported that, while they still held that
the position was quasi-diplomatic, they were satisfied with the
arrangements proposed by the colonial secretary. They suggested,
as a title, "High Commissioner of Canada in London". A brief
cable in February 1880 contained the recognition of Sir Alexander
Galt as high commissioner, and he sailed in March.[27]

Proposals that there should be a diplomatic representative of
Canada in London had more than once been made,[28] and Galt
was impressed by that aspect of his office. Shortly before sailing
for England he discussed with Macdonald the terms of his instructions, and wrote a memorandum embodying his ideas.[29] The
proposals are startling in their extent, though Galt pointed out
that he would not advise putting them all in the official instructions,
nor expect them to be carried out at once. The memorandum
reads as follows:

Nomination of Resident Minister marks a new era in Colonial
administration. To be attended with greatest probability of success, it
should be done with studied deliberation and formality. The minister should not present his credentials until the governments are prepared effectively to enter upon important negotiations, and his arrival
should be simultaneous with the announcement of such negotiations.

In my opinion it would be a grave error to allow the Mission to
assume the appearance of having its real duties in the Financial and
Emigration arrangements—which must inevitably arise if the advent
of the Minister be not marked by serious approaches to Her Majesty's
Government, and if the first impression relative to its importance be
formed by the British public through the announcement that the
Financial and Emigration duties have been assumed by the Mission.

To give due prominence to the concession made by the Imperial
Government in this respect, the arrival of the Minister should be
accompanied with the announcement of important international
negotiations. Subsequently—within from one to three months, but
not simultaneously, the minister should be instructed to take over the
supervision of finance and emigration—thus in the most direct manner, making it apparent to the government and people of England
that the real import of the mission is to be sought in its political aspect.

[27] *Canada, Sessional Papers,* 1880, no. 105.
[28] E.g., by Alexander Campbell in *Canada, Debates of the Senate,* 1874,
17.
[29] Enclosed in *Macdonald Papers,* "Sir Alexander Galt". Galt to Macdonald, March 11, 1880. Confidential.

Certain subjects have already been submitted to the British Government and remain in abeyance.

Of these the more important are—

The negotiation of treaties with foreign nations.

The Pacific Railway—and development of North West.

A review of commercial relations—pointing to an imperial customs union.

In regard to the first subject the object is to secure the thorough support of the imperial government. The appointment of a Canadian envoy is valuable and his information indispensable, but success will largely depend on the bonâ fide support given by the Foreign Office. This support will only be given when the views of the Imperial Government on other subjects are brought into accord with those of Canada.

The second subject is so connected with the last that they may be considered as one, because the principle of a commercial union is that of vital political identity and will be found the most powerful agent in arranging the others.

Circumstances peculiarly favour the present discussion of all these subjects.

The termination of all England's commercial treaties permits a change of policy.

A marked change of public feeling is growing up respecting free trade.

The agricultural distress is anxiously seeking a remedy.

The great North West relieves England from dependence on foreign nations for food—and opens illimitable field for emigration.

The Pacific railway thus becomes as necessary for England as for Canada.

Instead therefore of asking for guarantee, let a larger and more comprehensive proposal be submitted, to wit:

Practically a substantial alliance for certain specific national objects, based on the principle that produce and manufactures shall respectively receive more favoured nation treatment than those of foreign nations.

That the Pacific railway be constructed on joint account the cost to be recouped from the lands.

A system of aided emigration on joint account to be organized if desired by the imperial government.

The submission of such a proposal would amply justify the urgency of the government in desiring to appoint a minister.

It is in accord with the views of the government and people of Canada.

It would greatly conciliate public opinion in England—and if entertained by the Imperial Government would ensure their cordial support in foreign negotiations.

It would lead to united policy and action with the other colonies.

There is no record of Macdonald's reply to this memorandum. In part it coincided with the government's policy of making the office diplomatic or quasi-diplomatic, but the picture of an imperial alliance went far beyond any recorded policy of the government. Certainly the official instructions were the palest reflection of Galt's grandiose scheme.

III

Sir Alexander Galt was appointed under the great seal of Canada, and his instructions came to him from the secretary of state. General correspondence was to be carried on with the secretary of state; that on financial questions with the minister of finance; and on emigration matters with the minister of agriculture. Galt was to be chief emigration agent, and the instructions laid it down that the encouragement of emigration to the west of Canada was to be his first consideration, for only in that way could the financial burden of the west on the Canadian tax-payer be reduced. In the near future the management of the public debt and financial correspondence were to be transferred to the high commissioner. He was to carry on negotiations concerning the Esquimalt graving dock; assist the Canadian cattle trade; and sound out the British government on the delicate subjects of assistance to the Pacific Railway and a British zollverein. In foreign affairs he was to watch the fishery questions arising out of the Washington Treaty, remembering that the Canadian government did not wish to take the initiative in any negotiations on them. Careful instructions were given on commercial treaties. Treaties had been made since 1867 which affected the freedom of action of the dominion, and it was desired that Canada should be relieved from obligations as occasion arose, and not further committed without her approval. Whenever special arrangements in a treaty were desired in the Canadian interest the British government would be asked to accredit the high commissioner to the foreign power, to act in concert with the imperial representative.

In his short tenure of office (1880-1883) Galt put his hand to the multifarious tasks outlined both in formal instructions and private letters from the ministers. Much of his time was spent on securing immigrants, and—while other causes were at work— the numbers were multiplied during his years in London. A start was made toward trade treaties, but without tangible progress. The great plans of the Montreal memorandum foundered on the change of government in England, the failure of his hopes of being regarded as a diplomat, and the lack of money to establish a position in London which he felt might enable him to circumvent the caution of the colonial office. After a year in London he wrote to Macdonald. "I think you should insist now on your Representative being recognized as a member of the Corps Diplomatique. It is really the only proper definition of his rank, and the only way to ensure proper respect here. As a *Colonial* these 'arrogant insulars' turn up their noses at us all."[30] No such change, however, was made in the position of the office; and whether or not the Canadian government wished to have diplomatic status for the high commissioner, they were able to quote the existing arrangement against one type of parliamentary complaint. Sir Charles Tupper, Galt's successor, was criticized for doubling the rôles of high commissioner and minister of railways; and when he took part in the election of 1891, it was argued that a diplomat should keep free from party politics. In reply Sir John Thompson stated that the high commissioner "is nothing but the agent of the government living in London. His Excellency the Governor General is the medium of communication between this government and Her Majesty's Government, and no other can be had. . . . He does not occupy, either at home or abroad, such a position as an ambassador in the diplomatic service of the British Government holds."[31] A private letter from Macdonald to Lord Stanley, however, gives a somewhat different picture of the practice, if not of the constitutional position:

By degrees the Colonial Ministers [i.e., secretaries] have begun to treat the colonial representatives as diplomatic agents, rather than as subordinate executive officers and to consult them as such.

Canada has found it advantageous on several occasions to have Sir Charles Tupper dealt with as a quasi member of the corps diplomatique and I have no doubt the colonial secretary has been

---

[30] O. D. Skelton, *The Life and Times of Sir Alexander Tilloch Galt* (Toronto, 1920), 547.

[31] *Canada, House of Commons Debates*, 1891, 575.

assisted by his experience which Sir Charles gained during his service as a cabinet minister in Canada. We do not desire, however, to give him a "free hand" on any subject in discussion with the Imperial Government. He must take his instructions from the government here, as much as Sir Julian Pauncefote from Lord Salisbury and cannot travel out of "the four corners" of any minute on which his name is mentioned.[32]

Tupper, like Galt, had many duties: rescuing Canadian cattle from being condemned as diseased; encouraging immigration; furthering Canadian loans (especially those of the Canadian Pacific Railway); and generally making Canada known by speeches and a multitude of social activities. In 1885, during the North-West Rebellion, he was kept busy answering inquiries in England, getting information from Ottawa, and trying to correct the attitude of *The Times,* which obtained its news from a correspondent in Philadelphia. The conduct of foreign (as opposed to imperial) affairs was not the least part of his work, and the one which most closely relates to this study. In this Tupper inherited the negotiations for treaties with France and Spain, together with the constitutional question that had arisen in connection with them, that is, the status of a Canadian negotiator. From the first Tupper was not satisfied to be appointed as an advisor instead of a plenipotentiary. In his early months of office he had learned that an international conference was to be held at Paris to discuss the protection of submarine cables. Believing that this was a matter of interest to Canada, he suggested to Macdonald that he should attend, and the latter asked the governor general to cable a request to that effect to the colonial secretary. The latter then applied to the foreign office for credentials, and Tupper was duly appointed to represent Canada. He was pleased with the conference, and Canada's place at it, and on his return to London he wrote to Macdonald that "I feel some pride in the fact that Canada took her place in the international conference and on an equal footing with all the other Powers, and I may add that nothing could exceed the kindness and courtesy with which I was treated by all present."[33] In the following year the foreign secretary agreed

[32] *Macdonald Papers,* Letter Book 27. Aug. 15, 1890. When minutes were sent to the colonial secretary, copies were forwarded to the high commissioner.

[33] *Macdonald Papers,* "Sir Charles Tupper". Tupper to Macdonald, Oct. 31, 1883.

to Tupper's request that he be made a plenipotentiary jointly with
the ambassador, should the negotiations with Spain be officially
renewed. "This", he wrote, "is a very important point, and in
the light of Galt's reports a very important one scored for
Canada."[34]

On the one hand the conservative government was pressing
for plenipotentiary powers, and on the other was resisting the
claims of the opposition for direct negotiations between Canada
and foreign states. The debate—which reappeared periodically—
was chiefly on two grounds: which system of diplomacy would
be more advantageous to Canada, and whether greater independence in that one field would threaten the whole imperial structure.
The senate went over the ground in 1879, the commons in 1882,
both houses in 1891, and the commons again in 1892. In each
case there was a solid basis of agreement that Canadian interests
were not being adequately supported by the existing system of
treaty-making, and in each more general discussions of the whole
imperial question were the outcome. Edward Blake in the course
of a long speech, did not mince his words: "The history of the
diplomatic service of England, as far as Canada is concerned, has
been a history of error, blunder, wrong and concession". His
motion was that it would be expedient for Canada to obtain
powers for direct negotiation of trade treaties, either with another
British possession or a foreign state. Macdonald replied that it
was not the failure of the method, but the effect of unfavourable
circumstances. If Canada were to remain a dependency, England
could hardly grant the suggested concession.[35]

To some extent demands for direct relations with foreign states
reflected the long-held belief that English diplomats had done
little good for Canada. In part such demands were the result of
the slow speed at which negotiations moved. Those with Spain
dragged on but seemed always on the verge of success. Tupper's
instructions from Ottawa were to offer a reduction in the Canadian
duty on sugar in exchange for a reduction on Canadian exports
of fish, lumber, potatoes, flour, and certain manufactured goods
to the West Indies. In spite of all efforts no result was attained;
though some advantage did accrue to Canada from a British treaty

34 *Ibid.*, Tupper to Macdonald, Sept. 11, 1884.
35 *Canada, House of Commons Debates,* 1882, 1068 ff.

with Spain, providing for most-favoured-nation treatment. The local officials in Havana, however, proved to be a step ahead of the Canadian nationalists. The customs officials were convinced that Canada, being a nation, did not come under the British treaty, and were only persuaded to the contrary by word from Madrid.

The old system thus had its uses. In return for the concessions by Spain, certain West Indian sugars, raw hides, coffee, and tea were admitted into Canada free of duty. A further agreement was reached between Britain and Spain through an exchange of notes in June 1894 whereby advantages were conceded to the United Kingdom and the British colonies in return for the continuance of most-favoured-nation treatment to Spanish trade. Though not negotiated by Canada, this was not denounced by her, and therefore came into operation.

The long negotiations with France had a more successful ending, though not without many difficulties. Polite remarks were made by both parties on the affinity of old and new France, but the results were due not to sentiment but to a balancing of national interests. In the late autumn of 1892 Tupper was sent as a plenipotentiary to Paris for what proved to be the final round. On arrival he explained to Lord Dufferin, the British ambassador, the Canadian position. This, in brief, was to secure the admission of Canadian goods under the minimum French tariff and the removal of the *surtaxe d'entrepôt* as reciprocity for the existing favourable treatment afforded to French goods. The Canadian government, he explained, was no longer willing to reduce the duty on French wines. On the advice of the British embassy, Tupper's next call was at the office of the *République française* to secure favourable publicity. After a hurried visit to London to consult with Sir John Abbott, he was introduced by the ambassador to the minister for foreign affairs and officials of the commerce and customs departments. With the French commissioners Tupper discussed the actual figures of trade and the concessions that might be made by either party. Having failed to impress the French representatives with his picture of existing privileges and the attempts to establish steam communication, Tupper fell back on the proposition to lower the duties on French wines, books, soaps, and other articles. Proposals and counter-proposals were exchanged in meetings or by letter, Tupper keeping in touch with his government to obtain acceptances of each series of modification. The next step was the exchange of draft treaties. The final terms took the form of an "Agreement regulating the commercial relations between Canada and France in respect of customs tariff",[36] between France and Great Britain, signed for the queen by Lord Dufferin and Sir Charles Tupper as plenipotentiaries on February 6, 1893. The duties on French wines, soaps, nuts, almonds, prunes, and plums were reduced. Nineteen Canadian products—including canned meats, fish, fruit, timber, and wooden furniture, wooden ships, and boots and shoes—were to enter France, Algeria, and French colonies under the minimum tariff. In respect to these articles Canada was to enjoy most-favoured-nation treatment; while France and her colonies were to have complete most-favoured-nation concessions from Canada. The agreement was to be ratified by the parliaments of France and Canada.

After what he considered to be the successful completion of his labours, Tupper was surprised to find that his government was hesitant about its acceptance. A telegram instructing him not to sign until the terms had been received in Ottawa arrived too late. The principal points at issue were, first, a bounty to ships constructed in France, and, secondly, uncertainty as to whether the most-favoured-nation clause in the treaty applied to the trade between Canada and other British possessions. On the latter point the British government gave an assurance that it would not so apply, and the agreement was finally ratified in 1895, the Canadian parliament having passed an act (57 and 58 Vict., c. 2) in 1894 which empowered the governor general to proclaim assent at a date to be settled.

IV

In the same period as that of the protracted negotiations for trade treaties with European states the Canadian government was obliged to re-enter the diplomatic field in North America to settle the controversy once more raised by the apparently endless fishery dispute. The rejection by the American senate of the treaty of 1874 revived the arbitration provided for under the Treaty of Washington. For the board of three, the United States nominated

[36] The text is in *British and Foreign State Papers*, LXXXV, 28.

E. H. Kellogg; Canada, A. T. Galt; and the neutral arbitrator was the Belgian minister at Washington, Maurice Delfosse—named by the Austrian ambassador after the failure of the interested parties to agree on other names which one or the other submitted. The commission finally assembled at Halifax in June 1877, accompanied by legal advisers and other assistants appointed by the parties. Elaborate written cases were submitted by the British representatives (on behalf of Canada and Newfoundland) and by those of the United States. After a brief deliberation the commissioners, by a majority decision, awarded $5,500,000, payable over twelve years, as the balance due to Canada and Newfoundland for the superior value of their inshore fisheries. Kellogg dissented, and the award was received with general disapproval in the United States. In Canada there was mild satisfaction, which meant a good deal in view of the tradition of American diplomatic cunning and British defeats. Since it was an arbitration, it would hardly be proper to describe Galt's part as that of a successful Canadian advocate; but apparently his course was made easier by a conviction of the justice of the Canadian case.[37] Although the British brief called for a sum nearly three times as large, that can be put down to the usual technique of bargaining. In effect there seems little doubt that Canada had obtained a generous price—though for that she was to pay in international strain as well as in fish.

Whether it was because of American discontent with the decision, or because the arrangements in the treaty of 1871 failed to lay down an acceptable or complete set of rules, the fishery dispute flared up again before the ink was dry on the award; and the actions and counter-actions, claims and counter-claims threatened those friendly relations by means of which alone Canada could comfortably exist on the American continent. In 1885 the American government announced that the fishery clauses of the Treaty of Washington would be abrogated as from July 1—that is, in the midst of the season, a result which was only avoided by a temporary agreement to suspend action until the end of the year.[38] Following

[37] Skelton, *Sir Alexander Tilloch Galt*, 512.

[38] For the documents on this question see the British *Correspondence Relative to the North American Fisheries, 1884-1886* (United States, no. 1, 1887); *Further Correspondence Respecting North American Fisheries, 1886-1887* (United States, no. 2, 1887); *Canada, Sessional Papers*, 1887, no. 16. A full account of the negotiations, from the point of view of the American government, is in C. C. Tansill, *The Foreign Policy of Thomas F. Bayard, 1885-1897* (New York, 1940).

this suspension, the fishery question reverted to the pre-1871 position, and the Canadian government, vigorously enforcing protection of Atlantic fisheries, began to warn off, detain, or seize American vessels, to a number during 1886 of forty-nine, according to the American secretary of state.[39] The Canadian parliament passed a retaliatory act stopping the purchase of bait by American fishermen in Canadian ports, and permitting the seizure of any foreign vessel illegally entering Canadian waters, and congress replied with an act (happily not put into effect) empowering the president to prevent Canadian vessels from using American ports except in case of distress. The house of representatives would have gone further still by the stoppage of transit by land as well as sea—a measure of complete non-intercourse which it was induced by the senate to drop. Literally the waters were indeed troubled; and to the mutual seizure of ships were added other causes of friction: American discontent with the Halifax award, competition of Canadian fish with the interests of New England packers, an inveterate taste on the part of certain elements to twist the lion's tail (or that of the lion's cub), and a well-founded suspicion in the United States that Canadians were once more attempting to use their fisheries as a lever to secure reciprocity. Willingness to attempt a settlement was not lacking on either side, but by what machinery could it be discussed? The American government, its minister in London declared, would not deal with Canada.

Still less can the United States' Government consent to be drawn, at any time, into a discussion of the subject with the Colonial Government of Canada. The Treaty in question, and all the international relations arising out of it, exist only as between the governments of the United States and of Great Britain, and between those governments only can they be dealt with. If in entering upon that consideration of the subject which the United States have insisted upon, the arguments contained in the Report of the Canadian Minister should be advanced by Her Majesty's Government, I do not conceive that they will be found difficult to answer.[40]

The minister's intransigent position seems not to have represented the views of Bayard, the secretary of state, who had for some time been struggling to move toward a peaceful settlement, and who, in April, unofficially invited either Macdonald or Tupper to

39 *Canada, Sessional Papers*, 1888, no. 36C.
40 *Ibid.*, E. J. Phelps to Salisbury, Jan. 26, 1887.

discuss matters personally with him.[41] Tupper called on Bayard in May and proposed the holding of a conference in Washington. An exchange of letters after his return casts some light on the interview. Bayard, it now appeared, regretted the necessity of the indirect communication with Canada, made necessary by her "imperfectly developed sovereignty", but recognized that only the envoys of Great Britain could speak officially. He wrote warmly of the necessity of good relations with Canada, and welcomed a conference (as he said the president did), and presumed that Tupper would be a plenipotentiary. The British government, having been driven into a dispute in which it had no direct interest, readily accepted the proposal; and appointed Tupper, Joseph Chamberlain, and Sir Lionel Sackville West, British minister in Washington, as plenipotentiaries. The official instructions called first for a discussion, and if possible amicable settlement, of the North Atlantic fisheries, but allowed wide latitude on other subjects. "Full liberty is given to you to enter upon the consideration of any questions which may bear upon the issues involved, and to discuss and treat for any equivalents, whether by means of tariff concessions, or otherwise, which the United States' plenipotentiaries may be authorized to consider as a means of settlement." The Behring Sea fisheries might also be discussed if the American representatives were authorized to do so.[42] It was, and long had been, the Canadian aim to include the fisheries in a more general agreement that embraced reciprocal tariff concessions, but the difficulty was to get the Americans to broaden the agenda. Macdonald had prophesied that the whole procedure was "a snare laid by the United States Government to entrap England into a commission to consider the expediency of relaxing the terms of the convention of 1818";[43] and at the first regular meeting in Washington the British representatives spent three hours arguing against the American proposal so to limit the conference.[44] Tupper had nothing but praise for Chamberlain in that battle. On December 3 the British submitted a proposal that the fishery

[41] L. B. Shippee, *Thomas Francis Bayard* ("The American Secretaries of State and Their Diplomacy", ed. by S. F. Bemis, VIII, New York, 1927-8).

[42] *Canada, Sessional Papers,* 1888, no. 36C.

[43] *Macdonald Papers,* Letter Book 24. Macdonald to Lansdowne, Sept. 24, 1887.

[44] *Macdonald Papers,* "Washington Treaty, 1888", vol. VII. Tupper to Macdonald, Nov. 24, 1887.

privileges should be revived in exchange for a tariff agreement, but this was refused.[45] The meetings were then postponed while Tupper and Chamberlain went to Ottawa for consultation. Negotiations were continued in January, but with difficulty. At one point Chamberlain became "wildly indignant" and proposed to return to England,[46] but a treaty was finally signed in the middle of February. Though this also was rejected by the senate, a *modus vivendi* reached at the same time, providing for a system of licences for American fishermen, came into effect and remained in effect for over thirty years. Thus the Atlantic fisheries issue was laid to rest. Tupper, who pulled his full weight on the commission, reported that Chamberlain and West "could not have supported Canada with more untiring zeal than they have from first to last".[47]

The Behring Sea question, which the Americans had kept off the agenda at Washington, remained unsettled. The American claim was that it was necessary, in order to preserve the herds of seals, to prevent hunting during a part of the year. The Canadian government, however, supporting the interests of British Columbia fishermen, claimed that this was a subterfuge designed to enable American sealers to have a monopoly on the coast.[48] Meanwhile United States cutters were seizing Canadian fishing vessels on the ground that they were poaching.[49] Staving off an unfavourable settlement between the British and American governments, the Canadian government sent C. H. Tupper, minister of marine and fisheries, to Washington in February 1890 to meet the secretary of state, Blaine. The younger Tupper proved to be less fortunate than his father, both in establishing a working arrangement with the ambassador (Sir Julian Pauncefote) and in negotiations with the secretary of state. Tupper's status, it is true, was somewhat ambiguous, and Blaine bluntly said that he had not expected a Canadian representative, though he proved ready enough to talk

[45] E. M. Saunders (ed.), *The Life and Letters of the Rt. Hon. Sir Charles Tupper* (2 vols., London, 1916), II, 101.

[46] *Ibid.*, 109.

[47] *Macdonald Papers*, "Washington Treaty, 1888", vol. VII. Tupper to Macdonald, Feb. 10, 1888.

[48] Memorandum by G. E. Foster, 1888. Quoted in P. E. Corbett, *The Settlement of Canadian-American Disputes: A Critical Study of Methods and Results* (New Haven and Toronto, 1937), 43.

[49] *Canada, Sessional Papers*, 1887, no. 48.

to him.[50] Tupper believed that the Russian representative was "hand in glove with Mr. Blaine", and that Pauncefote was more anxious to reach a settlement than to push Canadian interests.[51] He protested that no British minister at Washington was in a position to take a firm attitude. "If Canadians", he protested, "cannot act for Great Britain in the negotiations of Canadian affairs the mother country should at least send out a strong and fearless man from home who would be indifferent as to the impression he might personally make upon the United States administration."[52] Tupper then concentrated his efforts on preventing Pauncefote from drafting a convention unfavourable to the Canadian interests. Actually no agreement of any kind was reached until 1891, when a temporary stop to hunting was decided on. At the end of that year the British and American governments agreed on an investigation by two commissioners, the former appointing G. M. Dawson of the Canadian Geological Survey and Sir George Baden-Powell. A year later the whole question was referred to an international arbitral tribunal, and the award was favourable to Britain and Canada.

Two decades of diplomacy had had diverse effects. An obvious one was the experience gained by the Canadian government and parliament in the problems and procedure of negotiation. In dealing with both European and American governments Canadians had encountered the advantages and the disadvantages of utilizing imperial machinery. While contemporaries were not agreed as to whether the balance was favourable or not, there was clearly a desire for at least a greater degree of control over diplomacy on commercial subjects. The progress made in that direction in the eighties and early nineties appeared to be halted by the dispatch of the colonial secretary, the Marquess of Ripon, to the governor general in June 1895, which laid down the principle that "to give the colonies the power of negotiating treaties for themselves without reference to Her Majesty's Government, would be to give them an international status as separate and sovereign states". That principle, however, was not pushed to an extreme in operation; and in 1907, when the Canadian government wished to open

50 *Macdonald Papers*, "Behring Sea", vol. I. C. H. Tupper to Macdonald, Feb. 26, 1890.
51 *Ibid.*, March 3 and 10, 1890.
52 *Ibid.*, April 11, 1890.

negotiations with France, the foreign secretary (Sir Edward Grey) ruled that it was the intention to prevent negotiations from being unknown to the British government; and explained to the ambassador in Paris that Canadians would be the negotiators, that they would doubtless keep him informed, and that he would sign an agreement with two Canadian plenipotentiaries.[53]

Changes continued to be made in constitutional practice in respect of commercial treaties. To some Canadians that development was almost an end in itself, but by others it was more properly judged as a means of achieving satisfactory relationships with foreign states. The subject matter of the negotiations was in most cases commercial, and frequently there was no political issue involved. But the line of demarcation was not exact, and the commercial merged into the political where the most fundamental external interests of Canada were concerned. Major changes in tariff arrangements with the United Kingdom or the United States involved decisions on policy in a field wider than commerce, and—so it seemed to contemporaries—decisions which would define the future relation of Canada toward the two great powers with which her fate was bound.

[53] *Canada, Sessional Papers*, 1908, no. 144.

Chapter VIII

CANADA, THE EMPIRE, AND THE UNITED STATES

THE foreign policy of any state is an expression of the attempt to maintain or establish a series of relationships with other countries, the whole being designed to promote security and prosperity. Any combination of a variety of factors, such as geography, race, historical connections, and economic position, may determine the nature of the policy adopted. Being made up of a series of relationships, foreign policy entails the balancing of one objective against another, and not infrequently the balancing of one state against another. Changing conditions at home or abroad, changing relations between two foreign states, lead to modifications of policy from time to time. Such a general definition may be applied to the foreign, or, to be more exact, to the external, policy of Canada. The alteration of phrase reveals the one unusual aspect of the position of the dominion. Canada was not a sovereign state but a unit within an empire, though grown beyond any known meaning of the word colony. That imperial connection, in itself a changing one, was constantly reviewed both by the mother country and its adult child. It brought obligations as well as advantages to both, the relative strengths of which were assessed anew by each generation.

As in the forties, Canadians in the last quarter of the nineteenth century were earnestly seeking to find an external policy best calculated to further the interests of their country. Theoretically there were, as usual, three simple answers: independence, annexation to the United States, or complete absorption within the empire. Each of these extremes had supporters, but more characteristic were the many compromises. Rather than accept the stark black and white offered by the doctrinaires, most Canadians chose a grey, allowing for almost endless shades according to the mixture. The force of attraction toward each of the extreme poles depended on the circumstances of the time. Independence made its appeal when fear of attack was absent, and when there was a weakening of imperial sentiment caused either by particular dissatisfaction with British handling of Canadian affairs or British coolness toward "the connection". Those who favoured annexation to the United States could similarly find arguments when imperial sentiment was low and some tangible economic advantage could be shown. The picture must be seen from two angles to be correctly interpreted. Strengthened relations with either the United Kingdom or the United States depended not only on the wishes of Canadians, but also on the policies of those other countries. That a bargain requires the action of two parties was amply illustrated for Canada in her trade relations with both great powers.

Circumstances combined in the eighties to bring to the fore in both Great Britain and Canada serious consideration of the future of the empire. In the mother country the influence of the "little Englanders" of the middle of the century was giving way before a revived imperialism firmly grounded on discernible interests and decorated by touches of emotion. Free trade lost some of its charm in the face of foreign tariff barriers and competitive industrialism in European states. The nationalism of the old world spread to colonial areas and threatened to shut out the British merchant. Livingstone's discoveries in tropical Africa created a fresh interest amongst the English, and a new era of expansion set in. Historians like Sir John Seeley and J. A. Froude put the movement in its setting, while Sir Charles Dilke portrayed the existing empire of his *Greater Britain*. Joseph Chamberlain led a succession of statesmen along the new path, while Cecil Rhodes showed again that the flag follows trade. Imperialism found its poet in Rudyard Kipling, who brought the empire within the understanding of every schoolboy.[1] The new imperialism embraced the self-governing colonies as well as the lands fresh to Europeans. The search for new fields of investment turned British eyes toward the more advanced colonies, and at the same time projects of greater imperial integration appealed to those who had no conscious economic motive.

For the average Canadian the tropical areas, with their ivory and rubber, their problems of slavery, policing, and railways,

---

[1] For an analysis of the nature and the literature of British imperial interests of this period see W. L. Langer, *Diplomacy of Imperialism, 1890-1902* (2 vols., New York, 1935), I, chap. III.

were romantic but remote. It was in the relations of the United Kingdom and the self-governing colonies that he had a direct interest. Like the Englishmen, he might see visions of a *pax Britannica*, of a world ruled and enlightened by British ideas and institutions; but, also like the Englishman, he was awake to an understanding of what that meant for him in the less distant future and with reference to his particular situation. Canada was a country deeply committed to external trade, with a great area to develop and defend, needing diplomatic machinery and support to sustain those interests. The receptive mood of the United Kingdom caused official and unofficial opinion in Canada to look more toward a closer alignment with her, but by no means without conditions, without frequent glances in other directions. Probably most Canadians who gave thought to the situation at all would have chosen, as the ideal, more favourable trade agreements with both the United Kingdom and the United States, without change in the political relation with either. A minority would have accepted, or even sought, closer union with Great Britain. A much smaller minority would have been ready for closer union with the United States as an accompaniment to extensive reciprocity. In either case critics could point to the danger of entangling alliances.

This broad question of external policy was many-sided. The chief aspects were political, economic, and military, each affecting the other, but each having temporarily a leading importance depending on the circumstances of the day. While bearing in mind the necessary connection between these aspects, the approach in the present chapter will be in the main from a particular side of the economic phase, which took concrete form in the choice between two paths: the one leading toward imperial preferential trade, with or without political federation; the other toward unrestricted reciprocity or "commercial union", with the shadow of political union behind it. For the major political parties there was dynamite either way, and both looked for compromise formulas which would encourage more voters than they alarmed. One group—for it never became quite a political party—had struggled to create a national point of view more original than the phrase-making of the older parties. The Canada First movement of the seventies had emphasized Canadian achievements, Canadian unity, and a Canadian character not merely a copy of the modes of other lands. Attacked from all sides the movement was driven from its brief attempt to form a political party, and its members went in varied directions; but its influence on political thought was lasting. For purposes of implementing plans for external policy there remained the two political parties: the conservatives, with traditions of imperial loyalty, and a belief in limited reciprocity; and the liberals, suspected of less imperialism, historically attached to low tariffs, and laying more emphasis on reciprocity. Such principles, if they had ever had any reality, proved almost meaningless in the face of events.

The plan for commercial union with the United States, thrown into the ring in 1887, precipitated an active controversy and caused alternative plans to be more definitely supported. The general scheme with its various forms of commercial union, unrestricted reciprocity, or a North American zollverein had been suggested for twenty years or more, both in the United States and Canada, but only became a real issue for a few years from 1887. The comparatively large support that it received in Canada at that time was due partly to local conditions, partly to the ability of its advocates. Canada was in the midst of a long depression. Trade had fallen off, the large immigration during the building of the Canadian Pacific Railway had ceased, the exodus to the United States was alarming, prices were low, the west was not filling up as had been hoped, and the United States threatened tariff retaliation over the fishery dispute. It was, in the words of Sir John Willison, "a time of gloom and doubt, of suspicion and unrest, of rash opinion and premature judgment".[2] Into the breach came Erastus Wiman, a New York business man born in Canada, with experience in journalism, and now president of the Great North-Western Telegraph Company. Wiman collaborated in the United States with Samuel Ritchie, an American with business interest in Canada, and Hezekiah Butterworth, a member of congress, who introduced a measure to provide for commercial union. In Canada he found the co-operation of H. W. Darling, president of the Toronto Board of Trade, Goldwin Smith, and others. Meetings were addressed during the summer of 1887, pamphlets written, and a commercial union league organized,

2 J. S. Willison, *Sir Wilfrid Laurier and the Liberal Party: A Political History* (2 vols., Toronto, 1903), II, 120.

with Goldwin Smith as president. Contemporary literature on the subject is almost entirely partisan and throws more light on the arguments meant for popular consumption than on the merits and demerits of an economic plan. The plan itself, in fact, needs little elucidation. It was proposed to remove all customs barriers between the United States and Canada, and to establish an identic tariff against third countries. In Ontario commercial union received the whole-hearted support of the Toronto *Mail*, and the conditional support of the *Globe*. The *Globe's* condition was that the arrangement should be purely economic.

That a customs Union between Canada and the United States would profit both countries in a pecuniary sense will scarcely be denied by anybody. It does not follow that the scheme should be embraced by Canadians. They have to enquire whether their entrance into such a Union would involve political consequences from which they are averse. . . . The Canadian people would make the worst of all trades if they bartered their sentiments for a Customs Union. In this matter we are entirely at variance with the *Mail*. Our contemporary believes, as we do, that a Customs Union would profit Canada, but it says:—"The only objection to it from this side of the line is that it might endanger British connection, but let us seriously ask ourselves if a people situated such as we are in this controversy can afford to be swayed by sentiment". To which there can be only one answer—if we cannot afford to be swayed by sentiment we are not worthy to draw breath as free men . . . the proposition is monstrous![3]

The *Globe* continued to hold to this condition, while supporting commercial union as an economic measure. It noted that all its former correspondents were in favour of the scheme, and "many of them are willing to go the length of annexation if they cannot get the benefit of enlarged trade with the United States in any other manner".[4] There is, in fact, ample evidence that many farmers throughout the country were enthusiastic supporters. The *Manitoba Free Press*, representing an agrarian element, remarked that "the cry against Commercial Union is distinctly a 'vested interest' cry". "What", it asked, "are our manufacturers compared with our miners, our fishermen, our Lumbermen, our farmers? Shall the millions be kept back for the benefit of the score or

[3] *The Globe* (Toronto), March 2, 1887.
[4] *Ibid.*, April 5, 1887.

hundreds?"[5] The Montreal *Gazette,* on the other hand, opposed commercial union on the ground that it would harm manufacturers, and that it would lead to political absorption. The Canadian Manufacturers' Association passed a resolution to the effect that unrestricted reciprocity would be disastrous to manufacturing, commerce, and agriculture. In Halifax the *Morning Herald* made almost daily attacks on what it called the "Wiman fad", which it declared would bring all the disadvantages and none of the advantages of annexation. Canada's markets would be open to American manufactured goods, without any comparable benefit in return. The *Evening Mail* also inveighed against commercial union, which, it argued, would result in a fifty per cent. higher duty on British goods. Other newspapers were divided on the issue. The Hamilton *Spectator* held that commercial union meant·annexation, while the Hamilton *Times* thought it would enlarge Canadian markets. The Montreal *Herald* and the Ottawa *Free Press* both argued that commercial union, because it meant prosperity, would avert annexation. The Toronto *World,* Ottawa *Citizen,* London *Advertiser,* and London *Free Press* were all opposed.

The Commercial Union Club issued a *Handbook of Commercial Union,* a series of papers supporting the project. In this, as in other publications in favour of the plan, it was denied that annexation, or even partial loss of independence, was necessarily a result. Goldwin Smith, who wrote the introduction to the pamphlet, defended commercial union again in his *Canada and the Canadian Question.* Amongst the pamphleteers James Young (of Galt) was one of the most active. Commercial union, he wrote, would threaten the independence of Canada, ruin her manufacturers without helping the farmers, discriminate against British trade, and remove the main source of the public revenue.[6] P. N. Facktz's pamphlet, *Canada and the United States Compared,* is more typical of a type of argument long familiar to Canadian readers. Canada, he found, was a country of great area and undeveloped natural resources, with a happy people and a rosy future. If commercial union were adopted annexation would follow, and Canadians find themselves under a corrupt government in a land where liberty

5 *Manitoba Free Press,* Sept. 5, 1887.
6 James Young, *Our National Future* (Toronto, 1888).

had perished, and where Chicago bankers played poker on steam yachts all Sunday afternoon.

Exhorted *pro* or *con* by newspapers, pamphlets, boards of trade, and farmers' institutes, the Canadian public also witnessed the passage of the commercial union project across the political arena. The liberals, as the low-tariff party, might be expected to be the more friendly. The new leader of the party, Wilfrid Laurier, was anxious to adopt either commercial union or unrestricted reciprocity, but there was some opposition to the move, and shortly after he had been elected leader he made a speech at Somerset, Quebec (August 1887) in which he refused to commit himself. "If I am asked at present for my opinion on the subject, I may say that for my part I am not ready to declare that commercial union should be adopted at the present moment. A great deal of study and reflection are needed to solve this question, for and against which there is much to be said."[7] Two months later, Cartwright, the former minister of finance, became the first political leader to support commercial union. "I am as averse as any man can be to annexation, or to resign our political independence, but I cannot shut my eyes to the facts. We have greatly misused our advantages. We have been most foolish and most wasteful in our expenditure. We have no means of satisfying the just demands of large portions of the Dominion except through such an arrangement as commercial union. There is a risk, and I cannot overlook it. But it is a choice of risks, and our present position is anything but one of stable equilibrium."[8] Other members of the party showed varying degrees of sympathy, but the liberal caucus held at the opening of parliament in 1888 decided for unrestricted reciprocity rather than commercial union; the difference being that customs houses would not be abolished, and that each country would be free in respect of tariffs against third parties. It was unthinkable that the conservative party should risk the cry of disloyalty or the disfavour of the manufacturers by adopting commercial union; but on the other hand it had never ceased—in spite of the other elements of the national policy—to seek reciprocity, and continued to do so. In 1887 Tupper went to Washington in another attempt to bargain for reciprocity in ex-

[7] Willison, *Sir Wilfrid Laurier*, II, 141.
[8] *Ibid.*, II, 138.

change for fishing rights.[9] The difference between the two parties on the tariff, then, remained one of degree. By the beginning of 1888 Sir John Macdonald was confident that the commercial union cause was lost. The federal elections, he wrote to Tupper, had all gone against it. Leading men of the opposition, like Alexander Mackenzie, James Young, and John Macdonald of Toronto, had denounced it. The rural press of Ontario, he claimed, opposed it. It was, in fact, "a dead duck—and I think Lord Lansdowne sees now that my policy as announced to him last spring of allowing the cry of Commercial Union to blaze, crackle and go out with a stink, without giving it undue importance was a wise one. The country here now by general consent have connected C. U. with annexation and repudiate both."[10] It remained to be seen whether parliament would ratify this judgment. The debate in the house of commons began on March 14 with a motion by Cartwright to seek free trade with the United States in manufactured goods and natural products.[11] Pointing to the emigration of Canadians and of recent immigrants, the slow settlement of the west, and the low figures of external trade, he argued that the proper course was reciprocity with the rapidly growing United States. All classes of the community would benefit; and even if direct taxation were then needed for revenue, the total burden of taxation would be no greater, and more fairly distributed. As to the effect of the proposed measure on imperial relations Cartwright claimed that, while Canadians should not feel any debt to English statesmen, a more prosperous Canada would buy more from England, and, further, would "act as a link of union and amity between the two great English races". A full-dress debate followed on the lines laid down by Cartwright; whether emigration was such a serious factor as it had been represented to be, and whether reciprocity would alleviate it; if agriculture and industry would benefit, or the latter at least be submerged without protection; the effect of removing customs revenue and replacing it by other taxes; and the influence of reciprocity on the political relations of Canada with the United Kingdom. Each point was taken up at length, and the arguments were serious and studded with

9 See above, 160-2.
10 Public Archives of Canada, *Macdonald Papers*, Letter Book 24. Macdonald to Tupper, Jan. 15, 1888.
11 *Canada, House of Commons Debates*, 1888, 144 *ff*.

statistics. The conservatives were careful to point out that the opposition had had no monopoly of a belief in reciprocity, and proposed in amendment that trade relations with the United States should be cultivated in so far as they did not conflict with the national policy. On the government side policy and flag-waving were at times brought in to reinforce statistics of trade, but liberal members urged that reciprocity was really a defence against annexation, and that the prospect of imperial preferential trade as an alternative was utterly unreal in the light of British fiscal policy. After three weeks of a debate which on the whole was maintained at a high level, the house divided on April 6, and the conservative amendment was carried by 124 to 67 on a party vote.

II

The campaign for commercial union gave a new stimulus to the movement for a closer integration of the empire, a movement which was by no means new, but had previously lacked wide support and appeared as somewhat academic. The interest of Canadians in the empire outside the United Kingdom was limited, but in some instances surprisingly active. The affairs of Ireland, and especially the home rule movement, were those most consistently watched. As the *Globe* pointed out, there were good reasons for this Canadian interest: there was a large Irish element in the Canadian population; the Irish question was of such concern in the United States that its peaceful settlement was necessary for good relations with Canada; and a settlement was also "necessary to the peace, the strength, the welfare, the influence and the glory of the Empire".[12] The *Manitoba Free Press* held that Ireland was now well governed, whatever had been the case in the past, and condemned in unmeasured terms the "cut-throats" who were guided by no patriotic interest.[13] Other papers were more critical of the British government. The Halifax *Morning Herald*, for example, frequently described Irish discontent, and labelled the British policy as reactionary. In 1885 a mass meeting was held in Halifax by Irish sympathizers. The *Evening Mail* of Halifax was also critical of the British government, and stated that the sooner the Irish obtained self-government, the better it

12 *The Globe*, April 18, 1887.
13 *Manitoba Free Press*, Oct. 27, 1887.

would be for the empire. The Saint John *Daily Telegraph* accused the Salisbury government of engaging in a controversy with the Tsar as a means of distracting attention from conditions in Ireland and England. In 1887 the Canadian parliament passed a resolution in favour of home rule, which, with other signs of sympathy, so encouraged the Irish nationalists that William O'Brien sailed for Canada to drive Lord Lansdowne (an Irish landlord) out of Canada. No other issue touched the Canadian people as intimately as the Irish one, but they were not oblivious to what was going on elsewhere in the empire. The annexation by France and Germany of islands in the western Pacific led the editor of the *Morning Herald* to draw a parallel between effects of this on Australia and a similar annexation of territory near Prince Edward Island.[14] The troubles in the Sudan in 1885 were closely followed with critical comments; in the same year the *Evening Mail* decided that the annexation of Burma by Great Britain would rescue the inhabitants from oppression and "make a fine addition to our possessions".[15]

Foreign affairs had long been extensively reported in Canadian newspapers, and were, therefore, presumably considered to be of interest to readers. But the editors went further than news, for they frequently commented on British foreign policy, not hesitating to point to mistakes; writing with such earnestness as to give the impression that Canadian interests were at stake—that is, that the strength of the empire depended in part on the success of British foreign policy, and that Canada was concerned in the strength of the empire. Again to refer to the editorial page of the Halifax *Herald*: the editor notes with satisfaction that the British government "have determined to act for once with promptness and fortitude" in preventing Turkey from sending troops to Egypt. A few months later, objecting to what he considered to be British weakness in resisting Russian advances toward India, the editor sweepingly described the cabinet as "the most conspicuously foolish and imbecile ministry that has ever ruled England for the past hundred years".[16] The exact significance to Canada of Russian imperialism may be seen in the apprehension in 1877-8 of Russian attacks on the west coast. An immediate relevance to Canada

14 *Morning Herald* (Halifax), Jan. 27, 1885.
15 *Evening Mail* (Halifax), Oct. 22 and Nov. 12, 1885.
16 *Morning Herald*, Jan. 20 and May 1, 1885.

was deduced from German imperialism in Samoa in 1887. Great Britain, the editor of the *Herald* suggested, should insist on the neutrality of Samoa and Hawaii, because of their strategic position with respect to Canada's new ocean route to Australia. Many other examples might be quoted, from this and other newspapers, to show the Canadian interest in British foreign policy. The outstanding case, because it most directly affected Canada, was policy toward the United States. Here Canadians were consistently inconsistent, since they demanded that Britain should be at once relentless in pursuing particular Canadian interests and conciliatory in order to establish good relations.

Though they never secured anything like a majority support in Canada, the imperial federationists alone wove together the many threads to make a logical pattern. In 1884 the Imperial Federation League was organized in London under the chairmanship of W. E. Forster, a former under-secretary for the colonies, and with various representatives of the United Kingdom and the colonies in attendance. Sir Charles Tupper, then high commissioner, was a speaker at the first conference. The resolutions adopted indicated in general the purposes of the league. They were:

That the object of the league be to secure by Federation the permanent unity of the Empire.

That no scheme of federation should interfere with the existing rights of local parliaments as regards local affairs.

That any scheme of Imperial Federation should combine on an equitable basis the resources of the Empire for the maintenance of common interests, and adequately provide for an organized defence of common rights.

That the league invites the support of men of all political parties.

No attempt was made to define the constitutional machinery by which these ends were to be procured, and the emphasis was laid more on unity than on federalism. While individuals worked out plans for a single parliament at Westminster with representatives from all the colonies, the spokesmen of the league on the whole refused to commit themselves to any one plan. Thus the league was able to attract the support of men who might have found an imperial parliament unacceptable. Certainly the general platform of the league had much to commend it: that there were matters of a local nature to be handled by the governing body of each unit, and also matters which affected several or all of the units. Canadians were, and long had been, very conscious that defence, foreign affairs, and trade had wide ramifications, which made them more than local subjects, and that at least raised the question as to whether there was any means by which they could be handled jointly. The whole project of closer imperial integration, in its various forms, was one for long and active debate in Canada.[17]

The Imperial Federation League in Canada was founded in Montreal in 1885, and three branches started—at Ingersoll, Peterborough, and Halifax—in the next two years. Colonel Denison was urged to be the president of a branch to be formed in Toronto, but he did not consider that the time had come for the country to spend money on imperial defence and refused. The branch did not materialize at that time, but only a year later a new factor led Denison to change his mind.

The progress the Commercial Union movement was making [he wrote] and the great danger arising from it, led my brother and me to discuss it with a number of loyal men, and on all sides the opinion seemed to be that active steps should be taken at once to work against it . . . and it was decided that the best policy was to advocate a Commercial Union of the British Empire as an alternative to the proposition of a Commercial Union with the United States, and that a scheme of Imperial Federation based upon a Commercial Union of the various parts of the Empire would be the best method of advocating our views.[18]

Toward the end of 1887 a branch of the Imperial Federation League was formed in Toronto, and wrote into its constitution a special clause stating that it looked toward imperial preferential trade. Denison made a vigorous speech at a public meeting held by the league, calling on patriots "to rally round the old flag and frustrate the evil designs of traitors". Believing that there were traitors in Canada, in touch with Americans who were working for annexation, Denison and his associates organized a modest

    [17] Representative opinions may be found as follows: PRO—G. T. Denison, The Struggle for Imperial Unity: Recollections and Experiences (London and Toronto, 1809); G. R. Parkin, Imperial Federation (London, 1892); G. M. Grant, Imperial Federation (Winnipeg, 1890). CONTRA—Goldwin Smith, Canada and the Canadian Question (London and Toronto, 1891); and writings of J. S. Ewart and Henri Bourassa. PRO and CON—S. C. Cheng, Schemes for the Federation of the British Empire (New York, 1931).

    [18] Denison, Struggle for Imperial Unity, 79, 85.

system of counter-espionage which produced at least some results. A written statement by Wiman in September 1888 directly connected commercial union with annexation, and this further confirmed the suspicions of the opponents of the first. While, therefore, the league in Canada never succeeded in establishing a definite programme, but rather contained men with varying views, it served for the time being as a focus for the opposition to closer connection with the United States and a generally sympathetic attitude toward imperial co-operation of some kind. The senate discussed imperial federation on a motion by C. A. Boulton that Canada might be accorded representation in the British house of commons. The motion was withdrawn without a vote being taken, but the debate gives some impression of the arguments of the day, both on the specific question of whether representation was feasible, and on the general issue between closer links with the United Kingdom or the United States.[19] A more direct alternative to unrestricted reciprocity was a proposal introduced into the house of commons for closer trade relations between Canada and Great Britain. D'Alton McCarthy, who led in the defence of the proposition, denied any hostility toward the United States, but claimed that Canadian trade would be more feasible with Great Britain, whose products were less in competition with those of Canada.[20]

Contemporary comments in the newspapers are some indication of public opinion on the imperial federation movement. The *Globe* was opposed to any of the constitutional plans put forward as unworkable and undesirable, and could see imperial relations only as static or less binding.

The loyalty of Canadians to-day is a reasonable loyalty. . . . But they see that, as all men acknowledge, a change in the relations of Canada with the Empire must one day take place. Whether it will be found best for Canada to remain in the Empire, as all would wish, or to make a further advance in the direction in which for some time it has been proceeding, and to take outside of the Empire the place of a loving child, an attached and devoted friend, is the question. . . .[21]

The Imperial Federation Conference of 1887 filled the editor with apprehension. Federation was "a grand jingo dream", with a danger of drawing Canada into imperial wars. The *Mail* also

[19] *Canada, Debates of the Senate*, 1890, 256 ff.
[20] *Canada, House of Commons Debates*, 1888, 1069 ff.
[21] *The Globe*, Jan. 23, 1885.

held that federation was out of the question, and had no strong popular support; but felt that defence was more necessary to discuss in days when "the belligerent spirit among the nations betrays no disposition to subside".[22] The *Manitoba Free Press* was sarcastic about the federation proposals, and concluded that "we are, as a people, well satisfied with our present relations. When there is a change it will be in a direction opposite to that sought by the Imperial Federationists." Canadians, said the editor, would never consent to pay taxes to be spent outside the country, nor did they wish to run the risk of being involved in British wars.[23] The Montreal *Journal of Commerce* found that "the proposition for an organized defence of common rights is entirely too vague to induce the Colonies to commit themselves to the principle [of imperial federation]".[24] The Halifax *Herald* was ready to contemplate federation as a future possibility, but not as an immediate necessity. In contrast to the *Globe,* it argued that, when a change came, it would be in that direction. The *Herald* welcomed the establishment of a branch of the Imperial Federation League in Montreal, remarking that "the British Empire must eventually be handled as a whole, of which no part is master and no part dependent".[25] The *Evening Mail* of Halifax was strongly in favour of an "Empire commercial union" as more desirable to Canada than one with the United States.[26] Such a plan would not be imperial federation, but would be a step toward it.

Such were the issues before the public, but they were reflected in only a distorted form in the election of 1891. The liberal party held to its project of unrestricted reciprocity, but vigorously denied that that implied annexation or any breaking of the imperial bond. Oliver Mowat claimed that only a fragment of either party was opposed to British connection. "A British subject I have lived for three-score years, and something more—I hope to live my life a British subject and as a British subject die." The conservative party, while hammering at the "veiled treason" of unrestricted reciprocity, undermined the liberals' appeal on trade grounds by letting it be known that negotiations were being initiated at

22 *The Mail* (Toronto), March 15, 22, April 6, 1887.
23 *Manitoba Free Press,* Jan. 16, 23, Feb. 3, 1887.
24 *Ibid.,* Feb. 3, 1887.
25 *Morning Herald,* May 12, 1885.
26 *Evening Mail,* June 11, Sept. 22, 1887.

Washington for a revival, in a modified form, of the limited reciprocity treaty of 1854. Having taken the edge off the liberal sword, the conservatives then made the most of an appeal to traditional loyalty, both to Canada and the empire. Sir Charles Tupper was brought from England to stump the country, and Macdonald—in what proved to be his last election—told the electorate that "a British subject I was born, a British subject I will die". While Mowat's similar confession was lost in the denunciation of an annexation menace, the "old man's" cry echoed throughout the country. In reality the election of 1891 settled nothing, save that the conservatives were returned to power for five years more, and that reciprocity, if obtainable, was to be restricted. Imperial preference, imperial federation, commercial and political relations with the United States—all remained to be defined and settled, and a choice—if choice there must be—made between them.

III

Neither the return of the conservatives in 1891 nor their defeat by the liberals five years later materially changed the character of the issues before the Canadian people. The several courses discussed before, centring around relations with the United Kingdom and the United States, continued to be discussed, and a choice was still to be made. In spite of the heat engendered, the elections were to some extent sham battles, for neither party stood committed to a definite policy in these important questions. The liberal party dropped its aim of unrestricted reciprocity, while the conservative administration in its last years of office found that Washington was unreceptive to the limited reciprocity that it sought. Both parties then settled down to an acceptance of moderate protection, modified, when possible, by special trade agreements. In the last years of the old century and the early years of the new, however, a number of factors combined to give a fresh setting to the Canadian problem of imperial and continental relationships.

The progress of protectionism in the United States, under the McKinley tariff of 1890 and the Dingley tariff of 1897, closed the door to reciprocity negotiations for more than fifteen years, until such advanced protection began to be questioned as a cause of the high cost of living. While on the one hand the road to

Washington was at least temporarily blocked, the movement for closer imperial ties received a new impetus. The jubilee of 1897 provided the occasion and the atmosphere for a unique gathering of empire statesmen in London, at a time when Joseph Chamberlain's new imperialism was seeking practical expression. In spite of the fact that he held what was normally considered a minor portfolio, that of colonial secretary, Chamberlain led his advance guard along new and even alarming paths—toward continental alliance in place of isolation, toward militant empire-building in South Africa, toward commercial union with the colonies, and even to a skirmish against the sacred citadel of free trade. The note was set by his speech at the Canada Club in the spring of 1896.

The recent isolation of the United Kingdom, the dangers which seemed to threaten us, have evoked from all our colonies, and especially from Canada, an outburst of loyalty and affection which has reverberated throughout the world. . . . is this demonstration . . . to pass away without a serious effort upon the part both of colonial and Imperial statesmen to transform these sentiments into practical results? . . .

We may endeavour to establish common interest and common obligations. . . . What is the greatest of our common obligations? It is Imperial defence. What is the greatest of our common interests? It is Imperial trade. And those two are very closely connected. It is very difficult to see how you can pretend to deal with this great question of Imperial defence without having first dealt with the question of Imperial trade. . . .

My . . . proposition is that a true Zollverein for the Empire, that a free trade established throughout the Empire, although it would involve the imposition of duties against foreign countries, and would be in that respect a derogation from the high principles of free trade, and from the practice of the United Kingdom up to the present time, would still be a proper subject for discussion and might possibly lead to a satisfactory arrangement if the colonies on their part were willing to consider it . . . it would undoubtedly lead to the earliest possible development of their great natural resources, would bring to them population, would open to them the enormous market of the United Kingdom. . . .[27]

Decisions on any changes in the imperial structure, whether political, military, or economic, must be made in Great Britain

[27] J. L. Garvin, *The Life of Joseph Chamberlain* (3 vols., London, 1934), III, 179.

and Canada (since neither the Australian nor South African colonies were as yet united) and in tariff questions must overcome the accepted policies of free trade in Great Britain and protection in Canada. That either country should make such a radical departure must have seemed improbable, but Chamberlain's gesture was followed by some encouragement from Laurier too.

Now the statesmen of Great Britain have thought [he said in June 1896] that the colonies have come to a time when a new step must be taken in their development. What is that? That there shall be a commercial agreement between England and the colonies. That practical statesman, Mr. Joseph Chamberlain, has come to the conclusion that the time has come when it is possible to have within the bounds of the Empire a new step taken, which will give to the colonies in England, a preference for their products over the products of other nations. . . . The possibilities are immense. . . . But Sir, if England is going to give us that preference, England would expect something from us in return . . . that we would come as closely to her own system of free trade, such as she has it, as it is possible for us to come. . . ."[28]

That nearest point, Laurier went on to say, was to adopt a revenue instead of a protective tariff; and such was said to be the liberal policy, although in reality the difference tended to be little more than one of name. A year later when Fielding introduced the first budget of the liberal government it was found to contain a preferential rate for English goods, 12½ per cent. at first and then increased to 25 per cent. This preferential rate was, from one point of view, simply a lower tariff, and as such alarming to not a few Canadian manufacturers. As an imperial move it was greeted with enthusiasm by members of the recently deceased Imperial Federation League and others who looked toward closer imperial relations. G. W. Ross, a member of the Ontario cabinet, told the British Empire League that the preference had not only "paved the way for the rapid development of Canadian commerce", but had "quieted for the time being, and I hope forever, the restlessness which prevailed in many quarters as to the future of Canada". Instead of the fluctuating markets of the United States, Canadians could now turn to the more certain ones of England; and at the same time the Canadian voice would be .

[28] Willison, *Sir Wilfrid Laurier*, II, 287.

more influential in the councils of the empire.[29] There were, of course, not lacking those who were equally vocal in condemning the preference as the thin end of the imperial wedge.

It was with such a background that the colonial conference met in London in 1897. In a sense the conference was an incidental result of the jubilee celebrations, but this very connection gave it an importance, not only because of the atmosphere, but because the jubilee brought the colonial prime ministers to England. Both in its personnel and its subject matter the third colonial conference had a new significance.[30] That of 1887 had touched on defence and trade, but had steered away from discussion of imperial federation. The Ottawa conference of 1894 had been concerned almost entirely with the Pacific cable, only stopping to give a passing blessing to inter-imperial trade. The third conference, in London in 1897, was described as informal as to its proceedings, but it was a conference of governments: the United Kingdom being represented by the secretary of state for the colonies, and the self-governing colonies by their prime ministers. Chamberlain's opening speech, almost the only part of the proceedings to be made public,[31] was a frank presentation of the thesis which he was already known to hold. The most important and the most difficult subject, he said, was the future relations between the United Kingdom and the self-governing colonies. He was not prepared to say whether the time was ripe for change: in England the idea of federation was "in the air", and he personally had thought of "a great council of the Empire" to which the colonies would send plenipotentiaries. But if the time should come when the colonies wished "to substitute for the slight relationship which at present exists a true partnership" with a share in the management of the empire, it would also have to be realized that "obligations and responsibility" must accompany control. If a representative body were to be established it would settle the related problem of imperial defence, the cost of which was now borne by the United Kingdom, although the army and navy were not even principally

---

29 G. W. Ross, *Preferential Trade with Great Britain and Reciprocity with the United States* (Toronto, 1897).

30 For a detailed study of the conferences from 1887 to 1907 see Richard Jebb, *The Imperial Conference: A History and Study* (2 vols., London, 1911).

31 *Proceedings of a Conference between the Secretary of State for the Colonies and the Premiers of the Self-governing Colonies at the Colonial Office, London, June and July 1897* (Cd. 8596).

maintained for local defence. On the question of commercial relations he referred to the value of a zollverein, but admitted the difficulties in the way. If the resolutions passed by the conference be taken as a test, its decisions were cautious and limited, but not without significance. It was decided (by a majority) that political relations between the United Kingdom and the self-governing colonies were "generally satisfactory under the existing condition of things". No decision was recorded on defence. It was agreed by the premiers that they should investigate the possibilities of tariff preferences to the United Kingdom. A separate resolution recommended the denunciation of treaties hampering the commercial relations between Great Britain and the colonies. The reference was to treaties with Belgium and Germany, which contained most-favoured-nation clauses standing in the way of such a preference. The case came up particularly in relation to the Canadian preference of 1897, but the British government had long been requested to terminate the treaties, which they now did. Finally, a unanimous resolution called for periodic conferences in the future.

Thus there emerge from the conference of 1897 one general issue and three particular ones, all of which continued to be discussed, at further conferences and between them, for many years. Two of these—the nature of the colonial conference and the defence question—will be examined in subsequent chapters.[32] The general problem of the political relations between the colonies and the United Kingdom runs through most aspects of the external relations of Canada. The particular phase of it which followed the conference of 1897 is closely linked with commercial policy, and may be considered here in that connection. The policy of the British government in respect of imperial relations was, for the time being at least, the policy of Joseph Chamberlain. Whatever may have been the opposition to it, in the government or outside it, it was the policy that was adopted and the one therefore with which the self-governing colonies were concerned. Those colonies differed in position, needs, and political development, and viewed the imperial question differently as a result. Their attitudes had some, but relatively little, influence on government and public in Canada. On the whole, and except perhaps in the case of

32 See below, chapters x and xi.

the Pacific cable, Canadians were ignorant and almost oblivious of the other colonies. Their interest was in the United Kingdom— by origin, trade, culture, defence, and government. It happened, however, that the man who was prime minister throughout fifteen years when these subjects were to the fore was a French Canadian, the first to hold that office in the history of the dominion. On the whole the French Canadians were little affected by the ties that bound their English-speaking compatriots to Great Britain. Their origin and culture were French; they put little emphasis on commerce; minimized the need for defence, even of Canadian territory; and had no reason to share in the imperial vision seen by other groups of Canadians. Cut away from France once and finally, they found their only *patrie* in Canada, which for them should be a part of the British Empire only so long as the established *modus vivendi* was retained. Wilfrid Laurier was descended from eight generations of Canadians, but his upbringing was unusual, combining English protestant with French catholic schools and associates. Nor did Laurier accept the traditional ultramontanism of the church in Quebec; indeed, one of the causes for which he stood was the separation of politics and religion, and the freedom to follow liberalism in the one without the accusation of being unorthodox in the other.

When Laurier went to the jubilee in 1897 it was his first crossing of the Atlantic. In London, as the prime minister of the only united dominion, he was given a leading part in the colourful ceremonies carried out in the almost mythical atmosphere of royalty and imperialism; and amidst it all he received a knighthood. In spite of the heady air, Laurier was cautious toward any commitment, and in fact returned without making any. He accepted Chamberlain's formula that responsibility must accompany control, and steered carefully away from both. Nevertheless, Laurier seemed in the eyes of some of his countrymen to be caught in the toils of imperialism—a suspicion which they thought to be proven by Canadian participation in the war in South Africa. He found himself threatened politically by the early stages of a nationalist movement in his own province, a movement of which Henri Bourassa was one of the earliest adherents and later the leader.[33] To such men Chamberlain was an arch-villain, insidiously

[33] For an account of this movement, see Henri Bourassa, Que devons-nous à l' Angleterre? (Montreal, 1915).

sapping at the autonomy of Canada, drawing her by subtle means into the maelstrom of imperial wars, imperial taxes, imperial control. It was not only in French Canada that such views were to be found. The nationalists among the English-speaking Canadians found an able pen in Goldwin Smith; but Smith was a liability as well as an asset, for his nationalism ended in the manifest destiny of annexation. It was J. S. Ewart, a lawyer of Ottawa, who took up the cause, and hewed to the straight and narrow line of Canadianism. Laurier had critics to the right as well as to the left. If the nationalists later broke with him because of the Boer War and the naval defence plans, it was the more imperially-minded Canadians who forced him into those limited excursions. Laurier, in fact, occupied a middle position; and it is a tribute to his political ability that for many years he escaped being crushed between the millstones. On a policy of imperial relations generally there is little difference between Laurier on the one hand and Macdonald and his successors on the other. There were, it is true, many conservatives who accused Laurier of being anti-imperial, but they never controlled their own party. Laurier could say with as much conviction as Macdonald that a British subject he would die, but the two were, in the practice of government, almost equally shy of commitments. Later the conservatives were to overthrow Sir Wilfrid by appeals to the flag, but it is notable that the administration which followed was as chary of positive measures as it had been prodigal of phrases. That a share in the control of imperial policy, or even consultation concerning it, entailed at least a moral obligation to bear the consequences became a dogma accepted by whatever party was in power.

In the decade following the Boer War there was active study and discussion of commercial policy as a part of the imperial relationship. Shortly before the colonial conference of 1902 the president of the Canadian Manufacturers' Association announced that the chief object of his organization was to bring all British countries into a closer union by means of a preferential tariff, and the president of the British Empire League in Canada called for an additional duty in all British countries on foreign goods to provide a fund for defence; while the Cassandra voice of Goldwin Smith repeated that no imperial zollverein could draw Canada away from the North American continent.[34] At the con-

[34] *Canadian Annual Review*, 1902, 108-9.

ference itself the Canadian delegates presented a memorandum intended to show that the preference had encouraged British imports, though they continued to refrain from using it as a basis for bargaining. In his opening speech Joseph Chamberlain recognized that the preference had arrested the decline of British exports to Canada, but the volume was still not great in relation to British imports from Canada. Even with a preference, he said, a protective tariff might effectually exclude British goods; and he looked wistfully toward a self-sustaining empire. The only resolution adopted by the conference on the subject of tariffs gave a blessing to the principle of preference, and recognized that a general system of free trade was not practicable.[35] While the discussions at the conference were not made public, then or since, it was the general impression in Canada that Laurier and his colleagues had been what their supporters would call cautious and their critics destructive. The vital issues of that conference, however, were not tariff levels but defence and an imperial constitution. Against commitments on either of these latter Laurier set his face like flint.

The conference had not long adjourned when the tariff question once more came to the fore. Through Joseph Chamberlain's campaign for "tariff reform", a direct assault was made upon the citadel of free trade as a means of attaining to that self-sustaining empire of which he dreamed. "A small remnant of Little Englanders of the Manchester School" clung to the strict application of free trade in a world in which foreign countries and the colonies as well had adopted protection. Freedom of interchange should be retained as a principle, but the power of negotiation and even retaliation be resumed. In parliament a storm of opposition was raised, not only by the liberal opposition, but also amongst the labour members and even some of the unionists. Nothing daunted by the traditional cries against a tax on bread, Chamberlain gave blow for blow, and a battle went on in newspapers and periodicals and on the public platform. The "tariff reform" project continued to be debated from its initiation in the spring of 1903, through 1904 and 1905. In Canada opinion was divided, but on the whole Chamberlain's policy was supported, though sometimes with reservations. R. L. Borden's comment on the opening speech was

---

[35] *Papers Relating to a Conference between the Secretary of State for the Colonies and the Prime Ministers of Self-governing Colonies; June to August, 1902* (Cd. 1299).

that the conservative party had been fighting for imperial preferential trade for ten years, and the veteran, Sir Charles Tupper, spoke of Chamberlain's "manly, straightforward and plucky stand". Most of the newspapers, especially the conservative ones, expressed approval, and various boards of trade passed resolutions in favour of the plan. Laurier was cautious in his comments but welcomed the idea of treaties of commerce between the British countries, each of which would have its own tariff. The *Globe* was cool about the plan, and in the province of Quebec some spokesmen, notably Bourassa, suspected that trade unity would be a step toward political unity.[36]

The Canadian preference to English goods remained as the original and solid form of imperial preference, and while it was often cited as advantageous to both countries, it was not always happily accepted by Canadian manufacturers.[37] While modified from time to time the Canadian preference nevertheless was retained: the rock on which the broader scheme was to be wrecked was the English aversion to duties on the necessities of life. Chamberlain had never quite converted the unionists and conservatives to tariff reform, but had made considerable headway. The fall of the government in 1905, and the accession to office of the liberals under Campbell-Bannerman (who had denounced the Chamberlain plan) removed it, for the time at least, as a political possibility.

IV

In the twentieth century both independence and annexation to the United States were still talked of but neither had any considerable measure of support. What did constitute a live issue was the revival of projects of reciprocity, a revival made possible by a changing attitude in the United States which in turn happened to coincide with the British decision to cling to free trade. The alternatives of reciprocity and imperial preference played somewhat

[36] For further Canadian comments see *Canadian Annual Review*, 1903, 306 ff.; 1904, 390 ff.; 1905, 448 ff.

[37] Edward Porritt, *Sixty Years of Protection in Canada, 1846-1907* (London, 1908).

the rôle they had in the eighties, but in a minor key and without any of the fighting spirit behind the former that the advocates of commercial union had shown. John Charlton made frequent references, in the house of commons and the newspapers, to the advantages of reciprocity, which he compared with the Chamberlain plan, to the detriment of the latter. But until there was some evidence of breaches in the American tariff wall any Canadian thoughts on reciprocity could not be much more than pious hopes. Even while the general belief in high tariffs continued to exist in the United States there were scattered indications of groups who saw advantages in reciprocity. In 1901 the National Association of Manufacturers held a National Reciprocity Convention at Washington, and in the next two or three years the movement began to gain momentum with the formation of reciprocity leagues in New England and the west, advocacy in the newspapers, by boards of trade, and delegations to congress in its favour. The arguments were usually that the Canadian market could be opened to American goods, and that action was necessary especially in view of the tendency toward more protection in Canada and the effect that the Chamberlain proposals would have on American trade with Canada. The advantages to American railways of reciprocal trade were often mentioned; and J. J. Hill, whose railways ran at various points to the Canadian border, was an active partisan in what was becoming a serious campaign.

In Canada, where, for thirty years, reciprocity had been energetically, at times frantically, sought, enthusiasm had calmed down or was being deliberately suppressed. It was recognized that any move must come from the United States, and there was a certain unwillingness to play once more the part of the unsuccessful suitor. Nor, indeed, was it certain that Barkis was now willing. The twentieth century had opened a new prosperity for Canada, with a relatively rapid development of the west and growing industrialization in the east. The Chamberlain tariff reform project offered possibilities of an alternative that was attractive to at least a part of the population, and might be upset by reciprocity with the United States. "Canada", said Colonel Denison in a speech in Toronto in 1903, "should avoid reciprocity as she would the plague."[38] In the same year the Canadian Manufacturers' Associa-

---

[38] *Canadian Annual Review*, 1903, 382.

tion passed a resolution against a reciprocity treaty affecting the manufacturing interests of Canada. In 1904 and 1905 much the same tone seemed to hold; that the United States had refused reciprocity when Canada wanted it, and that now the dominion was following other paths. The strength of economic and political nationalism as a barrier to reciprocity could not as yet be assessed, but there were indications that it was becoming a serious element. A further barrier, which might be manned by a quite different group, was the objection that reciprocity would endanger the imperial relation. There were, however, indications that an agreement limited to certain products would not be unacceptable; and probably there was much more desire for such an arrangement than public utterances would indicate. The exact state of Canadian opinion could only be tested when the question was put in a specific form.

In 1909 and the early part of 1910 the existing high protection began to be seriously questioned in Washington, and a variety of factors to lead toward negotiations with Canada. Impressed by the demands of certain groups, notably the newspaper publishers, for lower tariffs with Canada, by using complaints against the high cost of living, and dissensions within his own party, President Taft took steps to have the commercial relations of the two countries reconsidered.[39] The subject of immediate discussion was the legal necessity of applying to Canada the maximum rates of the Payne-Aldrich tariff due to the fact that the Canadian agreement with France was interpreted as a technical discrimination. When the department of state approached the British ambassador, Bryce informed the Canadian government of the department's desire for a conference, which the Canadian government suggested should be in Ottawa. There the American representatives suggested that Canada should offer her intermediate rate, but the Canadians denied that there was discrimination, though they finally agreed to the intermediate rate on a few articles as a token concession. A series of discussions, official and unofficial, then took place on the possibility of considering tariff agreements on a broader basis, during which the Canadian government expressed its willingness to hold such a conversation at any convenient time. Actual

[39] For an analysis of the American position, as well as other aspects of the subject, see L. E. Ellis, *Reciprocity, 1911* (New Haven and Toronto, 1939).

negotiations were conducted from November 1910 to January 1911. The Canadian proposals covered a small, the American a much larger, list of articles; and by the middle of January a compromise agreement was reached, under which most natural products were to be on the free list and the duty on a limited number of manufactured articles to be reduced. The agreement was to be brought into effect by concurrent legislation. In spite of some opposition, the necessary legislation was passed by congress before the end of July. It only remained for Canada to do its part.

The Canadian parliament consisted of two major parties, both of which in the past had emphatically announced their belief in reciprocity of some kind. Traditionally the liberals had been a low-tariff party, but of recent years had shown little disposition to pay more than lip-service to that faith. But, just as Taft had experienced pressure for reduced tariffs, so had Laurier. In a tour through the western provinces in the summer of 1910 he was besieged by demands for the ending of protection, and it seems clear that he was not a little impressed.[40] The caution of his government in meeting the American advances was marked; but the liberals found themselves in a favourable position for bargaining, and might well feel that the agreement was so satisfactory as to be invaluable for the coming election, and to offer a plank especially needed in view of the Quebec revolt over the naval question.[41] When the measure was presented to the house of commons the conservative members were in a flurry, believing at first that their constituents would fully support it. It was only after the lapse of some time that the opposition settled down to resist the passage of the bill. In thus dividing on party lines parliament followed the action already taken by most of the newspapers.[42] But even the early exceptions to the rule of party allegiance were significant, and as time went on they became more so. The manufacturing, financial, and transportation interests, through individuals or boards of trade, became more and more vociferous in their opposition. In Toronto eighteen prominent citizens, all liberals, voiced their opposition, and founded the Canadian National League

[40] The trip is described with documents in Edward Porritt, *The Revolt in Canada against the New Feudalism: Tariff History from the Revision of 1907 to the Uprising of the West in 1910* (London, 1911), chap. XII.

[41] See below, 285.

[42] Full analyses of public opinion and the parliamentary debates are in the *Canadian Annual Review*, 1911, and in Ellis, *Reciprocity, 1911*.

under the leadership of Z. A. Lash. Similar defections from the party ranks were conspicuous in other cities. One serious blow to the government was the decision of Clifford Sifton, one of the ablest of the liberal strategists, to throw his whole weight against reciprocity, and give aid in the west, where it was most needed. When the conservatives had blocked early passage of the bill, Laurier decided to go to the country, and thus precipitated an election which was fought almost entirely on external policies.

That the reciprocity agreement presented advantages to Canada was shown by the favourable reception that it first received. But the election was not fought on its terms but on its implications. Two arguments were mainly used by the conservatives and their liberal allies in English-speaking Canada. The first, which brought much tangible support to the campaign, was that Canada, having failed earlier to secure reciprocity, had built up a national economy with a heavy investment in railways and industries; and that both of these, being based on an east-and-west pattern, would be endangered by a sudden flow of north and south commerce. The second argument, appealing more to the general electorate as a whole, could be described by its opponents as pure flag-waving. Aided by indiscreet talk of annexation in the United States, orators pictured Canada as losing not only its connection with the empire but its very national being as well. Borden, in his last shot of the campaign, appealed on this ground: "I believe that we are, in truth, standing to-day at the parting of the ways. . . . We must decide whether the spirit of Canadianism or of continentalism shall prevail on the northern half of this continent." The issue, he said, was above party lines; it was for "the maintenance of our commercial and political freedom, for the permanence of Canada as an autonomous nation within the British Empire".[43]

In the province of Quebec the Laurier government was opposed by the nationalists on another aspect of external relations. The government's naval bill accentuated the existing fears of commitment to "imperial wars" and led to the formation of a nationalist party in the province where Laurier had hitherto been safe. Henri Bourassa, at first mildly supporting reciprocity, finally came out against it; not that he loved protection more, but the naval bill less. Thus was created that extraordinary alliance of the opposition

[43] Henry Borden (ed.), *Robert Laird Borden: His Memoirs* (2 vols., Toronto, 1938), I, 327.

in English Canada, with its appeal to the imperial tie, and the opposition in French Canada, loudly denouncing all signs of imperialism. Before that combination the liberal government, already beyond its prime, could make no effective stand. And with the fall of the administration was rejected the first—and perhaps the last—American invitation to a reciprocity agreement. A decision, whether wise or foolish, was thus at last made on one important aspect of external policy. The implications of that decision could not as yet be assessed. All that was certain was that reciprocity, in its proposed form, was rejected. But the purely commercial aspect of the issue had become mixed with wide political considerations—considerations which in themselves were confused and even conflicting. Had Canadians voted for what Borden had named "Canadianism" or for closer imperial integration? The answer lay in the future.

CHAPTER IX

EFFECTS OF EXTERNAL FORCES ON THE CANADIAN COMMUNITY

TRANSPORTATION and communications played an important part in the foreign relations of Canada as well as in her domestic economy. Postal and telegraph facilities formed links with the outside world, and—because of the geography of North America—were in part dependent on arrangements with the United States. Railways and waterways involved that and more, for they ignored the international boundary and invited traffic to follow the shortest or easiest lines.

Shortly after confederation Canada began to take stock of her internal waterways. A royal commission was appointed in 1870 to examine existing canals and consider the need for further construction. The majority report,[1] issued in the following year, showed the strong influence of the historic belief in the "natural" rôle of the St. Lawrence as the outlet for the American middle west. "Nature has intended the St. Lawrence", the commissioners wrote, "to be the great commercial highway of the west, and if it has not fulfilled its destiny to the extent it should have done, it is because the enterprise of man has endeavoured to divert its trade into other and artificial channels." The Erie Canal and the railways of New York State had certainly played havoc with nature's purposes, for only a small proportion of the posssible traffic passed through the Welland Canal. This fact, the commissioners stoutly maintained, could be explained by the inadequate size of the Welland and St. Lawrence canals. Their faith still strong in the prospect of prosperous traffic following improvement of canals, the commissioners urged that these should be deepened as soon as possible. For the Welland Canal, deepening, new locks, and an entirely new work for part of the route were completed in 1887, giving a depth of fourteen feet. Similar plans for the St. Lawrence

[1] *Canada, Sessional Papers,* 1871, no. 54.

were drawn up, and were carried to completion by stages; the whole being finished by 1903. If American traffic was to be encouraged to pass through Canadian canals, it was also true that Canadians wanted to make use of certain waterways in the United States. Even the dogma of the great river could not disguise the advantage of the Lake Champlain-Hudson River route to New York. In the absence of any Canadian canal until 1895 Canadian entrance to Lake Superior was dependent on the American canal at Sault Ste. Marie. The joint high commission at Washington made provision for the mutual use of waterways, but the terms of the treaty were in part only promises of recommendations to the local authorities, being the Canadian government on the one hand and the particular states concerned on the other.[2] On the ratification of the Treaty of Washington the president asked the governments of the interested states to take steps to carry it into effect. The governor of New York, the state most concerned, replied that no legal obstacles existed; but in 1874 the Canadian privy council declared that Canadian vessels had been prevented from passing through the Champlain Canal to the Hudson River, although American vessels had been permitted to go to any destination by way of the Chambly Canal; and the council asked that the British minister take up the question at Washington.[3]   A long diplomatic exchange followed between Hamilton Fish, the secretary of state, and Sir Edward Thornton, the British minister, the former using information from the governments of the states and the latter from that of Canada.[4] For a time an anti-climax was reached when the Canadian government was unable to quote any cases, but in the summer of 1875 it turned out that the Canadian right to use the Champlain route was virtually negatived by the decision that a vessel must discharge her cargo at the first port of entry, and that to proceed further would be to carry goods from one port in the United States to another. An escape from this dilemma lay in the power placed in the secretary of the treasury to designate any ports at which vessels laden with the products of Canada might discharge their cargoes; and in 1876 this was put into effect, with the result that Canadian vessels were on a parity with American in proceeding as far as Albany, by way of Plattsburg, Oswego, or Buffalo.

2 See above, 128.
3 *Canada, Sessional Papers*, 1876, III.
4 *Ibid.*, and *Canada, Sessional Papers*, 1879, no. 64.

This compromise on the navigation of the Hudson River by Canadian ships, carrying goods in bond destined for the port of New York, was regarded as a concession by the American government, which took the view that the Hudson was an internal waterway, not expressly opened by the Treaty of Washington. The St. Lawrence, on the other hand, was in part an international river, and for the rest of its course was, by article xxvi of the treaty, to be open for purposes of commerce to the citizens of the United States. In contrast to the American position, which apparently was to make such a concession for the benefit of Canadian rather than American interests, Canadians were anxious to encourage navigation of the St. Lawrence in order to swell the volume of business at Montreal, and thus to attract more shipping and lower the freight rates. To this end they were more than willing to allow American ships equal rights in the canals—except in the Welland to ships whose cargoes were then to be carried by rail or water to New York. The general objective was entirely consistent with an old policy, toward which the circumstances of the moment were to be bent. In 1882 tolls on the Erie Canal were abolished, and two years later the Canadian government attempted at once to meet this competition and to stimulate the through Canadian route by giving a rebate of 90 per cent. on all canal tolls on grain cargoes, whether Canadian or American, which were carried as far as Montreal and were shipped abroad. Was this discrimination? The Canadian government, in reply to protests, argued that it was discrimination against United States ports, and intentionally so; but not against American users of the waterway.[5] The American position was that it logically involved discrimination against American citizens. Two visits of Canadian ministers to Washington in 1892 failed to produce a settlement, though a number of compromises were suggested, including a Canadian proposal of withdrawal of the discriminatory tolls on the Welland Canal in exchange for navigation as far as New York. The American officials adopted strong language in description of the Canadian attitude and imposed tolls on the Sault Ste. Marie Canal as direct retaliation. Finally, in February 1893, the Canadian government capitulated and changed the system of tolls to one acceptable to the United States.[6]

5 *Canada, Sessional Papers*, 1892, no. 99.

6 J. M. Callahan, *American Foreign Policy in Canadian Relations* (New York, 1937), 423 ff.

Apart from a general desire to maintain friendly relations between the two countries, the result of the dispute may be explained by the superior bargaining position held by the United States. Both the Sault Ste. Marie and the Champlain canals were, at that time, monopolies which could be opened or closed at will. Moreover, it was not regarded as of major advantage to the United States to secure Canadian traffic. No doubt it would swell the business of the port of New York, but New York could in any case draw ample shipping. The Canadians, on the other hand, felt it necessary to give support to Montreal, and in general were desirous of attracting traffic to Canadian routes in competition with those of the United States. The principle extended to railways as well as waterways. The Grand Trunk Railway and the Great Western Railway were both designed on the assumption that they could obtain a generous share of the traffic between the American middle west and the seaboard. By securing a line to Chicago the Grand Trunk had a connection with American railways, and with lines to Montreal and Portland was in a position to carry goods in either summer or winter. A further indication of the belief that the cheapest route between Atlantic ports and Chicago lay through Canada was seen in the construction of the Canada Southern, an American-owned railway joining the New York Central and Michigan Central, and designed to obviate the loop around the south of Lake Erie.

The exploitation of what were conceived to be favourable geographical conditions never brought results on the scale that had been anticipated. The projects for a railway to the Canadian west gave a new turn to the issue. The Grand Trunk clung to its conviction that the logical route lay through the United States, by way of Chicago; but the governmental decision in favour of a line wholly on Canadian soil rendered the Grand Trunk plan impossible, since it could be realized only with the aid of public money. The decision to construct a railway to the Pacific coast by way of the northern shore of Lake Superior meant that that railway, completed in 1885, had to compete for traffic with American transcontinental lines, and to protect itself against drainage of business from its main line. The most vulnerable points were Sault Ste. Marie, the Red River Valley, and the Pacific coast. At these places where connections with American railways were, or could be, made, a variety of measures were adopted as defence against competition.[7]

Heavy investment in the Canadian Pacific and the later transcontinental railways—the Canadian Northern and the National Transcontinental-Grand Trunk Pacific—represented a commitment to a policy of east-and-west traffic in Canada which became a part of Canadian policy and formed a leading argument in the opposition to reciprocity in 1911. With the acceptance of the general strategy of Canadian railways the dream of the St. Lawrence Valley as the main route to the centre of North America faded. Yet much reality—and increasing reality—remained of railway relations with the United States. Beginning with through rail communication between Montreal and Boston in 1851, a network of connections between Canadian and American railways was gradually built up, realized in part by junctions at the frontier, and in part by ownership or operation of lines across the border. By 1933 there were fifty-five rail or car-ferry crossings along the border, all the way from New Brunswick to British Columbia. In the same year Canadian railways had control or trackage rights over 7,312 miles of rail in the United States, while American railways had a corresponding mileage of 1,556 in Canada.[8] The economic effects of such an interrelationship were far-reaching, enabling the commerce of one country to have easy access to that of the other. Each railway company concerned aimed, of course, to profit from the connection, and each therefore sought to attract traffic to its own lines. Because they were private companies, the railways conducted, to some extent, their own international relations, but were not reluctant to appeal to their respective governments against "unfair" competition. Official negotiations resulted on such questions as freight rates and bonding privileges.[9]

In the movement for the improvement of transportation by rail and water the chief emphasis was laid on satisfactory access to ocean ports in order to maintain and develop the foreign trade which was a major interest in Canada. With the progress of wheat-growing in the prairies, added to the staples for export in the

[7] G. P. deT. Glazebrook, *A History of Transportation in Canada* (New Haven and Toronto, 1938), 301 *ff.*

[8] A detailed study of this development is in W. J. Wilgus, *The Railway Interrelations of the United States and Canada* (New Haven and Toronto, 1937).

[9] See, for example, Callahan, *American Foreign Policy*, 394 *ff.*

east and centre, that object became of increasing importance. The possible outlets were the summer ports of Montreal and Quebec, the all-year ports of Saint John and Halifax, the new port of Vancouver, or the American ports of New England and New York. While the Canadians had struggled by diplomacy to secure use of the Hudson River route, and Canadian railways continued to obtain connections with American railways across the border, the investment in Canadian canals and railways demanded that both should be fed by ocean shipping at Canadian ports. Without that, both the Canadian Pacific and the Intercolonial railways would be meaningless, and the expensive canals would lead to a blank end.

From time immemorial the men of the maritime provinces and of Quebec had built and sailed ships, and had sold them abroad. The gradual replacement of wooden by iron ships, however, was fatal to the Canadian industry at that time, for local production of iron was quite inadequate to supply the new need. The highest figure for the Canadian production of wooden ships was reached in 1874, and in a dozen years this was reduced by three-fourths. Canadian foreign trade, therefore, had to be carried in ships of foreign manufacture—though not necessarily of foreign owner-ship. One of the most important of modern shipping lines was founded by a native of Halifax, Samuel Cunard; but in 1867 the Cunarders ceased to call at Halifax, since the volume of traffic on the New York route was so much greater.[10] The Cunard Com-pany, however, retained a Canadian connection by its service to the St. Lawrence ports. Another shipping line which originated in Canada was that controlled by the Allan brothers of Montreal. The company continued to use the St. Lawrence route in spite of the hazards of navigation and the competition with New York until increasing difficulties led to its sale to the newly-formed Cana-dian Pacific Ocean Steamships. The Dominion Line, organized in England in 1870, carried on a summer service to Montreal until 1894 when financial difficulties caused the sale of its ships, which, however, continued in service to Canada first under the British and North Atlantic Steam Navigation Company and then under the White Star Line. The impending completion of the Canadian

---

[10] For the history of ocean shipping in relation to Canada see Adam Shortt and A. G. Doughty (eds.), *Canada and its Provinces* (23 vols., Toronto, 1914), X, 589 ff.

Pacific Railway brought prospects of a complete Canadian route to the orient, with the advantages of through traffic for the railway and of general trade for Canada. As a first temporary measure the railway company chartered three steamships. In the meanwhile negotiations were being conducted with the imperial government on the project of a Pacific service supported by a mail subsidy. With the conclusion of an agreement, a ten-year contract was awarded to the Canadian Pacific in 1889 providing for a subsidy of £45,000 from the imperial government and £15,000 from the Canadian government for the carriage of mail to Hong Kong. The first three *Empresses* were built in England for the Canadian Pacific. An important trade was thus built up, both between Europe and the far east, and in oriental goods—particularly silk and tea—imported into Canada and the United States.

The sea-going shipping entered and cleared at Canadian ports amounted to 4,319,321 tons in 1868 and 14,175,121 tons in 1900. This satisfactory increase was due not only to the initiative of individual companies, but also to governmental aid by the improvement of navigation and by money subsidies. The channel in the St. Lawrence was repeatedly deepened, to twenty-two feet in 1877, and twenty-seven and a half feet in 1887. About 1900 work on a thirty-foot channel was begun. Concurrently with the improvement of the channel better harbour facilities were provided at Quebec and Montreal. The need for subsidies as an encouragement to direct steamship services to Canadian ports was early seen and constantly acted on. Considerable sums were paid to maintain a line between Canada, the West Indies, and Brazil; between Canada and France; and, in co-operation with the British government, to Japan, Australia, and South Africa. Subsidies were also paid to companies operating ships between Canadian and British ports, but in this case the steamship lines were handicapped by American competition.[11] As a further method of encouraging foreign trade some investigation was made in 1910 and the next three years of the possibility of control of the freight rates of the ocean steamship companies by common action of the imperial and dominion authorities. There was some discussion of the question at the imperial conference of 1911, but without

[11] Norma Claire Taylor, "The Economic Development of Canada's Merchant Marine" (unpublished M.A. thesis, University of Toronto, 1924), 25.

tangible result. In 1913 the Canadian government sent H. L. Drayton, head of the board of railway commissioners, to London to discuss the matter further, but again no agreement was reached.[12] The method of reaching freight rates by the North Atlantic Conference was under some criticism in Canada, and Drayton's report gives the impression that the charges were unduly high.

Communications, like transportation, played their part in the external relations of Canada. The two are closely connected, for the mails were dependent on the railway and shipping facilities available. The completion of the Intercolonial Railway and the Canadian Pacific Railway made it possible for the post office to send mail across Canada, and to connect with Atlantic and Pacific ports without being obliged to make use of American routes. The steady development of ocean shipping at Canadian ports also allowed for direct communication with a growing number of countries, and that with greater speed and regularity. The complicated position existing before the establishment of the Postal Union in 1874 entailed not only high rates of foreign postage, but varied rates according to the number of countries through which a letter passed and whether or not bilateral conventions existed. The situation caused not only expense to concerns engaged in foreign trade but also the necessity of arriving at rates for almost every letter. It was obviously advantageous, therefore, to secure entrance to the Union, but Canada was not admitted until 1878. Under the original constitution any one member could veto an application, and it happened that France exercised this power on account of a difference with Great Britain over sea rates. The situation was cleared up by the exertions of the British post office. Reductions of postage rates were subsequently made both within Canada and for foreign letters. The aspect of this which caused most interest was the project of imperial penny postage. Publicly advocated by an English member of parliament, Mr. Henniker Heaton, it was discussed at the colonial conference of 1887, but not adopted. Subsequently the plan was supported by the Canadian government, and came into effect in 1898 for the whole empire with the exception of Australia, which did not adhere to the arrangement until 1911. In 1899 the two-cent rate

[12] H. L. Drayton, *Ocean Freight Rates* (Department of Trade and Commerce, Ottawa, 1913).

was applied also to letters from Canada to the United States.[13]

Communication by telegraph and cable was another subject of importance for Canada in its external relations. In respect of telegraphs there is a double interest: the adequacy of the lines for the purpose of communication with the United States, and indirectly with British and foreign countries; and the connection between Canadian and American companies. In the years after confederation Canada had a network of telegraph lines that joined the main cities with each other and with American lines reaching to the border. The American company, Western Union, was associated in eastern Canada with the Montreal Telegraph Company; and in 1881 Western Union acquired lines in Nova Scotia and New Brunswick by taking over Jay Gould's American Union Telegraph Company. The Great North-Western Telegraph Company, incorporated in 1880, with its head office in Winnipeg, had Erastus Wiman, an American, as president. It absorbed the Montreal Company and the Dominion Telegraph Company (which owned the maritime provinces' lines), and thus the American interests of Western Union in Canada were consolidated, although the majority stock was held in Canada.[14] A cable from Newfoundland to Ireland had been successfully laid in the year before confederation by a private company, and other lines across the Atlantic followed. To complete Canada's cable communications with the outside world it remained to establish a Pacific cable. In the discussions of this, as in that of the imperial penny postage, commercial interests were mingled with political. The initiative in a project for an all-British, state-owned cable from Canada to Australia and New Zealand was taken by Sandford Fleming, and in the score of years from the first proposal to actual construction the pressure for the realization of the scheme came from Canada. With the coming completion of the telegraph to the Pacific coast in mind, Fleming began to formulate his plan for the cable, to be the continuation of the telegraph line.[15] Through the early eighties the Canadian government, with Fleming's assistance, collected

13 For an outline of the history of the Canadian post office since 1867, see Shortt and Doughty (eds.), *Canada and its Provinces*, VII.

14 H. Marshall, F. A. Southard, and K. W. Taylor, *Canadian-American Industry: A Study in International Investment* (New Haven and Toronto, 1936), 125.

15 L. J. Burpee, *Sandford Fleming, Empire Builder* (London and Toronto, 1915), 154 ff.

information which they placed before parliament. The Pacific cable was discussed at the colonial conferences of 1887 and 1897, and by other means in the intervals. Not a few obstacles were raised—the cost, the route, and the claims of existing commercial companies—but they were all in time overcome, and the Pacific cable was in operation in October 1902.

II

Before the nineteenth century was out Canada had a system of transportation that linked her to the United States, Europe, and the far cast, and that provided water or rail facilities from one end of the country to another. The greater part of the railway system had been built during days of depression, but in the faith that better times would come. Private investment in the railways, as well as government support by land and money, were a gamble on the growth of the country in the future. Without increased population, commerce, and trade the whole foundation of the structure would be gone. The late eighties and early nineties gave little ground for hope; stagnation was the dominant feature in Canada as elsewhere. It was only in the dying days of the century that confidence and optimism were rewarded, when the business cycle once more took an upward swing, and Canadians at least could see the future which they had predicted and on which they had staked the present. The mines of British Columbia and northern Ontario, the forest resources of east and west, the budding manufactures—all were ready for exploitation, and all called for labour. But the chief opening was in agriculture. The lands of the prairies were ready for working, but the labourers indeed were few.

The Canadian public and Canadian officials were convinced that they had in the west an asset of incalculable value, not only because of the richness and accessibility of the land, but because it had a scarcity value now that the American west was all but fully occupied. Immigrants would be welcomed, within limits, in other areas and occupations, but the big need was strong farmers for the virgin soil of the prairie. In the past Canada had never obtained immigrants in numbers comparable to her ambitions, and even the addition of such as had come had been more than offset by the drain of people to the United States. It has been calculated that net migration since confederation showed a loss in every year but one (1873) until 1901.[16] The inducement to migrate was primarily economic—the hope of people suffering from un-satisfactory conditions of life in town or country to better their lot in the new world. In some cases, too, groups in continental Europe were led to emigrate because of religious or political persecution. In the British Isles assistance and encouragement had long been given by private persons or organizations to emigrants to Canada and elsewhere. In the early twentieth century "about forty societies carried on the work of assisting emigrants, either by providing the passage in whole or in part, or in giving advice to intending emigrants, and putting them in touch with friendly societies or individuals overseas".[17] Trades unions continued to give some aid to members who wished to emigrate, though to a lesser extent than formerly.[18] The British government in this period took little direct responsibility for assisting emigration; but, under various statutes, boards of guardians, county councils, and borough councils were authorized to render assistance out of local rates.

In general, the efforts of organizations and of the government in the British Isles were directed toward giving assistance to those who were unemployed or otherwise suffering from economic hard-ships at home. The Canadian interest in migration was to secure enough suitable people to help to develop the country, by drawing them from wherever they could be found. The liberal government of Wilfrid Laurier came into office (1896) just as the economic horizon brightened. The vitality of a new government combined with better conditions to produce a fresh vigour and success in the search for immigrants. Agents and advertising matter were sent to the United Kingdom, the United States, and continental Europe. The department of immigration, under the stimulus of Clifford Sifton, adopted new methods and explored new fields.[19]

[16] Roland Wilson, "Migration Movements in Canada, 1868-1925" (*Canadian Historical Review*, XIII, June 1932). Cf. A. R. M. Lower, "The Growth of Canada's Population in Recent Years" (*Canadian Historical Review*, December 1932).

[17] W. A. Carrothers, *Emigration from the British Isles, with Special Reference to the Development of the Overseas Dominions* (London, 1929), 253.

[18] S. C. Johnson, *A History of Emigration from the United Kingdom to North America, 1763-1912* (London, 1913), 80 ff.

[19] J. W. Dafoe, *Clifford Sifton in Relation to His Times* (Toronto, 1931), 137 ff.

The results of the campaign in the United States were particularly striking; in 1897 only 9,000 immigrants came from the United States, but in 1912 the number had jumped to 133,000. Since the chief demand and the chief opportunity were for farmers in the prairies, it was open to the government to encourage their settlement in two other ways: by seeing that an adequate railway system was being provided, and by making land available on favourable terms. Even if railway branch lines could never quite keep up to the moving frontier of settlement, the Canadian Pacific's main line was rapidly being supplemented not only by its own branch lines but also by two additional transcontinental railways. In every step of railway expansion governments, both federal and provincial, gave aid by way of loans, land grants, or guarantee of bonds.[20] And because of its control over the natural resources of the west, the dominion government was able to organize the system of land grants so as to encourage settlement. From the first free-homesteading was provided for under a series of Dominion Land Acts, with conditions that provided against misuse by speculators in the attempt to attract immigrants. Lands granted to railways in aid of construction were sold by the companies, which were as anxious to secure the business that would accrue from the presence of settlers as they were to make a direct profit out of the land.[21] The railway companies also played an active part in the search for immigrants, carrying on an extensive campaign abroad with an enthusiasm that on occasion left them open to accusations of misrepresentation. Land companies and other private organizations also joined in the hunt for immigrants, whether to further their particular interests or in a more altruistic spirit of building up the dominion. The Canadian Pacific Railway followed as active a programme in securing immigrants as did the government; and, like the government, encouraged settlement by means also of aid to settlers after their arrival in the west.[22] Whatever the motive might be, the number of immigrants began to increase in numbers that were pleasing if not all that might be desired.

[20] For the relation of railways to settlement see W. A. Mackintosh, *Prairie Settlement: The Geographical Setting* (Toronto, 1934), chap. III.

[21] For the principles and practice of land grants see Chester Martin, *"Dominion Lands" Policy* (Toronto, 1938).

[22] For a detailed study see J. B. Hedges, *Building the Canadian West: The Land and Colonization Policies of the Canadian Pacific Railway* (New York, 1939).

From 1884 (during the construction of the Canadian Pacific Railway) the number of immigrants had gone down from a little over 100,000 to a paltry 17,000 in 1896. In 1903 it passed well over the hundred-thousand mark again; the two-hundred thousand mark was first passed in 1906, and the three-hundred thousand mark in 1911. The figure for 1913, of 400,870, was the all-time high.

Even the early twentieth-century enthusiasm for immigration did not entirely overshadow the caution of government and public in the selection of immigrants. The balance between quantity and quality was not always easy to adjust, and there were disagreements on the desirability of certain types of immigrants. The obvious objections were generally entertained toward physical disabilities, paupers, and non-white races. The first choice would be of families from Great Britain or the United States who would go on the land. These sources, however, were too limited for Canadian needs, and the government then turned to the continent of Europe. Investigation revealed that few immigrants could be secured from Germany, France, Belgium, or the Scandinavian countries, but that there were possibilities in Austria-Hungary and Russia of which Sifton had hopes.[23] The several immigration acts and orders-in-council in the fifteen years before the war were aimed at encouraging the growth of rural, and discouraging that of urban, population; this purpose arising in part from the already existing drift from country to town. The acts also provided regulations intended to keep out those who would become a charge on the country, or races which could not be assimilated. Between 1902 and 1912 some 60,000 persons were rejected at the ports or frontier, and 5,629 persons were deported.

The general policy, then, was to build up the rural population, by immigration, without departing too far from the existing ethnic basis of French and English. The largest group of immigrants was British, consisting of agriculturalists to western Canada and artisans to the cities of the east. The latter were employed particularly in the heavy industries that were rapidly developing in the period—for example, in and around Montreal. An effect of this on the province of Quebec was to accentuate a difference that already existed in some degree between the two races—that the

[23] Dafoe, *Clifford Sifton*, 141.

French were more often rural dwellers and the British urban. But no great problem of assimilation to the Canadian population as a whole was created, rather one of adjustment to new conditions.[24] Among those who went to the west were to be found agricultural labourers from large English farms, and the sons of yeoman farmers, of better education and imbued with some spirit of adventure.[25] For the most part these English farmer-immigrants were interspersed with other farmers, but one attempt, made in 1903, to form a wholly British colony at Lloydminster, Saskatchewan was an interesting but unsuccessful experiment. The colony was not only British in personnel, but intended to be so in social structure; the members of the colony were inexperienced in agriculture, and had little but misfortune until the population of the district became more mixed.[26]

Other experiments in the transplanting of groups from Europe to settle together in the west offered greater problems of assimilation, though they sometimes ended in a greater economic success. One of the most interesting examples was that of the Ukrainians, who left Russia partly because of political oppression, and partly because of economic hardships and lack of land. They were rural people, and settled in blocks in all three provinces. "Each settlement", wrote an observer, "is a little Ukraine in which anything of a foreign nature rarely intervenes to mar the even tenor of their ways."[27] While the children learnt English, the adult members of the families spoke Ukrainian. They brought with them their own culture and their own religion, the Greek Catholic Church. Some of their art, music, and literature tended to be overshadowed by that which already existed in Canada, and a rich heritage was in danger of being lost. To the attempts made in the public schools to plunge their children into the Canadian melting-pot the Ukrainians offered resistance, and a wise measure of toleration allowed a place for the Ukrainian language.

As in the case of many settlements of immigrants, the Ukrainians encountered economic difficulties, usually arising out of unproductive land. They worked on railway-construction or on older farms,

[24] L. G. Reynolds, *The British Immigrant: His Social and Economic Adjustment in Canada* (Toronto, 1935).

[25] A. G. Street, *Farmer's Glory* (London, 1932).

[26] Carrothers, *Emigration from the British Isles*, 247.

[27] C. H. Young, *The Ukrainian Canadians: A Study in Assimilation* (Toronto, 1931), 76.

however, and were able to maintain themselves, even if on a low standard. For Canada such problem as was created by the coming of the Ukrainians was not economic but cultural. Up to a point they enriched, by variety, the Canadian culture, but some conformity was necessary. That is to say, if foreign and unassimilated groups were multiplied, a time would come when the pattern would become so confused that national entity would be weakened.

The Doukhobors, who settled in southern Saskatchewan, were a much smaller group, but, because of their peculiar beliefs, can be regarded as a foreign influence remarkable in degree if not in size. The Doukhobors were an unorthodox religious sect who were persecuted in Russia because of their pacifist beliefs which forbade their doing the compulsory military service. Coming to Canada, first in 1899, they established a number of colonies organized on a communal basis. Some of them, indeed, broke away from communism and maintained private property, but with the majority difficulties were met in their first refusal to accept land grants as individuals or to pay taxes for roads. In deference to their beliefs, they were accorded exemption from military service. They proved to be a sober and industrious people, but, in the view of one who assisted the first migration, they got "drunk on theories and on superstitions".[28] The most remarkable demonstration of their emotional religion was a pilgrimage across country in 1902, after discarding their possessions and finally their clothes. Such activities could only be frowned on by majority opinion, and be handled as tactfully as possible by government officials. Such freakish behaviour contributed little to Canada; but it was foreign only in the sense that these families came from abroad; and it created no particularly Russian influence or connection.[29] Another, and a calmer, group of Russians were the Mennonites. The first members of this religious group to come to Canada arrived from Pennsylvania after the American revolution. From 1874 on several thousand more came direct from Russia, settling first in Manitoba and later further west. As a minority of Dutch extraction in Russia they formed in that country separate colonies as they were to do in Canada after their emigration. They were influenced in leaving Russia

    [28] A. Maude, *A Peculiar People: The Doukhobors* (New York, 1904), 232.
    [29] A full account of the Doukhobors is in J. F. C. Wright, *Slava Bohu: The Story of the Doukhobors* (New York, 1940).

because of a policy of assimilation there, and it might therefore be supposed that they would seek equally to maintain themselves as distinct groups in Canada. Their needs, however, were not extreme: religious freedom, exemption from military service, and some use of their own language (which was German).[30] Of the comparatively large German and Scandinavian elements in the population, a portion came from the United States, while many of the Germans in eastern Canada had been there for generations. It was generally found that both these racial groups were good settlers not only in the sense of their being industrious, but in that they readily fitted in with Canadian institutions and customs. An examination of the Magyar settlers in Saskatchewan showed that by origin they were farm labourers, and had naturally taken to the land in Canada. By inquiry from fifty-five families it appeared that at least thirty took Magyar periodicals.[31]

Oriental immigration created a problem quite different from that arising out of the presence in Canada of any other foreign group. The colour difference in itself was regarded by many Canadians as objectionable, and added to that were the differences in standards of living. The difficulty was greatly accentuated by the fact that most of the orientals settled in one province, British Columbia. Oriental immigrants came from three countries: China, Japan, and India. Each of these countries had a different relationship politically to Canada. India was a part of the British Empire; with Japan Great Britain had first commercial and later political treaties; China alone was not in a position to warrant special consideration. The first orientals to arrive in any number were Chinese from the United States, attracted to British Columbia by the gold rush of 1858, and amounting to some 2,000 in 1860.[32] Further immigrants then came directly from China, to a number sufficient to provoke an inquiry by parliament in 1879. Contractors on the Canadian Pacific Railway construction provided work for

[30] R. England, *The Colonization of Western Canada: A Study of Contemporary Land Settlement, 1896-1934* (London, 1936), 232 ff.

[31] E. H. Oliver, "The Settlement of Saskatchewan to 1914" (*Proceedings and Transactions of the Royal Society of Canada*, 1926).

[32] For detailed studies of the whole question of oriental immigration and its results see Cheng Tien-fang, *Oriental Immigration in Canada* (Shanghai, 1931), and C. J. Woodsworth, *Canada and the Orient: A Study in International Relations* (Toronto, 1941). *The Japanese Canadians* by C. H. Young, H. R. Y. Reid, and W. A. Carrothers (Toronto, 1938) is more concerned with standards of living.

further Chinese, and as many as 15,000 were estimated to have entered British Columbia between 1881 and 1884. Because of a ban on emigration from Japan before the revolutionary changes of 1867 Japanese were later in coming to Canada. There were perhaps 1,000 in Canada in 1896. The census of 1901 shows 4,738 and that of 1911, 9,067. Immigrants from India did not start to come until 1905, and the only large numbers of entries were in 1907 (2,124) and 1908 (2,623).

The presence of orientals became a main issue in British Columbia. The objections were, principally, on two grounds. The orientals, it was said, could not be assimilated—nor was it desirable that they should be. Mixed marriages were held to be out of the question, and there were not even ordinary social relations between the races. Whether it was in town or country, the orientals lived in groups, and lived, it was alleged, under unsanitary conditions that were a menace to the community. The second objection was that the orientals, who were virtually all uneducated labourers, deprived white people of work because they were prepared to accept lower wages. This had the effect either of keeping white men unemployed or of lowering the whole wage scale. From the mines the orientals moved to railway construction, and, when that was finished, to fisheries, agriculture, domestic work, and various other callings. In each of the occupations in turn, it was said, white men were dispossessed.

The provincial legislature and the British Columbia members of parliament struggled for years to secure exclusion. The legislature continually attempted to solve the problem by direct action, but its measures were disallowed by the federal government as beyond provincial powers. The federal government and parliament did, however, take a number of steps. More than one commission of inquiry was sent to the coast to investigate, and voluminous reports were made. Various means were also adopted to restrict immigration. In 1885 a head tax of $50 was imposed on every Chinese immigrant, and in 1900 the tax was doubled. Still the dam was not high enough to stop the flood of entries, and in 1904 the tax was raised as high as $500. That too failed in its purpose, and indeed it was interpreted as having the opposite effect by raising wages in a protected labour market, and so making it possible for newcomers to earn the tax in a short period.[33] Similar action could hardly be taken in respect of the Japanese because of political relations between their country and Great Britain. There was, however, the same cause for steps of some kind to be taken, for the immigration of Japanese was fast increasing, and their rate of natural increase was higher. The solution was found not by exclusion, but by a "gentlemen's agreement" of 1907 with the Japanese government by which passports were to be restricted, and the flow of labourers stopped.

In order to discuss Indian immigration with the British authorities, Mr. Mackenzie King was sent to London in 1908. He found a sympathetic hearing and a recognition that, on account of climate, manners, and customs, Canada was not a suitable place in which Indians might live. The government of India agreed to inform its subjects as to the conditions of Canada; steamship companies were warned not to use misleading literature; and the Indian Emigration Act made emigration of contract labour unlawful except to those countries which made provisions satisfactory to the government of India. The Canadian government, on its part, by orders-in-council, imposed as a condition that emigrants should be possessed of $200 and should pass by continuous voyage from their country of origin. Indian immigration, as a result of these obstacles, dwindled to almost nil.[34]

The fears felt in British Columbia were, by these various measures, partly appeased; but the problem of unassimilable races, threatening economic pressure on the white population, by no means wholly disappeared.

The population of Canada, which was constantly recruited by immigration, was equally constantly diminished by emigration. The door to the United States was, in those years, wide open, and thousands of men and women passed through it every year to seek opportunities of employment. A portion of these had only paused in Canada on their way from Europe and cannot be regarded as Canadians. Others were native-born or long resident, with Canadian background and ties; and their departure changed the balance of races remaining in Canada, and planted an increas-

---

[33] *Report of Royal Commission Appointed to Investigate the Method by which Oriental Labourers Have Been Introduced into Canada,* 1908. Quoted in Cheng Tien-fang, *Oriental Immigration in Canada,* 73.

[34] Cheng Tien-fang, *Oriental Immigration in Canada,* 142 *ff.*

ing element in the United States. An agent appointed by the Canadian government to investigate the number of Canadians in the United States concluded that in 1873 there were 800,000 Canadian-born residents there. About half of these were French, and half of these again were in New England.[35] Many of the Canadians went to the expanding American west, especially before the Canadian Pacific Railway opened a route to western Canada.

A broad distinction may be drawn between the English- and French-speaking Canadian emigrants to the United States in that the former mixed as individuals with the rest of the population, while the latter tended to form separate colonies and seek to avoid assimilation. The emigration of French Canadians, which had caused alarm as early as the forties, reached larger proportions after the Civil War and remained considerable until about 1890, when it diminished. It was in large part a movement of farmers to unskilled work in the factories of New England, where they, and their wives and children, were welcomed as employees by the managements of expanding industries requiring dependable workers at low wages. The motive of emigration, then, was economic, and seems to have been unmixed with any political or other discontent. The men went simply to seek profitable employment, without any of the bitterness of the *emigré*. Accustomed to the community life of Quebec, and with little or no knowledge of English, they early began to form small groups of their own. Separate French quarters—outposts of Quebec—grew up in the factory towns. The migrants were not infrequently resented by the English-speaking workers, in something of the same spirit that Canadians resented the coming of Chinese or other cheap foreign labour. Their going was no less regretted at home. Cries of distress continued to rise in Canada at the loss of thousands after thousands. The drain of people was regretted because it was held to impede the economic development of Canada, to weaken the French-Canadian group, and to detach so many from the church. Efforts at repatriation were made, and in 1875 the Quebec legislature voted $50,000 for that purpose, part of which was spent on agents to New England. The results, however, were meagre, and received little support amongst the spokesmen of the

[35] M. L. Hansen, *The Mingling of the Canadian and American Peoples*, vol. I, *Historical* (New Haven and Toronto, 1940), 168.

emigrés themselves.[36] If they could not be induced to return, it remained only to. encourage the maintenance of cultural links with a people who were voluntarily retaining many of their native traits. There might even result positive advantages.

Cette dépopulation en masse [wrote Hamon] est sans doute une calamité pour le Canada. Il eût été bien préférable de garder ces hommes au pays, où ils auraient fondés des familles de colons attachés au sol. Mais, d'autre part, elle a permis à la race française et catholique de jeter de profondes racines dans les Etats de l'Est, et qui sait le rôle qu'elle peut être appelée à jouer dans l'avenir?[37]

Had not the French long since learned the technique of maintaining their own national characteristics in face of an English government and population in Canada? The cases were not dissimilar. The binding forces were, in the main, three: language, religion, and education; and all three were interdependent. New England already had a large Roman Catholic element, but it was Irish. The immigrants were handicapped by ignorance of English and fitted with difficulty into the customs of the Irish parishes. Moreover, to do so would be to lose their entity, and this neither they nor their compatriots in Quebec would willingly see happen. A few French priests were established in New England before 1870, and after that date it became the rule. By 1890 eighty-six separate French Roman Catholic parishes had been established, most of which were served by French priests.[38] In 1911 there were said to be 202 parishes and 101 missions.[39] With the churches went convents and parish schools. The stress on separate education was the same as in Quebec, and where local conditions made it necessary for children to attend public schools the defenders of nationalism saw the defeat of their aims. "L'école publique", wrote one, "est le tombeau de la race française aux États-Unis."[40]

---

[36] A. R. Foley "French-Canadian Contacts with New England" (*Conference on Education Problems in Canadian-American Relations,* ed. by R. L. Morrow, Orono, Maine, 1939).

[37] E. Hamon, *Les Canadiens-français de la Nouvelle Angleterre* (Quebec, 1891), 11.

[38] G. T. Prior, "The French Canadians in New England" (unpublished M. A. thesis, Brown University, 1932), 67. Cf. Hamon, *Les Canadiens-français,* 89, who gives 120 churches or chapels.

[39] Adélard Desrosiers and P. A. Fournet, *La Race française en Amérique* (Montreal, 1911), 23.

[40] *Ibid.,* 35.

In 1890 there were fifty convents in New England, and these, with the parish schools, were educating 30,000 children. To Hamon the education of girls in convents was all-important because it was the women that maintained the French language.

Le couvent canadien-français sera donc avec l'église, la citadelle puissante qui gardera aux émigrés leur religion et leur langue. Là se formeront les jeunes filles qui devenues plus tard des mères de famille, parleront le français au foyer domestique et la feront parler à leurs enfants.[41]

Newspapers, many of them short-lived, were founded in various New England centres to maintain the language and corporate feeling of the French Canadians in the United States. Another force intended to maintain their entity lay in the French and Catholic societies, united in 1901 under the name of l'Union Saint-Jean Baptiste d'Amérique. Already there had been a number of conventions of the local societies; and in 1874 they were invited to Montreal to meet with the society there, and similarly in 1880 to Quebec.[42]

Organized resistance to assimilation, and conscious effort to maintain nationality, were not found among the English Canadians who migrated to the United States. The absence of a language difference, and the similarity of race with at least the predominant part of the American population, made it easy for English Canadians to fit into American society. They were, moreover, more of the business and professional classes than were the French-Canadian emigrants. In many cases they maintained links with Canada through friends and relations, or in some cases by sending their children back to school. There were many and frequent expressions of regret at the constant drain of educated men from English Canada, but no missionary effort such as marked the parallel relations in Quebec.

In the early twentieth century immigration became larger than emigration until the net gain in the peak year (1913) reached 217,914—slightly more than half of the total number of immigrants. The effects of this shifting of population on the character of the Canadian people cannot be defined with any accuracy, but some

[41] Hamon, Les Canadiens-français, 108.
[42] D. M. A. Magnan, Histoire de la race française aux Etats-Unis (Paris, 1912), 290 ff.

approach may be made to a study through the census returns. Since it is impossible to know what proportion of the newcomers passed on shortly to the United States, an analysis of immigrants has a limited value. A more fruitful method will be an examination of the population in the country, as shown in the census years. One series of categories is by place of birth. In 1881 the total population was 4,324,810. Of these approximately 86 per cent. were born in Canada, 11 per cent. in the British Isles and British possessions, 0.9 per cent. in Europe, none in Asia, and 1.7 per cent. in the United States. The total population in 1901 was 5,371,315. A large proportion—86.9 per cent.—was Canadian-born; only 7.8 per cent. born in the British Isles and possessions; 2.3 per cent. in Europe; 0.4 per cent. in Asia; and 2.4 per cent. in the United States. Ten years later the population had grown to 7,206,643. The Canadian-born were proportionately smaller— 77.9 per cent.; 11.5 per cent. were born in the British Isles and possessions, 5.6 per cent. in Europe, 0.6 per cent. in Asia, and 4.2 per cent. in the United States.

The population may also be divided by racial origins. (The census of 1891 did not include this category.) For the years covered, immigrants from the United States are not listed separately, as racial origin refers to origin before coming to this continent. In the lists that follow only the larger groups are shown, and Indians and Eskimos are omitted.[43]

Racial Origin	1881	1901	1911
Canada	4,324,810	5,371,315	7,206,643
British	2,548,514	3,063,195	3,999,081
French	1,298,929	1,649,371	2,061,719
German	254,319	310,501	403,417
Scandinavian	5,223	31,042	112,682
Ukrainian	....	5,485	64,315
Asiatic	4,383	23,721	43,213
Prince Edward Island	108,891	103,259	88,615
British	95,916	87,883	79,266
French	10,751	13,866	13,124

43 From *Seventh Census of Canada*, 1931, I, 710. Complete figures will be found there, divided into rural and urban.

Racial Origin	1881	1901	1911
Nova Scotia	440,572	459,574	492,338
British	342,238	359,064	380,205
French	41,219	45,161	51,919
German	40,065	41,020	38,894
New Brunswick	321,233	331,120	351,889
British	245,974	237,524	238,160
French	56,635	79,979	98,795
Quebec	1,359,027	1,648,898	2,005,776
British	260,538	290,169	318,799
French	1,073,820	1,322,115	1,606,535
Asiatic	7	1,600	2,343
Ontario	1,926,922	2,182,947	2,527,292
British	1,549,160	1,632,144	1,970,980
French	103,004	158,671	203,668
German	188,414	203,319	193,613
Manitoba	62,260	255,211	461,394
British	37,155	164,239	276,259
French	9,688	16,021	31,293
German	8,632	27,265	34,979
Scandinavian	952	11,924	17,644
Ukrainian	....	3,894	31,053
Saskatchewan	....	91,279	492,432
British	....	40,094	269,513
French	....	2,634	25,497
German	....	11,743	71,003
Scandinavian	....	1,452	35,157
Ukrainian	....	1,094	22,276
Alberta	....	73,022	374,295
British	....	34,903	215,174
French	....	4,511	20,600
German	....	7,836	41,656
Scandinavian	....	3,940	29,547
Ukrainian	....	634	17,584
British Columbia	49,459	178,657	392,480
British	14,660	106,403	266,295
French	916	4,600	9,341
German	858	5,707	12,726
Scandinavian	236	4,880	16,087
Asiatic	4,350	19,524	30,864

As in the case of the racial character of the population immediately after confederation, the later censuses must not be taken at their face value to represent the attachments of the population. It is true that the percentage of those of British origin diminished from 60.55 in 1871 to 54.07 in 1911, and that this decrease represented an increasing proportion of Europeans. But it is not clear that the change was reflected in changing views on external affairs. Moreover, if the racial composition is examined in detail, it will be apparent that the eastern provinces were hardly touched. Prince Edward Island retained about the same proportion of British and French. Nova Scotia, too, was little affected; and the German element there represented an early immigration. New Brunswick shows a larger percentage of people of French origin who had moved from Quebec into the northern part of the province. The only notable item in the figures for Quebec is the appearance of Japanese and Chinese, but it was not of great significance. Ontario retained its old racial characteristics. In the west there were more mixture and more diversity, as was inevitable from its place as the object of immigration. It can probably be assumed, too, that the European groups there were of recent origin. There might, therefore, be a distinction between the early German immigrants of Nova Scotia and Ontario and the much later groups in the prairie provinces. The most controversial issue arose out of the growing numbers of Japanese and Chinese in British Columbia.

In the period between 1871 and 1914 the population of Canada was basically British and French, those two together making up from eighty to ninety per cent. of the total. The French, however, were French-Canadian, less influenced by contemporary external influences than any other group of Canadians. They had, of course, cultural elements which grew out of their original mother-country, and which to some extent were fed by current French thought. But in respect of political ideas it must be apparent that they were the most native of Canadians. The ranks of the British Canadians, on the other hand, were constantly recruited by newcomers from the British Isles and from the United States. Those who came from the United Kingdom and the United States brought social and political ideas which they could relate, without undue distortion, to Canadian conditions. They readily obtained English or American periodicals, which had always formed one source of Canadian thinking. The position of European immigrants was very different. In some instances they were *emigrés* representing a dissatisfied minority, in others they came from purely economic motives. There is no indication of any serious attempt to introduce Russian, German, or Scandinavian institutions, but there was a tendency to cling to an old religion, language, or way of life. Such elements added variety—sometimes desirable and sometimes not—but never sufficient to change materially the character of Canada. The British and French basis remained the dominating force, and neither the institutions nor the external policy of the dominion appears to have been seriously modified by a growing diversity of peoples.

III

Enthusiasm for increased immigration was vociferous and real, but not shared by all classes of the Canadian population. While governments, railway companies, land companies, and employers painted a bright picture of a future Canada filled with energetic producers, the wage-earning class looked with some distrust on the whole idea. The immigrants were, and were bound to be, predominantly of the working class; and it was a question whether their coming did not endanger the level of wages and even of employment. Led by those of British Columbia, the Canadian labour organizations repeatedly took a stand against the admission of Chinese, Japanese, or East Indian immigrants, whose standard of living enabled them to accept lower wages and thus imperil the position of the white worker. Even of selected immigration there was some doubt, and at times opposition to it. Denials were made of the frequent statements that Canada had almost unlimited openings for immigrants. The annual report to the Dominion Trades and Labour Congress in 1906 expressed a not untypical point of view: "The fewer our people and the greater our wealth, the more ideal will be the existing conditions. We have no need of cheap peoples, they are an aspiration of the get-rich-quick man who desires to pile up a few extra thousands or hundreds of thousands of dollars at the expense of the future of Canada."[44] The least opposition was to agricultural workers going to the west, where there was an evident need of labour.

[44] *Canadian Annual Review,* 1906, 294.

The various labour organizations which took a continued interest in this aspect of external policy were, in their origin and character, materially affected by other influences from outside Canada; such influences being carried either by immigrants or imported books and periodicals. The early Canadian trade unions were based principally on English examples, and British influence continued to play a part. After confederation, however, American movements came to be the stronger, and even the predominant, forces affecting labour organization in Canada. With their legal status established under an act of 1872 (35 Vict., c. 30), which was almost a verbal copy of the British act of the previous year, Canadian unions were more free to develop, and indeed showed a rapid growth in an age of industrial expansion.[45] Individual unions had, even before this, become affiliated with parallel bodies in the United States. In the seventies and eighties Canadian labour followed British and American precedents by the linking together of local unions into larger bodies of various sizes and types. The Knights of Labour, which had a mushroom growth in the United States, for a time met with a welcome in Canada. The rival and successor, the American Federation of Labour, had a more lasting connection with Canadian organizations. The Industrial Workers of the World first obtained adherents in the Canadian west in 1906, and by 1911 claimed 10,000 followers. After conducting a strike on the Grand Trunk Pacific Railway in 1912, its numbers were cut in half. In 1913 it was vigorously denounced by the Canadian Federation of Labour as "attempting to overthrow the present forms of society by creating a state of industrial anarchy", and its radicalism prevented a wide support in Canada. The agents of the I.W.W., together with delegates of more moderate organizations, foreign groups in the cities, and visiting socialists, were not infrequently labelled as "foreign agitators".

While the main trend was toward international unions formed by the junction of Canadian and American units in various trades, there was, amongst Canadian labour organizations, a contrary opinion which believed in national rather than international organ-

---

[45] For the history of labour organization in Canada see R. H. Coats, "Labour Movement in Canada" (Shortt and Doughty (eds.), *Canada and its Provinces*, IX); H. A. Logan, *The History of Trade-Union Organization in Canada* (Chicago, 1928); Norman J. Ware and H. A. Logan, *Labor in Canadian-American Relations* (Toronto, 1937); and H. A. Innis, "Labour" (*Encyclopedia of Canada,* ed. by W. S. Wallace, Toronto, 1936).

izations. One main split began in 1902 with a secession from the Trades and Labour Congress. The latter continued in the faith of international unions and confined its membership to those organizations which had American affiliations. The seceding groups formed what was first known as the National Trades and Labour Congress, and later renamed the Canadian Federation of Labour. The Federation, always the smaller body, sought to be national and to include all Canadian unions. That position, however, it never attained, finding its strength, at different periods, in Quebec, Ontario, or the maritime provinces. The Trades and Labour Congress, while holding to the principle of international affiliation, aimed at being the representative organization of Canadian trade unions. Obstacles were found in Quebec with the rise of the Catholic and anti-international unions; in British Columbia, where the unions tended to follow their own course, with or without international connections; and in Nova Scotia. In the last the Provincial Workmen's Association shared the views of the Federation and eventually became affiliated with it. The Workmen's Association not only competed with the Congress, but in 1908 found its field directly invaded by the United Mine Workers, an international, and previously a western organization.[46] Both the Nova Scotia union and the company concerned (The Dominion Coal Company) resisted the efforts of the invaders to enlist the employees in an international union. The United Mine Workers called a strike in 1909, one which was accompanied by violence, and which broadened out into a general issue between national and international unionism. For the time being the invaders were repulsed with heavy financial losses, though such a decision proved to be the exception rather than the rule for international unionism in Canada as a whole.

In the many arguments arising out of the dispute in Nova Scotia it was pointed out that the "international" unions belied their name, since they had no affiliations with European trade unions. There were, of course, good reasons for the strong influence of the United States: geographical contiguity and similarity of conditions. There seems to have been in Canada no important body of opinion which sought affiliation with British labour unions; and there is no indication of more than a distant interest in the

[46] *Canadian Annual Review*, 1909, 297 ff.

first and second Internationals in Europe. In 1906 Mr. Ramsay Macdonald visited Canada, looking for "an understanding with the labour parties of the colonies so that there may be harmony and co-operation between ourselves and them", but any co-operation that resulted was only of a general kind.[47] There were, however, external forces affecting Canadian labour other than those coming from the United States. The plans and policies of labour organizations in Australia, New Zealand, Great Britain, and Europe were studied with some care, with a view to their lessons for Canada. Two themes were of particular interest: political action and socialist doctrines.

Manifestly any labour movement must aim at legislation as one means of achieving its objectives. The difference of opinion in the Canadian labour organizations was on whether or not they should intervene directly in politics by creating labour parties in the provinces or the dominion. British and foreign examples could be cited on either side of the argument. For some years sporadic attempts were made to further the desired legislation by running candidates for the various legislatures. In 1873 and 1874 the Ottawa Trades Council secured the election of labour candidates to the Ontario house. In 1883, 1886, and 1894 the Toronto Trades Council attempted, unsuccessfully, to elect candidates to either the federal or the provincial parliament. The Provincial Workmen's Association made several attempts in the eighties and nineties to elect candidates to the Nova Scotian Assembly, but with little success. The British Columbia labour organizations were most interested in political action, and in 1902 formed a Provincial Progressive Party. The question also was frequently discussed by the Canadian organizations as a whole. The Trades and Labour Congress, at its annual convention in 1894, adopted a general resolution in favour of direct political action, but with little result. The annual meeting in 1906 was the occasion for serious consideration of the organization of a labour party, the supporters of such a move being encouraged by the success of the labour party in England and the statement of the president of the American Federation of Labour in favour of political action. Again a general resolution was passed endorsing the sending of representatives of labour to federal and provincial parliaments,

47 *Ibid.*, 1906, 303.

and again the fruits were small. On the whole the Canadian labour organizations steered a middle course between the British emphasis on parliamentary action and the American tendency to minimize that method.

The various socialist programmes of Great Britain, Europe, the United States, Australia, and New Zealand were known in Canada and met with some acceptance. In January 1905 the Socialist Party of Canada was founded by Scottish and English adherents, together with some members from the United States and European countries. Its organization was planned to be provincial with a dominion executive committee, but its strength continued to be, as it started, in British Columbia, and the proposed national convention was never held. The principles of the party were strictly Marxian. The emphasis was on propaganda by lectures and pamphlets, and though the party had members in the provincial legislature, political activity was never its main method. The Social Democratic Party, including members who left the Socialist Party, was founded at Toronto in 1910. Based on British and German models, it continued to be centred in Toronto as the older body was in the west. An attempt to commit the Trades and Labour Congress to political socialism by a motion in favour of "absolute independent political action on the part of the working class with the collective ownership of the means of life as its ultimate aim" was voted down at a meeting in 1907.[48] Socialists from abroad—Britain, the United States, and Europe—toured the country from time to time. May Day parades—some of which were prohibited—were organized in Montreal, Toronto, and other cities. On the whole, however, socialism did not find wide support, though it was embraced by various small groups.

Amongst the farmers of Canada two foreign organizations had for a time a considerable success. The Patrons of Husbandry, or the Grange, was founded in Washington in 1867, and spread rapidly in the next few years. It was a fraternal society, organized in units, or granges, and aimed at collective action to cure such farmers' ills as high railway rates, undue profit by middlemen, heavy taxes, and high interest rates on loans. Canadian farmers with similar worries became interested in the idea and granges

[48] *Ibid.*, 1907, 283.

began to be set up in Quebec and Ontario from 1872.[49] The order
was incorporated in Canada as the "Dominion Grange of the
Patrons of Husbandry", and while it had a separate Canadian
existence its principles were taken from those of its American
parent. Membership grew rapidly until it reached its zenith in
1879 with an estimated 31,000 members. Ontario was the centre
of the movement; it had some success in Quebec and the maritime
provinces but almost none in the west. The activities of the
Grange included collective purchasing, a co-operative salt manufacturing company, a trust and loan society, and a projected bank.
While the Grange had some influence on legislation, it did not
attempt to organize a political party. Another farmers' order
imported from the United States, the Patrons of Industry of North
America, had somewhat similar organization and objectives, but
followed a different course. The Patrons of Industry, incorporated
in Canada in 1890, found strong support in the west. Unlike the
Grange, too, it entered the political field, but there met with
disaster in the federal election of 1896. Four members in the
house of commons did not constitute a party.

IV

The economic growth of Canada from the late nineties depended
partly on the improvement in general world conditions; and to
a large extent on the provision of adequate and costly modes of
transportation, together with increase of population. The financing
of all this development, both in the actual expense of railways
and the industrial and agricultural advance in which the new
population was to be employed, assured in turn a sound internal
financial structure with a supply of foreign capital. The political
union of the provinces opened the way for the utilization of what
credit was available within the dominion, and provided a more
favourable field for the foreign investor. The financial institutions
of the dominion, as of the old provinces, were modelled on those
of Great Britain and the United States; and as in the case of
so many other of its institutions, Canada had to decide on whether
the practice of its mother-country or of its neighbour was the more
satisfactory to follow. The banks of all the provinces had, before

[49] For the history of the Grange in Canada see L. A. Wood, *A History
of Farmers' Movements in Canada* (Toronto, 1924).

confederation, differed little from those of the United Kingdom: there were, however, some steps taken by the Province of Canada to introduce the "free banking" adopted by the United States. The act of 1850 (13 and 14 Vict., c. 21) was little used, but there remained some body of opinion which preferred the American system of a large number of local banks to the British system of few banks with numerous branches. By the British North America Act of 1867 exclusive jurisdiction over banking was given to the federal parliament, and in its early sessions there was discussion over the regulation of banks and currency. The first decision reached by the government was to organize Canadian banks on the American plan. The minister of finance, John Rose, prepared a series of resolutions to this end, and had the extra-parliamentary support of E. H. King, general manager of the Bank of Montreal. Resolutions were introduced into the house of commons, but the opposition proved to be so formidable that they were withdrawn. The two chief sponsors also left the field: Mr. King died and Mr. Rose resigned, to be succeeded by Sir Francis Hincks, who returned to the orthodox principles of British banking. Acts of 1870 were replaced in the following year by the first general Bank Act, to apply to all banks, and to remain in operation for ten years. The system of branch-banking was retained, and the proposal to base bank notes on dominion securities deposited with the receiver-general was rejected. In the decennial revisions of the Bank Act some signs of the old American heresy again appeared, but never became effective.

Decision on the type of currency to be used had already been made before confederation. In all the provinces the decimal system had been introduced, first as optional and finally as compulsory. It remained only for the dominion parliament to assimilate the currency of Ontario, Quebec, and New Brunswick. In spite of some opposition the currency of Nova Scotia was, in 1871, made uniform with that of the rest of Canada.[50] In contrast to the decision on the type of banking, no principle, other than that of convenience, was involved in the retention of the dollar currency, and only sentimental glances were cast back to the old régime.

If the currency was North American, the money used to build railways and promote industry was largely British in origin. Great

[50] Robert Chalmers, A History of Currency in the British Colonies (London, 1893).

Britain was, as she had long been, an exporter of capital on a large scale, and the Canadian provinces had in years past been materially benefitted by this fact. In the early twentieth century the flow to Canada rapidly increased.[51] Of a total foreign investment in Canada in 1900 of some thirty millions of dollars, a third was British. In subsequent years, as the total investment increased, the British proportion was higher. In 1905 the total first passed one hundred million dollars, of which about seventy per cent. was British. The external investment in Canada for the years 1900-1913 has been calculated as follows:

$$\begin{aligned}
\text{British:} &\quad \$1,753,118,000 \\
\text{American:} &\quad 629,794,000 \\
\text{Other countries:} &\quad 162,715,000 \\
\text{Total:} &\quad \$2,545,627,000
\end{aligned}$$

A further stimulant to Canadian economic life was in the establishment of English or foreign industries in Canada. To some extent this had long been the case: the Hudson's Bay Company, for example, had played, and continued to play, an important part in Canada, and the Grand Trunk Railway was largely an English company. American interests, too, had penetrated to Canada as early as the first half of the nineteenth century; began to take an important place after 1870; and expanded more rapidly at the end of the century.[52] Avoidance of the tariff was a leading motive in this movement; securing of raw material—especially wood products and metals—was another; transportation costs and adaptability to the market also played some part.

Labour, capital, and industry from abroad together constituted a large factor in Canadian economic life. In some cases there were complaints that foreign workers and foreign industries dispossessed Canadian workers or companies, but on the whole they added to a general growth far more than they displaced native people and enterprises. If to these there be added foreign trade it is apparent that the Canadian economy was largely dependent on external contributions and relationships.

[51] Jacob Viner, *Canada's Balance of International Indebtedness, 1900-1913* (Cambridge, Mass., 1924), 139.

[52] For a full account see Marshall, Southard, and Taylor, *Canadian-American Industry.*

CHAPTER X

THE CONDUCT OF HIGH POLICY: SUBJECTS AND METHODS

THE importance and variety of the external relations of Canada, increasing from year to year, threw a growing burden on the machinery of government, and led to an examination of the adequacy of that machinery. Though modelled in general on the British constitution, the Canadian system of government included two important characteristics not to be found in that of the mother country. When the union of 1867 was formed it was decided that a federation rather than a legislative union was best adapted to the conditions of the country, and subjects having any direct bearing on external affairs were assigned to the central authority. No exception was taken to George Brown's statement in the debate on the Quebec Resolution that "for all dealings with the Imperial Government and foreign countries we have clothed the General Government with the most ample powers";[1] and for purposes of external affairs Canada was virtually a unitary state. The other leading difference between the constitutions of Great Britain and Canada—that the latter was not a sovereign state—had a more serious effect on external relations. Within the limits of dominion powers, the parliament at Ottawa might exercise in respect of external relations the same supreme authority as did the parliament at Westminster. It was a fundamental principle of the English system that parliament should retain, in every branch of public affairs, the right not only to formulate policy, but also to hold such check as it might wish on the ministers and civil servants concerned. It has, however, been long recognized that parliamentary control is less easily exercised in foreign than in domestic affairs: not because the subject is more technical, but simply because it is foreign. Except in times of crisis, the electors

[1] *Parliamentary Debates on the Subject of the Confederation of the British North American Provinces* (Quebec, 1865), 108.

(and therefore the members of parliament) are less interested in, and often ill-informed on, foreign relations. Information may be withheld because of the necessity for at least some degree of secrecy in the conduct of diplomacy. Under the British constitution, and those which stem from it, the elected body discusses publicly such aspects of foreign policy as treaties and other engagements to an extent unknown under other systems of government, and at times to the embarrassment of the diplomats. On the other hand a study of the foreign relations of a democracy will also reveal that the diplomats may, and sometimes do, conduct conversations with foreign representatives which, without creating a binding commitment, go far toward an agreement just as real in practice. Examples of both types of cases may be taken from recent English history. When negotiations for an Anglo-German alliance were under way at the end of the nineteenth century, the German government saw, as an obstacle to the completion of a treaty, that it would either be made public by discussion in parliament, or, if it was not submitted to parliament, would have less value. An example of lack of parliamentary sanction is found in the relations built up by the diplomats of France and England between 1904 and 1914, the full implications of which were said not to have been known even to the whole cabinet.

With all its drawbacks, it has been accepted that parliamentary control of foreign policy is essential to democratic government. That principle was automatically accepted in Canada from the time of confederation, and in later years became a veritable dogma. In the Canadian, as in the English, parliament the subject of foreign relations might be introduced by means of a statement by a minister of the crown, by question and answer, by resolution, or by debate on a convention or treaty. From the very origin of the Canadian parliament the pages of the debates of the senate and house of commons are well larded with discussion of at least some aspects of external relations. The largest proportion of space is taken by commercial questions, especially actual or proposed tariff agreements. Reciprocity with the United States and the use of Canadian fisheries would probably come first in length, followed by the various aspects of imperial relations. The use of Canadian and American inland waterways received the attention of parliament from time to time, as did the few boundary disputes of the period. Political relations came up more often indirectly than directly, as at the time of the Joint High Commission at Washington in 1871 or in relation to imperial defence. Participation in the Boer War might well be regarded as a direct political question, but it is noteworthy that the Canadian parliament had nothing to do with the decisions that led to the outbreak of that war or to its conclusion. In political, far more than in commercial, questions it is apparent that the limitations of Canadian autonomy restricted the area and degree not only of the actual conduct of foreign relations but also of the policy by which it was governed. The escape from these limitations was a many-sided question, which will be examined later.[2] Given the geographical position, the stress on internal development, and the incomplete autonomy of Canada, it may not be an inaccurate generalization to say that parliament displayed a reasonable knowledge of, and interest in, foreign affairs. When the tariff was being considered members would present a formidable array of statistics. But they did not stop at factual material. Neither house was afraid to examine the very fundamentals of the external relations of Canada: independence, closer or looser political connection with the United States—all these found advocates, and all were debated with a disarming frankness. These were the very bases on which all other external policy of Canada was predicated, corresponding, for example, to the question raised in England as to whether isolation or alliances would be the wiser course. While the Canadian parliament thus continued on its way, doubts arose as to whether that part of the civil service which dealt with external relations was well designed.

The old system, untouched for forty years after confederation, was that external relations were conducted by various members of the cabinet and civil service, according to the subject, without any department or division of a department having particular responsibility, and without any recognition of a need for continuous attention or expert knowledge. The method of conducting matters with other British countries or with foreign countries falls into two aspects. The governor general in Canada and the colonial office in England normally constituted the sole channel of communication. The colonial office might, depending on the subject in question,

2 In Section II of this chapter.

niralty, war office, foreign office, or other depart-
:her link was added when the foreign office referred
broad. A reply to a dispatch from Ottawa might,
ient the completion of a process already having
several stages. There were, however, in practice
this cumbrous machinery. Commercial negotia-
tion. 	 1 states came to be direct in all but form, and the
Canadia.. 	 ited in them corresponded directly with the prime
minister. On 	 asions, as in the proposal for tariff discussions in
1910, the British ambassador in Washington communicated directly
with the governor general. The link between the governor general
and the Canadian government was usually the privy council, and
sometimes, on less important matters, an individual minister. An
incoming dispatch ordinarily went from the governor general to
the privy council, by which body it was assigned to the department most concerned in the subject. In due course the minister at
the head of the department reported back to the council, the report
became the basis of a minute, and the minute of a reply to the
original dispatch. The same process would operate for a correspondence initiated in Canada.

For many years the only criticism was levelled against the portion
of the machinery first described, that is of the communication
through governor general and colonial office. It seemed at times
hardly short of absurd that correspondence between the Canadian
and American governments should go by way of London, and
objections also were made to the process of negotiations on trade
matters with European governments. But, as modifications were
made which allowed Canadians virtually to negotiate commercial
treaties, and as direct communications with Washington became
more common, that criticism became less noticeable. Moreover,
it was fully realized that a radical change in the procedure would
materially alter the delicate balance of imperial relations. The
question then was raised—rather late, it is true—as to whether the
purely Canadian part of the machinery was adequate for the
purpose. Two facts stared an investigator in the face; nowhere
could there be found complete files covering even single cases in
external affairs—far less the full record of the external relations
of the dominion with any particular country, or during any particular period; and secondly, that there were no persons in the
civil service specially trained in foreign affairs, or even enabled

to specialize in that field. A practical proposal to end this situation, anomalous in a country which was no longer a colony and which had important external relations, was made in 1907 to the royal commission on the civil service by Joseph Pope, under-secretary of state. Pope advised that a department, or sub-department, of external affairs be set up, with its own staff, and with such files as it could collect from the various places to which they had found their way. While the report of the royal commission made only a passing and partial recommendation following Pope's memorandum, the original proposal was adopted by the government some two years later.

In 1909 Charles Murphy, secretary of state, moved a resolution in the house of commons that a department of external affairs be set up, presided over by the secretary of state, and with a deputy head and the necessary clerks.[3] In drawing up the plan the government had the advantage of the recent precedent in Australia, where a department with a similar name had been created. In both cases there was to be not a foreign office, as found in every sovereign state, but an office to handle both inter-imperial and foreign relations. The reasons for this are obvious: not only was it questionable whether there would be enough business for two departments; but—the more compelling reason—the two could not be separated, inasmuch as foreign relations were conducted through the colonial office. In other words, foreign and imperial relations were, to some extent, the same. Early in the debate, and again later, government spokesmen made it clear that no change was intended except in the purely Canadian organization, and no contrary opinion was expressed in the house of commons. The debate is brief and unimpressive. Speakers on the government side pointed to the growing volume of business in external affairs and argued the advantages of a separate organization. Opposition speakers were listless, and had little more to say than that things could go on as they were, without additional cost. The debate is in striking contrast to those on imperial relations or tariff questions. It is apparent that parliament had no appreciation of the fact that external affairs required expert administration just as did domestic affairs. And in some quarters it was to be long before this fallacy died. The act (8 and 9 Edw. VII, c. 13) passed

3 *Canada, House of Commons Debates,* 1909, 1978.

with little discussion or change. The point was made, outside parliament, that the phrase, "the secretary of state, as head of the department, shall have conduct of all official communications between the government of Canada and the government of any other country in connection with the external affairs of Canada . . .", was not an accurate description of the situation; and that, in view of the continuing rôle of the governor general, "care" should be used instead of "conduct". The substitution, however, was not made, and apparently no practical difficulty arose. The important change in the act was made in 1912 when the prime minister was made secretary of state for external affairs, an arrangement suggested when the original act was drafted, but not adopted at that time.

The machinery in force before the War of 1914 was therefore similar to that used in the United Kingdom, both on the parliamentary and administrative sides, but limited in its powers. The parliament of Canada retained a control over external affairs in so far as it wished and dominion autonomy allowed. A portfolio of external affairs, though not held by a separate minister, carried that subject into the inner councils of government. On the administrative side appointments were made but the development of the department in size was slow. Even by the end of the war there was only one officer included in the delegation to the peace conference. The Canadian machinery for the conduct of foreign affairs differed from the British in that the former was not only very small, but lacked diplomatic missions abroad, with all the flow of information that they involve.

II

Generally speaking, official relations between the Canadian and other governments were maintained through British channels. There were, however, modifications to this rule, important enough to justify a separate analysis. There were no permanent diplomatic agents stationed in Ottawa, nor were there Canadian agents abroad. In several cases Canadians were appointed as *ad hoc* plenipotentiaries, being, at least in form, representatives of the British government. In most instances appointments were made for the purpose of negotiation and signature of trade treaties, the relative place of the Canadian plenipotentiaries and their United

Kingdom associates changing from time to time. In one important case, however, that of the Washington joint commission of 1871, the subjects under discussion were more political than commercial. Though certain disadvantages existed in this indirect diplomacy, they were partly removed in practice; and Canada actually negotiated her own trade agreements with the aid of the experience and prestige of the British government. It was through the frequent negotiations with foreign governments, chiefly on tariff questions, fisheries, and the use of inland waters, that Canadians played their most active and most direct part in diplomacy. There were also, however, a number of officials and bodies which were more permanent, and were in some way related to the conduct of diplomacy. Representatives of Canada abroad were almost all non-diplomatic. Immigration agents in various countries were confined to their own subject. After confederation most of the provinces continued to appoint agents-general in London, as they had done before; but such officers could not in any way be described as diplomatic, having to do only with immigration and commerce. The office of high commissioner, described in a previous chapter, was in a different category.[4] Although the Canadian government had originally proposed that its representative in London should be diplomatic or quasi-diplomatic, constitutional objections had prevented that status being granted. Even after the department of external affairs was established the high commissioner continued to correspond with the under-secretary of state. A large proportion of the time of the high commissioners was occupied in promoting the financial, commercial, and immigration interests of the dominion, but they could be used for political questions as occasion arose, and were usually appointed as Canadian plenipotentiaries for the negotiation of treaties.

No consular appointments were made; Canadians, like other British subjects, being able to avail themselves of the services of the consular representatives of the imperial government.[5] There were, however, a number of foreign consuls in Canada, and their position had some significance as the only representatives of their countries in the dominion. The first report of the department of

---

4 See above, 150 ff.

5 Canadians paid fees for work done by British consuls which at least equalled the cost of the service. The first Canadian consuls were appointed in 1940.

external affairs contains a list of consuls and consular agents in 1910, showing that thirty-two states had such representatives in Canada. In most cases there were several officers, stationed at different Canadian cities.[6] Though the list does not make any such distinction, it is probable that the majority of the representatives were permanent residents, and that only the consuls-general or senior consuls were *de carrière*. Most of the head offices were either at Ottawa or Montreal. The procedure regulating the appointment of consuls was as follows: consular officers holding a commission from the head of the state required an *exequatur*, which was issued by the British government. In the case of those resident in Canada, the Canadian government was consulted as to whether the appointment was free from objection. In the case of those sent specially to Canada, that is, consuls *de carrière*, the appointment was made without consultation. For those consular officers appointed by a government or a superior consular officer a formal recognition, instead of an exequatur, was granted by the British government, after consultation with that of Canada. Temporary appointments might be accepted by the government of Canada, pending reference to the British government.[7] The Canadian government was consulted as to the establishment of new consulates, and on occasion it took the initiative in suggesting that approaches should be made to that end. It was, however, the status rather than the method of appointment of consuls that entailed questions of principle. After confederation, as before it, the general rule of the British government was that consuls were simply foreign residents. Special courtesies might well be extended to them, but none such as to entail change of status. They were not, for example, granted their request to have private entry to the governor-general's Drawing Room, for this was a privilege conferred on diplomats. From time to time one or more of the consuls protested that they did in fact occupy a position not analogous to that of consuls in sovereign states, but were doing diplomatic work that would otherwise be handled by embassies. For some years attempts by the consuls to act as diplomats were quashed. In 1876, for example, the Danish consul was discouraged

---

[6] *Canada, Sessional Papers,* 1910, no. 29 B.

[7] This procedure was later changed, leaving only formal action to the British government. See *Summary of Proceedings,* Imperial Conference of 1926, 26.

from acting as an intermediary in discussions over mutual rights of Danish and Canadian ships in the coasting trade. Again in 1881 Sir John Macdonald gracefully intimated to the French consul that the latter's views on trade negotiations were for the ear of His Majesty's government. In later years, however, principles were tacitly ignored to allow for the convenience of utilizing a representative of a foreign power resident in the dominion.

In what were at first described as "informal negotiations", the Canadian government discussed with the German consul-general the tariff quarrel between the two countries, and in 1910 the minister of finance and the consul reached an agreement for a settlement.[8] In the same year the minister signed an agreement with the Italian consul on tariff concessions.[9] The Japanese consul-general took part in the negotiations arising out of the immigration of Japanese, the Vancouver riots, and the relation of Canada to the Anglo-Japanese treaty of 1911.[10] The contrast between the formal status of consuls and the rôle they actually played was, therefore, marked. Answering a question in the house of commons as to the refusal of consuls to attend the Drawing Room, Laurier remarked that "the question . . . is an important one, not perhaps so much on account of the drawing room as on account of the duties which consuls-general now discharge in Canada. We have no diplomatic service in Canada, and the consuls-general are exercising by tolerance some, I shall not say diplomatic powers, but powers very often cognate to such. The question is one which should be settled, and the matter is now engaging the attention of the government."[11] In the following session the position of consuls again came up in the house, and on that occasion Laurier went further than he had before. The position of consuls in Canada, he said, like the status of Canada, could hardly be defined. Although Laurier had "often taken the view that we are now a nation", it was true that "we cannot have under present conditions diplomatic agents amongst us other than the consular agents who are entrusted by their governments with commercial functions. . . . By the force

[8] *Canada, Sessional Papers*, 1910, no. 10 G.

[9] *Canadian Annual Review*, 1910, 619.

[10] A. G. Dewey, *The Dominions and Diplomacy: The Canadian Contribution* (2 vols., London and Toronto, 1929), II, 291.

[11] *Canada, House of Commons Debates*, 1909-10, p. 853.

of things these consuls general have become with us semi-diplomatic agents, and many of the consuls have really performed diplomatic duties." Citing the cases of German, Italian, and American consuls as exercising diplomatic functions, Laurier admitted that "all this has been done without authority, and is contrary to the rules that apply among civilized nations". The position, he went on, should be regularized. "I think we should have an understanding with the imperial government that the consuls should have semi-diplomatic recognition amongst us.[12] Looking back at a practice with which he had been familiar, Sir Robert Borden concluded that it had been "both convenient and advantageous", and cited a case during his own period of office: that in 1913, when he had negotiated with the consul-general of Japan over Canada's adhesion to the Anglo-Japanese treaty of 1911.[13] Laurier's suggestion that the practice be regularized was never taken up, probably because the War of 1914 brought Canada nearer to participation in the more conventional diplomatic procedure.

Out of the appointment of officers abroad who were to promote Canadian trade grew the practice of utilizing these men for functions which were properly consular. The first step, in the nineties, was to nominate business men in the British Isles and the West Indies as "commercial agents" under the supervision of the minister of finance, with the object of receiving information from the localities on the possibilities of trade, and of supplying information to commercial firms there. When the department of trade and commerce was set up in 1892 the agents reported to it, but still gave only part-time services. In 1895 the first full-time commercial agent was appointed at Sydney, Australia, and subsequently others were sent to various cities. In 1907 the name was changed to "Canadian trade commissioners". The primary duty of the commissioners was to further the foreign trade of Canada, but as a matter of convenience they came to visé documents and handle immigration matters. But, while they incidentally did consular work, they could not be called in any sense diplomatic.

In all designs, projected or adopted, of machinery for the conduct of Canadian foreign relations, two immutable facts of Canada's position—her proximity to the United States and her

12 *Ibid.*, 1910-11, 953.
13 Sir Robert Laird Borden, *Canadian Constitutional Studies* (Toronto, 1922), 128.

membership in the British Empire—inevitably played an important part. The former led to exceptions in procedure and the creation of a special organization. The imperial aspect of Canada's position produced a much more complicated theme. As has already been pointed out, the relations of Canada with foreign states were carried on to a considerable extent through British officials. As the dominion developed in internal strength and national consciousness, differences of opinion arose as to the relative parts that should be taken by imperial and Canadian officers, and modifications were made from time to time. But that same growth of Canada also brought up an issue, with far wider implications and much less easily resolved. If this former group of detached colonies had become a single country with great resources and territory; if dependent status was steadily giving way to increasing autonomy; if Canada was, more and more, to determine and conduct her own foreign policy—was then that policy to be distinct from those of other parts of the empire? Such a complete break would generally have been regarded as undesirable and impracticable. But if there was to be a single policy or an integration of separate policies, by what means could either be accomplished? In the United Kingdom there were a complete mechanism, expert personnel, and a long tradition for the carrying out of foreign policy. In Canada and the other dominions none of the three was to be found. In the United Kingdom a realization of growing foreign pressure on the widespread empire and even on the island itself was leading to a desire for support from those parts of the empire which had grown to manhood. The dominions, for their part, saw the problem in the light of their various circumstances.

While there were as many approaches to the question as there were solutions offered for it, there could hardly be disagreement on the leading place taken by defence and foreign policy. The two were, to a considerable extent, interdependent, and any major plan for the one would also involve the other. In other respects, however, defence was a specialized subject, and will therefore be more fully treated in the following chapter. Turning now to foreign policy in general, it is apparent, as Mr. Duncan Hall points out, that common interests can be promoted only by a single authority or by co-operation between governments. In subdivision of the alternatives he finds that the common authority could be that of the British government or of an imperial federal parliament; and that co-operation between governments could be through intermediaries (corresponding to diplomats), or in direct meetings. All four methods were advocated, canvassed, and opposed; and three were in part adopted.[14]

The idea of an imperial parliament made up of representatives from all self-governing parts of the empire had the most obvious advantages and disadvantages; and many designs for such a body were put forward from time to time.[15] The general plan would provide for a parliament meeting in London, having control over matters of common interest, of which the most obvious were foreign policy, defence, and some amount of taxation. An imperial cabinet, responsible to this parliament, would also be required. It being a federal constitution, each component part—including the United Kingdom—would retain its governmental system for local affairs. Through the imperial machinery a single foreign policy could be evolved and carried out, supported by the whole empire. The defence effort could be distributed and integrated, with all the advantages of a single strategy and command. Having a voice in the determination of policy, no part of the empire would be committed to action—in peace or war—without its wish. The whole argument was, to some degree, built on the success of federalism in single countries—particularly in the United States and Canada. The parallel, however, was not exact. It would be a union of parts so divided geographically that attendance at a common parliament would offer difficulties. Furthermore, the federated countries would be so unequally represented—because of the wide differences in population—that the United Kingdom must be the dominant partner. Federalism was not an objective sponsored by Great Britain and opposed by the colonies. In both it found support, and in both severe criticism. Many people in the United Kingdom feared that their freedom of action would be restricted, without compensating additions of strength. While the dominions were far from being in agreement with each other, the effective Canadian opinion was that federation would spell

---

[14] H. D. Hall, *The British Commonwealth of Nations: A Study of its Past and Future Development* (London, 1920), 96.

[15] Of a considerable literature on the subject, S. C. Cheng, *Schemes for the Federation of the British Empire* (New York, 1931) contains the most comprehensive analysis of all the schemes, and of the arguments for and against them.

the loss of autonomy. An acute common danger might conceivably have overridden these objections, but no such overwhelming factor was felt to be present. During the War of 1914 that outside pressure, so effective in the confederation of Canada itself, was heavily applied, and an imperial federation was then once more discussed.

Direct co-operation on matters of common interest between the governments of the empire was realized in some degree through the meetings of the colonial (or later, imperial) conference. Beginning as conversations between the colonial secretary and members of the colonial cabinets, the conferences evolved into more organized and more authoritative discussions between prime ministers. While personal meetings and exchanges of views were undoubtedly helpful, there was a lack of continuity and of provision for implementing decisions by legislative or executive action. The conference remained a body with no continuous life and its members were helpless to do more than report back to their respective cabinets and legislatures. The conference of 1897 passed a resolution in favour of periodic meetings and that of 1902 voted more definitely for conferences every four years. Neither of these steps involved any essential change in the character of the conference, but that question came up in concrete form at the meeting in 1907. In 1905 Alfred Lyttleton, the colonial secretary, suggested in a dispatch to the various British governments that the title "colonial conference" should be changed to "imperial council", and that a commission or secretariat should be added to give continuity. Canada, alone of the dominions, objected to the proposals, Laurier's government seeing the thin end of the wedge of an imperial constitution, commitments, and curtailment of autonomy. The proposal was withdrawn before the conference of 1907, but the idea was discussed,[16] and it became apparent that there was no support for any radical change in the conference. In the end a resolution was adopted, naming the conference "imperial", and making it clear that the discussions were between governments. The resolution also attempted to bridge the four-year gap between conferences by advocating a secretariat and by allowing for subsidiary conferences on pressing or minor matters, to be attended only by those governments immediately interested. Both proposals bore

[16] *Minutes of Proceedings of the Colonial Conference, 1907* (Cd. 3523), 24 ff.

fruit. The secretariat was provided through a reorganization within the colonial office, and the first subsidiary conference was held in 1909 on military and naval defence. Once again, in 1911, a proposal for change was made, Sir Joseph Ward putting before the conference a plan for an imperial parliament, primarily for defence, and also for some aspects of foreign policy and taxation. Even less than the tentative idea of a council did this meet with any support, and the imperial conference remained as one between governments, with no legislative or executive authority.

Returning now to the four alternatives mentioned above, it is apparent that federation was unacceptable, and that direct co-operation between governments was realized in some degree through the imperial conference. Indirect co-operation of governments, by means of intermediaries, made little progress before 1914, since the only existing office which could have been utilized with respect to the relations of Canada, and the United Kingdom was that of high commissioner—an office which had remained non-diplomatic. There remained only the British government as a common authority in foreign relations. In certain fields—fiscal policy and relations with the United States—Canada kept the reins within her own hands. But in spite of adhesion to the doctrine of no commitments—or perhaps because of it—it was left to the British government to shape a foreign policy toward Europe that was technically not that of the dominions but in practice charted the course which they were to follow.

Relations with the United States, as with Great Britain, were of such primary importance as to suggest special governmental machinery. Diplomatic procedure, as has been mentioned, frequently departed from the strictly British channels to become more direct. In addition to this undefined method was a special body, the International Joint Commission, created to deal with boundary waters on the long frontier between Canada and the United States.[17] The commission had characteristics which gave it special significance: it was permanent, judicial, purely Canadian and American, and—while devoted to a special aspect of international relations—

---

[17] For the history of the commission and studies of its organization and operation see C. J. Chacko, *The International Joint Commission between the United States of America and the Dominion of Canada* (New York, 1932); *Papers Relating to the Work of the International Joint Commission* (Ottawa, 1929); and J. M. Callahan, *American Foreign Policy in Canadian Relations* (New York, 1937), 499 ff.

capable of extension to other fields. The origin of the idea of a body to deal with boundary waters is to be found in the International Irrigation Congress, which met at Albuquerque, New Mexico, in 1895. In addition to certain states of the union, Canada and Mexico were also represented. At the instigation of the delegates of the last two countries the congress passed a resolution inviting the United States to appoint an international commission to act with the governments of Canada and Mexico in "adjudicating the conflicting rights which have arisen, or may hereafter arise, on streams of an international character". In 1896 the British ambassador in Washington conveyed to the secretary of state the desire of the Canadian government to co-operate in the proposed plan, but found no readiness for immediate action. It was not until 1902 that the American government appointed its three commissioners, and the Canadian government then further delayed until 1905.

The International Waterways Commission was an experiment, and a fruitful one. Division of waters for irrigation and, increasingly, for electric power inevitably brought controversies and the need for agreement. Over such rivers as the St. Mary and the Milk, rising in Montana, and the Niagara the discussion had already begun when the first commission came into being. Its duties were to investigate and to make reports—with recommendations if required—to both governments. Such limited powers proved to be inadequate, and in the course of its reports the commission proposed that its powers be extended or a new commission established. Exploration and negotiation of a treaty to implement the suggestion went on over the course of three years. Many men had a hand in the process. Of the imperial representatives Bryce in Washington and Grey in Ottawa encouraged and facilitated the progress of the study. For the two governments immediately concerned, Root, Laurier, and Aylesworth were the ministers most closely associated with the work. The detailed negotiations, however, were shouldered by no one of these but by their appointees— George C. Gibbons and George Clinton, respectively Canadian and American representatives on the old Waterways Commission— made the first drafts of the treaty, which were then hammered into shape by Gibbons and Chandler Anderson, the chief counsel for the state department. Negotiations occupied a long period and were not without difficulties. Mr. Root, with thoughts of states' rights and the senate, at first resisted the Canadian proposal for a treaty which should lay down definite principles and give extensive powers to the commission. His alternative plan was for a loose arrangement, with each problem to be considered afresh as it arose. To Sir Wilfrid Laurier, on the other hand, such a commission was not worth creating. When Root finally gave way some further trouble developed by the insistence of the senate in making amendments, and Laurier seems to have become suspicious of their import and to have lost any enthusiasm he may earlier have had.

The process of negotiation, so largely direct between Canadians and Americans, foreshadowed an essential characteristic of the new commission. The Boundary Waters Treaty of 1909 was on its face a treaty between Great Britain and the United States, but its purpose was the creation of the International Joint Commission on which Great Britain had no representatives. By no one was Britain's exclusion thought to be other than a benefit to her. The active part she had earlier played in Canadian-American disputes had been necessary at a time when Canada had reason to fear military aggression, but it visited upon her both additional disputes with a great power with which she wished to be at peace and the criticism of the Canadians dissatisfied with the results obtained. It was hoped now that purely North American questions would be settled more readily by the simpler method of bilateral agreement, uncomplicated either by Anglo-American relations as such or by inter-imperial questions. The treaty, after defining boundary waters, and laying down rules for common use of them, provides for an International Joint Commission to consist of three commissioners on the part of the United States, appointed by the president, and three on the part of the United Kingdom, appointed by the king on the advice of the governor in council. Equal representation from each country raised the question as to whether the commission would divide on national lines and the unfortunate parallel of the Alaska Boundary Commission could be cited as evidence for such a fear. It proved, however, to be the case that most of the decisions were unanimous; and the only division on national lines was on a point of procedure. The powers of the commission were quasi-judicial, executive, arbitral, and for purposes of investigation and recommendation.[18] Both as defined in the treaty and from the cases considered by it, the work of the commission had to do primarily with boundary waters. It was provided, however, in article x of the treaty that "any questions or matters of difference arising between the High Contracting Parties involving the rights, obligations, or interests of the United States or of the Dominion of Canada either in relation to each other or to their respective inhabitants" might be referred to it, with the consent of the American senate and the governor in council, for investigation and recommendation. While other developments rendered this article less necessary in later years, it revealed both the temper of the agreement and the wide results that were expected to follow it.

The governmental machinery for the conduct of Canadian foreign relations was evolved over a period of years as the dominion grew in strength and confidence, partly by a process of trial and error, and as events showed the anachronisms in what already existed. It was natural, if unfortunate, that organization followed rather than preceded the issues with which it would be concerned: natural, because it was only the pressure of particular cases that proved the need for change; unfortunate, because in some cases international disputes might have been more easily settled if the new mechanism had already existed. The importance of the time-lag varied. The International Waterways Commission and the International Joint Commission, for example, were set up soon enough to handle the major cases. The Alaska boundary dispute, on the other hand, was settled by an *ad hoc* tribunal under circumstances which aroused the maximum of bitterness in Canada toward both the United States and the United Kingdom.

III

The determination of foreign policy for Canada depended in the main on three factors: geographical position, trade interests, and imperial connection—the three operating singly or in any combination. Canadian interest or activity spread over a wide area abroad, varying in intensity from one region to another.

[18] R. A. MacKay, "The International Joint Commission between the United States and Canada" (*Papers Relating to the Work of the International Joint Commission*, Ottawa, 1929).

In the Americas the dominating political entity was the United States, which tended to overshadow the foreign relations of Canada as of the other countries of the western hemisphere. But, while they had always to keep in mind the policies of the United States, Canadians were not unmindful of the lesser powers. Nearest at hand, in a position to control the approach to the St. Lawrence, was Newfoundland. That oldest colony had rejected federation with the other provinces in the original discussions, but there was reason to believe that, like Prince Edward Island and British Columbia, it might later become a part of the dominion. The atmosphere of confederation was not soon dissipated, and the final boundaries of Canada were still uncertain. For several years there was talk of union, both in the island and in Canada. For the latter the advantages were many. In the defence of Canada Newfoundland could not be ignored, but that consideration was given less attention in the days when the supremacy of the British navy was unquestioned. The place of Newfoundland in a shorter sea route to Europe was at times stressed; but the principal arguments were possibilities of extended trade, and—above all—the automatic settlement of the disputes over fisheries. Conferences between the two governments broke down on the refusal of Canada to take over the island's debt, but the Canadian government continued to express its general willingness for union, and the question was still an open one in 1914.

The acquisition of Newfoundland was generally thought to be desirable but not pressing. The boundaries of the dominion in the north were for a time brought into prominence by the fear that American zeal for the larger Alaska would be a prelude to general expansion northward. Fears were expressed, in parliament and the press, that American fishing in Hudson Bay might lead to a denial of complete sovereignty there. In the Canadian senate Paschal Poirier advocated a Canadian expedition to the pole, union with Newfoundland, and the acquisition of Greenland from Denmark. A. B. Aylesworth again drew attention to Labrador and Greenland, and the Halifax *Chronicle* editorially sponsored a Canadian "Monroe doctrine". This last was widely discussed by other newspapers, and was intended to embrace the islands of St. Pierre and Miquelon, should the United States attempt to purchase them from France, as it was feared she might do.[19] With the removal of the danger of this new stage of American expansionism (if it had ever been a real danger) the idea of a competitive Monroe doctrine fell into discard.

In the south, as well as in the east and north, was territory that was often spoken of as a possible addition to Canada. The dominion carried on a close trade connection with the British West Indies, built up in previous decades by Nova Scotia. Trade between these British colonies was never as great as it was felt it should be between two complementary economies, and Canadians had made many attempts to increase it, but without great success. Both in Canada and the West Indies it was primarily the hope of extended trade that led to the suggestions of political union. In 1905 isolated proposals changed to more general consideration. Canadian newspapers were divided in their views—some cautiously supporting union and others pointing to the problems that would arise from the racial composition and political immaturity of the islands. The Maritime Provinces Board of Trade and the Canadian Manufacturers' Association both went on record in favour of union, and individuals in various parts of Canada were found as advocates.[20] On sober second thought, however, Canadians decided that it was a step they were not yet ready to take, either at that time, or even years later in the full glow of nationalist consciousness. The Caribbean marked the southern boundary of the Canadian sphere of active interest in the Americas. With the republics of South America even trade relations were slight. Politically the republics were remote—even a little mysterious. Only once did a South American question impinge on Canada, and that only because of its effect on Anglo-American relations.

Repeated refusals of the government of Venezuela to respect the interests of foreigners led two of the powers mainly concerned, Great Britain and Germany, to apply pressure by means of a naval blockade in 1902. There is no reason to believe that Canadians saw that this action had any bearing on the dominion, but it soon proved to have an important indirect one. The United States, sensitive to any European intervention in South America, was particularly disturbed by it when taking place close to the

[19] *Canadian Annual Review*, 1903, 388-9.
[20] *Ibid.*, 1905, 487 ff.

proposed canal in the isthmus, and strain developed in the relations of the two European powers with the United States. Though desiring to avoid a further break with Germany, already opened by the failure of the alliance negotiations, the British government was even less willing to depart from its fixed principle of American friendship, and in 1903 consented to the American proposal of submission of the Venezuela dispute to the Hague tribunal. It was during the last months of the blockade, and when Britain was making its decision, that the arrangements for the submission of the Alaska boundary dispute to an international tribunal were finally made. The dispute was an old one. The boundary laid down in the treaty of 1825 between Russia and Great Britain antedated any accurate geographical knowledge of the region, and created problems common to all North American boundary questions. By 1867, when Alaska was purchased by the United States, the population of British Columbia was fully conscious of a northern development based on discoveries of gold, and saw in the southern extension of Alaska a barrier against the necessary access from the hinterland to the sea. After the entrance of British Columbia into the federation its legislature and government constantly called the attention of Ottawa to the need for defining the boundary, and the Canadian government in turn had negotiations initiated through British diplomatic channels. All attempts to reach agreement on the machinery for handling the dispute had, however, failed up to the end of the century. In a conference between United States and Canadian representatives at Washington in February 1892 the Canadians proposed that the dispute be submitted to "some impartial authority"; and that following an award a committee of experts be asked to report on the best way of delimiting the boundary.[21] The Joint High Commission of 1898-9, amongst other Canadian-American questions, considered that of Alaska, and the Canadian proposal for a tribunal of three narrowly failed of acceptance. The counter-proposal, for a tribunal of six—half British and half American—was unacceptable to Canada, and a British compromise plan of 1902, for the commission of six to include two neutral members, was rejected in Washington. Such was the position when Laurier went to the colonial conference of 1902, having promised his

21 *Canada, Sessional Papers*, 1892, no. 37.

colleagues not to yield to any English proposition for yielding to the American proposal. On his return, however, he confessed that he had agreed to such a commission, appointed by the two parties to the dispute. "Pressed for details he refused to go beyond the statement that he had no option but to yield the point".[22]

It remained, then, only to set the machinery in motion. In January 1903 a treaty was signed by the British ambassador and the American secretary of state, providing for a tribunal of "six impartial jurists of repute, who shall consider judicially the questions submitted to them", which plan was reluctantly accepted by the Canadian government. In February the bad news reached Ottawa that Roosevelt had appointed Elihu Root, the secretary of state for war, Senator Lodge, and Senator Turner. The Canadian government quite properly objected that none of these was an impartial jurist: the first being a member of the government that was a party to the dispute, and the other two having declared themselves against the Canadian case. It was, they complained, a violation of the treaty. On February 27 word came from London that the selection of American members was as much a surprise there as in Ottawa; that they felt it practically impossible to press for new appointments; were most unwilling to drop the whole negotiation; and could only suggest British members "who will meet the altered circumstances of the case". By the time the governor general sent a reply to this (March 6) the treaty had already been ratified (March 3), and, as the Canadian government pointed out, further discussion was precluded. They would not, however, consider the suggestion of matching the American representatives.[23] The British members, as appointed, were Lord Alverstone, chief justice of England, Sir Louis Jetté, lieutenant-governor of Quebec and formerly a judge of the superior court of Quebec, and A. B. Aylesworth, a Canadian lawyer. While the Canadian government then lived up to the letter and spirit of a treaty of which they had never approved, from the first they had good reason to suspect the good faith of the American government and the diplomatic support of the British.

Full study has been made of the arguments adduced by both sides, of the positions taken by the three governments concerned,

[22] J. W. Dafoe, *Clifford Sifton in Relation to His Times* (Toronto, 1931), 217.
[23] *Canada, Sessional Papers*, 1904, no. 46 A.

and in so far as it can be done—of the conversations that went on behind the scenes.[24] There is little disagreement on the main points, though the authorities differ as to the relative strength of the Canadian and American cases. On the whole it seems clear that the latter was definitely a stronger one; and, while there was a Canadian case, and it was argued by counsel of great ability, it would have been surprising if it had been upheld in any court. Unfortunately the tribunal of 1903 never lived up to the judicial principles laid down for it. Theodore Roosevelt as much as told the American members that they could find only one way; and, indeed, they seem to have needed no spur to run as partisans. No criticism has been made of either the appointment or actions of the Canadian members; yet they do seem to have been infected by the non-judicial atmosphere. Clifford Sifton, the British agent for the settlement, complained after his return that "Lord Alverstone did not stand by the Canadian commissioners".[25] Perhaps this was no more than an unfortunate phrase; yet it is hard to conceive of the Canadian commissioners finding in favour of the American case. The award, which substantially accepted the American claims, was signed by the three Americans and Alverstone. Jetté and Aylesworth refused to sign the award, and each voluntarily wrote an opinion with reasons for that refusal.[26] Both differed on several points from the majority decision. Aylesworth finished his statement with the remark that "the course the majority of this tribunal has decided to take in regard to the islands at the entrance of Portland channel is, in my humble judgment, so opposed to the plain requirements of justice, and so absolutely irreconcilable with any disposition of that branch of the case upon principles of a judicial character, that I respectfully decline to affix my signature to their award". Jetté concluded by saying that he "found it impossible . . . to concur in this arbitrary determination of a line which, although it does not concede all the territory they

---

[24] See, for example, H. L. Keenleyside, *Canada and the United States: Some Aspects of the History of the Republic and the Dominion* (New York, 1929), 210 ff.; Callahan, *American Foreign Policy in Canadian Relations,* chap. xix; L. M. Gelber, *The Rise of Anglo-American Friendship* (London and Toronto, 1938), chap. vii; Dafoe, *Clifford Sifton,* chap. viii; P. C. Jessup, *Elihu Root* (2 vols., New York, 1938), II, chap xix; O. D. Skelton, *Life and Letters of Sir Wilfrid Laurier* (2 vols., Toronto, 1921), II, 134 ff.

[25] Quoted in Dafoe, *Clifford Sifton,* 236.

[26] Printed, with the award, in *Canada, Sessional Papers,* 1904, no. 46 A.

claimed to the United States, nevertheless deprives Canada of the greater part of that to which she was entitled".

Under no circumstances would it have been easy for a tribunal consisting of three nationals from each party to the dispute to decide entirely on judicial principles. The character of the American appointments finally removed any possibility of such procedure, leaving the only alternatives as a deadlock or a diplomatic compromise. Canadians generally, would have accepted the former in a choice of evils, but British opinion favoured the latter. It seems evident that Alverstone, perhaps under pressure from his government, doubled the rôles of diplomat and judge in the general interest of Anglo-American understanding. On their return to Canada the two Canadian commissioners maintained a dignified restraint in comments on the award, refusing to achieve a cheap popularity by capitalizing on what was undoubtedly a very general resentment. A number of Canadians urged moderation, or supported the award as an unpleasant but necessary one; but on the whole opinion—especially in the press—was more or less violently critical.[27] It was taken for granted that the Canadian case was unassailable, and the general complaint was that Alverstone had submitted to the government's desire for peace at any price: the price being, as usual, the sacrifice of Canada. The tradition of the weakness of British diplomacy on behalf of Canada was already deep-rooted. Though not without some reason to support it, the argument was less often based on a study of the evidence than on sentiment and a naive assumption that the Canadian case was always right, and that right would always prevail.

Though not a few Canadians had had experience of diplomacy, they had done little to apprise the public of the real character and place of that art. Since the days of the Washington commission of 1871 Canadians generally had gained little appreciation of diplomacy as a process of bargaining, in which compromise and sanctions played a large part. The Alaska "panhandle" was classed with the jutting north of Maine. Neither of the two cases, as such, was studied seriously; nor could the average Canadian appreciate that firmness in pressing even a good case must be tempered by gauging the resultant friction. In 1903 there was reason to believe that Roosevelt's chauvinism was not mere acting,

[27] Canadian Annual Review, 1903, 365 ff.

and that it touched a highly responsive chord in the country. To talk of war was perhaps extreme; but there was a state short of war that would have been as unwelcome to Canada as to England. Given the circumstances, the best that could be hoped from the Alaska tribunal was a deadlock. To the British government this spelled a set-back to the *entente* policy pursued in Venezuela. To Canada it could bring no good; Alaska would still be a bone of contention, with a possible (though improbable) later settlement more in favour of the dominion. Bad relations between England and the United States would bedevil North American politics as well. If, however, Canada was dissatisfied with the results of British diplomacy, the only logical course was to conduct her own affairs directly—supplying the means and accepting the responsibility. It was a course which had more than once been proposed in the past, but never with the authority which Laurier now gave to it in the house of commons.

I have often regretted . . . that we have not in our own hands the treaty-making power which would enable us to dispose of our own affairs. But in this matter we are dealing with a position that was forced on us—we have not the treaty-making power. . . . I am sorry not only that we have not the treaty-making power, but that we are not in such an independent position that it is in my power to place before parliament the whole of the correspondence as it passed between the Canadian government and the British government. But we shall have that correspondence and it will be placed before parliament at the next session,—the whole of it, no matter what protest may come from abroad. . . . But we have no such power. Our hands are tied to a large extent, owing to the fact of our connection—which has its benefits, but which also has its disadvantages—the fact of our connection with the mother country making us not free agents and obliging us to deal with questions affecting ourselves through the instrumentality of British ambassadors. . . . The difficulty as I conceive it to be, is that so long as Canada remains a dependency of the British crown the present powers that we have are not sufficient for the maintenance of our rights. It is important that we should ask the British parliament for more extensive powers so that if ever we have to deal with matters of a similar nature again, we shall deal with them in our own way, in our own fashion, according to the best light that we have.[28]

[28] Quoted in Skelton, *Life and Letters of Laurier*, II, 155.

If this was a statement of policy it was one that was not implemented. In all probability Laurier, smarting under a sense of
injustice, spoke more strongly than he otherwise would have done.
Canada was already on the road to assume in greater degree the
conduct of her own affairs, but it needed more than the authority
of the British parliament to make the change. After the first
burst of indignation was over, it was questionable whether the
public would have welcomed such a radical departure in one step.
Moreover, while Canadians had in the past shown skill in diplomacy, there were no civil servants trained in, or even assigned
to, that special field; and it is significant that W. Sanford Evans
proposed that there should be a department of external affairs.[29]
In the establishment of that department in 1909, of the International Joint Commission in the same year, the procedure over
the French treaties in 1907 and 1909, and over the reciprocity
agreement in 1911 it may be argued that the Alaska affair played
a part; but it is equally probable that these changes would have
occurred in any case.

No one of the three countries derived much advantage from
the Alaska award. To the United States fell a strip of territory
barring the way to decaying mines in an undeveloped wilderness.
Great Britain secured some degree of reconciliation with the
United States at the cost of temporary but real discontent in
Canada. Canadian fears of American expansionism were once
more revived. The whole affair was a tempest in a teapot: but
of such stuff are international relations sometimes made.

The political relations of Canada outside the American continent were, in the period before 1914, almost entirely indirect:
that is to say, arising out of British, rather than Canadian, foreign
policy. But what is true of political policy does not so generally
apply to interests. Commercial advantages and selective immigration depended in part on satisfactory political relations with
foreign states. More basic still was the aim to preserve for the
empire as a whole a position in the world sufficiently powerful
that its independence could not be seriously endangered, and—
coming closer to home—that Canada could not be invaded. Thus
the balance of power affected Canada like other countries. But
unlike other countries with a small population she was drawn

[29] *Canadian Annual Review*, 1903, 366.

into these larger political issues not only on her own continent, but east and west as well. In the Americas there was no balance of power, and presumably never would be one. The dominance of the United States, however, was softened by a peaceful (if not always conciliatory) outlook. In the far east and in Europe the rivalry of the great powers, as they appeared after 1871, was assuming a pattern and a severity that was fast becoming the leading political fact of the period.

The power of Japan was first demonstrated in the Sino-Japanese war of 1894. For the British Empire the rise of a new great power in the Pacific had great implications. The United Kingdom had been the pioneer in opening China to trade, and was making heavy investments in railways, financial organizations, and commerce. Australia and New Zealand could not but be affected by the expanding power of Japan, and India too was within the Pacific sphere. For Canada the immediate pressure of the far east arose from Asiatic immigration, the attempts to limit which created a delicate political problem.[30] Less weight was placed on trade with the countries of the far east until the early twentieth century. When Great Britain made a commercial treaty with Japan in 1894 Canada was unwilling to accede to it unless she could retain the right to exclude both labourers and artisans; and even when the British ambassador had secured agreement to such a provision, the Canadian government delayed becoming a party to the treaty until 1906, by which time trade had assumed proportions sufficient to balance anti-Asiatic sentiment. While the policy of virtual exclusion maintained by the dominions did not help neither did it seriously hinder the good relations of Japan and the United Kingdom as written into commercial and political treaties. On the other hand the friction that might have resulted from the immigration difficulty was softened by the satisfaction felt in Tokyo over the Anglo-Japanese alliance. The first alliance, of 1902, was sought by Japan, and served her well in her war with Russia. The second treaty, in 1905, carried further obligations for both signatories, and was regarded as mutually advantageous. Canadians had no reason to criticize an alliance which paved the way to the voluntary limitation of Japanese immigration through the gentlemen's agreement and strengthened the defensive position

[30] See above, 208-10.

of the empire as a whole. The press of the United States welcomed the alliance of 1902 as a means of maintaining the open door.[31] When the treaty of 1905 was announced it could be said that "the Canadian press almost universally approves the arrangement and congratulates Lord Lansdowne upon his successful diplomacy".[32] During the imperial conference of 1911 the dominion representatives had, for the first time, an opportunity of discussing foreign policy—not in the conference itself, but in secret meetings of the committee of imperial defence. There Sir Edward Grey made a long statement of different aspects of British policy.[33] The Anglo-Japanese alliance, he said, had been most satisfactory and he hoped it would be renewed. Before doing so, however, it was necessary to reconcile it with British policy toward the United States. If the United States became involved in a war with Japan, Britain would be obligated to assist her ally. To avoid this he had proposed to the Japanese government that a clause should be included removing the obligation of either signatory from going to war with a power with which it had a general arbitration treaty. Written into the alliance, a clause (iv) to that effect saved England from difficulties with the United States by virtue of the new arbitration treaty. By this ingenious device Grey also removed a cause of worry to Canadian statesmen. Unfortunately the discussions following Grey's statement to the committee have not been published, but on the same day Grey was able to write to the British embassy at Tokyo that the dominion representatives had agreed cordially to the alliance.[34] There is every reason to suppose that, as far as Canada was concerned, this was the case. Leaving Anglo-American relations friendly, and easing the strain on Canadian-Japanese migration arrangements, the alliance still strengthened the position of the British Empire in the far east, and consequently in the world as a whole.

The alliance with Japan not only strengthened the position of Great Britain in the far east, but also relieved her of the necessity of maintaining a large naval force there, making it possible to divert ships to European waters. It was in the North

[31] C.-F. Chang, *The Anglo-Japanese Alliance* (Baltimore, 1931), 86.
[32] *Canadian Annual Review*, 1905, 421.
[33] G. P. Gooch and Harold Temperley (eds.), *British Documents on the Origins of the War, 1898-1914* (11 vols., London, 1927-1938), VI, 789.
[34] *Ibid.*, VI, 525.

Sea that they were now urgently needed. When the *Round Table,* a quarterly devoted to the affairs of the British Empire, was first published in 1910, the opening words were these: "The central fact in the international situation to-day is the antagonism between England and Germany". The events of the next four years more than justified the assertion. Canada had no part in foreign policy in Europe in the ten years before 1914: the ententes with France and Russia, the permission to the general staffs to conduct conversations on military and naval co-operation, and the attempts to prevent war in the Balkans. Nor did the Canadian government give advice in, or share responsibility for, British policy in the last hectic days from the murder of the Archduke Franz Ferdinand to the outbreak of general hostilities. It was not that Canada was deliberately excluded from British councils: it is probable that the British government would have welcomed consultation. But consultation, as successive Canadian governments had seen, involved responsibility; and they preferred to forgo the one in order to avoid the other. That they were none the less committed to the results of British policy was the anomaly of the position and the price they paid.

From the turn of the century, with the failure of Anglo-German negotiations for an alliance, the generally unfriendly attitude of Europe toward the war in South Africa, and the beginning of German naval construction on a large scale, the urgency and the burden of defence against a growing danger forced military and naval planning into the forefront of international relations. If no scheme was agreed on—though many were suggested—for a foreign policy drawn up and underwritten by all the self-governing parts of the empire, the problem of defence became, more and more, one for the dominions as well as the United Kingdom. Could Canada defend her own territory? Could she, and would she, share in a common effort to guard against the threat of German aggression?

CHAPTER XI

DEFENCE

THE word "defence", widely enough interpreted in all countries, has in Canada been stretched beyond all reasonable bounds. It is, perhaps, not without significance that this should be so: that no such terms as "war office" or "admiralty" should be current where frontiers are known as "boundaries", where the regular army has never been called by that name, where war, in fact, has never been visualized except as resistance to aggression. It is healthy that this should have been so, and, on the whole, consistent with the outlook and interests of the Canadian people. Yet Canada is not without military history and achievements; and, as in other states, the threat of force, even when not carried into effect, has played its part in her foreign relationships. It will be well, therefore, first to discover what is meant or implied in Canada by the word defence. Basically it has stood for the maintenance of territory already possessed, and with that purpose few Canadians have disagreed. Less obviously it has meant the defence of interests, such as trade, fisheries, or rights of citizens abroad. It has had a very real meaning as the defence of Canada's general political position in the world: protection against a serious loss of power or against a hostile alliance. It is tempting, but misleading, to draw an absolute distinction between defence of Canadian soil and imperial defence, for imperial defence itself has not one but several aspects. In some cases it has touched Canada directly. Even in the period after the withdrawal of the imperial garrisons the naval bases at Halifax and Esquimalt played a dual rôle: as part of the British naval system and as guards on the Canadian coasts. Other points, such as Newfoundland and the West Indies, might be regarded in part as indirect or outpost defences of Canada. Thirdly there has been the defence of the empire as a political organization of which Canada formed part and in whose strength she had a direct stake. For this the leading example would be the War of 1914. Finally came Canada's place in British wars whose outcome was neither a direct nor an indirect threat to Canada. For participation in these a much less obvious case could be made out, but events—such as the Sudan expeditions—proved that there was a case and that it had supporters.

Accepting the word defence, with its manifold meanings, it remains to examine in more detail the purposes for which military and naval power would be maintained, the local conditions to which they were related, their organization, and their use. Peace, consolidation, and economy in armament were naturally the desiderata of a country whose area was vast, population small, and political unity recent. A saturated power has no zeal for territorial expansion, but even the broad acres of the dominion left something to be desired. The jutting north of Maine was an old grievance with practical disadvantages that were real but not insuperable. Canadians would agree that they had been hardly treated, but had no idea of attempted revision by a show or use of force. Newfoundland would be a welcome addition to the federation, but that was a financial rather than a military problem. In the Arctic the claims of Canada might be disputed, but the major territorial dispute was over the boundary of Alaska. Here it was that Canadians, without fully realizing it, experienced a clear case of the delicate relation between diplomacy and armed force. Some Americans (including the president) hardly veiled their determination to resist any infringement of their rights, as they saw them. The success of diplomacy is explained not a little by the skill of the diplomat; but it is no accident that states capable of exercising strong military or naval force—and willing in the last resort to do so—have a card to play in international negotiations that no mere dexterity will take.

The connection between foreign policy and military policy may, under the happiest conditions, be made remote, but in no case can it be abolished. Armed forces have no meaning (leaving aside their police rôle) except in relation to possible but defined use against other states. It is the business of soldiers to fight when called upon to do so in the pursuance of, or as a result of, the foreign policy of the civil government. The first discussion of foreign policy between the representatives of the governments of the United Kingdom and the dominions was in the committee of imperial defence in 1911. The foreign secretary, Sir Edward

Grey, was invited by Mr. Asquith to give an exposition of the international situation, and began by talking of the aspect of defence that was then most to the fore. "The starting point", he said, ". . . of the consultation which we are now going to have on Foreign Policy, and the foreign situation, is really the creation of growing strength of separate fleets and forces in the Dominions. . . . It is possible to have separate fleets in a united Empire, but it is not possible to have separate Fleets in a united Empire without having a common Foreign Policy which shall determine the action of the different forces maintained in different parts of the Empire. . . ."[1] The nature and extent of armed forces are dictated in part by the capacity of a state to provide them and in part by the use for which they may be required. Military history is, to some extent, a theme in itself: in technical organization and the course of warfare. For the rest it is dependent on political policies and events. To say that a country wants peace may be the truth but not the whole truth. The real objective is peace on at least reasonably satisfactory terms. "Peace at any price" is almost a meaningless phrase, for there comes a point where national pride and national interest will demand the use of armed force, perhaps as the answer to the aggression of another state.

Military preparation in Canada in the generation before 1914 was governed by two sets of factors: domestic interests and external pressure. The period was one of rapid economic development, with industrial expansion in the central provinces and the peaceful conquest of the western. Financial and human resources were almost wholly absorbed in great railway schemes to make possible the settlement of the prairies and the exploitation of its agricultural land. To secure immigrants and retain them in the dominion, to build and finance transcontinental railways, and to promote the foreign trade which was a necessary corollary of the other two—these were the subjects before parliament and public. It is true that foreign trade in itself widened Canadians' outlook beyond their own boundaries, but for many years there was a peaceful world whose oceans were reassuringly patrolled by the ships of the British navy.

[1] G. P. Gooch and Harold Temperley (eds.), *British Documents on the Origins of the War, 1898-1914* (11 vols., London, 1927-1938), VI, 781.

External pressure might be applied by another American power or from beyond the coasts of the continent. From her immediate neighbours Canada had little reason to fear aggression. Relations with Newfoundland were not without friction. The fishery dispute trailed on for years, and there was an unsettled boundary between Quebec and Labrador. It would, however, have been absurd to think of a British dominion as a potential enemy. Newfoundland could be of military significance to Canada only if it were to come under the control of a foreign power—an eventuality of which there appeared to be no prospect. The only other land frontier marched with that of the United States, on the south and the north-west. Here, in one respect, the position was reversed: Canada being the weak power and its neighbour the strong. There were not lacking grounds for controversy—fisheries again, and boundary disputes—but Canadians were more and more assuming that war, or even serious friction, with the United States could be left out of account. It was true that in the United States there was loose talk of annexation as late as 1911, but it was not taken as a threat. After the settlement at Washington in 1871, unpopular as that may have been at the time in Canada, the old fear of American aggression, of manifest destiny, and of forced annexation steadily dissipated. While relations with the country against which Canada had erected defences for nearly two centuries at last became fixed and pacific, clouds came up from other directions. To England Russia was the bogey in the nineteenth century, and to Canada too in the seventies and eighties. At times attack on either coast was feared from the amorphous state which straddled the continents, and whose military strength was so consistently overrated. Thanks to her alliance with Great Britain in 1902 and to the settlement of the immigration question, Japan's growing power was not in these years regarded as involving any threat to the Pacific coast of Canada. The new danger, and the one which more and more dominated all planning for defence, lay in Germany's frank struggle for world power, and the appearance, for the first time in a century, of a fleet intended to challenge the supremacy of the British navy.

In retrospect there can be seen a change, not fully realized at the time, of the whole political position on which the defence policy of Canada was built. For decades before confederation and through the early years of the dominion defence for Canadians had meant protection against the United States. To aid them in this task they looked to Great Britain, whose great navy, professional army, and amassed wealth might redress the balance of the weak against the strong. In moments of England's troubles— the Crimean War or the Indian Mutiny—there were many volunteers in British North America ready to lend their swords in evidence of loyalty and common feeling. It was not, however, because England was weak or her national strength at stake that these men came forward. In the days of the American Civil War and immediately following it the withdrawal of the imperial troops from Canada was regretted—even resented. The weak still appealed to the strong for aid. In less than twenty years came the threat to the British position in Africa, ominous unpopularity throughout Europe, and the naval policy of Tirpitz and the Kaiser. Now Canada, with a new sense of security on her own borders, was forced for the first time to consider seriously the defence of the empire of which she was a part. It was no longer a question of gestures by individuals; it was a problem of national policy. The transition from the old balance to the new occupied some years; and the difficulty in understanding a change so close at hand was magnified by confusion of issues. To the opponents of imperial federation in all its forms the cry of the empire in danger smacked of a plot to lure the unwary into a political framework designed not for co-operation but dominance. Even to those not persuaded by either faith it was apparent that projects for imperial defence could never be wholly divorced from some type of agreement on foreign policy without which military or naval plans would be either meaningless or dangerous.

If Canadian defence policy be judged to have been anachronistic and its results to have been to some extent inadequate and inefficient, the governments immediately responsible must receive a measure of sympathy. Against what danger must they guard? Happily against no neighbours. Could they believe the old arguments of the federationists? Could the military burden on such a wealthy country as England be taken seriously in comparison to the burden on Canada of opening a pioneer country? It is not wholly surprising that the governments of these years steered by the star of immediate domestic needs, avoiding as best they could the rocks of provincial and racial cleavages. Defence policy tended to be based on compromise, with inevitable technical drawbacks—and some surprisingly effective results.

Canadian defence forces may be divided into military and naval. In both there were important links with the imperial arms; but the projects for an imperial defence organization were separate from the uniformity of drill, exchange of officers, and other convenient devices which were not intended to create a united force.

II

Fear of American aggression during and after the Civil War stimulated a new interest in the defence forces and was an important element in the confederation movement. But such zeal as was temporarily shown for expansion and improvement of the forces passed with the removal of the immediate danger. Little was left of the plans and talk of those years. The fortification scheme was dropped altogether and the money was spent on the Pacific railway. The regular army—or "permanent force"—had been started in 1871, and while it remained small, the principle soon became firmly established. The Royal Military College was opened at Kingston in 1876 and provided a mixed academic and military training of a high standard. Everything, however, seemed to combine against any forward movement in the militia. The North-West Rebellion of 1885 had no lasting effects. The financial depression which began in the late seventies, the expenditure on public works (especially railways), and peaceful relations with the United States all discouraged militia reform. Even the removal of the imperial troops from all points except the naval bases failed to encourage military preparations. It was what an historian of the militia has called "the dead period".[2] Expenditure was cut almost in half; the numbers of the active militia in training fell by a third; and the enthusiasm of officers and men waned.

The Venezuela scare of 1895 and more especially the experience of the South African War sounded a note of necessity that brought new life to the militia. Already there had been some slight signs of progress. The permanent force was reorganized and enlarged;

2 C. F. Hamilton, "The Canadian Militia: The Dead Period" (*Canadian Defence Quarterly*, VII, 1929-30).

the obsolete Snider rifles were partially replaced; government expenditure was modestly increased; and public interest somewhat
revived.[3] It was, however, after the South African War that the
main changes occurred. There were not lacking—and never had
been lacking—critics of the militia system: officers of the militia
itself, Canadian civilians, and the English officers appointed in
command in Canada pointed at times to weaknesses. The paper
strength of the militia was said to be misleading; the period of
training too short; equipment to be obsolete, incomplete, and
insufficient in quantity; the pay of both permanent and non-
permanent militia too small. No one questioned the quality of
the personnel, or their efforts to make the best of the situation,
but the handicaps were said to be too great. On the other hand,
the opposition to reform was influenced not only by parsimony
but by a disbelief in the necessity of military preparations on a
large scale. A comment in the Montreal *Herald* in 1902 on Lord
Dundonald's proposals for change is not untypical:

> Dundonald apparently shares a delusion dear to Hutton. He seems
> to think the people of Canada are concerned about being in readiness
> for war, or that if they are not they are to blame and should be
> stirred up. Any man who thinks that way—and all European soldiers
> do—fails to grasp the essential distinction between Europe and North
> America. With Europe war is a condition. With us it is a theory.[4]

The point of the *Herald's* attack was perhaps sharpened by
resentment against the prevailing rule under which the officer
commanding the Canadian militia was appointed from the British
regular army. It would be doing less than justice to the individuals
who held the position not to record that they made a valuable
contribution to the Canadian militia. They were able to bring
to the work training and experience wider than a Canadian officer
could obtain, and undoubtedly many of their criticisms were valid
and their recommendations wise. Many, indeed, of the improvements in the militia were due to one or other of these officers.
It was an arrangement, however, which was almost bound to lead
to trouble sooner or later. With few exceptions, the commanding
officers seem to have established good relations with the Canadian

[3] Hamilton, "The Canadian Militia: The Beginning of Reform" (*Canadian
Defence Quarterly*, VII, 1929-30).
[4] Quoted in *Canadian Annual Review*, 1902, 193.

officers, who welcomed their experience and were as anxious as they for reform. But it was not easy for non-Canadians to continue to hold the chief position in the Canadian militia, in a period in which Canadian autonomy and national feeling were growing, without arousing opposition. Especially was this true when the visiting commanders found it necessary to make criticisms publicly. The practical difficulty that arose was in the relations between the commanding officers and the ministers of militia. The division of powers was ill-defined, and each accused the other of usurping authority. General Hutton had a series of disagreements with the minister of militia, F. W. (later Sir Frederick) Borden. When Hutton returned to England in 1900 to take part in the South African War the question was bluntly asked in the Canadian house of commons if he had been dismissed because of friction with the government.[5] To this Laurier replied coldly that the matter was better not discussed, but nevertheless a debate ensued. Most of the members who spoke defended Hutton, but the point was made, by Borden and others, that it might be necessary in the future to appoint Canadians. In the course of his remarks Borden also denied that there had ever been improper political influence on the militia. That there had been such influence was a current charge, and one that arose in acute form during the period in which Lord Dundonald was commanding officer. Dundonald came to Canada in 1902 knowing something of the difficulties that had arisen and having been warned that he might well meet trouble. He was a soldier of considerable experience, both in peace and war, and proved himself to be sincerely anxious for the best interests of the Canadian militia. On his many tours of inspection he found much to criticize in the organization, equipment, and training of the militia, and in a number of public utterances was not slow in pointing to weaknesses which he believed to exist and changes which he thought should be made. From the first he claimed that his efforts were impeded by political interference.[6] A part of his report for 1902 was not presented to parliament, and in 1904 arose what has become known as "the Dundonald incident". The rights and wrongs of the affair may still be debated. To Dundonald it was a case of a minister insisting on an appointment in the army for party reasons; to the govern-

---

[5] Canada, House of Commons Debates, 1900, 323.
[6] The Earl of Dundonald, My Army Life (London, 1926).

ment it was an attempt to overrule its supreme authority.[7] Dundonald was dismissed; but before he left Canada made public his views, which, while bringing him some applause and sympathy, did nothing to ease what had become an intolerable situation.

Out of the tenure of the chief command by English officers came a paradoxical combination of results: the adoption of many of the reforms which they had urged, and the decision against similar appointments in the future. Both Hutton and Dundonald had urged the development of a self-contained militia in place of what the former described as "a collection of military units without cohesion, without staff, and without those military departments by which an army is moved, fed, or ministered to in sickness". The move toward an army complete in all branches began in Hutton's day and continued after it as a principal line of development.[8] Both results were found in the Militia Act of 1904 (4 Edw. VII, c. 23), the most important of such acts since confederation. Indeed, as Borden pointed out in introducing the bill into the commons, the existing militia law was practically the same as that before confederation.[9] The new régime, as defined by the act or as brought into effect under its permissive clauses, showed traces of national consciousness. The former rule under which imperial officers in the Canadian militia had precedence over Canadians of equal rank was abolished; and the imperial officer in command at Halifax was no longer automatically to take charge of the militia at the outbreak of war. More important than either of these was the provision that any qualified officer in the British Empire was to be eligible for the chief command, and not only an English officer as formerly. This provision was the answer to the previous friction between governments and general officers commanding, and was supplemented by a clause enabling a militia council to be set up. The council was said to be following the precedent recently established in England, where the army council, following the recommendations of the Esher Commission, had the secretary of state for war as chairman, with the military members as advisers.

[7] For Dundonald's case see *My Army Life,* chap. xxvi; for the government's see O. D. Skelton, *Life and Letters of Sir Wilfrid Laurier* (2 vols., Toronto, 1921), II, 196.

[8] For a summary of this process see C. P. Stacey, *The Military Problems of Canada: A Survey of Defence Policies and Strategic Conditions Past and Present* (Toronto, 1940), appendix B.

[9] *Canada, House of Commons Debates,* 1904, 205 ff.

Henceforward the minister of militia became the sole centre of authority, with the chief of the general staff as the senior officer. There was no longer any appointment comparable to that of the former commanders in chief. But the effect in practice, writes Colonel Hamilton, was that "the minister saw more of the technical men, the soldiers, and heard their case presented; and the influence of the soldiers, and more especially of the senior soldier, steadily grew. The result of a step which ostensibly lowered the footing of the soldier was to increase his influence in the working of the Department."[10] The act also provided that the permanent force might be raised from one to two thousand; that the period of annual training for the non-permanent force might be extended to thirty days; and that the pay of both branches of the militia be increased. In the years following 1904 expenditure on the militia was steadily increased from two and a half million dollars in 1903-04 to seven and a half in 1911-12. During the same period the number of men trained in the active militia rose from thirty-five to fifty thousand.

The memoranda of the new militia council in 1905 reflect official views of the new régime.[11] In their memorandum to the minister of militia the military members of the council pointed out that they had not "a clean sheet on which to draw out their plans, and they have constantly had to compromise between what was desirable and what was attainable". Their plans were not ambitious: gradual additions to the cavalry and artillery of the permanent force, and organization of the army service corps, ordnance corps, and army medical corps. The finance member of the council then explained in a memorandum the estimates for 1905-06, showing the increased expenditure in some detail. By 1910 the council was ready with a more elaborate report.[12] Some changes were reported: an inter-departmental committee for co-operation between the departments of militia and defence and of naval service; the appointment of staff officers to train candidates for the British staff college; and a mobilization committee at headquarters. But the formal picture drawn by the council looked less impressive when examined by soldiers. The

10 "The Canadian Militia: The Change in Organization" (*Canadian Defence Quarterly*, VIII, 1930-1, 97).

11 *Canada, Sessional Papers*, 1905, no. 130.

12 *Ibid.*, 1911, no. 35.

theme of the report of the inspector-general, Major-General Lake, was that the reduction of estimates had seriously impaired the efficiency and development of both permanent and non-permanent militia.[13] In the same year an outside opinion was given by Sir John French, who, as inspector-general of the imperial forces, had been invited to inspect the Canadian military forces. His report pays tribute to the men and officers available and to some aspects of their work; but the weaknesses he found were more conspicuous than the strength. He took "ability to defend the land frontiers of Canada" as the standard by which he formed his judgment, and his conclusions did little to give Canadians any sense of security. The peace organization he found defective in that the various arms of the service were not in correct proportions either in total or in any one district, nor did they have opportunities of training together. Units lacking in integration would have to be thrown together in time of war, when a further difficulty would arise from a lack of adequate mobilization plans. French made some suggestions for changes in the training of the permanent force, but on the whole wrote warmly of its efficiency. Some alterations, he thought, might be made in the organization of the staff. Whether the volunteer system would meet Canadian conditions could not, he thought, be decided until it had been given a fair trial, with a better organization, better knowledge in the higher command, and the qualifications for officers and the engagements of the rank and file in the militia being enforced.[14] Asked by the minister of militia to report on how far and in what manner Sir John French's recommendations could be implemented, Major-General Lake observed that on the whole they followed the same lines on which the militia council had been working. "There are", he wrote, "no proposals contained in Sir John French's report the adoption of which would involve any departure in principle from the policy which, under your direction, the militia council has pursued since its inception in 1904 . . . the extent to which progress in carrying out his recommendations can be made and the period which must elapse before they can become effective depends entirely upon how far Parliament is prepared to provide for the expenditure necessary."[15]

[13] *Ibid.*
[14] *Ibid.*, no. 35A.
[15] *Ibid.*, no. 35B.

Some at least of the recommendations made by French and endorsed by Lake were carried into effect. In eastern Canada the militia was organized in peace as it would be in war, into divisions each with a commander and staff, and each divisional commander was to control all the troops within his area. But still the reports of the new inspector-general, a Canadian, General Otter, pointed to continuance of the old weaknesses: shortage of officers and men, and inadequate qualifications. The last word before 1914 came from Sir Ian Hamilton, who inspected the Canadian forces in the summer of 1913. Organization, training, and education he believed had all improved. He found, however, that the active militia was still short of instructors, and that units were under strength. Above all he stressed the unreality of the paper liability for universal military service, and the absence in practice of any reserve.[16]

Such, in outline, were the military forces of Canada in the period between the withdrawal of the imperial troops and the War of 1914. Though theoretically based on universal service, the Canadian militia was in reality purely a volunteer force. Apart from the small permanent force, the militia suffered from scanty resources and sketchy training—in spite of the zealous efforts of many of its members. There was little that was distinctively Canadian about the militia. While frequently criticized as following too slowly or imperfectly the British army, it was nevertheless organized and trained on the methods of that army. From England came its drill, its weapons, and its training. Commanding officers for many years came from England, as did many of the staff of the Royal Military College. Canadian officers attended the English staff college. Advice came in generous amounts from English officers in Canada, either holding positions for a term or on special inspections. The colonial defence committee transmitted its views on Canadian defences to Ottawa. When changes were made they consisted in closer approximations to British practice: more modern rifles, organization, mobilization plans, relations between civil and military officials concerned in defence. A reading of either the reports of British experts or discussions by Canadians gives the impression that the excellence of the militia was

16 Sir Charles Lucas, *The Empire at War* (London and Toronto, 1921), I, 235-9.

in direct ratio to its likeness to its prototype. In addition to this technical relation of the military forces of the United Kingdom and Canada, was another and quite different one, found in the projects for concerted plans for imperial defence: organization for co-operative effort toward a common end.

III

Imperial defence, as has already been suggested, was not a single but a multiple problem, involving the defence of Canada, of near-by British territories, of far-distant colonies, and of imperial power as a whole. The protection of Canada itself was intended, after confederation, to be primarily a Canadian responsibility, with the understanding that in case of attack Great Britain would render assistance as she was able. The major part of the imperial troops had been withdrawn by 1871, though a garrison was left at Halifax. The military history of both Halifax and Esquimalt is of peculiar interest in that they alone played a dual rôle: as conveniently-situated ports for the British navy, which happened to be situated in Canada; and as strategic positions through which Canada might be invaded. The Canadian point of view, both in the government and amongst the public, was that the cost of maintenance should be shared; but the actual division was not so easily reached. When the world seemed peaceful Canadians tended to take the attitude that these bases were a British concern: when any threat loomed they emphasized the necessity of British naval and military forces being represented on both coasts. Because of this shifting atmosphere, and because of the impossibility of defining the relative values received by the United Kingdom and the dominion, the negotiations over the allocation of cost were protracted. Soon after British Columbia joined the federation her government pressed for the graving dock at Esquimalt, for which the dominion had promised in the terms of union to guarantee the interest on a loan. Correspondence then ensued between the provincial, federal, and imperial governments. The last agreed to contribute £30,000 on condition that the dock should be suitable in dimension and character, and that His Majesty's ships have preferential treatment there for fifteen years. The dominion government, for its part, offered a grant of £50,000 in lieu of its guarantee in the terms of union.[17] But in spite of these early offers there remained some disagreement, and contracts were not awarded until 1890.[18]

The maintenance of the defensive works and a garrison at Esquimalt was a more vital question which took even longer to settle. Here again the pressure came from British Columbia, through the provincial government and members of parliament, but the arrangements were to be made between the governments of the United Kingdom and Canada. The Russian scares of 1877-1885 drew attention to the weak state of defences on the Pacific coast, and temporary measures were taken to strengthen Esquimalt. Several years were then passed in correspondence between the Canadian and British governments, with proposals and counter-proposals as to how the responsibility for defence might be shared. It was not until 1893 that an agreement was reached under which the dominion government was to pay part of the cost of construction and the maintenance of the buildings and defence works, to pay for a detachment of Royal Marine Artillery, and to supply some troops to supplement the garrison. This, with modifications, continued to be the basis on which Esquimalt was maintained. No such controversy took place over Halifax, presumably because the British government regarded it as a more important naval base. It was suggested, however, that Canadian troops in the neighbourhood would be available in case of need. A step toward a share in the defence of Halifax was taken during the South African War, when a battalion was provided to relieve the British troops there for service elsewhere. A fuller responsibility for the defence of both ports was first suggested by the Canadian representatives at the colonial conference of 1902 in an offer to garrison both Halifax and Esquimalt,[19] and was formally renewed early in 1905. The offer was gratefully accepted, with the suggestion that the change might be made gradually, Canada in the meanwhile defraying the cost of such imperial troops as temporarily remained.[20] The proposal was accepted substantially as

[17] *Canada, Sessional Papers,* 1875, no. 64.

[18] *Ibid.,* 1890, no. 59G.

[19] No mention of this appears in the report of the conference, but in a Privy Council report of Jan. 20, 1905, it is said to have been "stated verbally" (*Canada, Sessional Papers,* 1905, no. 128).

[20] *Ibid.*

it was made, and in 1906 the last of the imperial troops left Halifax and Esquimalt. At the beginning of 1907 the Canadian government also took over the Halifax dockyard, though privileges for the royal navy were reserved. The changed position at the two ports coincided with the adoption of a new policy by the admiralty under which a local squadron was no longer to be stationed at either, but an equal or greater degree of security promised from the larger units in which the ships were thereafter to operate. To many Canadians, on the Atlantic and Pacific coasts alike, even one ship that could be seen was a more real protection than many that were far away. Feelings were mixed over the changes of 1905. Protests against the British abandonment of the stations were accompanied by expressions of satisfaction that Canada was accepting a greater proportion of the burden of defence.[21] The buildings and other property at Halifax were formally transferred to the Canadian government in 1910, and those at Esquimalt in 1911, subject to their being maintained in a state of efficiency, to a supply of fuel being kept, and other facilities being provided for the royal navy.

Excitement over the new policies for Halifax and Esquimalt arose not only from the importance of these two ports but because the decisions respecting them were related to the wider issues of imperial defence, then receiving a growing amount of public attention. No aspect of defence was as obviously a Canadian interest as that of the keys to her eastern and western coasts, but there were other problems that had to be faced, and on which some decisions had to be made. The story of the plans discussed in time of peace for co-operative imperial defence may be traced through the meetings of the colonial and imperial conferences. Referring to the programme of the first session in 1887 the colonial secretary wrote that "in the opinion of His Majesty's government the question which is at once urgent and capable of useful consideration is that of organization for military defence".[22] In the opening speech Lord Salisbury disclaimed any idea that "this proposal for Imperial defence is a mere contrivance on our part to lighten our burden, or that it results from any indolence or

21 For a summary of opinion in parliament and the press see *Canadian Annual Review*, 1905, 461 ff.
22 Richard Jebb, *The Imperial Conference: A History and Study* (2 vols., London, 1911), I, 8.

selfishness of ours", but went on to say, in an apparent *non sequitur,*
that "we desire that all should take their fair and legitimate part
in a task of which all ought to be proud".[23] Nearly half the
working time of the conference was devoted to considerations of
defence, mainly on naval problems of the Pacific, and the possible action to be taken by the Australian colonies. The Canadian
part in the discussions was meagre and negative. Sir Alexander
Campbell made what were to become regulation references to
the Intercolonial and Canadian Pacific railways as contributions
to defence, and virtually denied that the British navy was greater
because of any responsibility for the defence of Canada.[24]

Ten years elapsed before the next general discussion of defence
(for it was not taken up at the Ottawa session of 1894), and
then the pace was soon seen to be quickening. Joseph Chamberlain went straight to the point of arguing that the great military
and naval defences of Great Britain were necessitated largely by
her empire. Without this force behind her Canada would be
helpless in the face of disagreements with Japan, Russia, or the
United States, and become largely a dependent power. The
colonial defence committee, he said, had made some improvement,
but the position in the colonies in regard to defences was still not
satisfactory. As positive steps he proposed that regiments should
temporarily be exchanged between Great Britain and the colonies,
and that a colonial regiment thus in England might take part
in any military operations that occurred. The all-too-brief record
of the conference[25] contains no account of the discussion, but
it is evident that the colonial premiers made no promise of
anything more than an examination of the proposed interchange.
Sir Wilfrid Laurier attended his second colonial conference in
1902 without the South African War having shaken his inherent
nationalism; in London he faced Joseph Chamberlain, whose
imperialism had been fortified by the common efforts in that war.
From other colonies came representatives with no less conflicting
policies. In the preparations for the agenda, defence, amongst other
subjects, was suggested by the colonial secretary. In reply Minto

[23] *Ibid.,* 19.
[24] *Ibid.,* 55.
[25] *Proceedings of a Conference Between the Secretary of State for the
Colonies and the Premiers of the Self-governing Colonies, 1897.* (Cd. 8596,
1897).

was obliged to report that his ministers did not consider that "in the varying conditions of the Colonies there can be any scheme of defence applicable to all".[26] Taxed by the leader of the opposition with returning a discourteous reply, Laurier denied any such intention, but repeated that no useful purpose could be served by discussion of defence. The government would, he said, be ready to discuss the defence of Canada, but something other than that was intended by a school in England and Canada "which wants to bring Canada into the vortex of militarism which is the curse and the blight of Europe".[27] Defence, however, appeared on the agenda; and indeed the conference would have been entirely unrealistic if that had been excluded.

In his opening speech Chamberlain again pointed to the heavy burden of defence borne by Britain—a burden which was largely due to the existence of the colonies. But the colonies were no longer young and poor: they were rich enough to offer temptation to aggression and strong enough to assume a share of their own defence.[28] To introduce the subject of naval defence the first lord of the admiralty spoke on the position of sea-power and made in particular two points: that the task of the navy was not literally defence of certain places, but of destroying the enemy fleet; and that the maritime spirit of the empire and the sense of personal interest should be aroused by having more colonials in the navy. He had, he said, consulted the premiers, all of whom had offered money grants except Laurier, who had said that he was not able to make a similar offer, but that his government was contemplating the establishment of a local naval force. Figures were produced showing the *per capita* naval expenditure (Canada being nil), and a draft agreement on naval plans was made between the United Kingdom, Australia, and New Zealand; but the Canadian representatives remained aloof. On military policy more definite plans were put forward. The secretary of state for war advocated a highly trained, if small, force in each colony to be held in readiness for imperial service. To this the representatives of both Australia and Canada objected on the

[26] *Canadian Annual Review*, 1902, 106.
[27] *Ibid.*, 107.
[28] *Papers Relating to a Conference Between the Secretary of State for the Colonies and the Prime Ministers of Self-governing Colonies, 1902.* (Cd. 1299, 1902). The report of this conference is fuller than in previous cases.

ground that it would be a derogation of the principles of self-government. A parallel plan by New Zealand for an imperial reserve force appeared with the approval of the colonial defence committee; the committee also sponsored a paper by Lieut.-Colonel Altham, assistant quartermaster-general at the war office, which proposed that specified troops in each colony (3,000 in Canada) should be ready to supplement the British army in case of need. The Canadian policy was summed up in a memorandum (printed as appendix VI to the report) drawn up by the Canadian ministers regretting their inability to assent to suggestions of either the admiralty or the war office. Their objections arose, they said, "not so much from the expense involved, as from a belief that the acceptance of the proposals would entail an important departure from the principle of colonial self-government". They recognized that Canada should take over more of the burden of "self-defence", and held that while the Canadian militia had defects it was being improved. On the naval side they contemplated a naval reserve. In any defence schemes they wished to co-operate with the imperial authorities, so far as that was compatible with self-government. Implicitly the memorandum gave the impression that Canada should be increasingly responsible for her own defence; but it avoided any reference to activities outside Canada.

At the colonial conference of 1907 the Canadian policy in regard to defence was substantially unchanged: no commitments, no contributions to British naval or land forces, and no outside control over any part of the Canadian forces. But whatever the reason—whether it was that the atmosphere was better, or that the British government had learned wisdom—the conference proceeded more smoothly toward positive results. Progress, however, was least marked in regard to naval defence. Lord Tweedmouth, first lord of the admiralty, admitted British responsibility for naval defence. Colonial aid would be welcomed in any one of several forms, so long as consistent with control of strategy and unity of command.[29] The Canadian reply was made by the minister of marine and fisheries, L. P. Brodeur. The Canadian position, he said, was different from that of the other colonies and

---

[29] *Minutes of Proceedings of the Colonial Conference, 1907.* (Cd. 3523, 1907). A verbatim record of the discussions.

should be treated as such. He objected to a document showing that Canada had spent nothing on naval defence, citing the fisheries protection service, the naval militia, wireless stations, the hydrographic survey, and assumption of the dockyards at Halifax and Esquimalt. Canada was of one mind, he said, on the proposal to contribute directly to the British navy. A resolution moved by one of the representatives of Cape Colony in favour of the principle of colonial contributions in some form to the British navy was directly opposed by Laurier and withdrawn. It was on military defence that the conference reached positive agreement. Lord Haldane, secretary of state for war, explained how the general staff had grown out of the recommendations of the Esher committee of 1904, and suggested that the same principle might be applied to the empire, to meet what he described as "the desirability of a certain broad plan of military organisation". Sir Frederick Borden, after ascertaining that there was no idea of creating a body with authority in Canada, accepted in principle one with advisory functions, and in which there should be interchange of officers with the general staff of Canada. The proposal was then embodied in a general resolution and accepted by all the members of the conference.

It was on these lines that imperial military defence was to develop from then on. "The elaborate plans for pre-arranged contingents", concludes Colonel Hamilton, "thus dropped to a proposal for an Imperial general staff. This meant more than the civilian reader might suspect, for it carried the idea of establishing in the Empire common types of organization, co-ordinated plans for action, a common way of thinking on military problems, a common doctrine of war."[30] It was fully understood, and definitely stated over and over again, that no promise or guarantee was made by the dominions to provide contingents, and that there was no supreme military authority in Canada save that of its government. On the other hand, the Canadian government willingly entered into the plan for uniformity of education and organization, and for common discussion of military problems. Following the general agreement at the conference of 1907 a memorandum was drawn up by the general staff and circulated

[30] "The Canadian Militia: Imperial Organization" (*Canadian Defence Quarterly*, VIII, 1930-1, 244).

to the dominions at the end of 1908.[31] Further progress along the same lines was made at the subsidiary conference of 1909 (a form of additional conference provided for under resolution of the colonial conference of 1907, and called because of the immediacy of the German naval challenge). The military experts met together under the chairmanship of the chief of the imperial general staff and examined a memorandum submitted by him of "Proposals for so organizing the military forces of the empire as to ensure their effective co-operation in the event of war".[32] Recommendations were made by the experts designed to implement the general objectives of uniformity of training, equipment, and organization, for the relations of general staff officers in the dominion and the United Kingdom, and for the education of officers. These recommendations were then accepted by the full conference and the committee of imperial defence. "The result", Mr. Asquith told the house of commons, "is a plan for so organizing the forces of the Crown wherever they are that, while preserving the complete autonomy of each Dominion, should the Dominions desire to assist in the defence of the Empire in a real emergency, their forces could be rapidly combined into one homogeneous Imperial Army."

When the conference again met in 1911, under its new title of "imperial conference", progress was reported on the plans generally accepted in 1907.[33] The imperial general staff, although only two years old, was said to have made progress, and a Canadian section to be in process of formation. It was reported that officers of the Canadian permanent force were undergoing the same examinations for promotion as those in the British regular army. The army council expressed its willingness that the inspector-general should inspect overseas forces at the request of a dominion.[34] While these and other aspects of reorganization were going forward, an attempt was made to change the principles then being fol-

---

[31] *Correspondence Relating to the Proposed Formation of an Imperial General Staff.* (Cd. 4475, 1909).

[32] *Correspondence and Papers Relating to a Conference with Representatives of the Self-governing Dominions on the Naval and Military Defence of the Empire, 1909.* (Cd. 4948, 1909).

[33] *Papers Laid Before the Imperial Conference: Naval and Military Defence.* (Cd. 5746-2, 1911).

[34] Sir Ian Hamilton inspected the Canadian militia in 1913. See above, 264.

lowed by a revived plan for central political control over the defence forces of all parts of the empire. Although other aspects of defence were brought before the committee of imperial defence rather than the imperial conference, Sir Joseph Ward's project for an imperial parliament or council for imperial defence came, as a previous resolution, before the conference.[35] From the first of the discussion Ward's plan evoked little sympathy from any of the representatives of other parts of the empire, and frank opposition from most. In the course of being questioned, Ward admitted that his parliament would have authority to compel the dominions to make contributions to an imperial navy—an idea which was so far removed from practical politics as to be hopeless of achievement. With this motion withdrawn, the discussions of defence proceeded in the committee of imperial defence and at the war office and admiralty.

From 1911 until 1914 the organization of imperial defence lay, in the main, in two bodies: the imperial general staff and the committee of imperial defence. Both were advisory bodies, and both contained representatives of the dominions. The latter had no fixed membership, but dominion representatives might attend, as full members, as the occasion required. That the committee was also used in 1911 as the body in which foreign policy was discussed has been seen as having dangerous implications for dominion autonomy.[36] The fact was, however, that co-operation in foreign policy was not keeping pace with co-operation in military policy: in other words, the control over the development of situations in which the military plans might be called into play was virtually left by the dominions (so cautious about military control) to the British foreign office. The risk this involved was preferred, by Canada at least, to the more apparent risk involved in consultation and responsibility.

IV

In the last quarter of the nineteenth century wars and rumours of wars gave reality to the military policy of Canada in respect

[35] *Minutes of Proceedings of the Imperial Conference, 1911.* (Cd. 5745, 1911).

[36] See, e.g., Richard Jebb, *The Britannic Question: A Survey of Alternatives* (London, New York, 1913), 43ff.; A. G. Dewey, *The Dominions and Diplomacy: The Canadian Contribution* (2 vols., London and Toronto, 1929), I, 294 ff.

of both local and imperial defence. Fear of Russian attack, which had long been dormant, revived with the critical international situation in the near east in the years after 1877. Between the Crimean and the Japanese wars the strength of Russia was commonly over-estimated; and when the invasion of Turkey threatened an Anglo-Russian war many Canadians found cause for alarm, not merely in the danger to the United Kingdom but also in threats to their own shipping and coasts. And in the same period, while fear of American aggression had materially abated, good relations with the United States were not taken for granted. One Toronto editor conjured up unpleasant visions of difficulties with both Russia and the United States.

. . . we regard as absolutely fallacious the idea entertained in some quarters that there is anything in the Treaty of Paris [of 1856] which will prevent Russia from issuing commissions to vessels intended to prey upon the commercial marine of England and her colonies in case of war, and if the Canadian Government is hugging itself on a contrary notion and so neglecting to provide for possible contingencies, we fear they, and all people here who hold them, are destined to a rough awakening . . . any Power can at any time issue commissions to any vessel it pleases, and convert it into an addendum to its own belligerent navy. Moreover, it is quite on the cards that complications may arise between Great Britain and the United States in connection with this delicate point, and it will not do for us in Canada to be slumbering in a fool's paradise. . . . While Canada in fact has nothing whatever to gain, as a colony, by war between Russia and England, it has a very great deal to lose, and hostilities are sure to subject us as a colonial dependency to constant alarms and risks. This is a point which we fear is not yet realized by our people. . . .[37]

A few days later the *Mail* pointed to the danger of hostilities in the North Pacific. In fact the government was not slumbering, but had already discussed the defenceless condition of the Atlantic coast, and appealed to Britain for a fleet of fast cruisers.[38] When the dispatch reached the admiralty the reply was that the matter had long been under consideration; that the American Civil War had shown what damage could be done by a single fast cruiser; and that a considerable expenditure would be required to afford any adequate protection. "Looking", the admiralty reply continued, "at the very large mercantile marine possessed by the Dominion,

[37] Toronto *Mail*, May 7, 1878.
[38] Public Archives of Canada, *Macdonald Papers*, "Defence", vol. II. Privy Council Report, May 4, 1878.

it is only reasonable to assume that the Canadian government will avail themselves of their resources for the protection of Canadian ports and shipping", but suggested aid by the loan of guns.[39] Already the government had authorized the expenditure of $10,000 "in view of the precautionary measures now being taken for defensive purposes",[40] but apparently did not respond to the larger suggestion. Apprehension continued for some time. In 1879 reports were circulated that a Russian steamer from the Baltic was off the coast of Maine, and was laden with guns and seamen to supply commerce-raiders. In 1883 the senate discussed the defenceless condition of the Pacific coast. W. J. Macdonald, who brought up the question, spoke of the comparative nearness of Russian naval bases, the possibility of an Indian uprising in case of war, and the need for more protection by the royal navy.[41] In 1885 a similar concern for the Atlantic coast was expressed by the Saint John *Telegraph* in a suggestion that a Russian warship might quite possibly come into that harbour.[42]

Before the Russian danger had ceased to stir Canadian feelings the affairs of Egypt brought on a new and different type of military question. When Wolseley was organizing an expedition in 1884 to relieve Gordon, cut off at Khartum, he cabled a request for *voyageurs*, like those who had gone with him to the Red River in 1870, as steersmen for the Nile boats. A party numbering 367 was sent, made up in part of Indians and in part of lumbermen (for the *voyageurs* had all but disappeared).[43] The expedition reached Khartum too late, and as the situation in the Sudan became increasingly grave, New South Wales offered a contingent. Should Canada take similar action? Individual Canadians promptly offered to raise regiments, and there were suggestions that the government should send a contingent. From London Tupper cabled that Canada should send and pay for troops. "The cost", he wrote later, "would not be much and Canada cannot in my judgment afford to do *less* after what New South Wales has done. It will be repaid to the country in many ways and carry

[39] *Ibid.*, Admiralty to Colonial Office, June 10, 1878.
[40] *Ibid.*, Privy Council Report, May 22, 1878.
[41] *Canada, Debates of the Senate*, 1883, 118 *ff*.
[42] Saint John *Telegraph*, May 7, 1885.
[43] John Buchan, *Lord Minto: A Memoir* (London, 1924), 75.

out the expectations raised by your speeches here. . . ."[44] The
Week of Toronto rather surprisingly called for sending substantial
aid.[45] A more general attitude, however, was that expressed by
the *Mail* and the *Globe* of Toronto and the Saint John *Daily
Telegraph*.[46] Britain, the argument ran, was not in danger. Filial
loyalty might properly inspire individual offers of service, but
only a major crisis should lead the dominion to make an official
effort, at her own expense. A similar but more vigorous opinion
was expressed in the *Manitoba Free Press*, which commented that
"all the talk we have heard about Canada's fighting the battles
of England is very silly and quite likely to be hurtful".[47] In this
particular case the matter was decided by the outbreak of the
North-West Rebellion which required that all available Canadian
troops should remain in Canada. It was worthy of note that in
this, unlike the first Riel rebellion, imperial troops were not needed.

Ten years later the Venezuela controversy caused more than
a ripple in Canada, and had an interest in that it again involved
the possibility—though perhaps a remote one—of defence against
the United States. This also marked the last occasion on which
considerable preparations were made as defence against the United
States. But much the most important military event for Canada
between the period of the Civil War and Fenian raids and the
War of 1914 was the South African War. The decision to be
made by the Canadian government was not an easy one, since
the struggle with the Boers might be interpreted either as an
episode in the British imperial development or as a crisis of
dimensions sufficient to threaten the power and prestige of the
empire of which Canada was part. It was an imperial question
midway between the Sudan expeditions and the War of 1914. In
Canada, too, it might take the appearance of the repression of
one ethnic group by another, and so touch a delicate nerve.

In the summer of 1899, as the situation in South Africa
became more acute, several British colonies made offers of military
aid in the event of hostilities, and in Canada there were some
suggestions that their example should be followed. Both parliament

[44] *Macdonald Papers*, "Sir Charles Tupper". Tupper to Macdonald,
Feb. 27, 1885.
[45] *The Week* (Toronto), Feb. 19, 1885.
[46] February and March, 1885.
[47] *Manitoba Free Press*, Oct. 24, 1885.

and public, however, were slow in reaching that conclusion. On July 31 the prime minister introduced a resolution into the house of commons expressing sympathy with the British government in its attempt to secure equal rights for British subjects in the Transvaal. Whether or not this could be taken as an endorsement of British policy, it was not enough to satisfy the growing demand for more tangible aid. J. S. Willison, then editor of the *Globe*, bluntly told Laurier that he would have to send troops or go out of office, a conclusion with which Laurier was reluctantly forced to agree before long.[48] At the beginning of October events moved rapidly. On the third Joseph Chamberlain, the colonial secretary, who for three months had been angling for official promises of aid, cabled an acknowledgment of private "offers to serve in South Africa" and described the means by which they could be carried out.[49] On the same day Laurier had given an interview in which he said that while Canadian forces might be sent abroad in defence of Canada, the South African situation did not create any such menace. For this reason, and because parliament (which was not sitting) would have to grant the money, no troops had been offered. It has sometimes been said that Laurier's hand was forced by Chamberlain's cable: it is more probable that it was forced by the pressure of public opinion. Certainly he was in an uncomfortable position. Personally reluctant to take any action, not believing that the South African affair would assume large proportions, and pressed in his own province not to intervene, he found himself obliged either to do so, or to allow the opposition free play with public sentiment in most of English-speaking Canada.

Once the decision was made no constitutional difficulty was allowed to stand in the way. An ingeniously worded privy council report of October 14 showed the hope of the cabinet that it was possible to accept a very limited liability. After quoting Chamberlain's dispatch, the report states that,

The Prime Minister in view of the well-known desire of a great many Canadians who are ready to take service under such conditions, is of opinion that the moderate expenditure which would thus be involved for the equipment and transportation of such volunteers may readily be undertaken by the government of Canada without

[48] Sir John Willison, *Reminiscences, Political and Personal* (Toronto, 1919), 303.
[49] *Canada, Sessional Papers,* 1900, no. 20.

summoning parliament, especially as such an expenditure under such circumstances cannot be regarded as a departure from the well known principles of constitutional government and colonial practice, nor construed as a precedent for future action.[50]

On October 30, within a day of the last date set by Chamberlain, a battalion of over a thousand men sailed from Canada. As they had originally proposed, the British government were to bear all expenses from the time the troops landed, but one change was made in that the Canadians were to be kept as a separate unit. On November 2, after news of reverses, the Canadian government cabled an offer of another contingent, which, however, was not accepted until the situation had grown even worse in December.

Thus, when parliament met in February 1900 the Canadian government had, on its own authority, sent two contingents to a war that had already shown itself to be the most serious in which Great Britain had been engaged for half a century. The debates in both houses were prolonged and at times impressive. While the government enjoyed an almost unanimous support on main principles, criticism was not lacking. Some there were who held that more rapid and more generous aid should have been rendered, and in particular that Canada should have borne all expenses. Others objected to any participation. Even the breezy language of the privy council report could not disguise the fact that the government had acted without sanction of parliament, but the great majority agreed that, under the circumstances, this was justifiable. There were long discussions of the causes of the war, of the importance of South Africa to Great Britain, and of the interest which Canada had in the struggle. The general tenor of the debate was that British policy had been neither unreasonable nor aggressive; but a vocal minority, led by Bourassa, condemned the policy and the action of Canada in supporting it. The emphasis constantly laid on the position of Quebec revealed both the existence of an anti-war party there and the apprehension in the other provinces that that party might be dangerously strong. Constant protests were made that Quebec was "loyal", but it was also apparent that the most critical speeches came from members for Quebec constituencies. One further test of the government's policy came in the general election of 1900, an election largely fought

[50] *Ibid.*, no. 49.

on that policy, and in which an element of bitterness was all too apparent. The results of the polling were somewhat striking: in Ontario the government lost fourteen seats, and in Quebec it gained all but seven. It was easily apparent, therefore, that there had been no serious revolt in Quebec against Laurier; while the vote in Ontario must be explained not by any opposition to the war but, in part, by dissatisfaction at such cautious participation. The Canadian contribution to the war was not inconsiderable. The forces sent overseas consisted, first, of the second (special service) battalion of the Royal Canadian Regiment at a strength of 1,150 officers and men, under the command of a Canadian, Lieutenant-Colonel Otter. The second contingent, recruited at the end of 1899, included the Royal Canadian Dragoons (two squadrons), drawn largely from the permanent force, the Canadian Mounted Rifles (two squadrons), recruited in part from the North West Mounted Police, and three batteries of Royal Canadian Artillery, also recruited in part from the permanent force. In addition to the two first Canadian contingents were troops later raised in Canada, but not directly by the Canadian government. These included Lord Strathcona's Horse, of three squadrons, the expenses of which were met by Lord Strathcona; twelve squadrons of the South African constabulary; the 2nd Canadian Mounted Rifles; the 10th Canadian Field Hospital; and the 3rd, 4th, 5th, and 6th Canadian Mounted Rifles (these last arriving after the conclusion of peace). In all 7,300 men went to South Africa.[51] In Canada the 3rd Battalion, Royal Canadian Regiment, was raised to relieve the imperial garrison at Halifax. Citizens contributed to the Red Cross and Patriotic Fund organizations in Canada, and to provide insurance and other funds for the troops. Owing to the short term of enlistment parts of the forces returned to Canada before the end of hostilities, nor were the reinforcements adequate to keep the units up to strength. Apart from these weaknesses the Canadian troops played an active and efficient part in the war. Though lacking in training and experience on arrival in South Africa, they performed their duties satisfactorily, and at times with conspicuous success.[52]

[51] Hamilton, "The Canadian Militia: The South African War" (*Canadian Defence Quarterly*, VII, 1929-30, 537-42).

[52] For an account of the Canadian forces in the war see W. S. Evans, *The Canadian Contingents and Canadian Imperialism: A Story and a Study* (London, 1901).

While Canadians had thus played an active part in the war, their government had had no influence on the circumstances which led to its outbreak or on the methods by which it was conducted. It remained to be seen whether the Canadian government would exercise, or wish to exercise, any control over the terms on which peace was to be made. On several occasions the criticism was made in parliament that Canada had gone into a war for which she was in no way responsible, and the similar objection was raised against a purely English peace. In 1900 and 1901 Bourassa asked in the house of commons whether the government had been consulted on the conditions of peace, or intended to offer any opinion; and on both occasions the prime minister explicitly replied in the negative.[53] In 1902 John Charlton moved a cautious resolution asking for a magnanimous treatment of the Boers. In the debate that followed most of the speakers agreed with the prime minister that the Canadian parliament had a right to express such opinions, but that to intervene when peace was actually under discussion might prolong, rather than shorten, the war. Other members said that Canada had already been too free in expressing opinions.[54] The motion was withdrawn; and the Canadian participation in the South African War continued to be confined to its military aspect.

V

Naval defence was no less important to Canada than land defence, after confederation as before it; but so long as the British navy maintained unquestioned supremacy on the seas Canadians could and did expect that their coasts would be protected by that great force without their contributing ships themselves. For that reason there was in the dominion no pressure to formulate a naval policy until, in the twentieth century, the dominant position held since Trafalgar began to be threatened by Germany. Even then the Canadian government and parliament moved slowly to meet the new circumstances. Through the colonial conference of 1907 the Canadian attitude was almost wholly negative, being simply a refusal to make contributions to the British navy. In the follow-

---

53 *Canada, House of Commons Debates*, 1900, p. 6625; 1901, p. 1290.
54 *Ibid.*, 1902, p. 3316.

ing years, however, the vague suggestions of a Canadian navy began to harden into a positive policy. There had long been differing views in Canada on naval defence. One school of thought concurred with the view, presented at earlier colonial conferences, that the English burden of naval defence was materially increased by the existence of the colonies; and that the latter should consequently take steps to share that burden. Another held that British naval power was designed for defence of world-wide trade and was as large as it was because of a British conviction that sea-power, for an island dependent on sea-communication for its prosperity and very life, must be unquestioned. Those who held the former view suggested either a direct contribution of money or ships to the British navy (the plan most acceptable to the admiralty), or a Canadian navy acting, when occasion required, in concert with the royal navy. Occasionally, as at the time of the Russian scares, the people of both coasts at least were conscious of the need of naval protection, but otherwise the obviously superior power of the British navy prevented any feeling of necessity. It was only in 1909 when the German construction obviously began to threaten British supremacy that the Canadian people were aroused to a desire for action. There were, it is true, some who claimed that the danger was unduly, and even improperly, magnified; there were also those who continued to believe that naval defence was a British, and not a Canadian, responsibility. The effective majority, however, accepted the proposition that the threat was real, and that Canada must lend aid to combat it. In what form that aid was to be rendered remained a matter of disagreement.[55]

In the early stages of the naval question in parliament a remarkable unanimity appeared to exist. At the end of March, G. E. Foster moved a general resolution in favour of Canada defending her own coasts, and supplemented it by a speech in which he advocated a Canadian navy, and possibly an emergency gift of warships. Laurier (who was quite capable of language worthy of any imperialist) accepted Foster's policy, which he put in resolutions in the form of an amendment. The leader of the opposition, R. L. Borden, did no more than suggest some verbal changes, and the prime minister's motion, approving of expendi-

[55] For Canadian public opinion on the naval question see *Canadian Annual Review*, 1909. Pages 49-55 relate to the period before the parliamentary resolution; and pages 87-112 cover the period from the end of March.

ture for "a Canadian naval service in co-operation with and in close relation to the Imperial Navy", was passed without division, although some individual criticisms were made in the course of debate.

The scene then temporarily shifted to London. At about the same time as the Canadian resolutions the governments of New Zealand and Australia had offered battleships. The British government, in view of the actions of the three dominions, and of its understanding that the Canadian government intended to send its minister of militia and defence to England for consultations, proposed the holding of a subsidiary defence conference, as provided for by the colonial conference of 1907.[56] When the conference duly met at the end of July the admiralty submitted a memorandum expressing its preference for a single navy, but agreeing that the conditions in some of the dominions led them to prefer local naval forces. For those that followed this policy it was recommended that a distinct fleet unit should be the aim. Such a unit should include one armoured and three unarmed cruisers, six destroyers, three submarines, and the necessary auxiliaries. "The estimated first cost of building and arming such a complete fleet unit would be approximately £3,700,000, and the cost of maintenance, including upkeep of vessels, pay, and interest and sinking fund, at British rates, approximately £600,000 per annum." To these sums should be added the pay of persons in the auxiliary services, in training, sick, and in reserve. Ship-building and repairing establishments would be required, training schools, and sources of stores. While a dominion would thus provide its own navy complete, there should be uniformity in equipment, training, and discipline. It was understood that in time of war the local naval forces should come under the general direction of the admiralty. In the discussions that followed (of which only a summary was printed) between the British and Canadian representatives, a much less ambitious programme was considered. Given Canada's double seaboard, a fleet unit was recognized as unsuitable, and the admiralty, on ascertaining that Canada asked for two plans for naval forces involving a cost of £600,000 or £400,000 annually, suggested four cruisers and six destroyers or three cruisers and four

<hr>

56 For the correspondence see *Correspondence and Papers Relating to the Conference with Representatives of the Self-governing Dominions on the Naval and Military Defence of the Empire, 1909.* (Cd. 4948, 1909).

destroyers. During the period of construction and training the admiralty was prepared to lend two cruisers, and also volunteers from the royal navy to be paid by the Canadian government.

The apparently general support given to the Laurier-Borden programme was soon seen to represent the real opinions neither of parliament nor public. The conservatives showed the widest differences since their right wing denounced the plan as not calculated to give adequate or appropriate support, while in Quebec F. D. Monk led a revolt against the official policy of the party. The liberals suffered a similar defection in the province of Quebec, where Henri Bourassa attacked the whole idea of naval defence expenditure. Laurier, however, managed to hold his party together sufficiently to write into the Naval Service Bill, introduced into the commons in January 1910, substantially the terms of the parliamentary resolutions and of the agreement at the London conference of 1909. Five cruisers and six destroyers were to be built, if possible in Canada (if not, in England), and divided between the two coasts. The personnel was to be partly permanent, partly volunteer, with a naval college and a naval board. The Canadian government would control its navy, but might place it at the disposal of the admiralty in a crisis, subject to approval by parliament. The debate which followed was long, and ranged over the whole fields of strategy and—particularly—of imperial relations.[57] The official conservative opposition criticized the bill, not on its principles (to which they had already subscribed) but on a number of grounds. Firstly, it was objected that the government would be empowered, even in time of war, to withhold the Canadian naval forces from those of the rest of the empire. Secondly, the bill did not adequately provide for the unity of organization and action necessary for co-operation in empire defence. Thirdly, that no permanent policy should be entered on without being submitted to the people in a general election. Finally, it was held that the bill would provide no immediate aid, and that such should be given by a free contribution to the imperial authorities of money sufficient to pay for two dreadnoughts. The conservative programme was apparently designed to confirm adherence to the principle of a Canadian navy, while at the same time meeting the objections of the right wing by adding the offer

---

[57] The debates in both houses and public discussion are summarized in *Canadian Annual Review*, 1910, 146 ff.

of dreadnoughts. The bill, however, passed both houses, and a naval policy for Canada was at last written into the statutes.

The Canadian navy first materialized in two cruisers bought from the British government: the *Niobe* of 11,000 tons, commissioned in 1899, and the smaller *Rainbow,* of 3,600 tons, commissioned in 1892. It was announced that tenders for new ships would be called for, and a naval college opened at Halifax. Negotiations were also entered into with a British contractor for the construction of dry docks, one at Lévis and the other at Saint John. The two cruisers arrived in the autumn of 1910 at Halifax, where the naval station, together with that at Esquimalt, was taken over by the Canadian government. During the imperial conference of 1911 discussions between the admiralty and the representatives of Canada and Australia resulted in an agreement set forth in a memorandum.[58] The naval forces of the two dominions were to be under the control of their respective governments, but training and discipline were to be generally uniform with those of the fleet of the United Kingdom, and officers and men might be interchanged. The Canadian and Australian navies were to have their own naval stations, the limits of which were defined. "In time of war, when the naval service of a Dominion, or any part thereof, has been put at the disposal of the Imperial government by the Dominion authorities, the ships will form an integral part of the British fleet, and will remain under the control of the British Admiralty during the continuance of the war."

The conference at the admiralty was the last act in the naval programme of the liberal government. Already Laurier was engulfed in the reciprocity issue, and had been able to attend the imperial conference only because both parties had agreed to break the meeting of parliament for that purpose. Borden had demanded an election on the naval programme. An election indeed there was, but in so far as it turned on the defence question at all, its results did little to encourage the initiation of the conservative plan. The conservatives secured a working alliance (an "unholy alliance" as it has more than once been termed) against the government's naval programme; and this factor was an important one in their success at the polls. On the other hand, these

---

[58] See *Papers Laid Before the Imperial Conference: Naval and Military Defence.* (Cd. 5746-2, 1911).

opposition forces had no agreement on any positive alternative programme; and the conservative party—whether because of its own divisions, election strategy, or genuine conviction—had succeeded in breaking the unanimity of 1909. In the English-speaking provinces little was said in the campaign on the subject of defence; the issue there being reciprocity. In the province of Quebec, on the other hand, the liberal naval bill was the main issue. There the nationalists bitterly opposed it on grounds that it was a step leading Canada into Britain's imperialist wars, and was not necessary for the good of the dominion itself. The result was a defeat of the liberals in that province more than a victory for the conservatives; and certainly it was not a triumph for the policy of contributions to the British navy. Thus the conservative party which came into office in 1911 was hardly in a more happy position to secure united support on naval policy than it had been in 1909. In Ontario the imperial spirit had been enhanced by the arguments used against reciprocity, while in Quebec it had been further subdued by the oratory against the navy.

Although the Naval Service Act remained on the statute book no steps were taken by the incoming administration to implement it. The contracts were not completed, and the Canadian navy consisted only of the two cruisers already acquired. The conservative naval policy proved to differ in some important essentials from that of the liberals. Laurier had followed his doctrine of progressive Canadian nationalism by planning a Canadian navy which, even in time of war, might be kept distinct from the royal navy. To many conservatives this spelt non-participation or even neutrality in the major war which they believed to be not far off. Borden's naval policy was based on this acceptance of immediate necessity and on the hope—it was hardly more—that some method of collaboration in foreign policy might be worked out which would make feasible a single plan for naval defence. While in England in 1912 with three of his colleagues he had conversations with cabinet ministers and the admiralty on naval policy, and attended meetings of the committee of imperial defence. This body, while purely advisory in form, might serve, at least for the time being, to represent, and possibly to consolidate, the views of the various governments of the empire. On returning

from England Borden turned to naval policy.[59] The course which
he proposed was taken with the loss of F. D. Monk (the minister
of public works), who clung to the idea of a plebiscite. Some
of the conservative private members from Quebec also expressed
their decision to vote against the bill. Early in December Borden
introduced the Naval Aid Bill into parliament, providing for
$35,000,000 to pay for three battleships, to be incorporated in the
royal navy unless and until Canada decided to build a fleet of
her own. Whether the latter was to be done was left undecided.
Borden argued that the growing cost of, and need for, naval defence
for the empire made it necessary for the dominions to contribute,
adding that each dominion must preserve its autonomy, and that
"when Great Britain no longer assumes sole responsibility for
defence upon the high seas, she can no longer undertake to
assume sole responsibility for and sole control of foreign policy,
which is closely, vitally and constantly associated in that defence
in which the dominions participate". The liberal opposition held
to its policy of 1910 and brought forward amendment after
amendment. The debate dragged on for months until, early in
April, the government forced its bill through by the use of the
closure. In the senate the bill had a less successful course, for
there the liberal majority refused its passage with the formula
that it should be "submitted to the judgment of the country".

A virtual stalemate had been reached, partly because of sincere
differences of opinion and partly from party manoeuvring. The
government was unwilling to renew a debate which could only
have the same ending as before, and equally unwilling to reverse
its policy by sponsoring the liberal plan of a Canadian navy.
Not only was no progress made toward either a Canadian navy
or a contribution to the royal navy, but even the force already
acquired was not maintained in a state of efficiency. The personnel was allowed to dwindle, and the two cruisers were out of
commission.[60] Canada was thus left with no naval policy and
almost no navy. Yet the danger which had brought the issue to
a head was as real as the most pessimistic had described it. The

[59] See Henry Borden (ed.), *Robert Laird Borden: His Memoirs* (2 vols.,
Toronto, 1938), I, 399 *ff.*, and Skelton, *Life and Letters of Laurier*, II,
395 *ff.* Contemporary comments will be found in the *Round Table,* vols.
II-IV.
    [60] Colonel A. F. Duguid, *Official History of the Canadian Forces in the
Great War, 1914-1919,* General Series, I (Ottawa, 1938), appendix 30.

German navy was a fact, and the policy that lay behind it was translated into fact by the War of 1914.

That war introduced a new era into the naval and military affairs of Canada. And, more than that, it brought such sweeping changes in the whole field of external relations that the war may be taken as marking the end of one period and the beginning of another. That Canada should have—and consciously have—essential relations with the outside world was a traditional factor in her history. But in the years after 1914 she was to take a new place and a new initiative in the affairs of nations.

PART II

CANADIAN FOREIGN POLICY

CHAPTER XII

THE WAR OF 1914

THE spring and summer of 1914 came after long years of peace. Not for a century—not since the last world war—had Canadians fought on their own soil or seen their security threatened by any major conflict across the seas. It was not that Canada lacked a military tradition, but the stability of the *Pax Britannica,* coupled with the establishment of friendly relations with the United States, had long seemed to remove any serious danger. The South African War had demonstrated once more the fighting qualities of Canadian troops, but participation was on a small scale and in a limited theatre. It was in this same spring that plans were being prepared for the celebration of a hundred years of peace with the United States. That to most people seemed more in tune with what they knew than did the echoes of European diplomacy. Yet no reader of the newspapers could fail to be impressed in some degree by the signs of gathering storm. In the Germany of William II no secret was made of an ambition to gain world power built on naval as well as military strength. It was, perhaps, a far cry from a general apprehension to a belief in the imminence of war, but the international crises, following hard on each other's heels, became more alarming as they piled up unsolved problems. The murder of the Habsburg heir in an obscure Bosnian town was—so all reports said —a significant incident. To most people in North America it was also a little unreal; but it was not unobserved.

For Canadians concerned with public affairs, and for those in many forms of business, there were other and more immediate problems at hand. A busy session of parliament had reflected the uneasiness over a pause in the mushroom growth that had given rise to the optimistic description of the twentieth as "Canada's century". In facing this problem parliament was inevitably drawn into the traditional interest of Canada in her external relations,

291

though the particular aspects under discussion were far removed from warfare. The long hours devoted by the house of commons to the facts and policy of immigration show the emphasis laid on the growth of population. The year 1913 had brought a record influx, and there was a general zeal for a continuance of the quantity with a watch over the quality. Closely related to population, and inherent in an economy based on production of staples, was the attention that must be given to trade and the tariff. Connected with the peopling of the western prairies, and an indispensable aid to development, was the construction of railways. Heavy commitments had been made for the building of two additional transcontinental lines, the Grand Trunk Pacific and the Canadian Northern. For neither were the rails completely laid, so that they were then in their most expensive period. The references to "trade depression", unemployment, labour unrest, and "financial stringency" show the worries of the day. The long-delayed progress of Canada had seemed to be at last a reality, but now there were unpleasant signs that all was not well. Although there were "no figures available", it was evident that emigration to the United States was a serious offsetting factor to immigration. Borrowing abroad was becoming less easy. It was all disappointing and disturbing.

Meanwhile the world crisis was fast approaching as the last frantic efforts of diplomacy failed. News of what was going on, other than that reported in the newspapers, came from British sources. There was, it is true, a tiny Canadian department of external affairs, but no diplomatic representatives abroad, and no staff within the department to digest foreign intelligence. Canada was still, in its relationships to the rest of the world, in the last phase of colonial status. Nowhere was the reality of this more apparent than in the dependence of the Canadian government on London for information and direction on both political and military aspects. Such preparations as there had been for a possible war had been made by borrowing ideas, technical advice, and even personnel from the British Isles.

Some parts of the process of preparation could be carried on wholly by officials, but the naval question had long since become a public issue. The century that had passed without a world war had, in part at least, been possible because of the unchallenged supremacy of the British navy. When the latter, for the first time since Trafalgar, had been seriously threatened by German policy and actual construction, the position of the dominions had to be reconsidered. The response of the liberal government under Sir Wilfrid Laurier was the Naval Service Act of 1910, providing for the first time for a small Canadian navy which would supplement the royal navy. Two old cruisers were bought from the British admiralty, but before any further steps could be taken to implement the Act the election of 1911 brought in a new government. The naval policy of the conservative administration was evolved during the next year in consultation with the British authorities.[1] The decisions expressed in the new Naval Aid Bill were that the emergency was real; that it could not be met by the slow process of creating a Canadian navy; and that for these two reasons a contribution in the form of the cost of three dreadnoughts should be made. There could later be a Canadian navy, but something should be done right away in face of the German menace. Sir Robert Borden, who personally took an active part in the whole matter, was not unconscious of the objections to such a gift as opposed to a force under Canadian control, but was influenced not only by the need for effective action, but also by the possibility that he saw of Canadian participation in the direction of imperial policies. The bill was introduced into the commons in December 1912, and after a stormy passage was passed in May 1913. The senate (which retained a liberal majority) defeated the bill in about a week. Prevented thus from pursuing its own policy, the government, hoping to find a way out of the impasse, was unwilling to revert to the earlier legislation for a Canadian navy; so that by the summer of 1914 there was a personnel of only 352 officers and ratings, and there were virtually no ships.

The army was in no such sad state, and indeed had been increasing in size; but it was still very small. The regular army, or permanent force, included only three thousand men of all ranks, and the non-permanent active militia was up to 60,000, though the training was sketchy. The Dominion Arsenal was equipped to manufacture small-arm ammunition and some artillery shells. The rifle used was the Ross, a weapon which proved to be unsuitable both because it was different from that used by the

---

[1] See G. N. Tucker, "The Naval Policy of Sir Robert Borden, 1912-14" (*Canadian Historical Review*, XXVIII, March 1947, 1).

British army and because it was deficient in itself for conditions in the field. From a low point army estimates had doubled in five years, reaching $11,000,000 in 1913-14. Indications of disbelief in the likelihood of war appeared in debates on the estimates when one member of the commons described the expenditure on the arsenal as "money wasted", and another, speaking in June 1914, held that there was "no danger in sight . . . there is no emergency, in sight, and there will be none in our day and generation".

With a small army, a miniature navy, and no air force, Canada did not appear to be well equipped for a major war. In some other respects, happily, preparations for war were more advanced. Largely based on the work of the committee of imperial defence, plans were ready in Ottawa in respect of military and naval action. The "war book", adapted from the British one, provided in detail for the necessary steps in such civil matters as the control of shipping and cables. On this ground work the government was able, just before and after the outbreak of war, to add a series of emergency measures by the first shower of orders-in-council. The War Measures Act, passed in the special session of parliament, confirmed these early steps and gave extraordinary powers to the executive considered appropriate in time of war. To stem a run on the banks, authority was given for the increase of bank notes, for payment by the banks in their own notes instead of in gold or government notes, and for a moratorium; export of war materials and some other commodities was prohibited. Censorship was applied in stages. Control over enemy aliens was defined. By these and other means the government guarded domestic security and order.[2]

Such special powers conceded to the government reflected the attitude of parliament in the special session that began on August 18. The emergency was recognized not only in this way but also in the readiness of the provinces to call a truce in the perennial dispute over the respective jurisdiction of federal and provincial authorities, and to allow to the central government extraordinary powers. No major changes were made in the executive government itself until the time of the coalition, when two main cabinet committees were set up, one being the war committee and the

---

[2] For an account of emergency measures see A. F. Duguid, *Official History of the Canadian Forces in the Great War, 1914-1919* (Ottawa, 1938), I.

other the reconstruction and development committee. Behind the attitude of parliament and the provinces lay the remarkable unanimity of Canadian opinion on the issue of war. When Britain was at war, Canada was at war: that was constitutional and it was proper. More surprising was the almost unchallenged agreement that Canada should actively participate. This, it was realized, was for her to decide; and there was never any doubt as to how the decision would go. Everywhere the war was greeted with demonstrations of enthusiastic patriotism. In Montreal, Winnipeg, and other cities, crowds milled through the streets, singing patriotic songs, waving flags, and waiting for bulletins outside the newspaper offices. All the wild rumours, such as the sinking of the German navy, were greeted with cheers. Across Canada newspapers and individuals called for an army to aid the imperial cause. From the staunchest Tories of Ontario to the nationalists of Quebec there was hardly a dissenting voice.[3]

There were to be rifts later, but in the summer of 1914 there were but small indications of them. Canadians were largely of British and French origin, with the former in a distinct but not overwhelming majority. Many of the first were recent immigrants from the British Isles, but there had been virtually no immigration from France since the middle of the eighteenth century. In addition to these large groups were much smaller but not unimportant ones from various parts of Europe, including the now enemy states. The only question about the more recent arrivals from Europe was their loyalty to Canada, and on the whole not many problems arose in this connection. They had no significant political influence. The decisive question was whether the French and English Canadians could see eye to eye on the war. To judge from examples of the past they might not do so. The striking thing is that they did; for from all sides came cries for a truce to party disputes and a vigorous participation in the battlefield.

The government had not awaited the opening of parliament before making a start on the creation of a new army. On August 2 they asked London by cable for suggestions as to "the most effective means of rendering every possible aid", and expressed their confidence "that a considerable force would be available

---

[3] Analyses of opinion will be found in The Canadian Annual Review and in Elizabeth H. Armstrong, The Crisis of Quebec, 1914-18 (New York, 1937).

for service abroad". On August 6 the British government gratefully accepted the offer of an expeditionary force, which was
authorized in Ottawa by order-in-council on the same day. Recruits were accepted by means of the existing machinery in military divisions and assembled at Valcartier Camp near the city
of Quebec. At the beginning of October a great flotilla of thirty-
two vessels with more than 30,000 Canadian soldiers aboard set
sail with their naval escort (including H.M.C.S. *Niobe*). It was
to be the first of many such crossings in this war that called always
for more and more men.[4]

The quality of the first division was tested in its first battle
experience in France, where it proceeded after training in England. The battle of Ypres in April 1915 was marked by the
first use of poison gas. The horrible new weapon came drifting
across the trenches against troops that had no means of protection
against it. On their flank the French troops broke, but somehow
the Canadians held on and by their stand saved the whole salient.
There could be no doubt of the fighting capacities of Canadian
troops, and at Ypres they gained a reputation which was never
lost. In September the second division crossed the channel and an
army corps was now made of the two. In the first half of 1916
the third and fourth divisions were added, and in August the
whole corps was moved to its second field of operations in the
long and hard battle of the Somme. For the Canadians as for
the British on the Somme it was stiff fighting without much gain
of ground. Canadian forces did take Courcelette, but in the battle
generally they suffered 26,547 casualties.

In late 1916 and early 1917, some important changes were
made in the Canadian corps. The Canadian Expeditionary Force
had now reached such a size that it was found necessary to
appoint a minister of overseas military forces. Sir George Perley,
the high commissioner in London, was named to the new office,[5]
and, with the establishment of a Canadian general staff in Eng-

[4] For the organization of the Canadian Expeditionary Force see Duguid,
Official History. The same volume includes a history of Canadian military
operations in the first year of the war. For accounts of the whole period of
hostilities see Sir Charles Lucas, *The Empire at War* (London, 1923), II;
the *Canadian Annual Review;* and J. C. Hopkins, *Canada at War* (Toronto,
1919).

[5] The origin, organization, and functions are described in *Report of the
Ministry, Overseas Military Forces of Canada 1918* (London, n.d.).

land, the Canadian authorities were then in a position to take over responsibility for organization, training, and all supervision of the Canadian forces in the British Isles. In France they came under the operational control of the British command. In June 1917 a Canadian, General Currie, took over the command of the Canadian corps which had been successfully welded into a unit by his predecessor, General Byng. As the corps moved on to its great battles of 1917—Vimy Ridge, Hill 70, and Passchendaele —the problem of reinforcements became of ever-increasing concern. The fifth division, which had reached England, was broken up to reinforce the other four in France and Belgium, but the recruits in Canada were not appearing in sufficient numbers, and the government was faced with ways and means of finding them.

The government had already committed itself to a contribution of 500,000 men, and while there was some difference of opinion in the country as to whether this was excessive, it appeared to represent the majority view as well as that of the cabinet. Borden returned in May from a visit to England, convinced by the military position that conscription was inevitable, and invited the leader of the opposition, Sir Wilfrid Laurier, to join the government. The offer was refused, and for months the negotiations dragged on with Laurier and other leading liberals. There were now three related issues: conscription, coalition, and a wartime election. All through the summer and early autumn of 1917 the party situation was in a state of flux. The Military Service Act became law in August, but it was October before the union government was formed, and December before the general election confirmed that government in power. The pressure of the war had now brought about a situation in which sixty-two out of sixty-five seats in Quebec were held by an opposition that had won only twenty seats elsewhere, and virtually stood for a solid Quebec set against the other provinces on the major issue of the day.

Thus it was that a national unity which had already developed bad cracks gave way to a direct cleavage on racial lines. Some bitter things had been said about the failure of Quebec to contribute its share of soldiers, and while no accurate figures were available, calculations suggested great discrepancies between Quebec enlistments and those in the other provinces. Other and older disagreements between French- and English-speaking Canadians were revived, and it only needed the maladroit handling of both voluntary enlistment and conscription in Quebec to complete the destruction of the short-lived national unity. Resistance, passive or violent, to the draft in Quebec was a symptom of the rising discontent, and was at its worst in a bad riot in Quebec city in the spring of 1918. Moreover, the act did not even bring the men, and before long serious efforts to capture draft-evaders were dropped. With that restraint, and with the approach of victory, the racial bitterness in part subsided;[6] but the war had left its mark on national unity.

For their achievements in the first three years of war the Canadian corps had won a reputation as shock troops. In 1918 most of the troops missed any direct part in the grim struggle to hold the pressing March offensive of the Germans, but in July were on hand to take their share in the battle of Amiens. Against fifteen German divisions they advanced to a depth of fourteen miles, taking many prisoners and themselves suffering heavy casualties. Now as the tide swiftly turned they advanced to Arras, and so over the Canal du Nord to the battle of Cambrai in October. On November 11 they marched into Mons behind their own pipe-band and in company with the British 5th Lancers, who had returned after four years.

It was in the war on land that Canada had made its most notable contribution, but on sea and in the air Canadians had played no small part. The little Canadian navy of 1914 was multiplied to a personnel of some five thousand in 1918, and was able to man a fleet of small vessels occupied in convoys over the north Atlantic. No Canadian air force came into being, though one was in process of formation at the time of the armistice. But Canadian flyers in thousands (over eight thousand officers and eleven thousand airmen) were in the Royal Air Force, adding in both quality and quantity to that new and growing branch of the armed forces. Some, indeed, of the most famous air-fighters were Canadians.

The war, therefore, had revived the military traditions of Canada which had almost been forgotten in the long decades of peace. The hundreds of thousands who came back, and the tens of thousands who did not, alike created a new consciousness of national achievement and a new realization of the compelling

---

[6] For a detailed study see Armstrong, *Crisis of Quebec.*

power of foreign policy. The War of 1914 was to Canadians a great new human drama, both stimulating and tragic. It reached into every part of Canada and into every household, with its confused but loud *motifs* of personal heroism and suffering, mud, guns, and martial music. It was a story of personalities, told with a vividness and felt with an intimacy that the War of 1939 was never to reach. It broke on Canada in the summer of 1914 as the first great war, and it ended with the belief that it was the last.

In the long run the effects of the war on the Canadian economy were no less significant than they were on its armed forces. Quick action at the outbreak of war put an end to the financial panic which seemed to threaten, and thereafter war financing was smoothly and efficiently handled. The war produced some striking changes in public finance: the multiplication of public debt; the imposition of various new taxes, more particularly the first income tax; the war loans, which were the first federal loans to be floated in Canada, and which totalled nearly $1,850,000,000 by November 1919; and an important relative change from English to American investments in Canada. No one was more pleasantly surprised than the financial experts when the first war loan was over-subscribed by 100 per cent., and no people were more surprised than the Canadians when they found their new capacity to raise money and carry seemingly vast debts.[7]

Industrial and agricultural production kept pace with military effort. The increased demand for food was met by greater production. The favourable growing season of 1915 allowed for a jump in the yield of wheat from an average in the years 1910-13 of 204,712,000 bushels to 393,542,600, and, while that figure was not again reached, the next two years were well over average. The value of manufactured products rose slightly in 1915 and by 1917 was more than double the figure for 1910. This, and the increased exports, were due in large part to the need for food and instruments of war abroad. In the first autumn of the war a Canadian Shell Committee, consisting of local officials, a representative of the British War Office, and several manufacturers, was established. For about a year, contracts for munitions were made either by the Shell Committee or directly between manufacturers and

[7] See Sir Thomas White, *The Story of Canada's War Finance* (Montreal, 1921).

purchasing governments. While the process of providing facilities in Canada was fairly rapid, orders were comparatively small and irregular. It was not until late in 1915 that the Canadian munitions industry got into its stride, following the more vigorous methods of the British ministry of munitions, now under Lloyd George, and the change from the Shell Committee to the Imperial Munitions Board, with J. W. (later Sir Joseph) Flavelle as chairman. In addition to shells, aeroplanes and ships were constructed. The total expenditures of the board were enormous, amounting to $1,250 millions in three years. Even in 1915 the munitions industry had become the largest in Canada, and it continued to grow; resulting not only in an immediate multiplication of the figures of exports, but in the hurried growth of Canadian industry, which would have a more prolonged effect. In industry as in finance, Canada had experienced a process of change that under ordinary conditions might have been expected to take many years.

While the federal government was able to arrest the tendency towards provincial autonomy, and a degree of centralization was created in this period of crisis, the centrifugal forces had not been entirely dissipated, as was shown by the controversy between Quebec and Ontario. The conscription issue brought to a head the festering dissension in the country, and made necessary a coalition which many individuals had long before claimed to be necessary.

With these conflicting factors in mind it is not easy to measure any growth toward nationalism if the evidence is to be taken purely from the domestic scene. It can be said that the country went into the war united, though that unity was to some degree destroyed by opposite tendencies after the first year. The growth of industrial capacity and financial strength provided the foundation on which a more rounded economy and a more self-sustained entity could be built. There are indications of the growth of national self-assurance derived from effective military and industrial effort. It needed, however, some direction, some focus. If a sense of Canadian nationalism was to grow it must envisage both an overcoming of sectional differences and a Canadian point of view separate from, though not necessarily conflicting with, political affiliations outside Canadian territory.

The position of Canada within the British Empire is a main thread of Canadian history; changing always in its particular form, it offered to all generations a problem that never failed to arouse interest and controversy. At the time of the outbreak of war, autonomy in domestic affairs had in practice been effected, although there were certain vestiges of imperial authority which were technical rather than actual limitations. In its external relations Canada had moved only a part of the way toward autonomy. It had no diplomatic relations with other countries, no treaty-making power, and no separate status. To the outside world it was a colony, the channel to which was by way of the imperial government. Foreign policy, the results of which might affect it in greater or lesser degree, was made in London, and in that Canada had no voice. To the overwhelming majority of Canadians it was satisfactory that Canada should enter the war because the empire was at war. They were prepared not only to accept a state of belligerency which was held undoubtedly to exist, but to participate actively and in every feasible manner. The mother-country was in danger, and consequently the empire of which Canada formed a part was in danger. Some Canadians may have been influenced only by sentiment, but others could reach the same conclusion on grounds of interest.

To this context those of British origin or descent were necessarily in a different situation from those who were not. They might, and did, have a variety of views on the imperial relationship, but at least they could think in terms of their own mother-country. Those of French descent had no such relationship, no ties of blood. For a hundred and fifty years they had accepted the imperial authority as assuring to them liberty to maintain those institutions and ways of life that they most cherished. In the Province of Quebec, as elsewhere in Canada, there was no single view on the subject, but the majority there shared with the majority of other Canadians the belief that the country should take its part in the war. There were in all parts of Canada individuals who claimed that Canada was being dragged behind the imperial chariot, and others who thought that the Canadian government was being influenced to attempt too large an effort in the war, as well as those who agreed with the government's policy. The division was not on party lines, and only became so after conscription and the election of 1917.

Such controversies and differences were not without deep importance, but the new and the most significant fact was that Canadians were, from their own efforts, being hurried and shaken into a position in which they were obliged to re-assess their views on the position of Canada in the world. The sight of a great army led the Canadian government to take the steps which have already been described to transfer it, in so far as was practicable, to Canadian control. The Canadian navy, as it grew from such modest beginnings, was to come under Canadian authority at a later stage, and a separate Canadian air force was decided on in principle. Cause and result here operated in a defined field. But armed forces are only the instruments of policy, and every month of war drove home the lesson that men were fighting, munitions were being manufactured, and money was being poured out as a result of a situation which Canada had no part in making, and in order to reach a goal which was likely to be no less remote from Canadian control.

Both the economic and political aspects of imperial relationships were explored during the war. The Dominions Royal Commission, appointed in 1912, continued its work during the war. Composed of representatives of the United Kingdom and the dominions (Sir George Foster represented Canada) it toured Canada, amongst other parts of the empire, and made its final report in 1917 under the influence of wartime conditions. The following quotation from the report will indicate the line of approach:

The success of the action achieved during the war suggests that it is expedient that the Governments of the Empire should take steps, as soon as conditions permit, to secure the development of their natural wealth towards a definite and recognized object. In our opinion it is vital that the Empire should, as far as possible, be placed in a position which would enable it to resist any pressure which a foreign Power or group of Powers could exercise in time of peace or during war in virtue of control of raw materials and commodities essential for the safety and well-being of the Empire, and it is towards the attainment of this object that co-ordinated effort should be directed.[8]

The commission represented one phase of the long consideration—at imperial conferences, in parliaments, and in unofficial writings—

8 Quoted in W. K. Hancock, Survey of British Commonwealth Affairs; Vol. II, Problems of Economic Policy, 1918-1939, part I (London, 1940), 100. The section entitled "Economics of Siege" in which the quotation appears is a valuable study of contemporary thought on imperial economic integration.

of the desirability and possibility of closer integration of empire countries economically. Given a new urgency by the war, the decisions for all but immediate needs were left for a future date. There was, too, the same postponement of decisions on the character that political integration should take; but the developing practice evolved under pressure of war offered one experiment in imperial government which was important in itself and suggestive for the future.

For the early part of the war discussions between the commonwealth governments took the sporadic form of attendance at meetings of the British cabinet of any dominion prime ministers who happened to be in London. In practice this was far from sufficient for the Canadian government, which took the view that not only did it have no voice in the great decisions on strategy, but that it did not even get information. A somewhat heated letter from Borden to Perley (the high commissioner) in January 1916 was precipitated by Bonar Law's view that, while the Canadian government should be consulted, he saw no way in which that could be done. Borden wrote:

During the past four months since my return from Great Britain, the Canadian government (except for an occasional telegram from you or Sir Max Aitken) have had just what information could be gleaned from the daily press and no more. As to consultation, plans of campaign have been made and unmade, measures adopted and apparently abandoned and generally speaking steps of the most important and even vital character have been taken, postponed or rejected without the slightest consultation with the authorities of this Dominion. It can hardly be expected that we shall put 400,000 or 500,000 men in the field and willingly accept the position of having no more voice and receiving no more consideration than if we were toy automata. Any person cherishing such an expectation harbours an unfortunate and even dangerous delusion. Is this war being waged by the United Kingdom alone, or is it a war waged by the whole Empire?[9]

Borden's indignation grew not only out of a belief that in principle the dominions should be consulted, but also from a growing apprehension that British generalship left much to be desired.

[9] Henry Borden (ed.), *Robert Laird Borden: His Memoirs* (2 vols., Toronto, 1938), II, 622.

Whether or not this apprehension (which arose out of reports from Sir Arthur Currie) was justified, there was equal reason for full information and for consultation on the methods of conducting the war. It happened that Borden's point of view came very close to that of Lloyd George, who was critical of the generals and a believer in imperial policy reached by agreement. On coming to office at the end of 1916 Lloyd George first reorganized the United Kingdom cabinet, and then, in March 1917, set up two new bodies which should bring together the governments of the empire. The imperial war cabinet consisted of five members of the British war cabinet, the prime ministers of the dominions, a representative of India, and the colonial secretary. Parallel with this was the imperial war conference, of similar but larger membership.[10]

It was in the first of these bodies that the immediate problems of the war—strategy and supply—were discussed, and there was general agreement that it was a successful experiment. While it was decided that the general constitutional question of the empire should be left for a special imperial conference to be called immediately after the war, two tendencies were apparent. One was that the dominions would expect a continuing voice in foreign affairs; and the other was that the wartime bodies had so far served that purpose, and might form a model for permanent institutions.

During the war, Canadians might reasonably feel that, from their point of view, function had moved ahead of status. They were less conscious that, if an equation was to be reached, it followed that they must guard against an over-balance the other way. If foreign policy was to be on a common imperial footing, there must then be a combination of an agreed method and a readiness to take commitments. In the atmosphere at the end of 1918, however, the question of external political relations was not often envisaged in such simple terms. As hostilities drew to a close with Canadian fighting men taking no mean share of the burden, it is not surprising that the dominant Canadian feeling should have

10 See R. M. Dawson, *The Development of Dominion Status, 1900-1936* (London and Toronto, 1937) for an account of the wartime machinery. On Sir Robert Borden's position see also F. H. Soward, "Sir Robert Borden and Canada's External Policy, 1911-1920" (*Report of the Canadian Historical Association*, 1941); and the *Borden Memoirs*.

been that their country had paid its subscription to the society of sovereign states. A robust nationalism, bred of action, was manifesting itself. It showed immaturity and lack of experience in some of its expressions, and the country was not institutionally ready to play a part on the diplomatic stage. But if Canada was sufficiently a part of the world to throw munitions, food, and men into a war, it was surely entitled to take a place in the peace negotiations which it had helped to make possible.

CHAPTER XIII

PEACEMAKING

E VERY country that had actively participated in it was in some degree affected by the War of 1914. In some cases the effects were extreme: Austria-Hungary disintegrated under the additional stresses of war, and the empire of the Romanovs was torn down in bloody revolution. It was no less an opportunity for the triumph of nationalist movements, such as those which led to the placing on the map of Poland, Czechoslovakia, and Yugoslavia. Elsewhere belligerents experienced less fundamental changes. Some of them, like France or Serbia, saw their lands over-run or devastated in the course of military operations, with the inhabitants left homeless, penniless, and often starving. All contributed in the lives of their nationals, and from their treasuries.

The war arose out of a complexity of causes, immediate and underlying, some of which were carried through in direct or changed form to the plans for peace. As soon, however, as consideration was given to such plans, a whole series of national objectives arose. These were at least as much results of the war as they were causes. The idea of the League of Nations, for example, was an old one revived in practical form only because the war seemed to make it a pressing necessity. France and Belgium began to take stock of their frontiers with Germany. England thought of her interests in sea power, trade, and colonies; Italy of the completion of territorial unity; and Japan of predominance in the far east. The United States was determined to preserve intact the Monroe doctrine. As the possibility of a victorious conclusion became more hopeful, all the allied governments inevitably studied, from their own points of view, the terms which would best promote their own policies.

In this setting Canada was in a somewhat anomalous position. Technically she was not a sovereign state; and, although she had always had important relations with other countries, she was not recognized as an independent power, and had not herself carried on diplomatic relations with other states. There were Canadian interests abroad, but there was no Canadian foreign policy. Canada was a part of the British Empire, through which her diplomatic relations were conducted. For forty years or more Canadian governments had expressed views on foreign policy so far as it affected Canada, and had taken part in negotiations in which they were directly interested. The war had, in fact, come at one stage of a long development characteristic of the British Empire. Since it was organic, and capable of change as well as growth, that empire was never easily defined. To foreigners it was one thing; to its subjects it was any one of several other things, depending on their varying points of view.

One of the effects of the war on Canada was to make her more ready to take a direct place in the world of states. Her military and economic effort in the war had given her confidence, a sense of accomplishment, and added impetus to a slowly-rising spirit of nationalism. As the question of peacemaking arose it was inevitable that it should be linked in Canadian minds with this general constitutional one—if for no other reason than because it must be decided how Canada was to be represented. Late in October 1918 Lloyd George suggested to Borden by telegraph that he should be ready to leave for Europe to take part in discussions on the line to be taken "by the British delegates" at inter-allied conferences preceding the peace conference. Borden was ready to go, but replied that the Canadian government, press, and people expected that Canada would be represented at the peace conference. This, as Lloyd George pointed out, was a decision that could not be reached by cable.[1] In fact a group of four ministers and staff set sail without knowing whether or not they were a delegation.

What was the Canadian policy to be advocated by these ministers? Curiously enough it was primarily not so much a question of what they would advocate, but of how they could do so. They sought recognition of the right of representation not because they wanted the opportunity of securing territory or other objectives—not even

[1] The correspondence is printed in *Canada, Sessional Papers*, 1919, special session, No. 41 J. For a fuller account of Canadian participation and for bibliography, readers are referred to the present writer's *Canada at the Paris Peace Conference* (Toronto, 1942).

because they were deeply concerned with the form of world order —but because they wanted acceptance of Canadian status as a principle. Their position was not unique either by past or contemporary standards. Cavour had gone further by taking Sardinia into the Crimean War, not because she had any quarrel with Russia, but to secure the right to a seat at the subsequent peace conference. In 1918 South Africa and Australia took much the same view as Canada. But Sardinia, South Africa, and Australia all had in mind not only the establishment of the principle but also a means of expressing territorial ambitions. The Canadian government had no such specific objectives for which to prepare. Indeed there was little preparation of any kind except, apparently, some study of the constitutional aspect. No special committee or other group seems to have been set up to examine the issues likely to come before the peace conference, and certainly no standing organization was capable of undertaking such a task. The department of external affairs still existed in skeleton form only, and was in no position to supply background memoranda or experts on the various subjects of a conference. The only member of the department to go, in fact, was the legal adviser—a situation which was in line with the concentration by the ministers on legal or constitutional matters.

At the time that they left Canada the group of ministers and advisers did not know whether they were a delegation, but on one thing at least they had a firm policy. They felt—and it appears to have been the general view in Canada—that justice indicated a place at the peace table for a country that had played a man's part in the war. It could also be looked at from another side: that the war gave an opportunity for establishing a position which could with difficulty have been demanded under ordinary circumstances. Certainly this line of thought could by no conceivable reasoning be related to the factors which led Canada to enter and play an active part in the war, but was an objective which presented itself as growing out of it, and appropriately pursued as the occasion arose. It was most obviously in this way that Canada had been affected by the war; she had grown up internationally.

Grown up, but not yet reached maturity. There was no staff of permanent officials to study foreign affairs in general and the peace conference in particular, and in the available sources there is no hint of consideration in 1918 by the cabinet of current inter-national questions from a Canadian point of view. Similarly the public comment on the coming settlement, while not unintelligent, shows a lack of background of parliamentary discussion and recognized interest. It is not intended to suggest that a Canadian government and people were not capable of a more positive attitude. More than forty years before, Sir John Macdonald had shown himself a skilful negotiator when fisheries and other subjects of direct Canadian concern were under discussion in Washington. There were no such direct Canadian interests at the end of 1918, because the settlement was not to touch the Americas except indirectly. It was in Europe, the Pacific, and the far east that territory was to be transferred and the internal affairs of countries affected. On only one or two occasions did a proposal arise that would similarly touch North America, and then the Canadians were quick to express a view.

The Canadian group that set out for England in November was strong on the ministerial level, but with a team of advisers who, though able, could cover only a small part of the probable agenda. Sir Robert Borden, prime minister and secretary of state for external affairs, headed the group, the other ministers being Sir George Foster, minister of trade and commerce, A. L. Sifton, minister of customs, and C. J. Doherty, minister of justice. In London the imperial war cabinet met to examine a number of subjects that were to come up in Paris. As these were brought forward, Canadian policy was formulated, apparently concurrently with the discussions. Foster was put on a committee on reparations and accepted the general approach of Germany paying as much as she could. Borden queried the proposed procedure for the trial of the kaiser, and showed some interest in the Russian problem. He spoke with a new assurance and vigour on the necessity of good relations between Great Britain and the United States, which, he felt, might be imperilled by a grasping colonial policy. Here at least was a direct Canadian interest. On that, and even more on the representation of small powers, the Canadians concentrated in London. They also did a good deal of study, so that the curtain-raiser in Whitehall was a useful preliminary to the conference itself.

At least in degree, it was not until they reached Paris early in January that the Canadians realized the full implications of their own representation in the conference. They had too much tended to think of it as a constitutional problem within the British Empire. It was that certainly; and both Wilson and Lansing questioned what they regarded as multiple British Empire votes. Clemenceau was rather friendly towards the dominions which had shown a fighting capacity, but he had to be convinced that any small powers should have a part in the conference. The Canadians then had to support the claims of the lesser powers in the kind of argument that had occurred at so many previous conferences. From the point of view of the struggle for status a technical victory was won. The decision reached did not, it is true, give to Canada or any other small power much chance to participate in the work of the conference; but the dominions had a second string to their bow in their membership on the British Empire delegation. The arrangement for a panel allowed dominion representatives at times to attend the various bodies made up in whole or in part of the great powers, and always gave them a chance both to express views and to keep in close touch with what was really going on. In a practical way the dominions had the most advantageous position of any countries outside the great powers. They were always in touch with the centre as well as appearing in their own right as separate parties to the conference.

Properly speaking, peacemaking was in two stages: the preliminary conference, which was the discussion amongst the allies, and the conference itself which took the form of a written exchange between the allies and the enemy powers. With the first procedural questions out of the way, the conference (as it may be called for purposes of simplicity) settled down to a long list of substantive questions. In many of these subjects the Canadian delegation had no direct interest and no opportunity of participating, but in others they felt an immediate concern. Of the latter probably the major one was the projected League of Nations. From every point of view this came close to Canada. It involved her equality of status on international bodies, proposed commitments by the members that called for close study, and was intended to include the United Kingdom and the United States, the two great powers by whose policies Canada was always most affected. From the London days the delegation worked on the proposals. Lieutenant-Colonel O. M. Biggar, the judge advocate-general, and one of the two military experts, prepared there a series of memoranda analysing the various proposals. In Paris Doherty carried on the study in a memorandum which raised the general question of whether the league as projected was too much one of governments and too little one of peoples. By a queer twist of fate it turned out that, when for once the Canadian delegation had ideas to offer beyond their own country's status, they found that it was only on the latter and not on the former that they were being consulted.

It was not of course that the Canadian delegation were disinterested in membership. No serious problems arose about membership in general, and therefore of the assembly, since both the British and United States drafts had anticipated the inclusion of the dominions (though Colonel House ominously noted in his diary that the British would thus have six votes). Eligibility for the council, however, was not so easily established. On the supposition that great powers only would be represented on the council, Borden proposed that, as a temporary expedient, the British Empire should adopt the panel system. The conference's commission on the league, however, finally decided against a council made up exclusively of great powers. The Canadians then made assurance doubly sure by persuading Wilson, Lloyd George, and Clemenceau to sign a statement that the dominions were eligible.

Canada was not represented on the league commission, but the delegates kept closely in touch with its proceedings, and continued to devote a good deal of time to the practicability and implications of proposed articles. Some of their comments were on minor drafting questions, and they proposed that article VIII should include a prohibition of the private manufacture of munitions. The main criticism, however, was of article X, on the guarantee of political independence and territorial integrity. This was, and continued to be, a matter of major policy. Borden drew up a brief, and Doherty a lengthy criticism of the draft article. They felt that it had several serious defects. It assumed that "all existing territorial delimitations are just and expedient", though the peace conference had no authority to determine the legitimacy of such holdings, nor would any member state ever agree to such enquiry by its fellow members. From the Canadians' point of view there were special objections. Their country would be bound on all occasions, although it was a country with particular rather than general interest (to follow the language used by the conference to distinguish between great powers and others). Canada was a young country, with no reason to apprehend territorial aggression. There was, therefore, no mutual advantage. "Let the mighty, if they will, guarantee the security of the weak." To impose such an obligation on Canada and other nations smaller and less immediately concerned might imperil their whole attitude toward the league.

The point of view of the delegation toward the covenant was referred to Ottawa and approved by the cabinet. It was quite another thing to persuade the other countries. Borden's memorandum was circulated to the commission but apparently not discussed by it. The real obstacle to change lay in the conviction of the American delegation that article X was an essential part of the league, and of the French that it was the only portion that made any realistic approach to the problem of security. Having been jockeyed out of their plan for a league with an international army at its disposal, the French saw in article X the only solid guarantee in an otherwise uncertain scheme of protection. In this attitude they would, of course, be supported by a number of smaller European states which had an understandable fear of aggression. Whether they were right or wrong in their onslaught on article X—an onslaught which was to be repeated again and again in later years—the Canadian delegation at least perceived the difference in interest between what were to be known in the jargon of the twenties as the producers and consumers of security. They represented too, far more than did the United States delegation, a general attitude of the Americas that was soon to show itself with disastrous effect in the United States senate and subsequently in many questions of an international character.

Two other issues arose which similarly evoked a North American response from the Canadian delegation. The first of these was a Japanese proposal for an assertion in the covenant of racial equality. Between the readiness of the United Kingdom to accept a general statement and the firm opposition of Hughes of Australia, Borden tried to find a compromise that would be at once a gesture toward the oriental states and yet no possible commitment to accept their nationals as immigrants. In the end no compromise was found and the Japanese proposal failed. The interest of the incident is that it touched on immigration policy, which was a traditional Canadian contact with international relations. A second issue touching on local Canadian conditions was the proposed convention on air navigation. Preliminary studies had been made in England during the war, and the subject was later introduced into the peace conference. The Canadian ministers immediately began to think of the effects of any international control of civil aviation on their long border with the United States. The draft called forth a vigorous condemnation by Sifton, who described it in a letter to Borden as "the worst example we have yet seen of internationalism gone mad". Conversation with Lansing showed that the Americans too would think in terms of special arrangements for the common frontier, and a Canadian reservation was entered, expressing some objections and leaving the final word to parliament. Later the convention was approved, with a reservation allowing for bilateral arrangements with the United States. For similar reasons Canada did not adhere to two other conventions that grew out of the conference, one on the régime of navigable waterways and the other on freedom of transit.

The proposed labour organization was one of the major questions at Paris as far as the Canadian delegates were concerned. They represented a country of increasing industrial importance where the views of organized labour made up an important element in public opinion. The privileges and responsibilities to be incurred in membership in such an organization deserved careful study, and it was obvious that—unlike some other issues that played important parts at Paris—the labour charter would have a direct effect on Canadian domestic affairs. After the experience in connection with the covenant the delegation was watchful for any ambiguities in the right to full membership, or for any clauses that appeared to be undesirable from the Canadian point of view. For a time, indeed, there was more than an ambiguity, for, as it soon became apparent, officials of the United States delegation were opposing dominion membership of the governing body of the labour organization on the ground that it would mean multiple British voting. Borden was active in seeing the officials and finally Wilson himself, the latter proving to be ready to over-ride his labour experts. Conversations and re-drafts and discussions of procedure—all the processes typical of an international conference—led to a decision in plenary session satisfactory to the dominions. A story that is brief in the telling was long enough (in hours if not days) in the event.

Apart from some comments on details, the only other Canadian worry was a proposed clause which read: "In all matters concerning their status as workers and social insurance foreign workmen lawfully admitted to any country and their families should be ensured the same treatment as the nationals of that country". Now this raised a very awkward point, not unlike the Japanese proposal for a statement on racial equality. Here was the added complication that some provinces not only had fixed views on the presence of orientals, but had passed legislation barring orientals from certain trades. Various people tried their hands at re-drafts, and the accepted one was produced by Borden, at Balfour's suggestion, just in time for the plenary session of April 28. With a few polishes added, the now highly-innocuous clause read: "The standard set by law in each country with respect to the conditions of labour should take due regard to the equitable economic treatment of all workers lawfully resident therein".

The task which the peace conference had set itself was probably heavier than any similar body had ever assumed. The generally accepted objective was to produce a settlement and a world order that would facilitate the growth of democratic ideas, deal out justice to victor and vanquished, and set firm barriers against the revival of war as a means of settling international disputes. It has been easy to be cynical about both motives and results partly because cynicism is always easy, and partly because there has been ample ammunition left by the peacemakers themselves. The essence of the conference, however, was not that it was a collection of intriguers, but that it was a gathering of the representatives of thirty-two countries (excluding the enemy states) each of which had special problems and desires, and each of which felt quite honestly that it had a right in justice to attain measures which it required. By the time that the conference met many governments had formulated their policies in some detail, but for reasons which have already been indicated the Canadian delegation had no such running start. It was obliged to improvise as it went, to find the factual material where it could, and to evolve Canadian policy as circumstances made it necessary. Those questions which touched Canada most intimately have been mentioned. The delegation also turned its hand to various other matters that came before the conference. On reparations (pressed by demands in the parliament at Ottawa that Germany should pay) they supported in general the British thesis. All the delegates found themselves placed on various economic or political commissions and appear to have rendered a good account of themselves. Borden was named as chief British delegate to the proposed conference with the Bolsheviks at Prinkipo, looking to a negotiation which would have been as ungrateful as difficult; but the conference itself was called off because of disagreement on the agenda. Generally speaking, it is fair to say that the Canadian delegation was active and far-sighted in its pursuit of Canadian interests, and gave a good impression in its general work in the conference.

One last contentious question that arose was the signature of the treaties. Early in the conference Borden had sought and obtained agreement that the representatives of the dominions should sign separately. While this was readily cleared out of the way by a compromise,[2] some complications did arise from the decision of the United Kingdom representatives to sign for "the British Empire", which—in the days before the phrase "British Commonwealth" had come into usage—included the dominions. The latter were apparently therefore covered in two ways. The first consequence of this was when the colonial secretary informed Ottawa that his government hoped to ratify the Treaty of Versailles before the end of July. This raised a nice point. Since the United Kingdom plenipotentiaries had signed for the British Empire, ratification would be for the British Empire, including Canada. But the Canadian government was determined not to advise ratification until it had secured the approval of parliament. The anomaly was not overlooked when the treaty was brought down for approval by the special session at the beginning of September. In the house of commons a series of criticisms was made on this ground, perhaps the most vigorous being W. S. Fielding's description of the whole proceedings as "a colossal humbug".

What was more significant than this expected objection was the unwillingness of parliament to give any serious attention to the peace settlement as such. The debates in both houses appear long, but they are in fact devoted very largely to the constitu-

---

[2] Glazebrook, *Canada at the Paris Peace Conference*, 111-12.

tional implications. The ministers, who as plenipotentiaries had gone through the educational experience of the Paris conference, did their best to place before parliament the character of the treaties themselves, but with very little success, to judge by the substance of the debate. By September 4 the senate, and by September 11 the commons, had passed the resolution approving of the Treaty of Versailles, and little comment was made on the subsequent treaties as the same procedure was followed for each in turn.

Was the settlement satisfactory from a Canadian point of view? On the procedural side the answer was an affirmative from all those who had believed and argued that Canada was entitled to the status of a sovereign state both in the negotiation and signature of the treaties and also in the world organizations that had been set up at the same time. The other aspect of the settlement that evoked any real interest was the extent of the commitments undertaken under the Covenant of the League of Nations. Article X never ceased to be the target of criticism, for it appeared to commit Canada, as a member, to an indefinite responsibility in matters in which she might feel little concern. Since the settlement which the League was in part to uphold was one negotiated and approved by Canada, it would have been a logical process for her parliament to have discussed that settlement on its merits. Such, however, was not the mood of the time, nor apparently the stage of maturity which the Canadian people had attained in their thinking about world affairs.

It might be reasonable to ask the further question: What lessons did Canada learn from her participation in the Paris settlement? One practical answer was the need for governmental machinery devoted exclusively to the study of world affairs: or, in other words, the need for the development of a department of external affairs of a size commensurate with the government's new concern in that field. There are no published indications of any such conclusion, and indeed that department was for nearly another generation to be starved in size of staff. Diplomatic representation abroad was, in tune with constitutional development, early mooted, though not in effect for some years. Perhaps no government could have been expected to take steps still in advance of public and parliament. The atmosphere of the day in Canada was in many ways similar to that in the other English-speaking countries. Canadians were proud of their part in the war and conscious of the cost in men and money that would impose a burden, they thought, for many years. They shared the optimism of those who—unlike some of the exposed Europeans—looked towards a long era of peace based on the principles of democracy. The German armies had dissolved, the German navy was at the bottom of the sea, and provision was made for continued restriction of armaments. The threat had been met and was over; and in future any other aggression would have to run the gauntlet of collective action. The long struggle was finished. It had left deep wounds, but little apprehension of any repetition.

To return to the ways of peace was now the ambition of Canadians. Army and navy could safely be cut to a corporal's guard, and swords be beaten into ploughshares. It was hoped to convert to peacetime uses factories that had been making munitions, and to take advantage of the shortage of goods in the world to revive and enlarge foreign trade. Not that Canada could ever be the same in respect of its external relations as it had been before 1914. Official Canada had gained experience in the arts of war and diplomacy, and the public was to exhibit a marked degree of interest in world affairs—an interest that had existed only in a small degree before the war. Here, if properly encouraged and channelled, was one of the most important assets that a country with world interests could have. An informed and critical public opinion would in turn stimulate parliament to a close study of the government's foreign policy, and ensure that the degree and direction of Canada's activity in the foreign field was in accordance with the considered desires of the people.

So the Canadian people entered the post-war world, with experience drawn from participation in the final acts of international relations—the making of war and peace; and with hopes, ideas, and ideals for the new era. On the one hand were to be many shattered ambitions and misdirected efforts; on the other the real if intangible effect on national life of the lessons of experience.

Chapter XIV

POST-WAR CANADA

THE changes in Canada as a result of the war were considerable rather than radical. At no stage of history had Canadians lived an existence unaffected by the affairs of other countries. In the political, economic, social, and cultural fields the interdependence of Canada with other states had been strongly marked. The War of 1914 did not create either interest or participation in external affairs, for both had long existed. It did, however, increase the quantity and alter the character of both. Their share in hostilities and in peacemaking brought to Canadians a consciousness of having an active if minor rôle on the world's stage; but long before the deliberations of the Paris conference had been concluded the attention of the country was turned to peaceful pursuits in the post-war world. It was a world in which the triumphant ending of large-scale military operations well-nigh concealed the local struggles that continued to break out, and in which the conclusion of successful peace outweighed the unsettled causes of international friction. It had been a war to end war; and Canadians, like other peoples, hastened to divert the energy, the wealth, and the productive capacity that the war had evoked to the promotion of personal and national prosperity.

Amongst other effects the end of the war made possible a renewal of immigration, and discussions of policies, possibilities, and results ran through parliament and press. There is no aspect of external relations which has been of more direct interest to Canada and which has, over a long period, called forth such consistently similar arguments and counter-arguments. The country was large in area, with natural resources revealed in increasing quantities, and yet with a population small and growing slowly. Surely the answer was to open the doors to people from older lands, and so to build up a great population, as the United States had long since done? So far most Canadians in any generation would agree. At first blush the whole process appeared logical and easy. From more crowded lands would come people anxious to make new homes and to work in their various fields of endeavour. Production and demand would then interact so that wealth would increase with population, and the power and prestige of the country with both.

Thus it should be; and indeed in the decade before the war, with the wide west opening up to the tune of railway construction, such a process had seemed under way. In 1920 and 1921—before the economic slump cut the figures again—it seemed to have recommenced. In reality, of course, there had never been a simple procedure of adding population in direct ratio to the numbers of new residents that entered. Unfortunately there first had to be taken into account the considerable number of persons leaving Canada, particularly those going to the United States. Some of these were the recent immigrants themselves, passing on to the land of greater promise; others—and this was the serious problem—were the Canadian-born seeking greater opportunities. The effect in terms of statistics was that a favourable balance began to show only from 1901, and that in the peak year, 1913, while 406,065 persons entered Canada, 201,260 left it.[1] It was an old problem but, to the men who looked ruefully at it, one that was always new. By the decade of the twenties the situation, from the Canadian point of view, was in fact improving, although it gave at the time no less cause for worry. The position as it stood in 1921 was that there were in the United States 1,124,925 Canadian-born persons, representing 12.80 per cent. of the contemporary population of Canada.[2] They were settled for the most part in groups and so to some extent retained a consciousness of their origin, but the number that returned was small.

Men were leaving Canada for a country of greater and more varied opportunities. The advantages held by the United States must be due in great part to its vastly larger population. So the argument would come back to the same point: increase the inflow, with the result that it would not only change the balance but would in time build up a larger population that would make

---

[1] R. Wilson, "Migration Movements in Canada, 1868-1925" (*Canadian Historical Review*, XIII, June 1932, 157).

[2] R. H. Coats and M. C. MacLean, *The American-Born in Canada: A Statistical Interpretation* (Toronto, 1943), 24.

the country more attractive and so reduce absolutely the outflow. Here, however, a new difficulty presented itself. There were, it was true, large numbers of prospective immigrants, but could the country absorb them in the economic sense? In time of unemployment, such as in the depression which began in 1921, organized labour in particular was doubtful of the wisdom of introducing more people when there were not enough jobs to go round those already resident. In 1922 and 1923 the numbers of immigrants were materially reduced in consequence of the harder times in Canada.

Furthermore, there was constantly apprehension as to the political and social results of an indiscriminate lowering of the barriers against immigrants. For many years there had been severe restrictions on the entry of orientals on the grounds that their lower standards of living enabled them to compete unfairly with white workers and that their social characteristics introduced a permanently foreign element. Nor was it desired to have in Canada an undue proportion of people from certain countries of southern Europe. The racial balance must be maintained, which meant preserving the dominance of the French and Anglo-Saxon strains.

Debates on immigration in the house of commons took up long hours, and were similar in character to those in earlier and later years. Both government and opposition clung to a policy of "selective" immigration. Individual members would have defined that policy more closely by excluding, for example, orientals, professional labour agitators, and—that new menace—bolsheviks. It was generally agreed that more people were needed as settlers, to swell the ranks of industry, and to justify the expense of transcontinental railways. But the government must move cautiously: it must neither fling the gates wide open nor close them completely. It should, indeed, cling to that blessed word "selective", and the newcomers must be inducted into the Canadian way of life. References, as ever, were made to the loss of population to the United States, and to the desirability of repatriating those good citizens who had already gone there; though how this was to be done was never made clear.

An examination of the population as it stood under the census of 1921 indicates the ethnic composition in outline. There were at that time in Canada 8,787,949 souls in all. When broken down by place of birth the following divisions of the total population appear:

Canada   6,832,224
British Isles and possessions   1,064,795
Europe   459,325
United States   374,022
Asia   51,636

Looking at the provinces from east to west the picture may be studied in more detail, and with reference to racial origin as well as birthplace. The small population of Prince Edward Island had been born almost entirely in the Island itself, and with a scant proportion of races other than British. Nova Scotia and New Brunswick also had heavy proportions of Canadian-born, but with important minorities from the British Isles and Newfoundland, Europe, and the United States; and small groups from Syria and China. The Province of Quebec had two main elements—much the larger being Canadian by birth and French by origin (there was little French immigration to any province); and the other being English-speaking, made up of persons born in the province itself, in the British Isles, and in the United States. Europeans and Asiatics were not numerous. Ontario occupied a middle position, with large minorities born in the British Isles, in Europe, and to a lesser extent in the United States. The figures on ethnic origin show large European groups, particularly French who had come from the neighbouring province of Quebec. The three prairie provinces, from the nature and recent period of their settlement had large percentages of their population born outside Canada —in the British Isles, in Europe, and in the United States. In British Columbia alone was there any large body of orientals, chiefly Chinese, with lesser numbers of Japanese and East Indians.

Two attempts in the post-war years to control the ethnic character of immigration are of interest. One of the subjects for discussion at the imperial economic conference of 1923 was empire settlement. The special committee on this subject approved empire settlement in principle without introducing any new measures to facilitate it. The Canadian government continued its financial support of the passages of certain categories of settlers, agreed to assist in placing newcomers in employment, and extended loan facilities to ex-servicemen from other parts of the empire. These were positive moves to aid immigration. On the other side were new restrictions on the entrance of orientals. Renewed immigration of Chinese toward the end of the war once more brought on a series of debates and proposals. Without looking at all the several steps taken in the early twenties, the final arrangements may be noted. In 1923 a new act drastically curtailed Chinese immigration, limiting the permitted classes to government employees, Canadian-born children, merchants, and students. In 1928 a new gentlemen's agreement was reached which further curtailed the immigration of Japanese.[3]

No simple relationship can be established between the racial composition of the Canadian people and the outlook of the country. The French-Canadian population had some cultural but no political links with France. It was North American without being particularly influenced by the United States. It was, above all, *Canadienne*. The Germans of Nova Scotia and Ontario had lived in Canada for generations. Russians—of whom there were considerable numbers—were in large part religious refugees who had no sympathy with the Tsarist régime and no connection with the political parties of the opposition. Some groups, such as Doukhobors and Ukrainians, were good settlers and workers without being easily integrated. The oriental population was severely restricted, partly by virtual exclusion of newcomers, partly by the presence of few women and therefore the absence of natural increase. Even those that were in Canada, however, stood out as a separate element in the population and remained a subject of concern in British Columbia.

Immigration policy in the period between the first and second world wars showed no radical departures from its traditional form. It was cautious on both quantity and quality; and in general was a compromise between two conflicting ideas: that by immigration the Canadian people should measure up to the size of the country; and that the employment of Canadians, the standard of living, and the ethnic balance should not be endangered. Though never approaching the pre-war years, immigration reached respectable figures in the twenties. In the thirties, as a result of the depression, it dwindled to a trickle (as did emigration). The total increase in population as between the census years 1921 and 1931 was, in round figures, one and one-half millions. By means of immigra-

---

[3] On this subject see C. J. Woodsworth, *Canada and the Orient: A Study in International Relations* (Toronto, 1941).

tion the ethnic balance changed to the extent that the French and British groups together totalled 80 per cent. of the population in 1931 as compared with 83 per cent. in 1921.

External trade had always been an essential aspect of the Canadian economy, which was therefore invariably subject to the fluctuation of world conditions. In the first decade after hostilities these conditions went through two major changes. The high prices and great demands of the war period persisted until the latter part of 1920 when they were replaced by a depression lasting for about two years, which in turn was followed by a period of unequalled prosperity reaching its peak and end in 1929. Other circumstances arising during the same decade outside Canadian borders were also influential: for example, the heightening of American and, later, German tariffs, and the drop in ocean freights caused by an abundance of shipping and the opening of the Panama Canal.

Canadian export trade responded to these factors as it did also to developments within the country itself. In the years of the slump the farmers of the west were injured by low prices for wheat and by the United States tariff of 1921 with new barriers against agricultural products.[4] As had always happened, the consequent reduction in purchasing power affected sales by the industrial concerns of central Canada. By 1923, however, a general recovery was under way. Continued food shortages and low tariff walls in Europe made it possible for Canada to supply 38 per cent. of the wheat exports of the world as compared to 12 per cent. before the war. The volume of economic activity and the real income of the people both rose appreciably. In this respect British Columbia was the most fortunate region. Production and export of non-ferrous metals and of wood products were facilitated by hydro-electric power, and low transportation costs created by the Panama Canal and reduction of railway rates. The prairie provinces benefited by the last factor, by the sale of wheat, and by settlement and railway-construction. The central provinces expanded northward into the mining areas and continued to increase manufacturing industries that had been given an impetus by the war. The maritime provinces, on the other hand, suffered from the loss of the exceptional markets for fish and lumber that the

---

[4] *Canadian Annual Review*, 1921, 144 *ff.*

conditions of the war period had allowed, though a recovery was made on the basis of adjustment of railway rates, the commercial agreement with the West Indies, and the general effects of economic prosperity in other parts of Canada. Amongst the trading nations of the world Canada had come to occupy a relatively more important position, so that by 1928 she was the fifth of the exporting countries. In exports (which for most years after the war were substantially greater than imports) there was a marked rise in 1917 which, with the exceptions of 1922 and 1923, was held throughout the twenties. By 1929, indeed, the value in dollars of total exports was nearly double what it had been in 1916, and several times the value of earlier years. Much the largest buyers were still the United Kingdom and the United States, but now the latter was accepting more Canadian goods than the former, whereas in pre-war years the opposite had usually been the case. In types of goods exported vegetable products continued to be by far the most valuable, with wood and wood products second and minerals third. Looking at the other side of the picture it appears that Canada imported in the late twenties nearly four times as much from the United States as she did from the United Kingdom.[5]

The tariff, important to a trading country, was not generally revised between 1907 and 1930, although there were a number of changes in detail. It remained a protective as well as a revenue tariff, and continued to include imperial preference. As compared to other countries it was of moderate height, lower than the United States, for example, and higher than such countries as Sweden and Portugal. When in office the two main political parties followed much the same policies, although liberal members attempted in 1921 to revive the reciprocity agreement with the United States that had been signed in 1911 but on which the liberal government of the day had fallen. The move was in response to the increase of American protection of that year, but in practice the liberal party never pressed, and never again attempted to adopt, a low-tariff platform. The pressure for such a change came from the agrarian parties that in the provincial, and to some extent in the federal, fields showed a new strength after the war. The farmers' parties in Ontario and Alberta and

---

[5] The above paragraphs on economic development are based on the *Canada Year Book*, and on Book I of the *Report of the Royal Commission on Dominion-Provincial Relations* (Ottawa, 1940).

the new federal Progressive party vigorously criticized the traditional tariff policy on the grounds that it raised the cost of living and was drawn in favour of the industrial as opposed to the agrarian interests. On the other hand farmers' organizations on both coasts were less confident of the virtues of a low tariff.[6]

Importation of capital had been as essential a part of the Canadian economy as external trade in goods. From the days of the fur trade to the building of the transcontinental railways British capital had financed commerce and public works. The war brought a great change. The pressure on the United Kingdom treasury made it impossible after 1916 to pay in dollars for purchases of munitions, food, and other articles in Canada, and the British money market became closed for the time to Canadian borrowers. While it had proved feasible to raise in Canada comparatively large amounts of money for war purposes, the country continued after the war to import capital. The difference now was that it came for the most part from the United States. The extent of private American investment in Canadian enterprises was, in fact, one of the significant features of this period.

Two forms of investment may be noticed: purchase of government and other securities by individuals or corporations in the United States, and direct investment by means of ownership or control of branch factories, mines, timber limits, or other sources of production. British investment was largely in the former category, while American was more equally divided between the two. Available information does not permit of a break-down between the two forms of investment, but the following estimates of capital invested in all forms will give sufficient indication of the trends. The figures are in millions of dollars. In 1913 the total was 3,529.3, made up of British investment of 2,569.3 and American of 780. By 1920 the picture had changed. Of a total investment of 4,870.1 the British share was hardly changed at 2,577.3, while the American had gone up to 2,128.2. In 1922 United States investment for the first time exceeded that of Great Britain and by 1929 was materially larger.[7]

[6] See W. A. Mackintosh, "Canadian Tariff Policy" (*Canadian Papers, 1933: Prepared for the Fifth Biennial Conference of the Institute of Pacific Relations*, Toronto, n.d.).

[7] H. Marshall, F. A. Southard Jr., and K. W. Taylor, *Canadian-American Industry: A Study in International Investment* (New Haven and Toronto, 1936), 299.

For many years there had been a growing number of companies in Canada controlled by, or affiliated with, American ones, but the pace grew faster in the twenties. Of some 1,350 such companies that existed in 1934, 36 per cent. began operations between 1921 and 1929.[8] Calculations for the year 1932 show that there were then established in Canada 1,177 firms which were American-controlled or affiliated, and which together had a capital of $2,167,-249,508. They were responsible for widely varying proportions of the total value of Canadian production. In some cases the minority interest was high, and in the aggregate it amounted to 22.29 per cent. The factories and other enterprises should not, therefore, be regarded as wholly foreign in ownership, as they certainly were not in personnel employed. Manufacturing companies formed the largest group, with wood and paper products being the biggest item within it. Not far behind were the utility companies. Of these the producers of electrical energy employed the largest capital, though the natural gas concerns were responsible for 88.5 per cent. of all Canadian production (the largest percentage in any of the industries in question). Mining and merchandising companies had smaller but important stakes.[9]

Commercial enterprise, like emigrants, spilled over the border in both directions, for, in proportion to wealth and population, the Canadian investment in the United States was larger than that of Americans in Canada.[10] The need for raw materials, similarity of markets, cost of transportation, and search for new markets were factors influencing firms on each side of the border to spread to the other. In most forms of business activity the American investment in Canada was absolutely greater than the Canadian in the United States. This, however, was not true in the case of rail transport, for Canadian railways in the thirties operated or controlled more than four times as much mileage in the United States as did American railways in Canada. The principal reason for this extensive Canadian interest was geography. To reach ice-free ports the predecessors of the Canadian National Railways had secured lines to Portland and New London on the New England coast. For ready access to Saint John, New Brunswick, the Canadian Pacific had similarly built its "short line"

8 *Ibid.*, 19.
9 *Ibid.*, table V, opposite 24.
10 *Ibid.*, 175 *ff*.

through Maine. As a complement to its transcontinental line through the sparsely-peopled area north of Lake Superior the Canadian Pacific held the "Soo Line" through Minneapolis to Moose Jaw, Saskatchewan. The Grand Trunk had at one time an ambition to reach the Canadian prairies by continuing its Chicago line through rich territory. In comparison the United States railways had few such problems, with exceptions such as the Canada Southern that took the short cut north of Lake Erie.

The invasion of Southern Ontario by American railways was a blow to the Canadian companies that, following an established philosophy of Canadian transportation, had sought to compensate themselves for the limitations of local traffic by taking a share in American through-traffic. By the twenties this hope had almost gone, but adequate means of transport remained a national necessity for external trade as well as for domestic needs. War conditions combined with other factors to bring the Canadian Northern and the Grand Trunk railways—two of the three transcontinental systems—to their knees financially, and both fell into the lap of an embarrassed government. They were added to existing government railways to make in the early twenties the Canadian National System, which for the time at least proved to be a heavy burden on the treasury. The Canadian Pacific Railway, with a stronger strategic and financial structure, remained independent.

In the international aspect the objectives of Canadian transportation may be described as maximum and minimum. The first envisaged a use of Canadian waterways, railways, and ports for the commerce not only of Canada but of parts of the United States. The pull of the Erie Canal and of New York State railways to Atlantic ports largely defeated that hope, and left Canadians with the more restricted ambition of ensuring sufficient means of carriage for their own imports and exports, without losing too much of it to American rivals, and picking up what they could of American goods. Even for this was needed an elaborate network of railways across the country, canals to carry wheat, ore, and other bulky articles, and as good port facilities as could be provided. The new developments after the war—in addition to the nationalization of more than half the railway mileage—were the opening of an export route through Hudson Bay and the project of an enlarged St. Lawrence seaway. The first marked the triumph of an old argument (supported historically by the victory of the Bay as the fur-trade route) that the wheat of Manitoba and Saskatchewan should find its way to market by the nearer northern port rather than by the long trek to Montreal. Under pressure of strong local opinion the federal government proceeded to complete a line earlier begun, and in the autumn of 1931 two cargoes of wheat were shipped to Europe from Churchill. The improvement of the St. Lawrence route was intended to be international in operation as well as in respect of trade. The war delayed serious consideration of an American proposal of 1913, but after it an elaborate study was made by bodies representing both countries. A joint board of engineers worked out a plan for navigation and hydroelectric power which would allow for an eventual depth of thirty feet from Sault Ste. Marie to Montreal. A treaty embodying these proposals was in fact signed in 1932, but two years later was rejected by the American senate.

On the inland waterways the Canada Steamship Lines and other companies carried Canadian trade throughout the season of navigation. On the oceans Canadian concerns took some part in the shipping to and from Canadian ports. The Canadian Pacific Ocean Steamships plied on all oceans, and this company continued to increase its fleet and its routes after the war. The younger rival, the Canadian Government Merchant Marine, a subsidiary of the Canadian National Railways, started with an ambitious programme but suffered financial losses almost from the beginning of its history.

The philosophy and methods of organized labour in Canada had always been materially affected by the ideas and practices in other countries, and this was never more true than in the years after the war. While early trade unions in Canada were based largely on British experience, and while British parallels continued to have an effect, the dominating external influence in the twentieth century was American. In some cases, such as that of the carpenters and joiners, organizations originating respectively in the United Kingdom and the United States were amalgamated on both sides of the border in North America; in the case cited not without revolt by a number of locals.[11] The Canadian Trades and Labour

11 H. A. Logan, *The History of Trade-Union Organization in Canada* (Chicago, 1928), 132-5. See also N. J. Ware and H. A. Logan, *Labor in Canadian-American Relations* (New Haven and Toronto, 1937) on that particular aspect.

Congress had come to represent the principle of international unions and to be linked with the American Federation of Labour. There still remained, however, a body of opinion which preferred purely Canadian rather than international organizations. Two principal bodies represented the minority. One of these, the Canadian Federation of Labour, had a revival after the war, though it still included only a portion of the national unions. It was both nationalist and moderate, having no sympathy, for example, with the radicalism of the Industrial Workers of the World. The second body in question was the Federation of Catholic Workers of Canada. It also was opposed to radicalism and internationalism, though it did in a sense reflect an international influence since it was considerably influenced by the Roman Catholic Church, and by that church's views on the attitude of labour. The membership of the Federation was drawn from the Province of Quebec, and it was so closely linked with the thought of that province that it has been described as "a movement for French Canadianism rather than for Canadianism in an inclusive sense".[12]

The activities of labour organizations in the United States affected Canada in two principal ways. Because of the international affiliations of many Canadian trade unions, wage disputes or strikes on the American side of the border might well extend to Canada. Even if they did not, the close connection between the economies of the United States and Canada meant that a strike in the United States might seriously affect Canada. Examples of both effects may be taken from the year 1922. Strikes in the American coal fields both spread to some of the Canadian ones, and reduced the volume of coal imported into Canada. The American railway strike of the same year directly affected only American lines in Canada, but indirectly reduced trade between the two countries, as well as producing unrest in the Canadian unions.[13]

Such trends are clearly apparent in the period after the war, but they originated at a much earlier date. What was new was the increasing strength over a short period of imported radicalism in the Canadian labour organizations. The success of the bolshevik revolution in Russia gave fresh hope to those who had been advocat-

[12] Logan, *History of Trade-Union Organization*, 361.
[13] For a full account see *Canadian Annual Review*, 1922, 111 ff.

ing Marxian ideas, just as it reinforced the suspicions of those who had seen socialism never far behind trade-unionism. It was a period when labour, in company with the rest of humanity, was in a state of unrest in many countries. The disturbed and fluctuating economic conditions which followed the war seemed to threaten danger to those who were dependent on current conditions of prices, wages, and employment. Nor was the idealism that the war had stirred up confined to a hope of political democracy. It was no less applied to the social problems. On this unstable scene, then, came a mixed procession of old and new Marxians, foreign agitators, fanatics, and idealists to say their respective pieces into whatever receptive ears they could find.

The Industrial Workers of the World, which for some years had been regarded as the radical body in the Canadian labour movement, was banned in 1918, and even when that ban was lifted it did not show serious signs of vitality. The place on the left of the labour movement was taken in 1919 by the One Big Union, an organization created by western groups which had withdrawn from the Trades and Labour Congress after unsuccessfully attempting to change its course. The authors of the One Big Union reflected the idea of European communism, with approval of the Soviet System, abolition of capitalism, and belief in proletarian rule. It was a class movement, with the general strike as a mode of action.

A general strike, though given a date, did not in fact occur. There was, however, in the spring of 1919, a local general strike in Winnipeg in which the hand of the One Big Union was seen in varying degrees by observers. At least it is beyond doubt that some of the leaders of the O.B.U. were also leaders of the Winnipeg strike. The story of that episode need not be repeated here. What is important for present purposes is that contemporaries interpreted it as revolutionary, as a demonstration of international communism, at a time when there was some reason to fear the spread of that movement. And they saw to the fore in Winnipeg men who shortly before had been repeating the phrases of Lenin and Trotsky. Concurrently with the Winnipeg strike, but more as an answer to the general strike threatened by the O.B.U., parliament had taken two defensive steps. The Immigration Act had been amended so as to authorize the deportation of nationalized or non-nationalized immigrants who had advocated violence or demonstrated disloyalty. To the Criminal Code was added a new section, 98, defining as unlawful any association aiming at change by violence, and providing for the punishment of officers or members of such an association. During and immediately after the Winnipeg strike thirteen men were arrested and a quantity of documents seized by the police. Eight of the men were brought to trial. Correspondence and newspaper items used in evidence gave an impression of plans for revolution on the Russian model, and throughout Canada feeling ran high. On the one hand were those who believed that communism and revolution were being advocated, and on the other those who regarded the government as being swayed by the forces of reaction. More moderate labour men, both those connected with the Winnipeg strike and others, continued to deny charges of sedition and of dictation from Moscow; but there were indications that some foreign influences and foreign personnel were at work.

Communist activity in Canada did not end with the period of the Winnipeg strike. At the end of 1921 a successor to the O.B.U., known as the Workers' Party of Canada, was founded at a meeting in Toronto. The agreed platform was unblushingly Marxian:

1. To consolidate the existing labour organizations and develop them into organs of militant struggle against capitalism; to permeate the labour unions and strive to replace the present reactionary leadership by revolutionary leadership.

2. To participate in the elections and the general political life of the country.

3. To lead in the fight for the immediate needs of the workers, broaden and deepen their demands, organize and develop out of the every-day struggles a force for the abolition of capitalism.

4. To work for the overthrow of capitalism and capitalist dictatorship by the conquest of political power, the establishment of the working class dictatorship and the Workers' Republic.[14]

This frank acceptance of the views of the Third International was in itself alarming to contemporaries, and is interesting as a European influence filtered, apparently, through the United States. Its importance in effect, however, depended on the degree to which it was accepted in Canada. By the end of 1922 the

[14] Quoted in the *Canadian Annual Review*, 1922, 51.

new party claimed a hundred branches and 4,500 members. The "reactionary leadership" of the older unions, however, was not displaced, and indeed it was the opposition of the mass of organized labour in Canada that made the Workers' Party little more than a museum piece. Nor did it fare any better in the political sphere, where the various "progressive" movements of the day were moving along very different lines.

In another field organized labour was involved in world affairs. The Canadian delegation to the peace conference had included the secretary of the Trades and Labour Congress, and at Paris there were sessions on labour questions out of which arose the International Labour Organization. To the regular meetings of that body, the first at Washington and subsequent ones at Geneva, workers' representatives regularly went. Problems such as that of the eight-hour day, never matters of purely national interest, could now be discussed in a regular way in an international forum.

Many aspects of Canadian life—the character of the population, their occupations, the organization of business and of labour— were strongly and obviously influenced by the impact of world affairs. At the same time Canadians were becoming more conscious of a sense of nationalism which came from their part in the war and the peace, but were still far from pressing that sense to conclusions. In the cultural field there were signs of Canadianism particularly in the "group of seven" whose paintings of northern Ontario first became widely known through their first exhibition in 1920. But in literature and the arts generally there was more talk of national character than there were manifestations. Education and the churches continued to be firmly based on the external—primarily European—models on which they had begun.

The outlook abroad was many-sided. Immigration was desired and yet feared. Foreign trade was pressed with energy, and economic development within the country continued to be affected not only by trade but by the importation of capital. Politically Canadians were proud of their advanced status as a nation, quick to insist on their rights as such, yet cautious and reluctant when they saw themselves as committed to possible action as a result of participation in world affairs. There was thus a gap between their certainty of interest in such matters as foreign trade and their contradictory approach to high policy. In such a mood did Canada face the problem of foreign policy.

CHAPTER XV

THE APPROACH TO CANADIAN POLICY

LOOKING back on the war and the peace conference, neither parliament nor public was able to think of those great events in terms other than as new and important steps in the development of autonomy. The emphasis was all on status and recognition of nationhood. Few contemporaries could tear themselves away from this pleasing picture to analyse what in fact it meant, and—above all—what it implied. It meant that Canada had fought in a war that was the result of a policy over which her government had had no control, and about which it had known very little. Perhaps a Canadian foreign policy, had there been one, would have been no different from that of the United Kingdom. Certainly, as events stood in 1914, there could be little doubt that the Canadian interest in the conflict was so great that full participation was logical. And what was to be deduced from the position of Canada in the peace conference? That a Canadian delegation had ranked with those from the other small powers, and as such had had no influence at all on the terms of the treaties? Or that as members of the British Empire delegation the Canadian representatives had been kept well informed, and had had opportunities of taking part in the discussions of the great powers? Here was a dilemma that few Canadians liked to analyse, far less to resolve. To choose between the rôle of an independent, unattached small power and that of a colony in respect of foreign affairs was perhaps to put the issue in terms too stark and absolute. Perhaps there was some alternative that combined in some degree the advantages of both. The trouble, in 1920, however, was that the problem of finding—or looking for—that alternative was seldom honestly faced.

The real issues were almost entirely obscured by the cloud of status, which at its best is a negative thing, and at most a condition precedent to action. As one Canadian put it in a moment of cynicism, the national game was "I spy dominion status". Yet the issues were real enough, and apparent to all who cared to look. On the supposition that Canada had acquired the status of an autonomous power in international affairs (and that was a very doubtful supposition), by what means, and along what lines, was a foreign policy to be evolved and implemented? In the past the relations of Canada with foreign states had been conducted within an imperial framework. Canadians did, however, have virtually a free hand in various commercial negotiations; though, curiously enough, the difficulties which were at times encountered did not convey the obvious lesson that international agreement is not always reached readily. On the other hand, there was a tradition that British diplomacy on behalf of Canada was almost uniformly unsuccessful. No one, apparently, thought to add up and balance the cases, and to deduce from the result that negotiations might end in failure, whether carried on by British or Canadian representatives.

Least of all had Canadians learned to understand that diplomacy is but an agency of the state, and that its effectiveness depends not only on the wisdom of policy and the skill of diplomats, but also on the power and prestige of that state. A country must take responsibility for its own foreign policy, be the results good or ill. In some fields of foreign affairs the stakes are relatively not high; but in others they rise to the fundamental issue of security, of peace or war. Because there lay behind Canadian policy the strength of the United Kingdom, Canadian bargaining power had never been calculated. Canada, in short, had not stood on her own feet in the world. If she were to do so, it meant not just the appointment of agents here and there, but the establishment of a diplomatic service resting on an organization in Ottawa capable of analysing foreign affairs and preparing material for the government. It meant as a next step that that government must formulate policy in the light of world conditions, Canadian interests, and Canadian capacity. Finally it meant that the government must be prepared to accept responsibility for any necessary military preparations and military and diplomatic risks.

Such, in outline, was the issue raised by the War of 1914; and while there is no evidence that any responsible officials saw it in its entirety, there were some who pierced through the haze of status to find a constructive policy for which the progress of status called. Given the experience of being involved in a major war without any voice in the policy that led to it, what approach should be made by Canada toward a more acceptable régime? Since foreign policy is invariably derived from the particular conditions and aims of the country concerned, the first stage in such an inquiry would properly be an analysis of Canadian interests as related to external policy. There is no record of any effort to make at that time a specific estimate of Canadian interests. Perhaps the situation would have been clearer if those interests had been written down, but they were for the most part taken for granted. In later years a number of accounts were offered of Canadian interests in external affairs, the most penetrating of which was that by the first minister to hold, independently of the office of prime minister, the portfolio of external affairs.[1] The principles to which Mr. St. Laurent pointed underline the extent to which Canada had been, and continued to be, influenced by Great Britain and Europe. His starting point was the existence of two main cultural groups, whose relations with each other must not be adversely affected by foreign policy. Here were a fact and a deduction that no student of Canadian history and affairs could gainsay. It had been difficult enough to govern such a country in its domestic affairs, and the experience of the war period had shown how amity could be threatened by a foreign policy not acceptable to both groups.

His next three principles indicate the common ground on which the Canadian state is based. Belief in political liberty was inherited from English and French backgrounds "through the parent states . . . from the whole rich culture of western Europe". Respect for the rule of law was held by Canadians in contrast to a régime making for "the helpless plight of individuals who have been deprived of the primary right of an impartial administration of the law". Thirdly, policy must be based upon a conception of human rights. It was indeed to uphold these three related ideals that Canadians had fought the War of 1914, and for which they were to be ready to fight again. Regardless of the exact form of government, they were the principles that distinguished civilized men from savages. Canadians in every generation had, according to their lights, striven to protect and further them. They were as dear to W. L. Mackenzie as to J. A. Macdonald, as vital to L. H. Lafontaine as to G. E. Cartier. So obvious that they were often

---

[1] Louis St. Laurent, *The Foundations of Canadian Policy in World Affairs* (Duncan and John Gray Memorial Lecture, Toronto, 1947).

taken for granted, these principles evoked instant support if threatened from inside or outside the country.

Turning now to make some further deductions from the principles stated by Mr. St. Laurent, it may at once be said that the ties with the United Kingdom were ties of interest. Whether looked at from the point of view of common ideals or of Canadian dependence upon British power, the answer was the same: no break with the United Kingdom could conceivably be advantageous. It did not follow that there were no problems in the nature of intergovernmental relations. There were very real problems, and at times the consequent disputes on machinery made those seem ends in themselves rather than mere means to an almost-forgotten end. The maintenance of the empire—or the commonwealth as it was later called—was therefore a major Canadian interest; and it was one that had begun to assume a different—or rather variegated—hue. Throughout the nineteenth century the *Pax Britannica,* resting on sea power, had extended its comforting mantle to Canada; for part of that time leaving Canada still exposed to land attack from the United States, until in the last quarter of the century that problem too was dissipated. The German naval programme foreshadowed the end of that position, and German hostility to British policy in South Africa demonstrated the exposed position of an empire which could no longer live in splendid isolation. The Canadian stake in the continuance of imperial power was exemplified by participation in the Boer War and in the plans for support to the navy. As the German battle-ships sank at Scapa Flow, there was at least a temporary end to naval competition from Berlin, but the distribution of sea power did not return to the balance as it existed in the nineteenth century. Because of its partial exhaustion by the war the United Kingdom could never now expect to maintain more than parity with a United States whose economic resources had become increasingly strong. Nor indeed did it seem to be necessary to attempt naval superiority, for it had been since the nineties an assumption in British policy that there must never be a break with the United States.

The shift in the balance of naval power might, therefore, be no disadvantage to Canada. It might even represent an advantage, for Anglo-American friendship fitted in exactly with Canadian interest. In spite of the mythology of Canadian after-dinner speaking, that had not always been so. As late as 1905 Canadians were pressing their case on the Alaska boundary with little consideration—apparently with little understanding—of what was implied. With that period over, however, the arguments in favour of easy relations with the United States were unanswerable; and they could not be attained without similar relations between the United Kingdom and the United States. These were the two great powers with which Canada was closely associated. They must not be allowed to drift apart, for if they did Canada would have to go with one or the other—or fall between. That the two should work together in understanding and sympathy seemed much easier to Canadians than it did to the principals themselves. Did not both have the same set of values, the same love of liberty, the same belief in the individual, the same zeal for peace? That the answer was so obviously affirmative—and so obviously incomplete—was a mystery to Canadians, as to others.

It was with the United Kingdom and the United States that Canadian external trade was chiefly conducted, and from which Canada drew her capital requirements; and trade was, at any period of Canadian history, a major consideration. A mixture of ties—history, geography, common culture, political ideals, and trade—drew Canada into the orbits of both the United Kingdom and the United States. Links with other countries were less binding. France continued to be for French Canada a source of historical pride, and of intellectual stimulus limited by the encroachment of rationalism and gallicanism since the great revolution. Politically the Canadian interest in France was no stronger in Quebec than in other parts of Canada, for to all France stood as an ally of the immediate past and a bastion for the future against renewed German aggression. Other countries were for Canada sources of immigrants or fields for foreign trade. For the former Europe only was considered, though of course for the latter there was no geographical limit.

Given the character of the interests that have been outlined above, it remained to decide by what means they were to be implemented. Such a decision was too often seen through the simple formula of status slowly broadening down from precedent to precedent; and it was breezily assumed that it was only necessary for Canada to have the constitutional power to conduct her own foreign relations. Few Canadians, however, had the faintest idea of abandoning the advantages of British military and diplomatic support. All—or almost all—Canadians were agreed that their policy should in some way be related to British policy. Where they differed was in the way in which that could be done. A variety of plans, some definite and some hazy, were put forward. There were three main approaches.

The first was the revival of the project of a federal empire. The Imperial Federation League of the eighties had been formed to promote that idea, but had never committed itself to any particular scheme. The South African War gave a new stimulus to federalist thinking, and brought together in England an unusually able group of young men, most of whom had been officials in South Africa during the transitional period. Because of their youth and their association with the high commissioner they were known as "Milner's kindergarten". It was from this group that there came a series of studies on the future of the empire, with the idea of federalism as the central theme. A quarterly, the *Round Table*, was started in 1910 by the group in London; and in Canada —as in other dominions—a similar group, or "moot", took up the study from that side of the ocean. In Canada—and later elsewhere—study groups were organized to investigate imperial problems and consider solutions. In the war years the special subject for study was an imperial constitution that would carry into the post-war period the co-operation attained during the war. To these groups was submitted a memorandum by one of the London originators of the *Round Table*, Lionel Curtis, which formed the basis of study. In 1916 the memorandum was published as *The Problem of the Commonwealth*, as the personal views of the author, but representing to many contemporaries the agreed views of the *Round Table* movement. The book was aimed, wrote the author,

merely at showing what in the nature of things are the changes *which must be made* before a British subject in the Dominions can acquire self-government in the same degree as one domiciled in the British Isles. . . . . The main contention is this, that Dominion electorates must, in the not distant future, assume control of foreign affairs, yet cannot do so without deciding irrevocably whether they are to keep or renounce their status as citizens of the British Commonwealth. In plain words, the issue, as seen by the writer, is whether the Dominions are to become independent republics, or whether this world-wide Commonwealth is destined to stand more closely united as the noblest of all political achievements.

After an elaborate examination of the possible solutions, Curtis found himself driven by "an inexorable chain of reasoning" to the conclusion that there must be an imperial executive responsible to an imperial parliament elected in the United Kingdom and the dominions. The two bodies would deal with foreign affairs, defence, and finance; leaving to local parliaments all domestic affairs.

While there was in Canada a belief that some steps must be taken to tie together the parts of the empire in respect to foreign affairs, the particular plan proposed by Curtis met with little support. The Round Table groups, which had been consulted but took no responsibility for it, drafted a memorandum of "broad premises" which read as follows:

1. Canada has shown her determination to preserve and strengthen the ties which now bind her to Great Britain and other portions of the British Commonwealth.
2. Effective organization of the Empire must not involve any sacrifice of responsible government in domestic affairs, or the surrender of control over fiscal policy by any portion of the Empire.
3. But it is an inevitable development of responsible government in the Dominions that they should assume their proportionate share in the defence of the Empire, and should have a voice in determining its relation with other states.
4. We think, therefore, that as soon as circumstances permit, political leaders throughout the Empire, irrespective of party, should meet to consider the problem.

The memorandum, signed by a hundred well-known Canadians, was issued in February 1917. In April it was discussed in a public meeting held in Toronto, with Sir Edmund Walker, Canadian chairman of the Round Table and president of the Canadian Bank of Commerce, in the chair. J. W. (later Sir Joseph) Flavelle saw no reason to fear that "autonomy would be compromised by imperial federation", but N. W. Rowell expressed objections to centralized government.[2] One of the signatories of the memorandum, the prominent lawyer, Z. A. Lash, published his own views on the means by which the problem of imperial integration might

[2]*Canadian Annual Review*, 1917, 201.

be solved.[3] The "central authority" which he proposed differed from that of Curtis in that it was to be an "Imperial Council, having Executive and Legislative powers and consisting of the Crown and a small number of elected representatives from the United Kingdom and the Dominions, and representatives from India (not necessarily elected)". During a war its jurisdiction would be "practically unlimited for all purposes deemed necessary for the war", while in time of peace its jurisdiction would be limited. In general he was opposed to taxation by a central authority, and wished to preserve the sovereignty of the existing parliaments.

Direct opposition to the whole idea of a centralized authority was expressed by J. W. Dafoe, editor of the *Winnipeg Free Press*.[4] To Dafoe it appeared that the Curtis plan—against which he directed his argument—would turn Canada into a province in a new "British Nation". This reversal of the evolution of the empire would, he believed, meet with strong opposition:

> Here in Canada there are certain political facts that Mr. Curtis and his supporters should have the moral courage to look squarely in the face. Their scheme appeals to only a portion—certainly not to more than half—of the Canadians of British descent; to the remaining British Canadians it is anathema, as a denial of cherished political principles. To the non-British elements, comprising no less than forty-four per cent. of the population, it makes no appeal, except to a mere fringe affected by the social possibilities of the suggested innovation. If this question is forced into Dominion politics it will swallow all other issues. Until it is settled everything else will stand aside. The British-Canadian community will be rent in twain. A national party, dedicated to the task of preserving Canadian nationality, will inevitably arise; and the politics of this party will naturally be determined in large measure by the non-British elements, who will constitute a considerable majority of its membership.

As striking as the vigour of his rebuttal was the support which he admitted to exist for the idea of centralized machinery. As events proved, there can be no doubt that Dafoe's view was the one which was to prevail; and it may well be thought that the

[3] Z. A. Lash, *Defence and Foreign Affairs: A Suggestion for the Empire* (Toronto, 1917).
[4] See J. W. Dafoe, "Our Future in the Empire: Alliance under the Crown", in J. O. Miller (ed.), *The New Era in Canada: Essays Dealing with the Upbuilding of the Canadian Commonwealth* (Toronto, 1917).

enthusiasm for an imperial authority arose from a temporary atmosphere created by the war. Yet the problem remained as to the relation in foreign policy of one part of the empire with another. Dafoe's alternative was a perpetual alliance under the crown of the countries of the commonwealth. It was one that showed not a little foresight, but—for the time at least—it left many questions as to how the "alliance" was to operate. And, as things then stood, it left unchanged the position under which the foreign policy of Canada would in effect be formulated and implemented by the United Kingdom.

The plans for an imperial parliament or council were developed or supported by unofficial Canadians. They met with no encouragement from members of the government who, in Canada as well as in other dominions, consistently disapproved of any such machinery; so much so that they were liable to see centralizing conspiracies where none such existed. In spite of that, however, the Canadian government of the period was as deeply concerned as were individuals and groups of the public to find some method of putting an end to the ambiguous situation under which the country was exposed to the results of a foreign policy over which it had no control. To the prime minister, Sir Robert Borden, it had long been a matter of major concern, one that had been borne in upon his mind by the threat of war with Germany, and reinforced by the war itself. In the years immediately before the war Borden had firmly associated his proposal for a Canadian contribution to the naval defence of the empire with the demand for a voice in foreign policy; and he had expressed this view publicly. The machinery for co-operation, imperative in the conduct of the war, left at first a great deal to be desired; but it was this very fact that led to the institutional changes made in 1917 by Lloyd George's government. The success of the experiment brought hope of a more permanent structure on the same general pattern. The larger of the two new bodies, the imperial war conference, consisted of United Kingdom ministers not in the war cabinet, the colonial secretary (chairman), and dominion representatives. It was this body which passed in 1917 a resolution, no. IX, drawn up by Borden and Smuts and reading as follows:

The Imperial War Conference are of opinion that the readjustment of the constitutional relations of the component parts of the Empire is too important a subject to be dealt with during the war, and that it should form the subject of a special Imperial Conference to be summoned as soon as possible after the cessation of hostilities.

They deem it their duty, however, to place on record their view that any such readjustment, while thoroughly preserving all existing powers of self-government and complete control of domestic affairs, should be based upon a full recognition of the Dominions as autonomous units of an Imperial Commonwealth, and of India as an important portion of the same, should recognize the right of the Dominions and India to an adequate voice in foreign policy and in foreign relations, and should provide effective arrangements for continuous consultation in all important matters of common Imperial concern, and for such necessary concerted action, founded on consultation, as the several governments may determine.[5]

Accepted by all the governments concerned, the resolution firmly announced equality of status, the right to an "adequate" voice in foreign affairs, and the consequent need of "consultation". In introducing the resolution Borden pointed to the growing strengthening of the bonds of empire that came from autonomy in domestic affairs; and added to the points covered in the resolution the connection between foreign policy and defence, a relation which had been made familiar to him through the naval question. He made, too, a cautious reference to the imperial war cabinet as a possible guide in future development. This second body was a smaller one than the conference, being made up of the members of the British war cabinet, the dominion prime ministers, and the colonial secretary (representing the crown colonies and protectorates). Meeting concurrently with the war conference, it concerned itself largely with the immediate problem of the conduct of the war. In the summer of 1918, however, both bodies considered again the constitutional question. The discussion was initiated after agreement between the dominion prime ministers that their desire for direct communications between prime ministers should be accepted in principle. The resolution of the conference came before the cabinet in this form:

1. That this Conference is of the opinion that the developments which have taken place in the relations between the United Kingdom and the Dominions necessitate such a change in administrative arrange-

5 "Report of the Imperial War Conference, 1917," quoted in Dawson, *The Development of Dominion Status*, 175.

ments and in the channels of communication between these governments as will bring them more directly in touch with each other.

2. That the Imperial War Cabinet be invited to give immediate consideration to the creation of suitable machinery for the purpose.

Apparently the dominion representatives had meant by the second part of the resolution only the continuity (during the war) of the war cabinet. Both Lloyd George and Balfour, however, took it at its face value. The latter spoke of the means by which a single foreign policy could, in terms of a foreign office, be directed. Lloyd George made the proposal, fairly obvious under the circumstances, that there should be an informal committee to examine post-war machinery. This, however, was far from acceptable to the others. Hughes believed that Australians would be more worried by the commitments involved than pleased with the influence secured. Smuts was not ready to discuss post-war machinery; while Borden, who had spoken strongly as before on the need for a voice in imperial affairs, was not ready to discuss how that voice was to be heard. He shared with Hughes the fear that his own people would scent entanglements, following the Laurier tradition. He still believed in the theory of consultation but refused to discuss how it was to be achieved in time of peace. It is obvious, however, that all the prime ministers were impressed with the usefulness of the war cabinet, and what they were all ready to do now was to fill in the gaps between its meetings. The resolution as passed by the imperial war cabinet therefore included this point as well as the one on channels of communication:

I. (a) The Prime Ministers of the Dominions, as Members of the Imperial War Cabinet, have the right to direct communication with the Prime Minister of the United Kingdom, and vice versa.

(b) Such communications should be confined to questions of Cabinet importance. The Prime Ministers themselves are the judges of such questions.

(c) Telegraphic communication between the Prime Ministers should, as a rule, be conducted through the Colonial Office machinery, but this will not exclude the adoption of more direct means of communication in exceptional circumstances.

II. In order to secure continuity in the work of the Imperial War Cabinet and a permanent means of consultation during the war on the more important questions of common interest, the Prime Minister of each Dominion has the right to nominate a Cabinet Minister, either as a resident or visitor in London, to represent him at meetings of the Imperial War Cabinet to be held regularly between the plenary sessions.[6]

This in practice meant little for Canada. Direct correspondence between prime ministers had already been conducted. There was a resident minister in London, so that the only significance of the second part of the resolution would lie in its implementation; but this was prevented by the approach of the armistice and the gathering in London of ministerial groups from the dominions. The imperial war conference was then used for the discussion of peace terms, and, translated into the British Empire delegation, continued to operate at the peace conference in Paris. During the latter part of the war and through the peace conference, therefore, a means of consultation had been developed and its value proved. It was very much in the mind of Borden, as it was in varying degrees in those of the other prime ministers, that the same technique could form the basis of a permanent imperial machinery for the formulation of an imperial foreign policy. No further steps were taken at the time to examine in more detail the feasibility of that approach or even to reach an agreement on principle. On the other hand such a method was not dismissed.

Two methods which, at the end of the war, were principally discussed for associating the countries of the commonwealth in determining foreign policy assumed the establishment of either a single parliament for a federated empire or a body representing the several governments. There was one other possible method, which corresponds roughly to what Dafoe had labelled an alliance, but is better described as an *entente*. Under this régime each self-governing country of the commonwealth would both formulate and implement its own foreign policy. It might be that such individual policies would be in certain respects identical, because of similarity of interests and the practice of close consultation between governments. In that sense there would be common policy based on common aims. It would not, however, be properly described as a commonwealth policy, for it would represent only, on particular questions, a coincidence of views as between a group of sovereign states. The choice between the last two methods was

---

[6] The text of the resolution is in the *Borden Memoirs*, 828. The brief account in the memoirs has been supplemented by the unpublished Borden papers.

made pragmatically, gradually, and without announcement. In 1920 either way was open; and indeed up to a point there was still room for that compromise so acceptable to the British peoples.

Whatever road was followed the place of Canada in foreign relations would be in part dictated by the resources at her disposal. There was a growing appreciation amongst Canadians of the connection between foreign policy and power. The naval race before 1914 had driven the lesson part of the way home, and the war had made it very evident. The successful conclusion of the war, however, combined with the expectation of a long period of peace created in Canada, as in other countries, a disbelief in the necessity of maintaining large armed forces. On land the permanent force was less than 4,000 all ranks. The non-permanent active militia was large on paper but small in reality, and short in training and equipment. The Canadian navy was reduced to almost nothing. In 1920 the government accepted as gifts from the United Kingdom a light cruiser, two destroyers, and two submarines; and in 1922 even this miniature navy was reduced by putting the cruiser and the submarines in reserve. Of the three services only the Royal Canadian Air Force could show rising appropriations, explained apparently by its use for civil purposes.[7] In industry and man power it had been demonstrated that Canada had resources that could be used effectively in warfare, but in the twenties there was little to show as ready or in preparation.

Whether foreign policy was to be co-ordinated with the other members of the commonwealth or pursued independently it seemed clear that Canada expected by some means to have a voice in that policy. Theoretically all the machinery for the purpose existed. There was nothing to prevent parliament from devoting as much time as it wished to the discussion of Canadian interests and of the proper course to be pursued in general or in particular. Cabinet could place before parliament its views on foreign policy and receive support or criticisms. Throughout the generations parliament had indeed spent a good deal of time in deliberating on certain aspects of external relations, and more than once a question of commercial policy had been decisive in elections. Yet it was a far cry from reciprocity or the progress of autonomy to the point of view of a legislature responsible for passing on decisions on

---

[7] C. P. Stacey, *The Military Problems of Canada* (Toronto, 1940), 85-92.

high policy, and keeping an eye on the independent place of the country in relation to the world scene. Despite their length, the debates in the commons on the Treaty of Versailles show little evidence either of knowledge of the subject or appreciation of the advantages and obligations involved. The ministers completely failed to dissipate the atmosphere of an academic debating society. The weakness was curable if any real sense of responsibility were introduced; but the members of parliament mirrored accurately enough the public. Bismarck once said cynically of Italy that it developed an appetite in foreign affairs before it grew teeth. With the notable exception of the war Canadians for the most part relied on the teeth of others; for they continued to depend on British strength, either because they were opposed to the drift toward autonomy in that field, or because they were wholly pre-occupied with a constitutional question.

There was one other portion of governmental machinery that needed more than a change of attitude. Foreign affairs, like other subjects, require a body of trained specialists. The department of external affairs, created in 1909, had in 1920 a staff of three men outside the clerical ranks. Of these one was the under-secretary and one the legal adviser. There was no increase in staff until 1927; and in 1929 there were still only seven men in the department in Ottawa. In the early twenties there were no diplomatic missions, and the only office abroad of a comparable nature, that of the high commissioner in London, was little concerned with world affairs. At this time, then, when Canada was deliberating the method by which she should conduct her relations with the rest of the world, the government had no intelligence sources of its own abroad and no staff in the capital to analyse international affairs as seen from there. A flow of information came from London, but its value was limited in view of the lack of experts to digest it and relate it to other material. Even the technique of international relations was little understood in Ottawa, with the result that frequent inquiries were addressed to London on questions of procedure. Curiously enough this anomalous situation does not seem to have impressed either government or parliament. Perhaps that was the price that had to be paid for the way in which the whole question was being approached. The British tradition was strong in Canada, and on the whole that supposed the method of trial and error rather than the acceptance of any known rules. Because, in both Canada and the United Kingdom, people preferred to ignore a logic that might prove to be more apparent than real, the commonwealth was allowed to develop not as a brittle structure made from blue-prints, but as an organic body blessed with an amazing capacity to adjust itself to a variety of situations. In foreign affairs the events of the twenties began to demonstrate the needs of a country faced for the first time with concrete situations calling for the formulation and implementation of policy.

Chapter XVI

THE EARLY TWENTIES

IN the generation since the peace settlement of 1919-20 two basic questions on foreign policy have been presented to, and in the end answered by, Canadian governments. In outline they are these: Should there be a combined commonwealth foreign policy? Should Canada accept a global responsibility for the maintenance of peace? The first was raised in a serious way only in the early years. The second runs through the three stages into which world events divided the whole period: the years up to the Manchurian episode and the accession of Hitler, in which time peace appeared to be secure; the active challenge to collective security followed by the outbreak of war; and the attempt after that war to make a lasting peace.

In less than thirty years Canadian foreign policy developed, almost imperceptibly, from nearly nothing to a solid and mature position. Until recently—even in the thirties—a common generalization by Canadians, as ill-considered as it was dogmatic, was that there was no Canadian foreign policy. For the most part such language reflects on the part of its authors an ignorance of the character of foreign policy; a vague theory that a foreign policy consists of a series of assertions and commitments, as definable and unchangeable as a concrete object. Such has had, as will be seen, an obstructive effect on the proper development of policy. There was, however, this element of truth (even if it was not intended) in such generalizations: that until Canada could decide whether her policy was to be individually formulated and implemented, or alternatively to be part of a combined commonwealth policy, its development was bound to be slow and incomplete. For the rest criticism should have been directed—as of course it often was—at the character of the policy itself or the portion of governmental effort devoted to foreign affairs.

It will be useful to recapitulate briefly the main factors affecting the foreign relations of Canada as they stood in the year 1920. Emerging from the war with a new sense of national power, Canadians looked towards a place in world affairs comparable to the effort they had found themselves capable of exerting. Membership in the peace conference, in the League of Nations, and in the International Labour Organization was seen as recognition of a direct rather than a colonial standing in the world, and it was confidently hoped that sovereign states would accept the changed position. As against this trend were conflicting considerations. The war and the peace settlement had shown the strength of the commonwealth as a unit as well as the growing strength of the various dominions. By entering the League of Nations Canada had, it is true, acquired status; but it had also accepted obligations about which it was far from happy.

As yet, however, the clouds in the international sky were small and distant. Talk was not of war but of disarmament and lasting peace. Certainly the meagre armed forces of Canada seemed to reflect a confidence that they would not be needed. The great army built up a few years before was reduced to a skeleton, the air force subsisted largely on its civil usefulness, and little came of the tentative plans for a navy. In the latter part of the war the admiralty was working on a scheme for a single navy maintained by all parts of the commonwealth, but such a plan, with the political implications inseparable from it, was not acceptable in Ottawa. Rather the policy favoured was to establish a Canadian navy, technically similar to the navies in the rest of the commonwealth; and to obtain advice on this the Canadian government expressed its interest in a visit from a United Kingdom expert. Lord Jellicoe's visit in 1919 led him to propose alternative fleet units ranging in cost from $5,000,000 to $25,000,000. Actually the government went no further in 1920 than to accept from the United Kingdom government a light cruiser, two destroyers, and two submarines. The old *Niobe* and *Rainbow* went to the scrapheap.

It would not seem from this modest venture that naval defence was of serious concern in Canada. In one sense it was not, for there was little belief in any threat to Canadian security. On the other hand the wider problems of sea power raised political issues of major importance, and affected Canada as they did the great naval powers. They were tied too to questions of major Canadian interest which were brought together at the meeting in London in June 1921. The official description of this meeting was a "Conference of the Prime Ministers and Representatives of the United Kingdom, the Dominions, and India, held in June, July, and August 1921". It was also at the time referred to as the imperial cabinet, and has commonly since then been known as an imperial conference. One function that the conference did not perform was the constitutional one assigned in 1917 to a postwar meeting. Discussion of the character of the empire or commonwealth (both names were still used) was simply shelved, but in practice it was impossible to deal with foreign policy without making *de facto* decisions on commonwealth relations.

The one question of foreign policy before the conference of 1921 that affected the dominions as well as the United Kingdom was naval rivalry. There were in 1921 three naval powers in the world: the United Kingdom, the United States, and Japan. The first clung to its traditional view that superior sea power was essential to its peculiar circumstances; the second was challenging the British claim to supremacy; while Japan, in pursuit of its Pacific ambitions, was ready to spend half the government revenue on the armed forces. Both the western governments were concerned over the undue expansion of Japan on the Chinese mainland and over the islands of the Pacific, but were far from agreeing with each other either as to how to combat this threat or as to what their own relative strengths should be. In the United States a big navy element was seeking to continue the large-scale building begun during the war, while triumphant isolationism prevented such a force from becoming a bulwark of the League of Nations.[1]

Canada's interest in the situation was partly as a Pacific power, but much more because of its effect on Anglo-American relations. Dominating the naval question proper was the political one of whether the treaty between the United Kingdom and Japan, a treaty which had reduced the dispersion required of the royal navy, was to be continued. It was on this aspect of the problem that Canadian interest was centred. "If there is one dominion," the prime minister told the house of commons, "to which, more than

[1] The American position is traced in detail in Harold and Margaret Sprout, *Toward a New Order of Sea Power: American Naval Policy and the World Scene, 1918-1922* (Princeton, 1940).

another, the question of the renewal [of the treaty] is of importance
it is to the Dominion of Canada . . . a portion of the British Empire
standing—if I may say it—between Great Britain on the one hand
and the United States on the other."[2] American opposition to the
Anglo-Japanese Treaty of 1911 was given more weight in Ottawa
than in London, and the Canadian government, at least as early as
February 1921, expressed its opposition to the known British policy
of renewal. The future of the treaty was then discussed in June at
the conference in London. The treaty was a commonwealth interest,
not only because it had been renewed with dominion approval in
1911, but because it continued to be important strategically to
Australia and New Zealand, the representatives of both of which
vigorously supported its continuation. The Canadian government,
relatively little concerned with security in the Pacific, had an
equally genuine interest: the old one of trying to avoid a breach
between the United Kingdom and the United States. Opposition
to renewal was expressed at the conference, as it had been in previous
correspondence, with energy and success, by the prime minister,
Arthur Meighen. After a sharp debate the decision of the conference was against renewal and in favour of the alternative of a meeting by the Pacific powers on restriction of armaments and agreement
on policy in that area. The idea of a conference was not new, going
back in one form or another for several months. After the usual
"informal" clearing of the air, invitations were issued to the four
principal allied powers in August for a meeting at Washington "to
participate in a conference on the limitation of armaments, in connection with which Pacific and Far-Eastern questions would also
be discussed."[3]

The Canadian position at the London conference can as yet be
described from only incomplete sources.[4] Obviously the rôle of
Meighen there has been over-dramatized and over-simplified. Without detracting from the skill of the prime minister's handling of his
case, it should be remembered that he was not introducing new
arguments but stressing ones already known. His constructive con-

---

[2] *Canada, House of Commons Debates,* April 27, 1921.

[3] *Papers Relating to the Foreign Relations of the United States, 1921*
(Washington, D.C., 1936), II, 18 *ff.*

[4] The full record of the Conference has not been made public. For an
account of the Canadian position see J. B. Brebner, "Canada, the Anglo-
Japanese Alliance and the Washington Conference" (*Political Science Quarterly,*
L, March 1935, 45).

tribution seems to have been to give a more accurate account of American opinion than the foreign office was at first receiving through its own channels. It should be remembered that he was persuading not only the United Kingdom government to change its policy—the simple and common interpretation—but arguing as well against the firm views of Australia and New Zealand. Hughes was just as vociferous on one side as Meighen was on the other. Perhaps the most significant aspect of the conference of 1921 was that it designed a commonwealth foreign policy. The various units of the commonwealth came with conflicting views, the case was argued back and forth, and an agreed decision was reached and pursued—as it turned out— by a similarly common action.

Nor is it wise simply to assume that the decision made was the wise one. From the general, as well as from the Canadian, point of view, it had real advantages. It reduced serious friction between the United Kingdom and the United States, and it opened the way to reduction of naval armaments and political agreement on the far east. The success of the policy so warmly advocated by Canada must, however, be judged also in relation both to the actual achievements of the Washington conference and to the long-range results of the Washington decisions.

Pending some more general agreement to replace it, the Anglo-Japanese Treaty was for the time being left in force. Meanwhile there were discussions as to the best procedure for handling political questions in the far east, which, it was generally recognized, had an essential connection with any attempt to reduce naval armaments. The British proposal was for a preliminary discussion in London, or alternatively in Washington, on Pacific questions; an arrangement which would have the additional advantage of allowing for the presence of the dominion prime ministers before they dispersed. If this plan had been adopted it is probable that at the naval conference proper the United Kingdom would have represented the British Empire. Since, however, the plan was unacceptable to the United States, it was left for the one conference at Washington to deal with the whole agenda. It also followed that the dominions would have to be represented in some way.

That way was the same as the method followed at the Paris peace conference. Just as the imperial war cabinet of 1918 moved to Paris as the British Empire delegation, so the meeting of prime ministers of 1921 moved to Washington as another British Empire delegation.

The same protection was given to dominion policies, by providing that each government must consent before the delegation could pursue any course, and that each government should separately sign any agreement which affected it. Both then and later there was criticism of this arrangement on the ground that it failed to recognize dominion autonomy, and it was pointed out that the American government had neglected to address separate invitations to the dominion capitals. It would have been much more surprising had it done so, for all the contemporary evidence suggests that both the United Kingdom and the dominion governments assumed that there would be a single delegation. The state department was from the first concerned that allowance should be made on the British delegation for dominion representation in some form, and the American ambassador, in a conversation with Curzon, went out of his way to "present your tentative suggestion of five or six delegates to avoid possibility of future criticism from Dominions that might be based upon assumption that they were barred out of adequate participation through any plan or act of yours."[5] Curzon's bland assumption that two or three representatives would be enough was puzzling to the Americans and would have been wholly unacceptable in the dominions. Smuts wanted separate invitations, but Meighen had apparently been going on the assumption of a single delegation and one invitation to London. He did, however, require dominion representation on that delegation, and in August was asking Lloyd George by telegraph as to the "method by which it is proposed to provide representation of Canada on British Empire Delegation."[6] It must be assumed that counsels more modern than Curzon's prevailed in London, for in the end there were seven British Empire delegates, an arrangement which seems to have been regarded as satisfactory by Sir Robert Borden, the Canadian appointee.

Borden, who had resigned as prime minister a year and a half before, had shown his capacity for negotiation at the Paris conference and played again a real part in Washington. In addition to a private secretary he was accompanied only by the legal adviser of the department of external affairs (though even that meant one-third of the officers of the department). The course which he

[5] Ambassador in Great Britain to the Secretary of State, August 26, 1921. *Papers Relating to the Foreign Relations of the United States, 1921*, I, 63.
[6] The exchange of telegrams is printed in Dawson, *The Development of Dominion Status*, 217.

followed was clear and consistent with that pursued by Meighen in London.[7] The immediate objective was to reconcile the policies of the British Empire and the United States in the far east and in respect of naval building generally. In both these subjects individually Canada had also some interest: in the first because she was a Pacific state, and in the second because any limitation of tonnage would apply to the empire as a whole. A further and related objective was to explore the possibilities of bringing the United States within some general agreement designed to preserve peace, for only in that way could be overcome the situation created by the refusal of the United States to join the League of Nations. His early private conversations with Americans best tell the story. On November 9 he saw Root.

I explained to him my personal view that the greatest success obtainable at this conference would be an understanding (an alliance being both impossible and undesirable) between the British Commonwealth and the American Republic. With this he most heartily agreed. I explained to him the attitude of Canada with regard to the Anglo-Japanese Alliance, and I found him fully aware of the position that Mr. Meighen had taken. I then explained to him the view that had been advanced by the Australian and New Zealand Prime Ministers, and my desire to find some solution which would obviate their difficulties. He spoke very strongly of the disastrous effect upon American public opinion of a renewal of the Alliance. It had been formed, he said, to afford security against Russia, and perhaps against Germany. Any danger from those countries had disappeared, and the alliance at present was regarded by the people as an alliance between Great Britain and Japan against the United States.[8]

A talk with Lodge brought much the same response. On November 23 Borden had "a brief, but very important, interview with Hughes," the secretary of state. In the course of that he moved on to the more positive proposal arising out of the complications

---

[7] Sources for the Canadian participation in the Washington Conference are principally the admirable "Report of the Canadian Delegate" (*Canada, Sessional Papers, 1922*, no. 47), and the unpublished papers of Sir Robert Borden. The "Report of the American Delegation" (*Papers Relating to the Foreign Relations of the United States, 1922*, I) is a useful companion account of the conference as a whole. See also Gwendolen M. Carter, *The British Commonwealth and International Security: The Role of the Dominions, 1919-1939* (Toronto, 1947), chap. II.

[8] This and succeeding quotations are from 'Notes by Sir Robert upon the Disarmament Conference at Washington" in unpublished papers of Sir Robert Borden.

placed in the way of disarmament by the French requirements for security.

I told him I imagined that he must have in mind some proposal which would prevent the outbreak of hostilities; that this might be accomplished if the United States would be willing to agree to an arrangement by which the various nations would bind themselves not to commence hostilities until after investigation of their differences by a permanent international tribunal. I referred him to the treaties, about 30 in number, into which the United States had entered about 1914 and which contained such provisions. It seemed to me that these precedents would enable the United States to enter upon the project of establishing an international tribunal for the purpose indicated, as my proposal, if carried out, would not bind the United States or any other nation to any definite action in the final result. Thus the difficulties which had prevented the United States from accepting the Covenant of the League of Nations would not present themselves. Mr. Hughes said that precisely the same idea had been in his own mind; that he thought it unwise to broach it at present until some of the difficulties in the existing situation had been cleared away; but that he hoped that something of the kind might be accomplished.

At the same time Borden took up with Balfour the suggestion that the delegation should formally raise with the Americans the need for some means of peaceful settlement of disputes, although it was clear that it was necessary to move cautiously. Borden was impressed by the fact that reduction of armaments alone was not enough, and hoped to find some means of introducing the principle of arbitration and of meeting the French demand for security. Nothing, of course, came of the project at the time, though it did find expression in a diluted form in the Pact of Paris of 1928.

In conformity with his general interest in Anglo-American relations, Borden was active in the negotiations for a naval agreement. On at least two occasions he intervened with good effect. At the outset the United States delegation made a concrete proposal for the method of limitation, and Borden at once urged Balfour to accept it warmly "in spirit and principle", and it was this phrase which Balfour used. Later on, however, in the British delegation the naval experts began to press for modifications, and evoked a vigorous statement from Borden. The resources of the United States, he argued, would enable her "easily to out-distance the

Empire in any race for naval supremacy." Surely it was best to accept the American offer. "The naval experts," he later wrote in his diary, "imagine that they are broad-minded when in reality they look at the nation and the public exchequer as merely a convenient means of keeping up a great naval force which they regard as an ideal condition." On a related subject, limitation of land armament, Borden was encouraged by Hughes to speak when it appeared that the French delegation feared that conditions were likely to be imposed on them that would prejudice their security. In a passage quoted verbatim in the report, Borden dismissed any such idea, but stressed the desirability of disarmament on land, though with due regard for the French interest.

In the end, of course, only naval and not land limitation proved to be possible, and that, on the lines of the original American proposal, was incorporated in the five-power treaty. Under this agreement there was to be limitation on the tonnage of capital ships and aircraft carriers. For the former a proportion was accepted as follows: for the United Kingdom and the United States, 5; for Japan, 3; and for France and Italy, 1.75. On the political side the four-power treaty (United Kingdom, United States, France, and Japan) expressed the agreement of each signatory to respect the rights of the others in their insular possessions in the Pacific and called for consultation should any controversy arise. It was this treaty which took the place of the Anglo-Japanese alliance. The nine-power treaty was an attempt to protect the integrity of China and the open door. One further of the group of treaties may be mentioned as Borden had been active in the sub-committee which prepared the way for it. This was the agreement on the Chinese customs tariff. On that subject, which had wide ramifications, Borden had spent a great deal of time during the conference, showing a concern both for Chinese autonomy and for the protection of Canadian interests in relation to tariff agreements.

Without attempting a full description of the Washington conference, some stress has been laid upon the importance of it as seen from Canada at the time. It marks an attempt to approach postwar security through the means of a single commonwealth policy, and as such is the lineal descendant of the practice begun in 1917 with the formation of the imperial war cabinet. As it turned out, both the four-power and the nine-power treaties proved ineffectual to achieve their objectives of restraining Japanese imperialism and supporting the Chinese state. It does not follow that a continuation of the alliance, by keeping Japan "grouped", would have produced any better result; but the long story of Japanese expansion from Mukden to the fall of Hong Kong suggests caution in appraising the wisdom of the Canadian onslaught on the alliance. The five-power treaty was, on the whole, the most successful of the attempts at limitation of armaments. Technically it had very little effect on Canada, which continued to maintain only a miniature navy. To the extent that it—combined with the dropping of the alliance—contributed to an Anglo-American *rapprochement,* it did, however, have a direct importance.

There is one curious passage (para. 46) in Borden's report on the Washington conference which should be noted.

While the provisions of the [five-power] Treaty limit the total naval power which the British Empire as a whole is permitted to maintain, they leave entirely untouched the question of co-operation in the maintenance of that power. This question stands exactly where it stood before the conference, for the decision of the Parliaments of the Empire. The subject of Imperial co-operation was not discussed at Washington, either in the British Empire Delegation or elsewhere; it was unnecessary to consider it for the purpose of the Conference, nor were the delegates authorized to discuss it.

This apparently gratuitous information is at first puzzling. Surely no one would suppose that an international treaty would deal with the domestic affairs of the empire? Or that imperial co-operation would be discussed at a conference which had nothing to do with it? On second thoughts, however, it is evident that these glimpses of the obvious reflect the Canadian obsession on the theory and practice of imperial relations, as also Borden's conviction— which he had now held for more than ten years—that defence and foreign policy were inseparably connected. Just before the opening of the Washington Conference, Borden had told the Lawyers' Club of New York that "the voice of the British Commonwealth in world affairs must not be the voice of the United Kingdom alone, but the voice of all the British self-governing nations. This principle has been wholly accepted both in the United Kingdom and the Dominions. The precise method by which it shall be worked out in actual practice has not yet been fully determined, and is surrounded by difficulties of undoubted gravity, but not incapable of solution."⁹ Lord Milner's statement of six months earlier shows a weariness of such remarks as the one just quoted. "Incessantly of late years, and with increasing emphasis, dominion statesmen have claimed the right to have a voice in determining the foreign policy of Great Britain. Nobody can dispute—nobody, as far as I know, has disputed—the justice of that claim. The only difficulty is to find out how it can be done. It is a purely practical difficulty. There is, as far as I know, no difference of principle."¹⁰

In truth, the rather pompous phrases to which Borden resorted barely conceal the fact that neither he, nor any other responsible person, knew "how it can be done." Canadians were then just in the process of moving away from Laurier's negative formula of no consultations and no commitments toward a realization that there would in fact be commitments, in the sense of results, arising from British foreign policy, whether there was consultation or not. They knew that no plan for a federal empire would be acceptable. During the immediate post-war years they were implementing foreign policy in two ways: separately, and through commonwealth machinery. The transition from these parallel methods to a concentration on the first is gradual and has a complication of causes. On the Canadian side of the ocean the retirement of Borden removed the leader of the school of thought that hoped for the evolution of a commonwealth machinery for foreign policy that would combine a single voice with the autonomy of each unit. With the accession to power of the Liberals under W. L. Mackenzie King in 1922 came not an abrupt change of policy but rather a coolness toward the Borden thesis. There were also, however, other forces operating against common policy, not the least of which was a disregard of its practice by the United Kingdom government.

The Chanak incident was a major, perhaps the effective, event that halted the progress of commonwealth policy by consultation. The events are well known. In September 1922 the Greeks were being pursued by Kemal's Turkish Nationalists, and after the withdrawal of French and Italian forces the British were left alone at Chanak to hold the Straits against the advancing Turkish troops. Caught by the failure of his policy in the near east, Lloyd George telegraphed an enquiry to the Australian, New Zealand, and Canad-

---

⁹ *Canadian Annual Review*, 1921, 81.
¹⁰ *Ibid.*, 78.

ian governments as to whether they wished to associate themselves with the action of the British government and to send contingents if war broke out. It appears that the United Kingdom government had failed to keep the dominions informed of the developing situation or of its own intentions; and certainly the virtual appeal for assistance had no background of consultation. New Zealand replied promptly that it would send a contingent, and Australia less enthusiastically promised assistance. In Canada Lloyd George's telegram arrived at midnight on Friday, and for some reason the decoded copy did not reach the prime minister until Saturday afternoon. Meanwhile he had seen a press release issued in London notifying the world of the contents of the cabled message. On Monday, after a meeting of the cabinet, the prime minister made the following statement:

As already mentioned, the only communication which our Government has thus far received with respect to the situation in the Near East from the British Government is a cable despatch marked secret, the contents of which, without the sanction of the British Government, we do not feel at liberty to make public. It is the view of the Government that public opinion in Canada would demand authorization on the part of Parliament as a necessary preliminary to the despatch of any contingent to participate in the conflict in the Near East. The Government is in communication with members of the Cabinet at present in Europe, as Canada's representatives at the League of Nations, and with the British Government, with a view to ascertaining whether the situation that exists in the Near East is one which would justify the summoning of a special Session of Parliament.[11]

It was soon evident that public opinion ranged all the way from opposition to any participation to numerous offers of military service. Parliament was not summoned, but the various leading politicians made statements, the leader of the conservative opposition claiming that the government should have said "Ready, aye ready; we stand by you." It is not difficult, however, to make a case for the government's attitude. It was, it is true, a signatory of the virtually defunct Treaty of Sèvres, but so were a great many other countries which did not feel called upon to support British policy. Unlike Australia and New Zealand, Canada had only an indirect interest in the Mediterranean route to the east. The public announcement, it will

[11] *Ibid.*, 1922, 181.

be observed, while certainly lacking in warmth, gave no negative decision. As the crisis abated, an occasion for sending troops did not arise.

The conference at Lausanne, resulting in the treaty of peace with Turkey, was the sequel to the Chanak episode in imperial as it was in international relations. The course followed by the United Kingdom and the Canadian governments in regard to Lausanne is incomprehensible unless it be assumed that both were now blowing cold on common policy based on agreement and common action. The Chanak affair had evoked on both sides of the Atlantic so much criticism, so much pointing of the moral, that no minister or official could have failed to see that the arrangements for the conference at Lausanne brought up just the same question of consultation. When, therefore, on October 27, 1922, London informed Ottawa that it was sending two plenipotentiaries there was no protest. "Plenipotentiaries," the telegram ended, "are fully acquainted with the Imperial aspect of the problem and with the keen interest taken by the Dominion Governments in its solution."[12] As far as the Canadian government was concerned, there was no indication of a keen interest—quite the opposite. When, as an explanation of the failure to invite the dominions, a French demand that Tunis, Algeria, and West Africa be treated equally was cited, even this absurd argument was not challenged. The available evidence suggests that the United Kingdom on the one hand made not the slightest effort to revive either the Paris or the Washington precedents, and that on the other the Canadian government avoided any opportunity of suggesting that it should be directly represented. The latter did, however, make clear as the correspondence proceeded that it would not be bound by any action that the former might take, and that it would be involved in treaty-making either wholly or not at all.

The attitude of the Canadian, and perhaps to a lesser extent the United Kingdom, government is in part explained by a parallel development in the method of making treaties by members of the

---

12 The correspondence and Mackenzie King's statement in the house of commons are printed in Dawson, *The Development of Dominion Status,* 258 *ff.* The correspondence is printed in *Correspondence with the Canadian Government on the Subject of the Peace Settlement with Turkey* (Cmd. 2146, 1924) and in *Canada, Sessional Papers,* 1924, no. 232. See also A. G. Dewey, *The Dominions and Diplomacy: The Canadian Contribution* (2 vols., London, 1929), 147 *ff.*

commonwealth. Beginning at the end of 1922 the Canadian and American governments had negotiated for an agreement for the protection of halibut in the North Pacific. A common interest in fisheries had, of course, for a long period been a matter of discussion between the two countries through a variety of procedures. When in this case the nature of the treaty had been settled, the Canadian government raised the question of how it should be signed.[13] Having received through the colonial office full powers for Ernest Lapointe to conclude the treaty, the Canadian government then proposed that he alone should sign it. ". . . the treaty being one of concern solely to Canada and the United States, and not affecting in any particular any imperial interest, the signature of the Canadian minister should be sufficient . . ." London accepted the request with good grace, and by doing so agreed to the establishment of an important precedent. The American senate, however, was not so ready, and sought to add a condition that "none of the nationals and inhabitants and vessels and boats of any other part of Great Britain [sic] shall engage in halibut fishing contrary to any of the provisions of this treaty". To this attempt to introduce an imperial interest, and so, apparently, to avoid a treaty concluded with Canada alone, the Canadian government refused to accede; and since it was apparently ready to sacrifice the treaty rather than give way, the senate finally abandoned its condition.

Whether this episode be regarded as a struggle for status or simplicity—or both—it did initiate a new phase in commonwealth relations, and one the implications of which called for general commonwealth consideration. If a dominion could now negotiate and sign a treaty entirely by itself, that not only meant a constitutional change, but raised the practical problem of any effects such a treaty might have on other members of the commonwealth. This was a new problem only if seen in respect of dominion initiative; the halibut treaty, for example, might affect fishermen from the British Isles. On the other side of the picture, however, the United Kingdom had long been making treaties that might affect the dominions. In recent times the dominions had been protected in one of two ways: either by being consulted as to whether they wished to be included in the treaty, or (for a short period) by joint action in negotiation. The Lausanne case, therefore, was not so much new

---

[13] The correspondence is in *Canada, Sessional Papers*, 1923, no. 111a.

as a reversion to an earlier practice. The existing position, however, was that two units of the commonwealth had separately been making treaties without there being any organized method of consulting about possible results for other units.

Such was the situation that faced the imperial conference of 1923. Although it was only two years since the meeting of prime ministers in 1921 a good deal of water had flowed under the imperial bridge. At the time of the earlier meeting there was still a strong opinion in favour of a single policy, and indeed the most positive achievement of that conference was to carry out a single policy by means of a single delegation. Somehow or other—no one quite stopped to ask why—that opinion had almost disappeared, and the whole trend was in the opposite direction. The conference of 1923 neither accepted nor rejected a return to that method of foreign relations: what it did was to provide for an actual practice of a quite different kind. It should be noted, however, that this was taken as one of two alternative methods, the other being the one of a British Empire delegation. A committee drew up a resolution which is admirably clear and was unanimously approved by the conference. It read as follows:

1. *Negotiation*

(a) It is desirable that no treaty should be negotiated by any of the governments of the Empire without due consideration of its possible effect on other parts of the Empire, or, if circumstances so demand, on the Empire as a whole.

(b) Before negotiations are opened with the intention of concluding a treaty, steps should be taken to ensure that any of the other governments of the Empire likely to be interested are informed, so that, if any such government considers that its interests would be affected, it may have an opportunity of expressing its views, or, when its interests are intimately involved, of participating in the negotiations.

(c) In all cases where more than one of the governments of the Empire participate in the negotiations, there should be the fullest possible exchange of views between the governments before and after the negotiations. In the case of treaties negotiated at International Conferences, where there is a British Empire Delegation, on which, in accordance with the now established practice, the Dominions and India are separately represented, such representation should also be used to attain this object.

(d) Steps should be taken to ensure that those governments of the Empire whose representatives are not participating in the negotiations should, during their progress, be kept informed in regard to any points in which they may be interested.

2. *Signature*

(a) Bilateral treaties imposing obligations on one part of the Empire only should be signed by a representative of the government of that part. The Full Power issued to such representatives should indicate the part of the Empire in respect of which the obligations are to be undertaken, and the preamble and text of the treaty should be so worded as to make its scope clear.

(b) Where a bilateral treaty imposes obligations on more than one part of the Empire, the treaty should be signed by one or more plenipotentiaries on behalf of all the governments concerned.

(c) As regards treaties negotiated at International Conferences, the existing practice of signature by plenipotentiaries on behalf of all the governments of the Empire represented at the Conference should be continued, and the Full Powers should be in the form employed at Paris and Washington.

3. *Ratification*

The existing practice in connection with the ratification of treaties should be maintained.[14]

The main part of the resolution has been quoted verbatim and deserves careful study. It clearly describes a procedure which was sensible, elastic, and adequately met the imperial situation as it had come to exist. Mackenzie King, in moving on June 21, 1926, for the approval by the house of commons of the committee's resolution, referred with justifiable satisfaction to the halibut treaty, and pointed out that,

. . . the Canadian position as taken was maintained absolutely by the Imperial Conference as a whole. Not only did the Ministers of other self-governing Dominions take the position, in giving their assent to the resolution, that what Canada had done with respect to that particular treaty was done in a right and proper way, but the conference went further and said that with respect to similar

[14] The *Summary of Proceedings* and *Appendices* are published as *Canada, Sessional Papers*, 1924, nos. 37 and 37a. Neither gives any account of the discussions that led up to or followed the resolution.

classes of treaties in the future the procedure there adopted should be the one to be followed.[15]

In the half-dozen years after 1919 any consideration of Canadian foreign relations must give due place to the developing commonwealth relations. The best reason for such weight is that, even from a purely constitutional point of view, no government could long operate foreign relations without running into the fact of imperial machinery. There were, as there always had been, wide differences of opinion as to what changes should at any time be made in the imperial framework; and Canadians never seemed to tire of talking sense or nonsense on what the empire was or should be. Like King Charles's head in Mr. Dick's memorial, the imperial tie frequently turned up where it did not belong. Parliament or public were not quick to learn to discuss foreign affairs on their facts and merits; they had an almost incurable weakness for ventilating instead their various and varying views on the empire. There were, however, undoubted signs that Canadians were paying more attention to the study of international affairs. In 1921 the League of Nations Society of Canada was launched in Ottawa with an impressive list of officers and spread, through numerous branches, across Canada. In the press, in the universities and schools, and in various clubs could be seen reflected the growing desire for knowledge, the growing realization that treaties and alliances and diplomacy were not just remote things belonging to an older and outmoded world. The modest attention given to foreign affairs by the house of commons suggests, however, that the subject was still not regarded as one to which constituents required that their members should give an attention comparable to domestic questions. It was to be some time before the earnest study made by many groups throughout the country progressed beyond the dangerous stage of formulas and dogmas to an appreciation of the relationship between events and policies.

In the first years of the twenties, however, there is some evidence of a desire in Canada to think and act directly in foreign affairs, as well as to regard them as means to an improved status. This

---

15 In respect of representation at the inter-allied conference of 1924 on the Dawes plans there was a difference of opinion between the United Kingdom and Canadian governments. In the end a compromise was reached by which Canada was represented only on an imperial panel. See *Canada, Sessional Papers,* 1924, no. 309; *Canada, House of Commons Debates,* July 4 and 17, 1924.

tendency is seen both in the formation of policy and the machinery for its implementation. For the latter the question at issue was direct Canadian representation in Washington.[16] There had been talk of this for decades arising out of the good reason that for countries with as much business between them as the United States and Canada the route via London was indirect and apparently a needless complication.[17] No government, however, before 1914 took seriously the idea of assuming from Great Britain the responsibility for conducting diplomacy. It was easy to criticize the British handling of Canadian interests, but a very different thing to try to do better. It was only with the growth of national consciousness during the war that a Canadian government began to look at plans for diplomatic representation in the United States. There had been effective machinery for particular purposes. The International Joint Commission, established by treaty in 1909, was a standing body that might deal with the use of waters on the international boundary, with boundary questions submitted by either government, or indeed with any question that both governments might wish to submit. Though valuable in a limited sphere, the commission was not in fact employed on as wide a range of subjects as under the treaty it might have been.[18] Its specialized character is also demonstrated by the fact that its continued existence was not affected by the later establishment of a diplomatic mission.

In the last year of the war it was found necessary to set up a Canadian War Mission in Washington to deal with questions, as the order in council put it, "largely of a business and commercial character". The mission was to represent the cabinet and departments in negotiations with American departments of government. It was not diplomatic. It was to keep the British embassy generally informed, and in turn to be informed by the embassy of its negotiations with the American government in so far as they affected

---

[16] On this subject see H. G. Skilling, *Canadian Representation Abroad* (Toronto, 1945), chap. V.

[17] The degree of complication may be seen by one example. A routine inquiry took the following route: United States fisheries authority to secretary of interior; secretary of interior to secretary of state; secretary of state to British ambassador; British ambassador to foreign office; foreign office to colonial office; colonial office to governor-general; governor-general to secretary of state for external affairs. After being considered by the appropriate Canadian authorities the reply was sent back through the same succession of steps.

[18] On the origin, scope, and work of the commission see C. J. Chacko, *The International Joint Commission between the United States of America and the Dominion of Canada* (New York, 1932).

Canada. This obviously useful channel was, again, intended for a specific purpose, but when it was proposed to wind up its business a month or so after the armistice, the government considered it "very essential" that arrangements should now be made for "permanent Canadian Representation at Washington."[19]

The war mission apparently covered a narrower field than the kind of representation originally intended, and was something of a compromise. In October 1917 Borden telegraphed to the high commissioner the government's decision that war conditions made a direct channel necessary, and that it was proposed to appoint J. D. Hazen, minister of marine and fisheries, "and to give him the designation of High Commissioner or some suitable title". In matters concerning the empire as a whole he would consult with the British embassy, while in purely Canadian matters he would communicate direct with the United States government. Perley, after discussion with the colonial secretary, found that the latter approved of the idea, but suggested two conditions: that the appointment should be for the duration of the war, and that Hazen should be attached to the embassy, "though remaining entirely under your control". Borden was ready to accept the first condition, subject to reconsideration at the end of the war, but thought that the other (which had already been suggested to him when he was in London) would not only alter the character of the position but make it difficult to secure the services of a suitable man. To this Long replied that if the Canadian was to have diplomatic status that raised a constitutional question which he must take up with his colleagues. If the diplomatic unity of the empire was to be preserved it would be necessary for the Canadian representative to be connected with the embassy, though he could "settle matters of local interest with the United States government." The Canadian government's reply is of interest.

For many years questions of great importance arising between the United States and Canada, respecting disputes as to delimitation and use of boundary waters, the management of international fishery waters and many other subjects have been disposed of by commissioners appointed by the two governments or by conference between United States and Canadian officials and with excellent results. At present Canadian Food Controller, Canadian Fuel Controller, and Canadian

---

[19] Borden to Rowell, Dec. 10, 1918, in unpublished papers of Sir Robert Borden. The account which follows is based chiefly on those papers.

Board of Grain Supervisors confer directly with corresponding Boards in United States and quick and efficient co-operation is thereby secured. To these methods of procedure, I am not aware that any constitutional objections have been or can be urged. They have developed naturally by ignoring old forms which have lost their meaning and adopting direct and business like methods of communication. It is vitally important that such development should continue. Canada has now double the population with which United States commenced national career and practically same number as inhabited British Isles during the early Napoleonic wars. Her relations with United States are of most intimate and important character and commercial and business relations between the two countries are naturally closer than those between United Kingdom and United States. Lord Bryce told us that three quarters of work of Embassy in his time related to Canada and the ratio will probably be maintained. Yet hitherto Canada has had no representation on Embassy nor in any permanent direct way. Thus her interests have sometimes suffered from oversight or lack of information. Obviously the situation cannot continue. My proposal involves a suitable and dignified status for Canada's representative, but there is no desire to create anything in the nature of a separate Embassy. After discussion with the Ambassador who is in Ottawa, I am convinced that there will be no insurmountable difficulty in accomplishing this. Hazen will probably visit Washington in immediate future and before appointment. . . .[20]

At this stage it becomes somewhat difficult to understand what the points of difference were between London and Ottawa. They seemed to agree that there should be suitable representation. What Borden meant by "a suitable and dignified status" is far from clear, but if it was not intended to be separate diplomatic status it does not seem to clash with the United Kingdom view. However, this vigorous if vague statement of policy by Canada was followed by an anti-climax, the Canadian government deciding in November that it would leave the whole question until after the election, giving, apparently, as reasons the scarcity of accommodation in Washington and the fact that Hazen had accepted a judicial appointment. At the beginning of February 1918 the war mission was set up as an alternative, and it was only at the end of the year, as has been mentioned, that the impending closing of that mission revived the problem of representation.

[20] This exchange of despatches is printed in the *Borden Memoirs*, 1002, 1004.

It was not until October 1919, two years after the original correspondence, that the Canadian government seriously revived the question. This time it was in more explicit terms. A Canadian, under the instructions of the secretary of state for external affairs, should be His Majesty's minister plenipotentiary and envoy extraordinary, dealing with the United States government in matters affecting Canada. The Canadian diplomatic establishment, however, was to form part of the British Embassy. There should be continuous consultation between the minister and the ambassador, and any disagreement must be referred to the respective governments. To this the United Kingdom government agreed, with the additional suggestion that the minister should take charge of the embassy in the absence of the ambassador. Following this agreement it was then necessary to take up the matter with the American authorities. It then turned out that Washington was as much, if not more, concerned for the diplomatic unity of the British Empire as was the empire itself. There was much talk of the nature of an announcement which it was felt had to be made, although the Americans would have preferred that the move be treated quietly, as a routine matter. When the announcement was made on May 7, 1920, jointly in the United Kingdom and Canadian parliaments, it explained the position of the proposed Canadian minister, and emphasized that it would not interfere with diplomatic unity.[21]

No appointment was made. This proved puzzling to the Canadian parliament (as well as to others) which annually voted funds for a mission that was not set up. Why no action was taken by the conservative administration is not clear, unless it was that it found no suitable person to fill the post. A more practical difficulty—whether or not it was a reason for the delay—was that Canada was proposing to operate at least a close approximation to a foreign service without having any staff either for abroad or at home. The department of external affairs was absurdly small, and lacked expert knowledge. During the correspondence about the Washington appointment it became apparent that no one in Ottawa seemed to know what letters of credence were; and an ingenious effort to secure precedence for a Canadian minister by quoting the Bavarian example gave way before an expert opinion from the foreign office. Whatever the explanation (and it was not given to parliament) the

21 The text of the announcement is in the *Borden Memoirs*, 1006.

government never pursued its highly complicated plan of a mission that was separate and not separate, taking directions from a government that had no body of officials for that subject. With the fall of the government in 1921 the succeeding liberal administration took no action on a plan in which the party had never believed; for, while the new prime minister, Mackenzie King, had supported the project of representation, he had opposed associating it with the British embassy. The liberal alternative waited until 1927.

The abortive plans for representation in Washington have been examined at some length because they throw light on the current stage of Canadian development in foreign relations. The central issue is certainly the attempt to combine direct relations with the one foreign country in which Canada had major interests with a safeguarding of commonwealth foreign policy which at that time was a practice as well as a theory. Diplomatic unity was, as has been shown, common ground for British, American, and Canadian governments; and at the very time when the Canadian government was being evasive in the house of commons on why it had done nothing about the Washington appointment, it was—apparently happily—being represented at the disarmament conference through an imperial delegation.

It is equally true that—also at the same time—Canadian policy was being expressed through another medium by delegations firmly kept distinct from those of other parts of the commonwealth. When the League of Nations was formed Canada and other dominions were accepted, not without hesitation, as separate members. In the discussion on the terms of the covenant and at the annual assemblies that met under it the Canadian views put forward show the emergence of a national foreign policy that was to last for some twenty years. Because it was strongly flavoured with isolationism that policy has been regarded as negative. It was far from being so—as far as was British isolationism in the late nineteenth century. It was a policy which derived both from general and local conditions. With the only possible aggressor subdued, peace seemed fixed. Throughout the British Commonwealth there was a general tendency in governments and public to limit commitments. In the United States, which could not fail to influence Canada, an almost fanatical isolationism was triumphant. Within Canada there was a wide range of opinion from those who were prepared to accept the full implications of the covenant to those on the other extreme who still recoiled from the "vortex of European militarism". A middle position, pretty consistently followed by successive governments, probably represented the views of the bulk of the population. On the face of it there seems to be a contrast between the eagerness of Canada to be a member of the League and its constant harping on the virtues of peace, and an apparent reluctance to support the kind of league that could maintain peace. Such a contradiction (by no means peculiar to Canadians) is explained in part by special circumstances. Canada's insistence on full rights in the League, including eligibility to the council, was so coloured by the ambition to secure thereby recognition of status that the decision on acceptance of the covenant was at least as much influenced by constitutional growth as by belief in the merits of the plan as such.

Furthermore, Canadians found it hard to see any real danger to their own country. Their geographical position in the early days of flying insulated them from Europe or the east. The oceans, of course, could be crossed; but had not the royal navy always stood guard? Moreover, there was now also a great American navy; and while it was true that the United States renounced any participation in collective security, the philosophy of the Monroe doctrine could be considered to apply throughout the Americas. From all this came, in the words of a later Canadian representative, the theory of the "fire-proof house"; or, to use the jargon of the day, Canada was a producer but not a consumer of security. The history of the country, indeed, showed no lack of military capacity or of readiness to share burdens in time of crisis. It did, however, show resistance to making commitments designed to achieve security, even to the extent that receding colonialism allowed for such action. Taken together such considerations formed a strong and understandable background for the attitude taken on specific issues.

Throughout the twenties and thirties the consistent Canadian view of international organizations was that their value lay in the means provided for consultation, and consequently for peaceful settlement after discussion and perhaps compromise. On the other hand there was a marked reluctance to accept commitments to participate in the threat or use of force as a means of ensuring peaceful settlement. This central issue had first come up when the covenant was under construction at Paris, and at that time the delegation made the first Canadian onslaught on article X.[22] The government had defended the article, as a part of the treaty it had signed, against opposition in parliament, but took the first opportunity, at the first assembly in 1920, to move that it be struck out of the covenant.[23] As an amendment to the covenant the Canadian proposal was referred to the committee on amendments, and by it to an international committee of jurists. Running the whole gamut of committees the amendment to delete such an important article was soon seen to be a lost cause, though it continued to be defended in the second assembly by Doherty. The amendment was still standing on the agenda when the third assembly met in 1922. "It did not appear that the proposal had found favour in any quarter in the Assembly," stated the delegates to that assembly.[24] "It had, on the contrary, aroused marked hostility. The French representatives were particularly strong in their objections to the elimination of the Article. Many of the smaller nations too were disposed to regard the Article as a protection against aggression and naturally did not look with approval on the proposal to strike it out." This remarkable discovery, apparently, led the government—now a liberal government—to change its tactics, and to propose instead of deletion the addition of what are euphemistically called in the report of the delegates "a few explanatory words". It was proposed to add the following to the existing article:

. . . taking into account the political and geographical circumstances of each state. The opinion given by the Council in such cases should be regarded as a matter of the first importance and should be taken into consideration by all the Members of the League who should use their utmost endeavours to conform to the conclusions of the Council; but no Member should be under the obligation to engage in any act of war without the consent of its parliament, legislature or other representative body.

[22] See above, 311-12.

[23] On Canadian policy in the League see W. E. Armstrong, *Canada and the League of Nations: The Problem of Peace* (Geneva, 1930) ; G. M. Carter, *The British Commonwealth and International Security;* S. Mack Eastman, *Canada at Geneva: An Historical Survey and Its Lessons* (Toronto, 1946).

[24] *Report of the Canadian Delegates to the Third Assembly of the League of Nations (Canada, Sessional Papers*, 1923, no. 36). This and subsequent annual reports are very brief, and give only the most sketchy account of the proceedings and of Canadian participation in them.

The new amendment was held over for the next assembly, the council meanwhile to arrange for its detailed study. By this time two things had happened. One was that article X had been so much studied that there was increasing doubt as to what in fact it did mean. During the same period, too, the assembly had also been debating amendments to article XVI, though in this case the Canadian delegates—rather surprisingly—were less to the fore. The other new circumstance was that the search for security had now moved into alternative and parallel channels, so that the states most concerned with exposure to aggression were pinning less hope on article X. In the fourth committee still another approach was tried. It appears not to have been suggested by the Canadians but by the Swiss and Belgian delegates in the first committee of the assembly. It was now proposed, in view of the difficulty of securing agreement on an amendment, that an interpretative resolution be put forward in its place. The wording by a sub-committee, as modified by proposals of the British delegation, was as follows:

It is in conformity with the spirit of Article X that, in the event of the Council considering it to be its duty to recommend the application of military measures in consequence of an aggression or danger or threat of aggression, the Council shall be bound to take account, more particularly, of the geographical situation and of the special conditions of each State.

It is for the constitutional authorities of each Member to decide, in reference to the obligation of preserving the independence and the integrity of the territory of Members, in what degree the Member is bound to assume the execution of its obligation by employment of its military forces.

The recommendation made by the Council shall be regarded as being of the highest importance and shall be taken into consideration by all the Members of the League with the desire to execute their engagements in good faith.

"The difference between the Canadian amendment and the interpretative resolution," W. E. Armstrong points out, "was that the former placed the responsibility of making a decision on the national Parliament, whereas the latter left it, as it is under Article X, a matter for the Council."[25] The assembly came close to the necessary unanimity when the resolution was before it. Twenty-nine states,

---

[25] Armstrong, *Canada and the League of Nations*, 85.

including France and Belgium, voted for it. Twenty-three were absent or abstained. One only—Persia—which had consistently opposed the resolution, voted against it. The resolution failed, therefore, though the president of the assembly made the curious decision that "I shall not declare the motion rejected, because it cannot be argued that in voting as it has done, the Assembly has pronounced in favour of the converse interpretation."

Leaving the subject on this note gave room for a continuing Canadian tradition that the interpretation had really been accepted. Obviously it was not Canada alone that sought to whittle down the clauses in the covenant which required member states to participate in sanctions. There were, in the case of Canada, intelligible reasons for the view it consistently took. In the main these have already been stated. The apparent remoteness of danger was one. Another was the tradition, previously applied to the United Kingdom, that the country should not be committed in advance but that parliament should decide as each case arose. Thirdly was the hope that the opposition of the United States to the League, centring as it had on article X, might dwindle if the covenant were revised. In this connection Canada not only shared the universal belief that no league could be fully effective without the participation of the United States, but had a particular desire to see its powerful neighbour following the same course as itself and the United Kingdom.

The attitude toward article X and the other enforcement clauses of the covenant was repeated in respect of contemporary projects for increasing the effectiveness of collective security. At an early stage it came to be recognized that reduction of armaments was dependent not so much on the technical question it raised as on the previous solution of the problem of security. States were not willing to give up their own defences unless they were satisfied that some alternative security was assured. A series of attempts was made to formulate a scheme acceptable both to the exposed states and to those which had little apprehension of aggression. In the third assembly a resolution (no. XIV) was adopted which stated this relationship of security and disarmament and proposed a general defensive agreement as a means of making the second possible. In principle military assistance was to be given by states in the same region. At the request of the assembly the council sent this resolution to all member governments of the League, asking for each government's conclusions as a guide for further drafting of what at this stage was called a treaty of mutual guarantee.[26] In its reply the Canadian government stated that it did "not see its way to participate". It noted the regional arrangement, but as a part of the British Empire could not see how a plan could be devised that would meet these conflicting considerations—that is to say the North American and imperial connections.[27] A similar, though more elaborate comment was made when the fourth assembly passed to the governments for their views the text of the Draft Treaty of Mutual Assistance (the name having been altered) intended to carry out the purposes of resolution XIV.[28] Though professing sympathy with the objects of the treaty, and encouraging consultation on the possible causes of war, the Canadian government defined its various objections.

The position of Canada in the British Empire is such that, in spite of the fact that the application of the Treaty to the continent of North America is by its terms conditioned upon its ratification by the United States of America, the question of Canada's adherence to it has a more practical aspect than it would otherwise have. Apart from indications that the government of the United States of America was not likely to find the plan acceptable in principle, Canada has already indicated disapproval of the interpretation of the terms of Article 10 of the Covenant as implying an obligation upon her to intervene actively under that article. The proposed Treaty creates an obligation wider in its extent and more precise in its implications than any which Article 10 could be interpreted as imposing, and it proposes, moreover, to transfer the right to decide upon the scope of action Canada should take from the Canadian Parliament to the Council of the League of Nations. It is true that, for the purpose of deciding upon the assistance to be given by Canada, the Council would include a Canadian representative and that the draft limits the liability of a signatory in another continent to measures not involving naval, military or air operations. But the presence of a Canadian representative on the Council would hardly compensate for the, at least nominal transfer of authority, and, again, Canada's

---

[26] Circular letter from the president of the council, Oct. 23, 1922, in *League of Nations, Official Journal*, Feb., 1923, 174.

[27] The text of the reply is in R. A. MacKay and E. B. Rogers, *Canada Looks Abroad* (Toronto, 1938), 327.

[28] Circular letter from the secretary-general, Oct. 25, 1923, in *League of Nations, Official Journal*, Dec., 1923, 1520. The letter quotes the assembly's resolution and transmits the relevant papers.

position in the British Empire affects the protection afforded her by the continental limitation of which in any event the utility is uncertain since it appears doubtful if hostile action can widely or indeed safely be undertaken by any State upon the principle of limited liability.[29]

From even the second, and longer, of the two replies it is not easy to follow the Canadian argument; nor is any further light cast by the statement made in the house of commons (which was far from the practice of dissecting its government's actions on foreign policy). Some aid is given, however, by collating the note with the text of the treaty. The preamble was obviously a red rag, for it gave as the purpose "a scheme of mutual assistance with a view to facilitate the application of Articles X and XVI of the Covenant". Apparently, then, the assembly was attempting to strengthen the very articles which Canada wished to weaken, and that by giving under article V authority to the council which Canada claimed for its own parliament. In other words it was the direct opposite of Canadian policy as expressed again and again at Geneva. It seemed to Canadian eyes certain that the United States would have nothing to do with the proposed treaty, and while that would under article XVIII make the treaty non-applicable in North America this was no protection to Canada—which saw no prospect of aggression in North America—but did signify a further blow to Canadian hopes of finding a bridge between American and European policies. In effect the government saw itself dragged into sanctions either because liability could not, in fact, be limited or because the British Empire was a world state.

The rejection of the draft treaty was unanimous by all portions of the commonwealth. They shared, perhaps in varying degrees, the objection to further and specific commitments; and certainly they shared the view put forward by Canada that for them the regional scheme was unreal and unworkable. As one authority has phrased it,

The apportionment of liability on continental lines cut fatally across the structure of the British Commonwealth with its world-wide responsibilities. Either some parts of the Empire might be at war while others remained at peace—a situation regarded at that date as intolerable—or Great Britain and her Dominions would be

[29] MacKay and Rogers, *Canada Looks Abroad*, 328-9.

subjected to a wholly disproportionate share of the burden of resisting aggression in all parts of the world.[30]

Neither in this nor in the succeeding League plan for security was it a question of one part of the commonwealth influencing others or of common policy reached by conference, but of identical policies reached, it is true, with some consultation but principally from individual decisions. The Protocol for the Pacific Settlement of International Disputes, adopted by the fifth assembly, was, like its predecessor, submitted to member governments for their approval. The emphasis was on arbitration and the solidity of article XVI of the covenant. While the complicated regional scheme was dropped, the protocol provided for sanctions otherwise similar to those of the draft treaty. In this case the United Kingdom government did attempt to provide for the conclusion of a common policy, and as a means suggested an imperial conference. That government, as it told all dominion governments, was "greatly impressed with momentous character of question". It involved compulsory arbitration and "sanctions of the most drastic character". Furthermore, it "necessarily brings to the forefront far-reaching problems affecting the security of the Empire, and its future relations to the countries of Europe and the United States of America."[31] An imperial conference proved impossible to arrange because of sessions of some of the dominion parliaments. The Canadian prime minister, while unable to attend a conference, agreed that it was "highly desirable that similar attitude should be adopted towards Protocol by countries of British Empire which are members of the League of Nations". The phrasing is not without significance, for there is a real difference between a single policy and a similar attitude.

To some extent views on the protocol were exchanged between the various dominion capitals, but there is no reason to believe that any important change was made as a result. The Canadian reply to the secretary-general of the League, dated March 10, 1925, was consistent with previous statements, though less complicated because the protocol was less complicated. While expressing con-

[30] G. M. Gathorne-Hardy, *A Short History of International Affairs, 1920 to 1938* (Oxford, 1938), 59.

[31] Telegram of Dec. 19, 1924, to all dominion prime ministers, *Protocol for the Pacific Settlement of International Disputes: Correspondence Relating to the Positions of the Dominions* (Cmd. 2458, 1925).

tinued belief in the League and in peaceful settlement, the reply was firm that,

> . . . we do not consider it in the interests of Canada, of the British Empire or of the League itself, to recommend to Parliament adherence to the Protocol and particularly to its rigid provisions for application of economic and military sanctions in practically every future war. Among the grounds for this conclusion is the consideration of the effect of the non-participation of the United States upon attempts to enforce the sanctions and particularly so in the case of a contiguous country like Canada.[32]

By 1925, then, it appeared that Canadian policy toward collective security had been fully declared. Contemporary students may now be spared, as representatives then at the assembly would gladly have been spared, the almost inevitable Canadian self-congratulation on the virtues of international relations in North America. The unguarded frontier and the century of peace became too well advertised to be of further interest in Geneva. Behind the barrage of words however, lay some pertinent facts. Canada considered that she had no military problem in North America, either from land or sea attack. She did, however, have a political problem in her constant pursuit of a formula that would unite the English-speaking world. No government of the period would involve the country in commitments wider than those they were trying to pare down in the covenant. No government would take any action calculated to discourage the United States from re-entering world affairs; and no government would willingly complicate its position in the commonwealth.

So far all the schemes for increasing collective security had met unanimous refusal throughout the commonwealth (and a fortiori the disapproval of the United States). When, however, the persistent Europeans turned to another method of attempting to put real bulwarks against war there came a difference in United Kingdom and Canadian policies. Regional security had entered into the draft treaty as one element; it now took first place in what became the Locarno treaties. The Treaty of Mutual Guarantee of 1925 was of great importance in ushering in the most optimistic period since 1914. The "spirit of Locarno" was a very real thing at the time, but it was an atmosphere created not by speech-

[32] MacKay and Rogers, *Canada Looks Abroad*, 329.

making alone but by what looked like a lasting settlement of the Rhine frontier. The initiative came from Germany, was picked up in London, and finally accepted by France. There were two essential features in any agreement that was to be of value: that Germany and France should mutually renounce aggression, and that the United Kingdom should add its outside guarantee. That the British government was prepared, if reluctant, to do; but it did so without help or hindrance from the dominions. They were kept informed of the progress of the negotiations but did not participate in them. Exactly how that situation arose has never been made quite clear. Lloyd George (of Chanak fame) vigorously called the kettle black, whereupon Austen Chamberlain (foreign secretary) rightly pointed to the attempt at an imperial conference to discuss the Geneva Protocol, and equally reasonably described Locarno as an alternative to the protocol.

Be that as it may, neither the United Kingdom nor the Canadian government made any criticism of the other. Probably it suited the Canadian government to be free from negotiation of a treaty which it would hardly have supported and to which it never adhered. There are obvious paradoxes in the situation. When the draft treaty was up for discussion one of the Canadian objections had been that it was unreal to suppose that regional obligations would fit a world-wide empire. Yet nothing could have been more unreal than to suppose that a war over the Rhine frontier could be other than a world war in which Canada, in its own interest, would participate. To all intents and purposes, although the letter of the routine under the 1923 imperial conference was observed, Canada had willingly dropped back into the position under which high policy was made in London. It is almost certain, however, that the Canadian public on the whole would have opposed adherence to what could so easily be represented as a treaty of only European concern. Moreover there was common ground for the government's opposition to both the draft treaty and Locarno. That was the now-sacred "parliament-must-decide" formula which would have been undermined in either case.

Gone now were the attempts to strengthen collective security on a global basis. It was generally understood that the obligations under the covenant were weakened rather than strengthened by the battle that had been waged over them, and no general buttresses had been run up to hold them from outside. With the guarantee of the Rhine frontier, the inauguration of the Dawes plan, the entrance of Germany into the League, and signs of increasing prosperity everywhere, it seemed that peace and prosperity had succeeded the troubled years immediately after the war. For a brief spell the international scene began to look much more pleasant.

Over five years the main episodes that have been reviewed show the direction of Canadian policy and the effect that it had on international relations. No attempt has been made to examine every international negotiation in which Canada was concerned. An indication of these may be found in the annual Report of the Secretary of State for External Affairs. The second half of the decade showed for Canada, as it did generally, new trends in international affairs. While in essentials Canadian policy remained unchanged, some important new steps were taken. In general these amounted to more freedom of action and more machinery for that action. At the imperial conference of 1926, at which everybody seems to have been cordial about everybody else's foreign policy, emerged the declaration on equality of status. Like Magna Carta, the statement was important not so much for what it said as for what it came to represent. By laying the ghost of imperial control, the conference left the way open for freedom of action in foreign policy.

CHAPTER XVII

THE LATE TWENTIES

IN the troubled generation since the beginning of the first world war only the short span of the late twenties stands out as a time both of apparently solid advance and of hope for the continuation of peace and prosperity. From the combination of advantages in those years no country benefited more than Canada, dependent as it was on foreign trade, and standing only to gain—in population, prosperity, and peace of mind—from a world devoted to the arts of peace. With the generally favourable trend went factors particularly advantageous to the Canadian situation. The cautious and tentative steps taken by the United States back from complete isolation augured well for the reconciliation of British and American policies, an end, of course, always dear to Canadian governments. The settlement of the problem of dominion status disentangled, so far as legal forms could do, constitutional growth from foreign policy.

The glamour surrounding the recognition of dominion status obscured at the time, and has partially obscured since, the common sense which put in workable form the position of the self-governing units of the commonwealth in respect of foreign policy. So far at least as that theme of the development from 1926 to 1931 is concerned, the process was not a struggle between a conservative metropolitan power and peoples struggling to be free, but the last phase of the long effort to invent forms and practices that would save an old empire from breaking because it was inelastic. There were extremists of both kinds: those who held that complete independence was desirable or at least inevitable, and those who clung to the hope of centralized machinery. Both groups, however, were minorities without influence on the course of change, which was in the direction of co-operation between countries with traditions and basic interests in common. There continued to be talk of "sentiment" as the tenuous link of empire, but such talk was wholly misleading. It was not sentiment, not even trade, that caused the peoples of the commonwealth to maintain their novel relationship but an undefined recognition of common interests. To suggest that the "gains" of the process of constitutional change are to be found in concessions to the dominions is to miss the point: the gains lay in the agreement on formulas for co-operation.

The imperial conference of 1926,[1] at which the policy decisions were made, reached two main conclusions. The first, and widely-publicized one, was the recognition that the self-governing communities of the empire were equal in status both in domestic and external affairs. The second was that "the principles of equality and similarity, appropriate to *status,* do not universally extend to function". From this sensible starting-point came the positive decisions in respect of foreign affairs. A committee was recommended to work out the principle that each dominion should have power to give extra-territorial operation to its legislation. That committee, or conference, met in London in 1929 and recommended a "declaratory enactment". Approved by the imperial conference of the following year, the decision appears as clause 3 of the Statute of Westminster. By a similar process dominion parliaments became free to enact merchant shipping legislation.[2]

In respect of the negotiation and signature of treaties the conference of 1926 amplified and clarified the decisions reached at the conference of 1923. A study of representation at international conferences led the conference of 1926 to the conclusion that no difficulty arose in regard to conferences called by the League of Nations. For international conferences called by a foreign power at which more than one part of the empire wished to be represented there were three alternatives: (a) common plenipotentiaries holding full powers issued on the advice of all participating parts of the empire; (b) a single empire delegation; (c) separate delegations.

Turning to the general conduct of foreign policy, the conference of 1926 reached this conclusion:

We went on to examine the possibility of applying the principle underlying the Treaty Resolution of the 1923 Conference to matters arising in the conduct of foreign affairs generally. It was frankly

---

[1] *Imperial Conference, 1926: Summary of Proceedings* (Cmd. 1768, 1926).

[2] The relevant parts of the reports of the three meetings will be found in A. B. Keith (ed.), *Speeches and Documents on the British Dominions, 1918-1931: From Self-government to National Sovereignty* (Oxford, 1938).

recognized that in the sphere of defence, the major share of responsibility rests now, and must for some time continue to rest, with His Majesty's Government in Great Britain. Nevertheless, practically all the Dominions are engaged to some extent, and some to a considerable extent, in the conduct of foreign relations, particularly those with foreign countries on their borders. A particular instance of this is the growing work in connection with the relations between Canada and the United States of America which has led to the necessity for the appointment of a Minister Plenipotentiary to represent the Canadian Government in Washington. We felt that the governing consideration underlying all discussions of the problem must be that neither Great Britain nor the Dominions could be committed to the acceptance of active obligations except with the definite assent of their own governments. . . .

The conference then went on to suggest that the procedure described for treaties might be taken as a guide in relation to other international negotiations. The total effect, then, was that each unit of the commonwealth had independent powers of legislation, and that for negotiations—whether or not leading up to a treaty —a flexible procedure was accepted which combined arrangements for consultations and co-operation with freedom of action.[3] All this, however, was to be read in the light of the fact that the United Kingdom had the major share of responsibility, and the principle that no one part of the commonwealth was by unilateral action to commit any other part. It was probably impossible to go further with the analysis of these two latter considerations, yet they left untouched a fundamental problem that was to give trouble in the future as it had in the past. To accept or avoid active obligations might seem a simple choice, and superficially it was. Canada, for example, did not adhere to the Locarno Treaty. It did not, at a later period, participate in any guarantee of Poland or in the partition of Czechoslovakia. Yet when these dykes were washed away by the Nazi flood Canada was just as much affected as it would have been if it had signed as many agreements as the United Kingdom. On paper, perhaps, the

---

[3] The treaty procedure worked out in 1923 and 1926 on the whole operated smoothly. Dawson, in *The Development of Dominion Status*, 112, cites a number of such cases. An exception, however, was the case of the Anglo-Egyptian negotiations of 1927, when the Canadian government was obliged to point out that the United Kingdom government had not followed the rules. For a valuable note on this case see A. J. Toynbee, *Survey of International Affairs, 1928* (Oxford, 1929), 279.

procedure laid down allowed for consultation on all aspects of foreign affairs, and therefore covered any line taken by the United Kingdom which might at any time involve the dominions. In regard to the actual position in the twenties and thirties, however, Canada had maintained a theoretical policy of limited liability, which, so far as treaty obligations were concerned, it could maintain. By doing so it inevitably left itself open to the results of British policy if these were deemed to become Canadian interests. It was too late—if it had ever been possible—to close that gap by the creation of imperial machinery and the pursuit of a single policy. The only remaining answer was a fuller knowledge of, and participation in, world affairs.

One condition that had to be fulfilled before such a change could even be attempted was to build up a body of experts at home and a foreign service abroad. The former had always been within the competence of the Canadian government, involving no agreement by foreign states or even by the United Kingdom. There were, of course, not lacking contemporaries who appreciated the need, and some slight progress was made. The number of officers in the department of external affairs (including the under-secretary) rose from three in 1927 to five in 1928 and to seven in 1929. This is not impressive for a department which had existed for twenty years and it was obviously inadequate if foreign affairs were to be given the study that the interests of Canada required. On the other hand it is probable that the governments of the day (even before they were overtaken by the need of stringent economies) had no desire to defend in parliament a budget swollen to anything like the level that serious growth would have involved. To make an argument in defence of such an expenditure it would have been necessary to enlarge on Canada's participation in foreign affairs, and thus to invite criticism from a parliament and press unaccustomed to think in terms of foreign relations as a professional occupation, and on the whole reluctant to accept the idea that foreign offices were needed in the purer air of America.

Paradoxically enough the main advance of the period was in the establishment of offices abroad. A foreign service, of course, rotates around the country which it represents. Because the government is at the home capital, it is from there that instructions come, there that reports are received and digested, and normally there that the personnel is trained. For reasons that have been suggested there was little building at the centre. On the other hand there were reasons for establishing offices abroad. To contemporaries they were a mixture of practical need and prestige. The right of legation fitted in with the current emphasis on status, and its acceptance has always been regarded as a sign of constitutional growth. To have set up offices around the world for reasons of prestige alone would have been absurd, and both conservative and liberal administrations had always laid genuine stress on the practical need. In other words the functions of the offices would as much express the increased volume of Canadian affairs with other countries as their very existence would symbolize the stature of the country.

The first move was in Geneva, when an official misnamed "Canadian Advisory Officer to the League of Nations" was posted in 1925. Certainly the officer was not to advise the League of Nations, but to keep the Canadian government informed, to act as adviser to delegates, and to be in touch with officials of the League and the International Labour Office. In 1938 the name was changed to "Permanent Delegate of Canada to the League of Nations".[4] There can be no doubt of the value of this office, not only for the performance of the duties mentioned but because Geneva was a listening-post for the affairs of Europe and the world. Because it was not a diplomatic appointment, however, it caused less stir than the delayed action on representation in Washington. The original plan of the Borden government had not been implemented by the conservatives before their fall from power, nor did the liberal government act until 1927. In that year a Canadian envoy extraordinary, and minister plenipotentiary presented to the President of the United States letters of credence issued by the king and naming the Honourable Charles Vincent Massey as minister "with the especial object of representing in the United States of America the interests of our Dominion of Canada."[5] Neither the minister nor his staff had been in the department of external affairs, though the commercial secretary, M. M. Mahoney, had been the department's agent in Washington since the closing of the war mission. In 1927, indeed, the staff in Washington alone was larger than that in Ottawa. That

    4 Skilling, *Canadian Representation Abroad*, 166.
    5 The text of the letters of credence is in W. P. M. Kennedy (ed.), *Statutes, Treaties and Documents of the Canadian Constitution, 1713-1929* (Toronto, 1930), 712.

part of the earlier plan which had provided for the attachment of the Canadian minister to the British embassy was dropped.

Two more legations were set up in this period. In Paris it was only a question of transferring the office of the commissioner-general for Canada into a diplomatic mission. Non-diplomatic representation at the French capital dated back to 1882, and from then until 1911 the office represented both the federal and Quebec governments. In 1928 the change was made. If there were to be any Canadian diplomatic representatives abroad there could be little quarrel with starting in Washington where there was the greatest volume of business. Paris was obviously the next move, both as one of the major capitals of Europe and as the first mother-country of Canada. At the same time the intention to establish a legation in Tokyo was announced, and implemented in 1929. As Paris was to Europe, so Tokyo was to be to the far east. In the parliamentary discussion of these moves emphasis was laid by the government on the value of missions in Europe and the far east, and on the help that they would give in maintaining good relations between foreign countries and the British Empire as a whole. Members of the opposition questioned both arguments, some denying the value of Canadian legations and others fearing the end of the diplomatic unity of the commonwealth.

Here for a time the development of the foreign service ended. Since 1921 the office of the high commissioner in London had been brought under the jurisdiction of the department of external affairs; and while, of course, it did not have diplomatic status because it was within the commonwealth, it performed much the same function as the legations. There were no Canadian consulates, although consular functions could be performed at London, Washington, Paris, and Tokyo. For the rest Canadian citizens, as British subjects, availed themselves of the services of United Kingdom consulates throughout the world. In three years Canada had set up the beginning of a diplomatic service, thus being provided at least with the nucleus of a machinery for carrying out foreign policy in the régime initiated by the imperial conference of 1926. It was, of course, only the beginning. Reporting from abroad could cover a limited part of the world and business with other countries could only in part be conducted through Canadian channels. The department of external affairs was as yet too small either for the desired specialization or to train enough officers for service abroad. Yet, as compared to a decade before, it was a considerable step toward acquiring the means of formulating and implementing foreign policy. For, if the Canadian government was to be able to act in this field with wisdom and success, it must look forward to obtaining its own knowledge of international affairs and to carrying out its decisions through its own professional staff.

The lines of policy were laid in the early twenties, and indeed had roots reaching back to long before that. In these last "post-war" years no strong outside pressures were put on Canadian policy under which it might show strength or weakness, and no determined parliamentary drive was made to alter its course. It is, therefore, a comparatively calm period in which policy may be examined, following its earlier definition and preceding the years of growing crisis which begin as the period closes. In doing so the problem may be approached from two angles: the range of policy in space, and its range in kind.

The first needs little elaboration. Theoretically two interests were universal. As a country dependent on external trade Canada would gladly do business with any part of the world. In practice, however, only a fraction of her trade reached beyond the United Kingdom and the United States. Membership in a world organization, the League of Nations, similarly created a technical relationship to all parts of the world; and, while this was far from being meaningless, it was modified by the cautious policy that the government had pursued in respect of obligations under the covenant. The British Commonwealth, of which Canada formed part, also spread throughout the world. The extension of Canadian interest thus caused is not easily definable. Relations with the other dominions had yet to become intimate. The vital connection was with the United Kingdom and through it with other parts of the commonwealth or empire. The empire as a great power was one of the essential bases of the Canadian position in the world. The foreign policy of Canada could differ in degree but not in kind from that of Great Britain. In any major crisis the two policies must converge.

The path to Europe lay through London more than it did through Geneva. The French origin of Canada, while it had an important internal influence, had little or no effect on foreign policy. Rather it was because the United Kingdom was inevitably tied to Europe that Canada was also so tied. This had little to do with constitutional controls or the lack of them, although the two factors were—

perhaps unavoidably—confused in the minds of contemporaries. Although the situation was seldom expressed by Canadians in such simple terms, the balance of power in Europe meant just the same to them as it did to the people of the British Isles. To both its overthrow would spell a threat to the security of the United Kingdom, the centre of power in the commonwealth. Individual or direct relations with European states were less compelling. Migration brought no political ties. The Vatican was the centre of the faith of a large proportion of Canadians, but there was no resultant attachment to the Kingdom of Italy. Canadian relations with the U.S.S.R. did little more than follow the course pursued by London. The Canadian government was concerned to encourage trade and discourage propaganda, and when in 1927 the two became obviously entangled, it terminated the official commercial relations.

The different countries of the Americas were of varying interest to Canada. From every point of view the United States was a major influence on Canada, as it had always been. The British West Indies had for long been of commercial interest, but periodic suggestions that they might be politically joined to Canada met with a cool reception. There was no land-hunger in a country that was still expanding into its own territory. To most Canadians Latin America seemed more distant than Europe. Trade with the republics was small. There was no tradition of common political effort in the past and no expectation of co-operation for the future in war or in peace. From time to time individuals suggested that Canada should join the inter-American system, but there was a marked lack of enthusiasm on both sides. To the United States Canada came close to being one of the "dominions whose foreign relations are controlled by European states".[6] To the extent that any of the Latin republics favoured Canadian entry it was suspected that it was to offset the predominating influence of the United States. To Canadians membership offered little apparent advantage, particularly in view of the fact that it could not be expected to improve relations with the United States. On the other hand to join would be to make another commitment at a time when it was desired to curtail the existing ones.

[6] Quoted in F. H. Soward and A. M. Macaulay, *Canada and the Pan American System* (Toronto, 1948), 22. On the general subject see also J. P. Humphrey, *The Inter-American System: A Canadian View* (Toronto, 1942).

The extent of Canadian interest in the far east is not easy to assess.[7] Trade was larger than with Latin America but still a small portion of the total. Canadian missionary effort in China and Japan created a link that partially offset the discouragement of Canadian immigration policy. The vigorous opposition in 1921 to the renewal of the Anglo-Japanese Treaty should not be construed as an indication of a major political interest in the far east. Geographically Canada was a Pacific as well as an Atlantic state, but there was never any question of equality of interest in the two oceans. The somewhat unusual force of Canadian policy in 1921 sprang not from direct concern with the far east but from a desire to avoid friction between the United Kingdom and the United States.

Such in outline is the range of Canadian foreign interest, looked at geographically. Turning to an analysis of policy by subject it will be seen that there were three main elements: relations with the one land-neighbour, views on collective security, and trade policy. The choice of Washington as the capital to have the first Canadian diplomatic mission is one indication of the importance placed on relations with the United States; and the description by the under-secretary of state for external affairs of the legation's first year outlines its activities:

The legation has been fully employed from the day of its establishment. . . .

Among matters which have engaged the attention of the legation have been the following:

The many problems connected with boundary waterways.

The numerous questions connected with the movement of persons across the international border, and especially the situation created in Canadian border towns, by the alteration of the United States regulations in April, 1927. This question occupied the attention of the legation for many months until a satisfactory settlement was reached which protected the interests of the two or three thousand Canadians, born outside Canada, who were principally affected.

Many questions connected with the United States Tariff and trade between the two countries, of which the most important was the embargo declared on milk shipments from parts of Eastern Canada to the United States in March, 1927.

The allocation of radio broadcasting channels and other radio matters of international importance.

[7] On the general subject see C. J. Woodsworth, *Canada and the Orient: A Study in International Relations* (Toronto, 1941).

The means of co-operation between the two Governments in the suppression of smuggling, both by land and sea.

International flying; international fishery questions; the extradition of criminals.

In general the protection of the interests of Canadian citizens in a very wide range of matters, principally connected with immigration, deportation, arrest and imprisonment, settlement of estates, and claims against the government of the United States.[8]

The mission, in fact, devoted itself to workaday matters that were weak in drama but important for the people of Canada. Rum-running from Canada during the days of American prohibition produced problems that might well have led to friction between states that were less ready for amicable settlements. The sinking of the Canadian ship, *I'm Alone*, by a United States Coast Guard vessel, for example, instead of leading to an "incident", was quietly handled through diplomatic channels and settled by joint judicial decision. Negotiations toward the construction of the St. Lawrence deep waterway as a joint project by the two countries continued throughout these years. In the various matters currently being discussed with the United States there was little that could be called high policy. Where the foreign policies of Canada and the United States came into that field was not in bilateral relations but in the wider stream of world affairs, in the general question of security against war.

The cautious reappearance of the United States in world affairs in the late twenties was, from the Canadian point of view, a most desirable tendency. Furthermore, the main theme now was reduction of armaments by agreement amongst the great powers, and divorced from general plans of military aid to the victims of aggression. Those commitments that were asked of the lesser powers did not involve sanctions, but were concerned with consultation and arbitration. All this well fitted the Canadian book. As far as the Canadian armed forces were concerned they could hardly be reduced further than had already been done. With no belief in threats to their own security, Canadians could freely encourage reduction of armaments by others; and, it must be admitted, in doing so indulged in particularly bad examples of platitudinous sentimentality and effortless superiority.

[8] *Report of the Secretary of State for External Affairs for the Year Ended March 31, 1927* (Ottawa, 1928).

It was appropriate that the declaration on equality made in the report of the imperial conference in 1926 was followed the next year by the election of Canada to the council of the League. The election (the first of a British dominion) marked the final recognition of the eligibility agreed upon at Paris in 1919. So much for status. On the side of function the election brought Canada into direct contact with the discussions on a general agreement for the reduction of armaments. Nearly two years earlier the council of the League had set up a preparatory commission to lay out the ground for the proposed general disarmament conference; and Canada, as a member of the council, automatically became a member of the commission. The commission, however, was not confined to members of the League, so that both the United States and the Soviet Union were represented on it. On the formation in 1927 of a sub-committee on arbitration and security Canada was represented on that body as well. It was inevitable that the contribution of Canada to the prolonged discussions on disarmament should be a minor one, not only because it was a lesser power but also because Canada was neither a seriously armed power nor one that felt the need of armaments. From the point of view of the development of Canadian policy, however, the government's attitude toward the various questions that arose concerning disarmament is of interest.

For purposes of simplicity three main types of approach to the reduction of armaments may be distinguished: technical or political discussions in the commission and the sub-committee; a series of international agreements bearing in various ways on the general problems; and conferences between certain of the great powers on limitation of naval armaments. Since the last affected Canada only indirectly it may be dismissed in a few words. On the invitation of the American government the United Kingdom and Japan sent representatives to a three-power conference in Geneva in 1927. No agreement, however, was reached and the conference dissolved. The London naval conference of 1930, which included also delegations from France and Italy, resulted in a treaty which extended the scope of the Washington agreement of 1922. By no stretch of the imagination could Canada at that period have been called a naval power, and as far as her indirect interests were concerned they were well met by agreement between the United Kingdom and the United

States. There were Canadian representatives on the British Commonwealth delegations at both conferences.

As the various aspects of disarmament came before the commission, the Canadian representatives voiced opinions that were clearly in line with the general Canadian outlook.[9] Compulsory military service was undesirable, and chemical warfare should be made impossible. On several occasions stress was laid on the salutary influence of public opinion as contrasted with the machinations of governments. The Rush-Bagot agreement was trotted out from time to time, and references made to the value of conciliation and investigation. The danger of regional agreements becoming military alliances was also pointed out by the Canadian representative.

It is in relation to the series of special international agreements that Canadian policy is most clearly expressed. Growing out of the suggestion of an unofficial group in the United States there was signed in Paris in August 1928 the General Treaty for the Renunciation of War (or Briand-Kellogg Pact). The plan, though not a new one (it was little different from an assembly resolution of 1927), was significant in that it represented the degree to which at that time the United States was willing to re-enter the area of collective security. By the treaty the contracting powers renounced war as an instrument of national policy and agreed that disputes between them should be settled by pacific means. There is in the treaty no suggestion of sanctions and no reference to existing or new machinery by which disputes were to be resolved. Canada was a separate and original party to the treaty, as were the other dominions, through an invitation from the American secretary of state, acting on the suggestion from London that it was not sufficient to address only that government. The reply of the Canadian secretary of state for external affairs to the invitation to become an original party to the treaty shows an enthusiasm that is in marked contrast to the comments on the earlier projects involving sanctions. It is also a brief essay on Canadian foreign policy.

. . . The Government of Canada is certain that it speaks for the whole Canadian people in welcoming the outcome, in the proposed multilateral pact, of the discussion initiated almost a year ago between the Governments of France and of the United States. It is pleased to find that in this attitude it is in accord with all His Majesty's

[9] For the Canadian position in respect of discussions on disarmament see Armstrong, *Canada and the League of Nations*, chap. VIII.

other governments. The proposals of the United States Government, by their directness and simplicity, afford to the peoples of the world a new and notable opportunity of ensuring lasting peace.

The Dominion of Canada, fortunate in its ties of kinship and allegiance as well as its historic and neighbourly friendships, and with half a continent as its heritage, is less exposed to the danger of attack or the temptation to aggression than many other lands. Yet the Great War, with its burdens of suffering and of loss, brought home the danger which all countries share, and led Canada to turn with hope to the efforts to build up effective barriers against war which took shape in the League of Nations; it will welcome the present proposals as a manifestation of the same striving for peace.

The question whether the obligations of the Covenant of the League would conflict in any way with the obligations of the proposed pact has been given careful consideration. His Majesty's Government in Canada regards the League, with all its limitations, as an indispensable and continuing agency of international understanding, and would not desire to enter upon any course which would prejudice its effectiveness. It is, however, convinced that there is no conflict either in the letter or the spirit between the covenant and the multilateral pact, or between the obligations assumed under each.

The pre-eminent value of the League lies in its positive and preventive action. In bringing together periodically the representatives of fifty states, it builds up barriers against war by developing a spirit of conciliation, an acceptance of publicity in international affairs, and a habit of co-operation in common ends and a permanently available machinery for the adjustment of differences. It is true that the Covenant also contemplates the application of sanctions in the event of a member state going to war if in so doing it has broken the pledges of the Covenant to seek a peaceful solution of disputes. Canada has always opposed any interpretation of the Covenant which would involve the application of these sanctions automatically or by the decision of other states. It was on the initiative of Canada that the Fourth Assembly, with a single negative vote, accepted the interpretative resolution to which the Secretary of State of the United States recently referred, indicating that it is for the constitutional authorities of each state to determine in what degree it is bound to assume the execution of the obligations of this Article by employment of its military forces. The question of sanctions has received further consideration by later Assemblies. It is plain that the full realization of the ideal of joint economic or military pressure upon an outlaw power, upon which some of the founders of the League set great store, will require either an approach to the universality of the League contemplated when the Covenant was being drawn, or an adjustment of the old rules of neutrality to meet the new conditions of co-operative defence.

In any event, if, as would seem to be the case, the proposed multilateral treaty does not impose any obligation upon a signatory in relation to a state which has not signed the treaty or has broken it, any decision taken to apply sanctions against a member of the League which has made war in violation of its Covenant pledges would not appear to conflict with the obligations of the treaty. . . .[10]

Little comment is needed on this note. Its main interest is two-fold. It describes, both in general and in relation to obligations under the covenant, the Canadian position as seen from Ottawa. Secondly, it shows that Canadian policy had changed in no essential since the Paris peace conference. Whatever other criticisms may be levelled at that policy it cannot be called inconsistent.

The government's attitude toward the optional clause of the statute of the permanent court of international justice was also in line with the persistent Canadian belief in peaceful settlement separated from sanctions. The principle of compulsory jurisdiction of the court had been accepted by Canada as early as the first assemby, and was repeated in the telegram to the League secretariat in connection with the Geneva Protocol. In 1926 the imperial conference agreed that it was premature to accept the optional clause, and it was understood that no one of the governments would make any move toward acceptance without discussing it with the others. Again the Canadian view on the optional clause was repeated in the League assembly in 1927; and early in 1929 the government initiated discussions with other commonwealth governments. In the autumn all the commonwealth governments separately made statements in the assembly accepting the optional clause subject to the exclusion of intra-commonwealth disputes.[11] It was this latter question which had, of course, made it necessary for the commonwealth governments to act in unison.

The sub-committee on arbitration and security, of which Canada was a member, prepared what, when adopted by the ninth assembly, was known as the general act for the pacific settlement of international disputes. The act, intended to supplement the optional

[10] The text of the note is in MacKay and Rogers, *Canada Looks Abroad,* 330.

[11] The United Kingdom text is in A. J. Toynbee, *Survey of International Affairs, 1929* (Oxford, 1930), 77. The Canadian position was discussed in the house of commons on March 31 and April 9, 1930.

clause, provided for settlement either by conciliation, arbitration, or judicial decision. When discussed at the imperial conference of 1930 there was agreement on the desirability of the proposal, subject to the exclusion again of intra-commonwealth disputes. Canada acceded to the general act in 1931, thus rounding out its obligations to renounce war as an instrument of policy and to accept instead peaceful settlement of all international disputes.

A vital aspect of Canadian foreign policy as studied in kind is the furtherance of that international trade which had always been an essential element in the country's economy. To the average Canadian—and therefore to the average member of parliament— trade was more understandable, and so more important, than eso- teric plans for dealing with international political relations. The years from 1926 to 1929 saw a markedly rapid rise in the volume of exports. While the national income as a whole went up to 125 per cent. (1920=100) in 1926 and to 148 per cent. in 1928-9, exports increased in the same years to 161 and 172 per cent.[12] While the various parts of Canada did not benefit equally from this important source of wealth, the general effect was to stimulate production within the country and to encourage that expansion which—how- ever disastrous its later effects—was a dominating feature of Cana- dian life at the time. Buyers of Canadian goods were more scattered than they had formerly been. The United Kingdom's share of Canadian exports had fallen from more than a half to a third of the whole. The decline in purchases by the United States was less. The proportion taken by other foreign countries had risen in a generation from a twentieth to a fifth. The other noticeable change was the larger Canadian purchases from the United States.[13]

It is not easy to see that the great prosperity of the late twenties had an appreciable effect on Canadian foreign policy. National wealth was not diverted to armaments, nor did increased popula- tion and economic power lead to the acceptance of commitments to maintain by force the peace of the world. Given the comparative calm in world affairs which marked these years it would have been surprising if such a change had taken place. In the case of Canada, therefore, the world depression which began with dramatic sudden- ness in New York in the autumn of 1929 made in itself no important

[12] *Report of the Royal Commission on Dominion-Provincial Relations,* Book I, 117.
[13] Full tables are in the *Canada Year Book.*

change in the general lines of Canadian foreign policy. It was, of course, no coincidence that armed aggression grew out of the depression, flourishing on the preoccupation of governments with the immediate problems of prices and unemployment, and seeking to pursue national ambitions at a time when they were least likely to be opposed. It is true that in Canada, as elsewhere, the efforts of government were concentrated on the domestic scene. As a means of combating the depression changes were made in the tariff from 1930, all designed to increase protection by higher rates and wider coverage or to aid exports by treaty. To this extent Canada shared in the nationalism that was the recourse of states in the thirties, whether for purposes of aggression or of economic assistance, or both.

It is nevertheless clear that Canadian foreign policy was little altered by the violent change from prosperity to depression. The atmosphere, of course, was different. Instead of an expectation of continued peace and expanding trade, Canadians were faced with the march of armies and shrinking markets. What in the late twenties had been no more than an unconvincing potentiality now became a fact. Collective security had once been represented as a form of insurance against possible risks: in the thirties it was challenged by a series of unilateral acts. Canada, therefore, like other members of the League, was called upon to make a number of decisions as each challenge threatened or actual breach of the peace occurred. From the time of the writing of the covenant Canadian governments had consistently opposed commitments to maintain by force the *status quo*. That had been in the post-war years. Now that not only the *status quo* but the whole fabric of peace was threatened, the same policy was in fact continued, as the "peace-loving" states retreated from position to position before the reality of military force.

CHAPTER XVIII

THE CHALLENGE

THE eight years from the beginning of Japanese aggression in Manchuria to the outbreak of war in 1939 witnessed a series of challenges met by the dwindling free world with as flabby an answer as may be found in the modern history of relations between states. Instead of finding a compensating strength in their own positive beliefs, the governments and peoples of the western world watched numbly the brisk and ordered advance of the dictatorships, while they themselves mumbled formulas in which they no longer had faith and waited, like Mr. Micawber, for something to turn up. As the pendulum swung dully from threats of collective action to undignified retreats, the democracies sought refuge in the theory that if the settlement could not be held it might be modified: a process known to its supporters as "peaceful change" and to its critics as "appeasement".

In this depressing period Canadian governments and people acted and talked little differently from their fellows. As citizens of a minor power they felt less responsibility for leadership than they attributed to the great powers, and in effect followed the lead—or lack of it—given by the great powers. It is not, therefore, intended to suggest that any deficiencies or lack of foresight in policy were peculiarly Canadian; or, indeed, that the pursuit of a different policy by Canada might have changed the course of events in the far east and Europe. As, however, this is a study of Canadian foreign policy and not of world affairs it is appropriate to examine in some detail the narrower theme.

Two main and related pressures explain the situation facing in the thirties those countries which wished to maintain the peace and, in general, the settlement reached after 1918. The first in time was the economic disaster that was bringing misery and threatening a breakdown over an increasing area. It was more than the ordinary depressions which had come from time to time. "In 1931," wrote

Toynbee, "men and women all over the world were seriously contemplating and frankly discussing the possibilities that the Western System of Society might break down and cease to work."[1] Step by step after the collapse of the New York stock market in the autumn of 1929 the rot spread across Europe. In May the *Credit-Anstalt* in Vienna was no longer able to carry itself, and, although it was heavily supported by the Austrian government and the Bank for International Settlements, confidence in Austrian finance generally was shaken. In July one of the great German banks, the Darmstädter Bank, was unable to open its doors. In September came the most violent shock to world finance when the pound sterling went off the gold standard. Throughout 1932 the finances of most of the other countries of Europe showed major troubles, and by 1933, in the great creditor country, the United States, bank "holidays" in state after state culminated in the closing by the president of all banks in March. Parallel with the financial symptoms of disorder went the other signs of acute depression. Unemployment reached serious heights everywhere and in some cases affected considerable proportions of the possible workers. Foreign trade shrank by alarming figures. Everywhere governments struggled to stem the flood by various devices: public works provided some employment, and protective tariffs were used as a means of capturing a share of what business was left. The world economic conference, held in London in the summer of 1933, was an attempt to approach on a broad front the common economic evils that beset the world. Its failure suggested that economic nationalism was a stronger force than internationalism.

In more ways than one the depression was a cause of the political pressure directed against the post-war settlement. Broadly speaking, the states of the world had been sorting themselves into two categories: those whose interests lay in the maintenance of the settlement, and those which sought major changes in that settlement. In the latter group were found not only those defeated in the War of 1914 but also such victors whose gains were far below their ambitions and demands. Leaving aside the minor powers, there were three great powers—Germany, Italy, and Japan—which looked for an opportunity to press for what they considered to be their proper places in the world. Desire for expansion of territory and—

[1] This idea is brilliantly developed in the section "Annus Terribilis 1931", in A. J. Toynbee, *Survey of International Affairs, 1931* (Oxford, 1932).

in the case of Germany—freedom from restraints—came first from the treaties of peace themselves and were nourished by grievances and national pride. Economic disorder in all those countries strengthened the determination to find new sources of raw materials, new lands for their peoples. In Germany the national socialist party found a fresh source of support in voters harassed and bewildered by unemployment and poverty. Moreover, the defences of those states which upheld the settlement were badly sapped by their own economic troubles, and their attention was diverted to the pressing problems of escaping complete national bankruptcy and collapse. If under such circumstances collective action faltered in respect of financial agreements there was little expectation that it would avail against the armies of aggression.

It is in the setting created by the development and interaction of these two themes that Canadian foreign policy in the thirties must be examined. The conservative government which came into office in 1930 shared the general belief that a declining trade must be propped by a protective tariff. With prices of Canadian staple exports falling disastrously and a limited market even at prices below the cost of production, the new government steadily raised the general tariff level by about 50 per cent. to afford protection to both agricultural and industrial products. Another Chinese wall, the Hawley-Smoot tariff of 1930, already stood across the border, barring from the United States a number of Canadian primary products. Since, as always, the bulk of Canadian trade had been with the United States and the United Kingdom, it appeared that the only remaining field for bargaining on tariffs was with the latter. At the imperial conference of 1930 the prime minister, R. B. Bennett, proposed that there should be a general plan of imperial preference, and that the discussion of this matter—which did not proceed far at London—should be continued in an adjourned session of the economic section to meet at Ottawa within the next twelve months.

It was, as it proved, to be two years before the Ottawa meeting, since the governments of Australia and New Zealand found that the summer of 1931 was inconvenient. Meanwhile, and in anticipation of the expected meeting, a vigorous debate took place in the Canadian house of commons on government policy. In the course of a lengthy speech on the Address the leader of the opposition, W. L. Mackenzie King, criticized the whole approach of the government to the imperial conference in London and to the proposed adjourned session in Ottawa. He accused the prime minister of playing a lone hand in respect not only of parliament but even of his own cabinet; and, by raising tariffs as a preliminary to bargaining, of coming close to an attempt to coerce the United Kingdom government.[2] In reply the prime minister described his policy of imperial preference, arguing that it was supported by the other dominions and was consistent with Canadian policy followed since the time of Sir Wilfrid Laurier.[3]

By the time the doubly-postponed conference met in Ottawa in the summer of 1932, during the depth of the depression, the new conservative government in London had followed Canada into protective tariffs. Agreement was not easily reached, and hard bargaining was the order of the day. In the end, however, the United Kingdom accepted free entry of many Canadian goods, both natural products and manufactured articles; and Canada provided additional preferences on certain British products. Actually there was a series of bilateral agreements as between the various parts of the commonwealth, but for Canada the main consideration was in sales to the British Isles, and these did in fact rise materially. Thus a commonwealth front was constructed in conformity with the economic nationalism of the day.

It is not surprising that unemployment, bankruptcies, and general economic misery— facts which came so close to their every-day life —were of more immediate concern to most Canadians than was the armed conflict in remote Manchuria. Yet it was the successful challenge to the system of peaceful settlement of international disputes that marked the beginning of the pre-war period; and which showed the way to those other states which sought to pursue their ambitions by whatever means might be successful. Japan had long desired to extend her control into Manchuria; and now that the powers supporting the *status quo* were preoccupied with home affairs the time seemed ripe for prying loose an outlying portion of the shaky Chinese republic. All the catch-words and techniques that were to be used over and over in subsequent years were taken as a veneer for stark aggression. *Lebensraum* must be found for the teeming millions of the crowded Japanese islands. The Chinese

---

[2] *Canada, House of Commons Debates,* March 16, 1931, 22 *ff.*
[3] *Ibid.,* 58 *ff.*

themselves had provoked the combat. The local population needed help in its desire for the independence of Manchuria. And so on with all the half-truths and non-sequiturs that were to form the pattern for eight years in the east and in Europe.

Following an explosion on the South Manchurian Railway on September 18, 1931 the Japanese forces seized Mukden near which the explosion had occurred. By early February of 1932 all Manchuria was in Japanese hands. Neither the League of Nations nor the League in association with the United States had been able to arrest this process. It happened that, at the time of the Mukden incident, the council of the League (including representatives of both China and Japan) was in session at Geneva, and the Japanese representative quickly brought the matter before the council under article XI of the covenant. No means of settlement are prescribed in that article, which provided only that the League should "take any action that may be deemed wise and effectual to safeguard the peace of nations." Whether the action was wise or not, it certainly did not prove to be effectual. The first move of the council—and one with which the United States expressed its concurrence—was to try to get the troops withdrawn as a preliminary to an examination of the dispute. As the Japanese went their way in Manchuria, the council's efforts proved completely vain; and in December it was decided to send a special commission to examine the question on the spot. As the commission was getting under way the American secretary of state sent, early in January, identical notes to the Chinese and Japanese governments announcing that the United States would not recognize any *de facto* change in the east accomplished by means contrary to the Pact of Paris. The "Stimson doctrine" brought at first no response from the other powers, but in March it was accepted in terms if not in name by a resolution of the assembly of the League. Neither this stand taken by the assembly nor the invoking of articles X and XV of the covenant by the representative of China on the council seemed to have any deterring effect on the Japanese government, which, in the middle of March, set up an "independent" state. On March 12 (the day after the assembly's resolution on non-recognition) the "minister for foreign affairs of Manchuquo" informed fifty-two governments that certain named provinces (those in Manchuria, with Jehol added) "have united themselves to establish an independent government severing their relations with the Republic of China and have created 'Manchuquo', the State of Manchuria, on March 1, 1932 . . ."

Such, in outline, was the situation which the Canadian government, in company with other governments, faced. Not being at this time represented on the council, the government had its first opportunity of expressing views on the Manchurian question when that was referred to the assembly in March under article XV of the covenant. The Canadian delegate, Sir George Perley, suggested in the course of a brief speech that the assembly should work on the basis of the following considerations:

1. We should stop further bloodshed and bring about a real and effective armistice;

2. We should distinguish between the rights of a case and the manner in which those rights are realized and enforced;

3. We should affirm as solemnly as possible the fundamental truth that no infringement of the territorial integrity, and no change in the political independence, of any Member of the League of Nations which is brought about by force in disregard of the undertakings of Article 10 of the Covenant can be recognized as valid and effective by other Members of the League.[4]

Here was safe doctrine; but it is interesting to find a Canadian spokesman making a deliberate reference to article X. It is true that the approach in the speech is more from the point of view of the "Stimson doctrine" than from that of the article itself, which is an undertaking not only to respect but "preserve" the territorial integrity and political independence of other members of the League; but it is interesting that Perley should cite an article against which Canadian governments had so persistently protested. If it had been worth while, it would not have been difficult for some European delegates to ask whether Canada had changed its mind on the value of that article.

In the house of commons J. S. Woodsworth, leader of the Co-operative Commonwealth Federation party and one of the members best informed on foreign affairs, expressed disappointment at the Canadian attitude, and elicited the reply from the prime minister that he "did not think it would be wise . . . that we should endeavour, with the slight knowledge that we possess . . . either to blame or

[4] League of Nations, *Minutes of the Fifth Meeting, General Commission, Special Session of the Assembly, March 8, 1932*, 7. Quoted in MacKay and Rogers, *Canada Looks Abroad*, 334.

praise this country or the other in matters so serious as those involved
in the then differences between Japan and China".[5] It was a curious
point of view that a country which was a member of the League,
and had an established department of external affairs and a diplomatic mission in Tokyo should have no more than a "slight knowledge" of a major international question; but a few weeks later,
on May 25, when the subject again came up in the commons, the
prime minister came down to more solid ground by asking members
to examine the sanctions provided by the covenant and consider
whether they would be prepared to accept "what was involved in
endeavouring to put these sanctions in force against either China or
Japan". On November 21, several weeks after the publication of
the report of the Lytton commission,[6] Woodsworth again tried to
draw some indication of policy from the government by the direct
question: "What, if any, is the policy of His Majesty's government
in Canada in regard to the situation in the far east and to the
Lytton report?" Bennett refused, however, to make "individual
preliminary declarations" before the discussion of the report by the
assembly.

"Were I to declare to-day an attitude which is in my mind with
respect to some of these matters, it might not only become embar-
rassing but might render the influence of this dominion absolutely
useless as far as the problem itself is concerned, for my antecedent
judgment would be upon facts which might be varied by reason of
concessions between powers or by a new attitude being taken . . .
Almost any problem is capable of being completely altered by . . .
a changed attitude . . . of those primarily responsible for its solution."[7]

No doubt there was an argument for leaving room for compromise
by avoiding any inflexible policy; but it so happened that when the
assembly was re-convened at the end of November the government
appeared to be still in search of a policy. The Canadian delegate,
C. H. Cahan, a member of the cabinet, in speaking on the Lytton
report expressed views which were "more or less personal", though
he thought they were opinions in which his government would
concur. Speaking on December 8, Cahan doubted whether the
Chinese government fulfilled the condition of having a strong

[5] *Canada, House of Commons Debates*, April 7, 1932, 1826.
[6] League of Nations, *Appeal by the Chinese Government: Report of the Commission of Inquiry.* The report was published on October 2.
[7] *Canada, House of Commons Debates*, Nov. 21, 1932, 1367 *ff*.

central government, which was a "clear assumption" for any member of the League. After giving in simplified terms the Canadian view of the meaning of article X of the covenant, Cahan thought that the assembly could not "wholly disregard" the statement made by the Japanese delegate that his government had had no connection with the independence movement in Manchuria. After the expression of these apparently personal views Cahan stated two points on Canadian government policy. Skating around the starting-point of the commission's proposals—that Manchuria, though having a large measure of autonomy, should remain under Chinese sovereignty—Cahan fixed on the recommendation that China and Japan should make bilateral treaties on economic matters, and offered the Canadian experience with the international joint commission. Secondly, he represented his government as "a life-long friend of Japan", anxious that a solution be found which Japan could accept.

Though this friendly attitude toward Japan was not unsimilar to the attitudes of the United Kingdom, Australia, and France, there was criticism both in Geneva and in Canada at the views expressed by Cahan. Meanwhile to the committee of nineteen (on which Canada was not represented) was given the task of pursuing the course of conciliation; and only when that proved hopeless—because of Japanese intransigence—did the committee propose to the assembly that no consideration be given to recognition of "Manchuquo", and that the report of the Lytton commission be accepted.

At this point (February 24, 1933) the Canadian representative was sent instructions to vote in favour of the committee's recommendation. The instructions, tabled in text in the house, noted the failure of conciliation and the gravity of the situation created by that failure.[8] To continue a study of the dispute the assembly created a new body, the far eastern advisory committee, composed of the committee of nineteen with representatives of the United States, Holland and Canada (the U.S.S.R. refusing an invitation). There was talk of an arms embargo, but the only action of that kind was when the United Kingdom placed an embargo on arms to both Japan and China, with Canada beginning to follow the lead. The resignation of Japan from the League, announced on March 27, 1933, ended this chapter of the long struggle in the far east.

[8] *Ibid.*, Feb. 24, 1933, 2430-1.

As far as the development of Canadian foreign policy was concerned the Manchurian affair brought no change. It is significant, however, for that very reason; since it showed that a policy adopted in comparatively placid years could be retained when the whole future of collective security was threatened by unilateral action in defiance of treaties. Concurrently with the crisis in the far east Canadian policy was being expressed in the world disarmament conference. After years of preparation the conference for the reduction and limitation of armaments opened in Geneva on February 2, 1932. Representatives of fifty-nine states gathered to consider a broad approach to a goal toward which steps had already been taken by the reduction in the treaties of peace of the armaments of the defeated states, by the voluntary reduction of those of many other countries, and by the successive agreements amongst the naval powers. As the president of the conference, Mr. Arthur Henderson, pointed out in his opening speech, the governments were at the same time confronted with "a situation of such extreme gravity as that which now exists in the Far East", and must relate the question of disarmament to "the grave economic and financial crisis for which most nations are at the moment trying to find a solution". If the first of the two factors was a discouraging one for a conference attempting to reduce armaments, the second might well be used as an argument for cutting an expenditure which in total was very large.

For Canada, where armaments had been allowed to sink back to a low level, the decision to be made was not whether her own forces should be reduced but the definition of her attitude on collective security. It raised, therefore, the same problem as the contemporary far eastern crisis. In the study of disarmament over the previous ten years it had come to be fully realized that, in the words of a Spanish observer, "the problem of disarmament is not the problem of disarmament. It really is the problem of the organization of the World-Community".[9] It was, in other words, a particular approach to the central issue before the League, or in this case before the powers represented at the disarmament conference: were the states collectively prepared to guarantee each other against aggression? If the answer was yes, then the security obtained by national armaments could be in part replaced by the security obtained through the promise of aid. If the answer was no then it could hardly be ex-

[9] Salvador de Madariaga, *Disarmament* (New York, 1929), 56.

pected that those countries which were apprehensive of attack would willingly lower such individual barriers as they themselves felt capable of erecting. For some time appreciated as the central problem of general reduction of armaments, this question was inevitably emphasized by the fact of the use of armed force in China and by the failure of the League to meet individual force with collective force.

In his speech in the course of the opening debate, the Canadian representative expressed the usual approval of the principle of disarmament, reminded the conference of the fortunate and virtuous state of Canadian frontiers, and warned the conference against sanctions.

We think . . . that this organization of peace can best be achieved at this time by emphasizing the prevention of conflict, rather than the punishment of aggression; by building up machinery for conciliation, rather than providing for sanctions; by using the League of Nations as a channel through which international public opinion can express itself, rather than by developing it into a Super-State. In adopting this view, which we genuinely consider to be a constructive one, we are convinced that we are not merely serving our own interests, but the true interests of all nations as well.[10]

The other Canadian interventions in the conference were on less controversial questions. The Canadian government supported the gradual abolition of the private manufacture of armaments, though regarding the internationalization of manufacture as impracticable.[11] When international control of aviation was discussed the Canadian representative repeated the view expressed at the Paris peace conference, that internationalization in North America was impracticable and unnecessary.[12]

It was on the use of sanctions as a means of preventing or stopping war that international relations were to pivot in the next few years. Starting in the atmosphere of the Manchurian affair the conference was soon under the shadow cast by the revival of extreme nationalism in Germany. When Adolf Hitler became chancellor in January 1933 it was evident that the author of *Mein Kampf* would do nothing to allay the apprehensions of France and Belgium that Germany

[10] *Report on Conference on Limitation and Reduction of Armaments, Geneva 1932-1934* (Ottawa, 1934), 26.
[11] *Ibid.*, 45.
[12] *Ibid.*, 16.

was a continuing threat. On October 15 Germany withdrew from the conference, after the delegates had failed to secure acceptance of the thesis that Germany should be accepted, for purposes of disarmament, as on a basis of equality with the other great powers. A few days later the German government gave notice of withdrawal from the League. In an atmosphere of uncontrolled nationalism, of wars and rumours of wars, the disarmament conference maintained a nominal existence into 1935; but, with the failure to arrive at any effective agreement on collective security, the powers looked more to rearmament than to disarmament and the conference ended in failure.

The dominating issue in international relations was now settling down to a struggle between those countries which in general sought to maintain the settlement of 1919-20 and those which not only desired change—as they had for fifteen years—but were prepared to secure their ends by force. Japan had first shown the way along that road. In Europe the decisive event was the accession to power of the national socialist party in Germany and the increasing indication that the new government intended to free that country from at least some of the restraints put upon it by the Treaty of Versailles. The vigorous nationalism in Hitler's speeches was implemented by a series of breaches in the treaty. In March 1935 compulsory military service in Germany was restored. In June a treaty was concluded with the United Kingdom by which the latter accepted a German navy 35 per cent. as powerful as its own. In March 1936 Hitler announced the rearmament of the Rhineland, thus breaking both the Treaty of Versailles and the Locarno agreement. This last act, as an early example of Hitler's success in taking calculated risks, began to earn for him amongst his own people a reputation for second sight and for judgment shrewder than that of the general staff.

Europe sought to draw itself together in defence against the German threat. France and Russia announced a treaty of mutual assistance. In April 1935 representatives of France, the United Kingdom, and Italy met at Stresa to consider the situation arising from German rearmament. The first declaration represented their general conclusion:

The Three Powers, the object of whose policy is the collective maintenance of peace within the framework of the League of Nations, find themselves in complete agreement in opposing by all practicable means, any unilateral repudiation of treaties which may endanger the peace of Europe, and will act in close and cordial collaboration for this purpose.[13]

Partly as a result of the Stresa meeting, the council of the League established a special committee, known as the committee of thirteen. On this the Canadian government agreed to be represented though making it clear that in doing so it did not commit itself to the principle that sanctions were automatically invoked in the case of repudiation of international obligations. Acting on instructions the Canadian representative, W. A. Riddell, made a statement in opposition to the proposition that article XI of the covenant could be used as the legal basis for the application of sanctions in the event of a breach of treaty.[14] The studies of sanctions, which were the responsibility of the committee, were a direct result of the course being followed by the German government, and the attempt to use article XI derived from the fact that the covenant did not provide otherwise for such a situation. As it happened, however, before any conclusion had been reached on how to deal with the German problem, the Italian-Ethiopian dispute had reached a point where it provided the immediate emergency and took a form that fitted readily into the articles of the covenant. In a very real sense it was still the threat of German power and aggression that dominated international relations. Without the opportunity of moving underneath that shadow it is more than unlikely that Italy would have taken so bold a course in defiance of the powers defending the *status quo.*

Fearful of German armies at the Brenner Pass, Mussolini had for a time acted in concert with France and the United Kingdom in attempting to set barriers against the German advance; but with the misguided opportunism that had for so long plagued Italian foreign policy he began to plan a forward movement in Africa under the favourable conditions created by the German moves. Already in January 1935 the Abyssinian government had appealed to the League under article XI, and then in March it invoked article XV. By the time the assembly came together in September the Abyssinian

[13] The whole resolution is printed in A. J. Toynbee, *Survey of International Affairs, 1935* (2 vols., Oxford, 1936), I, 159.

[14] The text of the statement is in W. A. Riddell, *World Security by Conference* (Toronto, 1947), 93-5.

affair was in the centre of the stage. In the course of the Canadian election campaign both liberal and conservative leaders had played down the possibility of sending troops overseas. In the debate in the assembly the Canadian representative hoped for a peaceful solution and stated that Canada would join with other members "in considering how, by unanimous action, peace can be maintained."[15] By October the neutral members of the council agreed that Italy had resorted to war in disregard of article XII of the covenant, and pledged themselves to action under article XVI. The assembly followed up by appointing a "co-ordination committee" to consider the action to be taken under article XVI; and that committee set up in turn a smaller committee—which became known as the committee of eighteen—including a representative of Canada. Thus the Canadian government was in a position to follow up the question of sanctions placed before the earlier and exploratory committee of thirteen. At the first meeting of the committee of eighteen the Canadian delegate, G. H. Ferguson, called for firm and immediate action:

The sole problem before the committee was to decide what sanctions the delegations could all agree upon that afternoon and put into application immediately. Let them show the world that the League was no longer to be scoffed or laughed at, but that it meant business, and that when a breach of its Covenant took place it proposed to deal with the aggressor in the proper way. Otherwise the League and the Assembly would lose prestige and influence in the world and might as well be dissolved. If the delegations were not at Geneva to see that the Covenant was carried out, there was no purpose in their being there at all.

He suggested that the committee could perhaps deal at once with the question of the arms embargo, upon which all members might be able to agree. As time went on there would perhaps have to be some method of adopting progressive sanctions from time to time, but surely this was something—perhaps with regard to a financial sanction or the arms embargo—that could be announced to the world tonight in order that it might be known that the League was taking some action.

[15] This, with the texts of other Canadian statements and related documents, will be found in Department of External Affairs, *Documents Relating to the Italo-Ethiopian Conflict* (Ottawa, 1936). The Canadian position may also be followed in Carter, *The British Commonwealth and International Security*, and in Riddell, *World Security by Conference*.

Again on October 14 Ferguson called for rapid action. On that day the conservative government was defeated, and on the following day the retiring prime minister telegraphed to the delegation to delay action until instructions were received from the new government. By the time that the liberal government assumed office (October 23) the co-ordinating committee had put forward proposals for sanctions under five headings:

1. Prohibition of export of arms and munitions to Italy.
2. Prohibition of loans and credits.
3. Prohibition of all imports from Italy.
4. Embargo on certain exports to Italy.
5. Mutual support in the results of the application of economic sanctions.

The first indication of the policy of the liberal government took the form of a press release by the secretary of state for external affairs (W. L. Mackenzie King) on October 29. Declaring again the adherence of Canada to the aims of the League, the statement noted that "successive Canadian governments have opposed the view that the League's central purpose should be to guarantee the territorial status quo and to rely upon force for the maintenance of peace". In the existing dispute however, there was "no room for doubt" as to where the responsibility for the outbreak of war rested, and the Canadian government would apply the proposed sanctions. It was to be understood, however, that no commitment to military sanctions was considered to be involved, and that the acceptance of economic sanctions in this case did not establish a precedent. Following the statement, the decision to take part in sanctions was implemented by successive orders in council.

Meanwhile there had been talk in Geneva—both informally and in the committee of eighteen—of the extension of sanctions to a point where they would form an effective obstacle to the continuance of Italian aggression. W. A. Riddell, formerly alternate delegate, had now taken Ferguson's place on the committee of eighteen. Convinced of the need for further sanctions, he had spoken in support of suggestions that sanctions should be made sufficiently comprehensive. On November 2, believing that this question would arise shortly, he telegraphed for instructions; but seeing that the opportunity to speak was to come before a reply could be expected, Riddell found himself in a quandary not unfamiliar to diplomats. Choosing to take the opportunity offered he then proposed that the list of sanctions be extended to include petroleum and derivatives, coal, iron, cast iron, and steel. Only after the proposal had been made did the answer come from Ottawa that "no action of any kind was to be taken . . . without specific instructions from the government."[16] Finding that Riddell's proposal was, not surprisingly, given a good deal of publicity in the English newspapers as an important lead by the Canadian government, that government issued a press release on December 2 claiming that Riddell's proposal was no more than "his own personal opinion, and his views as a member of the Committee—and not the views of the Canadian Government". Canada did not propose to take the initiative, but "with regard to future developments, Canada will continue, with other Members of the League of Nations, to consider the changes in the situation as they arise, including any proposal for the revision of economic sanctions". The government, the prime minister told the house of commons, had decided against immediate repudiation of Riddell's action ". . . only because we were most anxious not to take any step which might possibly embarrass the situation in Europe or which might appear even remotely to indicate an exception on the part of Canada to what was being done by other parts of the British Empire".[17]

It is interesting to note that in both the Manchurian and Ethiopian questions Canadian representatives to the League had spoken without the book. Whether or not this suggests some imperfection or lack of experience in the Canadian practice of diplomacy, there seems little mystery on what Canadian policy was in relation to collective security. It followed, indeed, the lines laid down in the early twenties. Successive Canadian governments had emphasized the value of the League as machinery for the discussion of international questions and for the conciliation and arbitration of disputes between states. Equally they had shown doubt of sanctions as a means of enforcing League decisions, and in particular had stood out against any idea of automatic obligations to enforce sanctions. It might be added that previous governments had been as reluctant as that which took office in 1935 to take the lead in formulating League policies. It did not follow that sanctions were ruled out,

---

[16] *Canada, House of Commons Debates*, 1936, 92 *ff*. The whole of the prime minister's statement of Feb. 11, should be read in conjunction with the sources mentioned in the previous footnote.

[17] *Ibid.*, 95.

and in the case of Ethiopia those agreed by the co-ordinating committee were accepted by the Canadian government. It is possible, as was indicated, that more stringent sanctions might have been accepted had they been proposed in the same way. It was only from the fame of leadership that the government backed with such rapid steps.

There have been attempts to examine the motives for this modesty in the Ethiopian case, and suggestions have been made that it was because of the pressure of isolationist opinion and the sympathy felt for Italy in the Province of Quebec. The fact that it was the acting secretary of state for external affairs, Ernest Lapointe, who made the statement of December 2 has been cited as evidence of Quebec pressure. Some critics have carried the issue further by indicating that the cold water poured by the Canadian government was a reason for the failure of the League to agree on oil sanctions and so to arrest Italian aggression. It is fruitless to follow into the realm of speculation; but it does not seem probable—taking into consideration the fact that oil sanctions were already under discussion—that the Canadian action was, or could have been, decisive. At most it was a refusal to take a place in the van, a position which has disadvantages as well as advantages.

The most interesting aspect of what came to be called the "Riddell incident" was not that it marked any change in policy but that it gave new stimulus to Canadian thinking on foreign policy. By the middle thirties, with the possibility of a war involving Canada as more than an academic question, there was an appreciable volume of writing and talking on current questions in international affairs and on what Canadian policy should be in general or in particular. In a brief space it is not possible, and for purposes of this study not necessary, to sift through the mass of articles in newspapers and periodicals, of papers read to various organizations, and the occasional debates in parliament, which together constitute the evidence for expressed public opinion. There are, however, certain characteristics of Canadian thinking on the subject which may usefully be examined.

In the first place it is noticeable that the approach was not, as might be expected, from the starting-point of Canadian conditions and interests but largely focussed on poles outside the country. There were the two traditional ones—the United Kingdom and the United States—with the addition of the more recent interest in the League of Nations. To some extent the three were not mutually exclusive: it was, for example, an important consideration that the commonwealth countries were members of the League of Nations while the United States was not. Obviously any foreign policy must be related to other countries and international organizations, but a peculiarity of the Canadian outlook was the degree to which it responded to the policies of other countries or was dependent on doctrinaire views of what Canadian connections should exist. This was as true of those Canadians who advocated detachment from any or all of the outside forces mentioned as of those who argued in favour of close relationship with one or more. There were understandable reasons for this situation. It was not until after the War of 1914 that Canada had ceased to be in a semi-colonial status as far as foreign affairs were concerned, a position which inevitably created in that field a peculiarly intimate relation with the United Kingdom. For other reasons—such as contiguity and economic interests—relations with the United States were unusually close. It was as logical as it was traditional that Canada should in foreign affairs follow— or at least not diverge from—the policies of those two great powers; and further to do anything possible to ensure that no choice had to be made between conflicting policies. It was in this connection, as well as on general grounds, that Canadians regretted the absence of the United States from the League of Nations.

A second characteristic of the trends of public opinion in Canada, and one which overlaps with the first, was a desire to place into neat categories all those Canadians who admitted any views on foreign affairs. The labels varied in detail, and ingenious writers invented various sub-divisions. In the main, however, it was supposed that any one individual could be placed in one of three groups: isolationists (or non-interventionists); "imperialists" (or supporters of a British front); and collectivists.[18] There is no doubt that there were at any given time men and women who held such ideas. Nor indeed was there much in them that was new, apart from the complication caused by the establishment of the League of Nations. The newspapers of a century earlier reflect the then current—and frequently vigorous—views on relationships with the United Kingdom, whether Canada should take part in "British

[18] For an examination of these schools of thought see MacKay and Rogers, *Canada Looks Abroad*, 263 ff.

wars", whether isolation on the North American continent was possible and desirable, and so on. The discouraging factor as seen from the point of view of the formation of intelligent Canadian opinion, was the assumption that people could so easily be put in pigeon-holes—and stay there. In reality a strong supporter of the League might or might not, according to particular circumstances, at the same time approve of British policy. Those who believed in non-intervention in some situations need not be suspected of having such closed minds that they would be isolationists to the end of time.

Not only were Canadians supposed to be capable of simple classification and readily to be frozen into groups, but apparently also they were to remain frozen. Opportunism, if considered at all, was thought to be undesirable. There is little indication, as one turns the pages of journals of opinion in the thirties, that the foreign policy of a country must be recognized as subject to modification— even to radical change—as the world situation alters. The intellectuals of the thirties can have found little comfort later in their confidence in formulas, in classification, in deciding on a foreign policy as frozen as their own opinions. In no previous period of Canadian history had there existed such facilities for the study of foreign affairs. Newspapers and periodicals carried a considerable proportion of foreign news; new organizations, such as the League of Nations Society and the Canadian Institute of International Affairs, provided for mutual study; speakers were always available to discourse before audiences of all kinds and sizes on various aspects of world affairs. Interest in international affairs was undoubtedly wide; but when applied to Canadian foreign policy it was so overcast with formulas and meaningless phrases as to lose a good deal of its value as a democratic control over government.

It has earlier been suggested that the policy of the Canadian government toward the Italo-Ethiopian dispute was not inconsistent with the policy pursued in general in the previous fifteen years. Looked at from another point of view it may be seen as more positive, more laden with commitments than can be found in any previous case outside actual participation in war. The controversy which arose over the government's disavowal of its representative's action led to an emphasis on the negative rather than the positive. The fact that the government had refused to take the initiative in extending sanctions was of more value as news than the fact that it had accepted and implemented all the other measures proposed by the co-ordination committee, and left the way open for similar action on any other measures proposed to it. The criticisms of those who felt that Canada missed an opportunity of leading the way in the defence of collective action were more than matched by the government's apprehension that it had already gone too far for its own public opinion, and at least must not be represented as doing more than cautiously accepting responsibility resulting from a proper interpretation of the covenant and acting in the light of the particular situation presented.

In the press release of October 29 the secretary of state for external affairs had laid it down as the government's policy that "it does not recognize any commitment binding Canada to adopt military sanctions, and that no such commitment could be made without the prior approval of the Canadian Parliament". The emphasis which continued to be laid by the liberal government of Mackenzie King on the principle that "parliament must decide" seemed to the government's critics to amount to a fetish, and to represent an unwillingness to give any lead in foreign policy. On the other hand it suggests an alternative to the attempts by groups in and out of parliament, to insist on decisions taken previous to the event. It is easy to see now the weaknesses in both approaches. To work by formulas ignored the shifting character of international relations, and, in its extreme form, threatened to commit parliament to fixed action regardless of circumstances. The reluctance of the government to express views on foreign policy added to the unreality of debate and concealed from a potential enemy the opposition which he might expect to encounter.

This very reticence on the part of government is explained by another passage from the same press release in which it was stated that the future participation of Canada in League action would take the form of "such . . . policies as are appropriate for a country in the geographic and economic position of the Dominion, and as will ensure unity and common consent in Canada as well as the advancement of peace abroad". Here, as seen by the liberal government, was the crux of the situation. The African war, more clearly than the far eastern one, had shown the dangerous trends in world affairs; had shown that collective action consisted in more than conciliation and discussion, in more even than economic sanctions, which had come to be regarded as a form of warfare to be answered by guns. The next few years were to reveal that there was lacking in other countries which were opposed to aggression the readiness to take active steps to stop it until the eleventh hour. The situation in Canada was, therefore, by no means unique; but it was the situation with which the Canadian government had to deal. Political leaders of generations earlier had sadly remarked that Canada was a difficult country to govern. It had become no easier by the thirties; and sectionalism and cross-currents complicated foreign at least as much as domestic policy. Whether or not the government of the day had reached any conclusion on the foreign policy that it would regard as desirable or likely, at least it alone was in possession of the full information on which an appreciation of future probabilities could be based. It evidently chose, however, to avoid statements that would accentuate the divisions of opinion that obviously existed in Canada; and to rest on the principle that parliament would decide whenever a decision became necessary. For the present the atmosphere was to be reminiscent of the old Laurier policy of no commitments.

The years 1937 and 1938 brought a series of challenges to the statesmen of the peace-loving states, the response to which was uniformly ineffective. As the international situation went from bad to worse Canada was in the ambiguous position of a spectator making pointed comments on a game in which his favourite team was losing, and into which he was apprehensive of being drawn in the clothes that he wore. Defence estimates were raised moderately but in spite of opposition from those members of parliament who wished to commit Canada to neutrality in any kind of conflict. The Spanish Civil War stirred deep emotions in individual Canadians. Some hundreds of volunteers went to fight for the republican cause, and others felt that it was the crisis of the developing conflict between democracy and fascism. Other Canadians, particularly in the province of Quebec, associated the republicans with communism and attacks on the church. Canada was not represented on the committee on non-intervention in Spain, but the government followed a similar policy by placing barriers against assistance to either party, by means of men and materials.[19] Throughout all this time public opinion continued to be as varied as it was vocal, and the government for its part continued to avoid any statements that would

[19] F. H. Soward and others, *Canada in World Affairs: The Pre-War Years* (Toronto, 1941), 63. See this work on Canadian policy and expression of opinion in the years immediately before 1939.

conflict with its determination to avoid prior commitments to any line of action. Only in the mounting estimates for defence did the government show its hand, and in that it was accused both of going too far and not far enough.

The Munich settlement of the Czech crisis demonstrated the continuation of the policy of appeasement. Greeted with enthusiasm by both government and public in Canada, it appears to have been effected without even the expression of any Canadian views. The white paper issued in Ottawa in September 1938 contained only United Kingdom documents,[20] and the Canadian government seems to have regarded the whole transaction as the responsibility of London. As elsewhere, opinion in Canada shifted completely not long after the Munich decisions, and there were superficial evidences of a determination to halt the aggressive Hitler in his track. Such emotional outbursts, which ignored almost completely the military position, can however be taken more as a further part of the spectator's criticism of the game than a readiness to plunge into it. There was, of course, still uncertainty as to the extent of Hitler's ambitions, and there were many men who honestly believed that he would in fact be content with the acquisition of the German Sudetenland. On the whole, however, there was a growing feeling that the Czechs had been sacrificed in vain, and that Munich had solved nothing. With the entrance of German troops into Prague in March 1939 any doubts as to the extent of Hitler's designs were dissolved.

From that time there began to be a new note of realism in discussions on Canadian foreign policy. "If," the prime minister told the house, "there were a prospect of an aggressor launching an attack on Britain, with bombers raining death on London, I have no doubt what the decision of the Canadian people and parliament would be." It was still to be understood, however, that parliament would decide in any particular circumstance. Speaking at a dinner on August 8, the prime minister reminded the audience that there were to be no decisions beforehand: "One thing I will not do and cannot be persuaded to do is to say what Canada will do in regard to a situation that may arise at some future time and under circumstances of which we now know nothing." With the news of the German-Soviet treaty, measures for military preparation were

[20] Department of External Affairs, *Documents Relating to the German-Czechoslovak Crisis, September, 1938* (Ottawa, 1938).

taken, and it was promised that parliament would be called if all efforts for maintaining peace were unsuccessful. As a part of those efforts the prime minister addressed to the heads of the governments of Poland, Italy, and Germany telegrams urging a peaceful solution of "the momentous issues of this period".[21]

On September 1, the day that the mechanized German army began its devastating *blitzkrieg* in Poland, parliament was summoned to meet in special session on September 7. The speech from the throne, calling for a declaration of war, was followed by a brief and sober debate. Opposition was insignificant and agreement was reached without a division. With the approval of parliament and the authorization of the king, a proclamation was issued declaring that a state of war existed as from September 10. As yet it was not known what in military terms that would mean. The C.C.F. in the special session failed to obtain a decision that no forces would be sent overseas, but after the short campaign in Poland the seeming stalemate gave colour to the view that the Maginot Line would hold. It was only with the beginning of the real German campaign in the spring of 1940 that the character of the war became evident. Canadians, who had entered the war by decision of their own government and parliament, saw western Europe invaded step after rapid step, saw the British Isles threatened, saw the prospect of the free world being overwhelmed by an alien and hated system. With the first Canadian division on guard in England since the end of 1939, the Canadian government and people forgot their old uncertainties and their old differences, to throw their united strength into the decision on which everything in the future depended.

That the Canadian government had itself decided the course to take was—for what that was worth—an acknowledgment of sovereign status. More important than that, it was a means of national unity as well as a demonstration of it. It was a fulfilment of the liberal pledge that parliament should decide on the basis of particular circumstances. It was also true, however, that parliament was dealing with a situation not only fully developed, but one arising out of policies over which the Canadian government had exercised virtually no influence. Not, as in the days before 1914, could this be attributed to a surviving colonial status. At least in the thirties the Canadian government and parliament had all the powers necessary

<hr>

[21] Department of External Affairs, *Documents Relating to the Outbreak of War, September, 1939* (Ottawa, 1939).

and proper for the formulation and conduct of foreign policy. Canada was, no doubt, a minor power, yet for many long months it was to stand as the second power opposing the German advance across the world. The war itself was a final demonstration—if such were needed—that Canada was tied by her own interests to the critical issues in international relations. A lingering confidence in the Laurier policy of no commitments had once more been answered by an acceptance of the greatest commitment. In the new era Canadians, with other free peoples, asked themselves whether it was not more realistic to accept fully extensive but defined obligations to action designed to prevent another great war.

CHAPTER XIX

CHANGED POLICY IN A CHANGED WORLD

THE story of Canadian foreign policy runs through a bare thirty years. There is, of course, a long background of interest in many aspects of world affairs, and of participation in some of them; but it is only since the first war that constitutional development toward sovereign status brought with it the corollary that Canada should formulate and conduct its own foreign policy. An attempt has been made in preceding chapters to show against the backdrop of Canadian interests and the character of the world scene how a policy was worked out and the necessary means of implementing it were found.

It has been suggested that Canadian policy in the twenties and thirties was basically clear and consistent, while retaining sufficient elasticity to allow for modifications in the light of changing international forces. As was appropriate in a democratic country many criticisms were from time to time levelled at this policy. Without attempting to recapitulate them all, it is pertinent to examine the charge that Canadian foreign policy was negative both in the sense of a lack of initiative and in failure to take a positive line calculated to maintain peace. Both aspects of the charge may be pressed with some conviction, but should be finally judged only within their setting. Canada was a newcomer to international relations of other than a commercial character, and lacked not only experience in this field, but also the tradition of balancing risks and calculating consequences. While the desire to secure recognition of status led in the direction of independent views and actions, that drive was checked by a cautious desire to retain the advantages of the British connection and, as far as might be, to follow a line not dissimilar to that taken by the United States. Such an inclination was more than a meaningless relic, for Canadian interests and objectives continued to be closely allied to those of these two great powers; and to have failed to recognize a community of purpose and the advantages of being grouped with such powerful friends would have been short-sighted and senseless.

In the years after the first war when the exposed European states were anxious to build protective walls against the danger of future aggression, the same compelling need was not felt by the countries —those of the commonwealth and the United States—with which Canada had the closest ties. There were, in fact, from the point of view of general outlook, three groups of states: those which sought, by whatever means might present themselves, to restore their lost positions; those which feared the impact of aggressive methods; and those which had little apprehension of danger. It was to the last group that Canada belonged; and shared with her heterogeneous companions a mistaken optimism in the continuance of peace, or, perhaps more accurately, refused to face the growing signs of coming disaster. It does not follow that successive Canadian governments were helpless in the grip of circumstance, or unable to attempt, by persuasion of others and acceptance of responsibility themselves, to steer the peace-loving states into a course better calculated to maintain the peace. The concurrence, however, of Canadian policy with that of other English-speaking states was not only the result of a desire to keep in step with powerful friends. The prevailing failure to recognize the grim realities even of the thirties was fully shared by a Canada physically removed from the scenes of strife, and occupied with the tasks of economic development, as absorbing in the lean years as in the prosperous ones. There were, indeed, voices raised in favour of more concrete support of collective security, but they made little impression on a majority opinion ranging from hopeful detachment to dogged determination to keep out of all war, preventive or otherwise.

The springs of Canadian foreign policy, then, may be traced readily to domestic convictions and the echo which they found in those states with which Canada—for the best of reasons—was most closely associated. It will have been observed, however, that Canada was, according to her own lights, a firm supporter of the League. The League which she desired to see was concerned more with consultation, compromise, and arbitration than one empowered to call forth gleaming swords at will. Her governments did their best to persuade other members to accept that same view and to pattern the League to that type. Throughout the twenties the Canadian vote was cast against automatic sanctions and the authority of the League's organs to encroach on national sovereignty. Even in the thirties Canadian representatives were found to be sounding notes of caution. Yet when sanctions were decided on the Canadian government was ready to live up to the obligations that it had assumed under the covenant, and was not slow in implementing agreed decisions.

That the world was plunged once more into general war is a condemnation both of the authoritarian states that willed it and of those that, hating war, watched the developing tragedy with dull eyes and idle hands. That the system of collective security failed to prevent disaster is the responsibility of Canada no less than of other countries. As the flames spread in Europe and the far east, as men died in far lands to save their fellows from slavery, the moral of the inter-war period was all too painfully apparent. It was a moral that had a double impact on Canada, for it derived not only from the ground common to many states, but as a delayed and repeated lesson from an earlier period. While there had for some time been an element of isolationism in the Canadian outlook, the record shows that that was never the dominating factor. What was more effective was the general resistance to making prior commitments, an attitude which in Laurier's day led to the erection of a previous barrier by means of a reluctance even to enter into consultations. In the days before 1914 the general formula was directed toward imperial relations, and meant that Canadian governments were cautious in respect of consultation with the United Kingdom on matters of foreign policy. The war that followed shook this belief in two ways. It showed that Canada had gained nothing by this caution, and had in fact merely become involved in a war without expressing any view on the circumstances that led to it. Secondly, the system of common imperial policy that operated from 1917 to 1922 was the negation of the old principle of avoiding consultation. As against these corrective forces, however, was set the atmosphere already described in the states that believed themselves distant from any threat of further aggression. In effect, therefore, the opposition in Canada to making commitments received a new support from both domestic and external sources.

The speed and unanimity with which Canada entered the War of 1939 gave the denial, if that were needed, to any charge of doctrinaire isolationism, and demonstrated again the elasticity of Canadian policy. Moreover, it raised once more the question in Canada, as indeed it did in other states, of the wisdom of paying heavy premiums on insurance against war. This, then, is the main theme that calls for careful analysis in the years of the war and in those that immediately followed. Of the direct Canadian effort in the war itself the story must be left to the specialized studies of its various aspects.[1] No apology will ever be needed for the wholehearted way in which Canadians participated in that war. From its early stand against an invasion of the British Isles, through the Italian campaign to the advance across France and into Germany, the army lived up to the high standards set in the first war. Starting from almost nothing, a Canadian navy was built up that took a major share in keeping open the North Atlantic life-line when the submarines made that look like an almost impossible task. Through the Commonwealth Air Training Plan, in the Royal Air Force, and in the Royal Canadian Air Force, Canadians too helped to defeat the might of the great German air force and to make daring attacks on German centres of production. By well-designed controls and plans the Canadian economy was switched over to a war footing and proved to be a major source of the essential supplies needed in such vast quantities.

For the first autumn and winter of the war there was comparatively little action. Orders for munitions only trickled in from the United Kingdom, and there was genuine doubt as to whether any large numbers of Canadians would be called into the armed forces. All doubts were dispelled by the smashing, terrifying German advance in the spring of 1940. With France and the low countries eliminated and Italy jumping, as it thought, to catch a share of the spoils, the commonwealth found itself alone, and Canada stood as in strength the second power attempting to stem the march of one of the most powerful and most fully prepared states that had ever tried for world domination by force of arms. Fighting a losing battle for month after month, Canadians turned to their heavy task in nothing of the atmosphere that marked the first war. No one thought of this as a war to end war and there was little of the glamour that comes from personal heroism and achievement. Heroism there was in plenty, but the mechanized nature of the war made it unemotional, grim, business-like—as the machines that it em-

---

[1] For an account of the literature on this subject see G. deT. Glazebrook, "Canadian Foreign Policy in the Twentieth Century" (*Journal of Modern History*, XXI, March 1949, 44).

ployed. Contrary to any detached calculations that could have been made between 1940 and 1944, the war was won. Yet VE-Day and VJ-Day were passed not in the jubilation of 1918 but in relief only that the immediate goal was reached, and with little optimism that it marked the achievement of lasting peace. The world was too troubled a place for anyone to hope for the carefree days of the twenties again.

By the end of the period of hostilities Canadian external policy had already been markedly changed and was in the post-war years to follow lines in some respects quite different from those of the pre-war years. It is not easy to fix any exact date on which the change began, or to identify it with specific events of the war years. There can, however, be found certain factors—both within and outside the country—which together explain the new situation as it has been since 1945.

The very fact of the war and of the nature of the Canadian response to it may be taken as the starting-point. As in 1914-18 the national effort in the war was itself a spur to nationalism; and, even more than in the first war, the second brought a compelling responsibility when the margin between victory and defeat was so narrow, when the toppling European powers left so narrow a base on which to rebuild the defences of the free world. A consciousness of responsibility together with a growing sense of achievement brought maturity in outlook on world affairs, and, with it, a surer and more ready hand in foreign policy. The department of external affairs, though thirty years old at the outbreak of war, had grown slowly over that period, and on the outbreak of war took heavy burdens with a staff still very small. For the best of reasons—purely practical ones—it began rapidly to grow in size during the active period of the war. Between 1939 and 1941 high commissioners were sent to all the dominions and Newfoundland, and legations were opened in Argentina, Brazil, and Chile. Consulates were established in Greenland and in St. Pierre and Miquelon to deal with matters arising out of the war. That the work increased far more rapidly than the staff is an indication that foreign affairs were becoming an everyday essential in the business of government.

It was not so much the pattern of policy that changed as the approach. It was still appropriate to plan in harmony with the United Kingdom and the United States; but now the objectives were starkly drawn, and formulas were replaced by hard realities.

Canada now was fighting for its free life, and diplomacy, which had once seemed to many Canadians a mere frill, was a necessary instrument of defence. Constant relations with other governments, on large questions and questions of detail, were needed in the many-sided struggle. Canada was in the somewhat ambiguous position of a minor power playing, for a time at least, a major role. By 1941, when the Soviet Union and the United States had both entered the war, the major questions were for the most part decided by the three great powers. Although the Canadian contribution to the allied cause had increased absolutely, it was now relatively less significant than it had been in the early years. Though for that reason the Canadian voice in allied councils was not that of a major participant, the war remained the dominating problem in Canadian life, and with it everything that contributed to the war or led out of it.

. Foreign policy, therefore, became more compelling and more of a practical issue than ever before. Moreover, foreign policy was at last freed from the complications of status in the empire or commonwealth. Canada entered the war of her own will, put into it at least a fair share, and had no constitutional objectives to be tied up with it. The commonwealth countries were partners in a great enterprise having, it is true, more intimate relations than those normal between states, but dealing with each other on business-like terms and with no reason to think in terms of status. Ministers and officials of the United Kingdom and of Canada met frequently during the period of hostilities and found no reason to bother themselves or each other with questions of relative stature and status. That stage was passed. The imperial conference of 1926 had accepted equality of status and noted an inequality of function. The first was worked out through years of legal development and practice; and the imperative task of waging war automatically emphasized function. The strain of the war on the United Kingdom further drained resources that had never been fully restored after the first war; while on the other hand, the different circumstances in which Canada was placed tended to result in her being strengthened rather than weakened by a mushroom growth of industrial power. Thus, not only did disparity in status receive a final quietus, but disparity in function between the self-governing parts of the commonwealth became less.

The whole balance of power was in fact changing. If there was now an end to any doubt as to complete Canadian control over the formulation and implementation of foreign policy, there was also an end, in degree at least, to the protection that had so long come from the naval and financial strength of the United Kingdom. France, the first mother-country of Canada, suffered a partial and then a complete occupation after a humiliating defeat in the short campaign of 1940. The long-term result was to weaken the principal state of Western Europe and the one with which Canada had not only historical links but also a continuing community of interest. Meanwhile the military collapse of France and the institution of the Vichy régime called for a series of decisions in Ottawa. It was decided to maintain diplomatic relations, though the same course was not followed by the United Kingdom. The French minister remained in Ottawa and a Canadian chargé d'affaires maintained an office in London, and made occasional visits to Vichy. On the other hand, the Free French were made welcome in Canada; and from observing the relative activities of the two groups, a stranger might well have wondered which of the two offices was that which represented France. This dualism came to an end in November 1942, when the French resistance to the allied landing in North Africa made it necessary to terminate recognition of the French government.

Preponderant power was now shifting to the Soviet Union and the United States. Though there was little sympathy in Canada with the doctrine of communism, the sacrifices made by the Russian people as the German armies drove deep into the Soviet Union, and the tremendous national effort that stemmed and turned back an apparently irresistible advance, awakened a respect and fellow-feeling amongst Canadians which for a time overshadowed the old suspicions. Later they were to be revived in a more active form than ever in face of the fusion of militant communism with the traditional expansionism of the tsars. In spite of appalling losses in men and property, the Soviet Union emerged from the early campaigns as a more powerful state than before, and with a new confidence bred of military achievement.

The United States was becoming the only other world power of comparable strength. Long before Pearl Harbour, the American and Canadian governments had progressed far toward co-operation in the defence of the continent and indeed beyond that to support of the Canadian war effort generally. In August 1940 the Canadian prime minister met the American president at Ogdensburg, across the St. Lawrence from the Canadian shore, and there discussed "mutual problems of defence in relation to the safety of Canada and the United States". It was there agreed to set up a Permanent Joint Board on Defence, which should study "the defence of the north half of the western hemisphere".[2] The other major step was in the economic field. A second meeting of the prime minister and the president, this time at the president's house at Hyde Park in April 1941, resulted in an agreement described in the Hyde Park Declaration:

Among other important matters, the President and the Prime Minister discussed measures by which the most prompt and effective utilization might be made of the productive facilities of North America for the purposes both of local and hemisphere defence, and of the assistance which in addition to their own programme both Canada and the United States are rendering to Great Britain and the other democracies.

It was agreed as a general principle that in mobilizing the resources of this continent each country should provide the other with the defence articles which it is best able to produce, and above all, produce quickly, and that production programmes should be co-ordinated to this end.

While Canada has expanded its productive capacity manifold since the beginning of the war, there are still numerous defence articles which it must obtain in the United States, and purchases of this character by Canada will be even greater in the coming year than in the past. On the other hand, there is existing and potential capacity in Canada for the speedy production of certain kinds of munitions, strategic materials, aluminum, and ships, which are urgently required by the United States for its own purposes.

While exact estimates cannot yet be made, it is hoped that during the next twelve months Canada can supply the United States with between $200,000,000 and $300,000,000 worth of such defence articles. This sum is a small fraction of the total defence programme of the United States, but many of the articles to be provided are of vital importance. In addition, it is of great importance to the economic and financial relations between the two countries that payment by the United States for these supplies will materially assist Canada in meeting part of the cost of Canadian defence purchases in the United States.

In so far as Canada's defence purchases in the United States consist of component parts to be used in equipment and munitions which

---

[2] See the order-in-council of August 21, 1940, printed in R. M. Dawson, *Canada in World Affairs: Two Years of War, 1939-1941* (Toronto, 1943), 310.

Canada is producing for Great Britain, it was also agreed that Great Britain will obtain these parts under the Lease-Lend Act and forward them to Canada for inclusion in the finished articles.

The technical and financial details will be worked out as soon as possible in accordance with the general principles which have been agreed upon between the President and the Prime Minister.[3]

With the period of American belligerency, the co-operation in war between the neighbouring countries grew ever closer. The Alaska Highway and the Canol project, designed to facilitate possible operations in the war with Japan, are examples of the ease with which joint endeavours could be carried out on Canadian soil. Valuable and appropriate as the approach was, it could not but raise the problem of relations between a great and a lesser power. Any idea of American expansionist aims was long since dead on both sides of the border, but it was important to ensure that arrangements entered into for a specific purpose in time of war were not allowed to drift on when their immediate object had been fulfilled and when they might begin to cause embarrassment. Canadians did not fail to see that the old problem which had existed in relations with London should not be revived, in another form, in relations with Washington. The foreign policy that began to emerge toward the end of the war and immediately after it was thus designed by a country changed within itself, and looking at a world no less changed. Once more there was a concurrence of, and mutual reaction between, conditions at home and abroad. Germany and Japan were problems not primarily of future aggression but in their relations to the balance of power. Those two powers were, for the time being, otherwise outside the play of international dealings. With a weakened United Kingdom and a France yet to rediscover its place in Europe and outside, the direction which world affairs were to take depended on the U.S.S.R. and the United States. It was not to be long before those two showed themselves as the leading members of antagonistic groups, the friction between which was to give the key-note to the post-war years.

Just as the Canadian mood of the early twenties was similar to that in the countries with which Canada had her closest affinities, so that of the forties coincided with the atmosphere in the commonwealth and the United States. And now the similarity between the

[3] *Ibid.*, 321.

thought in Canada and in the other countries was even greater, for the United States showed no sign of retreating from an active part in world affairs: on the contrary, it was apparently determined to play fully the leading part which its power and interests suggested. Throughout the commonwealth and the United States the will to make a durable peace reinforced by an association of the nations was no less strong than it had been a quarter of a century earlier. In the forties, however, that hope was accompanied by a shrewder appreciation of the difficulties, combined with a greater readiness to pay the price of peace. It remained, of course, to see how and to what extent this general point of view would be translated into action. Turning now to the particular case of Canada, an examination of the development of policy may be concentrated on two main themes: discussions of the treaties of peace, and the organization and activities of the United Nations.

Profiting from the experience after 1919, it was decided that the treaties of peace and the association of the nations should be approached separately. As in similar cases of peacemaking, the question at once arose of the comparative authority of the great and lesser powers in drawing up the terms. In 1919 this problem had been largely solved for Canada by membership in the British Empire delegation in addition to direct representation through her own delegation. Since this procedure was not revived, it was all the more important for the government to find some way in which it could effectively express any views it wanted to present. The precedent set in the case of the treaties with Italy and the minor powers was not a happy one. Before the general conference had assembled in Paris in the summer of 1946, the great powers had already taken the treaty through the drafting stage, so that the lesser powers could not put forward their suggestions until after the texts had become comparatively firm. The prime minister suggested, in moderate terms, dissatisfaction with the procedure. "We in Canada," he told the plenary conference, "felt that the measure of our participation in the war against aggression would have warranted a similar measure of participation in the decisions of peace. In the event these hopes are not being realized."

It marks the change since 1919 that the Canadian delegation was fully prepared by previous study of the subjects to come before the conference, and adequately provided with expert advisers. The general point of view was first expressed by the prime minister in his opening speech:

Canada's interest in the successful outcome of the deliberations of the conference is obviously less immediate and direct than that of some of the participating countries. Clearly, there are many countries represented here that will be more closely and directly concerned with the specific solutions of questions of territorial boundaries, population transfers, war damage indemnities and so on. I can only say that Canada has no specific national interest in the adoption of any particular formula for the solution of individual conflicts and differences which, in the aggregate, will constitute the general settlement. But we have a vital and compelling interest in the kind of settlement that results from their deliberations. Our principal duty and interest lie, it seems to me, in helping the countries more directly concerned to work out agreed solutions which are fair and likely to endure. Our concern as a nation is to see that, as far as we can help to make them so, the peace treaties will be based upon broad and enduring principles of justice and equity. Canada seeks no territory, no reparations, no special concessions of any kind, but we do seek to build a lasting peace.

As the conference proceeded the Canadian delegation took an active part in its work, finding somewhat more direct concern with particular points on such matters as boundaries.[4] In the middle of September one of the Canadian delegates, Mr. Claxton, said that,

In a profound sense Canada, like other non-European belligerents, is directly involved in the task of peace-making. Canada has in the last thirty years fought throughout the whole duration, from the very beginning to the very end, of two terrible wars, both of which had their origins in the European Continent. How did it come about that a country so far from the centre of conflict took up arms in these two successive struggles? It was because our government and people knew that both the national interests of Canada and the principles on which our very life depended were at stake in the conflict. With this experience behind us and with our knowledge of how small the world has become, it is apparent that the future peace and prosperity of everyone depends in part on what is done here.

[4] For a brief account see Brooke Claxton, "Canada at the Paris Conference" (*International Journal*, II, Spring, 1947, 124). There is a bulky collection of documents published by the United States Department of State, *Paris Peace Conference, 1946* (Washington, n.d.).

As the settlement with Germany approached—or at least the allied discussions of it—the note of interest was sounded more clearly, and there was a growing tendency to go much further than generalizations by proposing specific solutions for particular problems. Here again, however, the procedure being followed made it difficult to interfere at the crucial drafting stage. In January 1947 the Canadian government was invited to present its views to the special deputies for forwarding to the council of foreign ministers. After asking for "a full part in discussions both on questions of procedure and of substance", and having received no reply, the government decided to present in writing its preliminary views, still maintaining that adequate discussions should follow. The Canadian submission[5] marks an important stage in the development of policy, for it emphasized the substance of the treaties, regarding the procedural question as important only because on it depended the adequate presentation of those views. As things then stood it was impossible to discuss clauses—there was no means of doing so—and the submission therefore could do no more than state principles which, it was suggested, should underlie the settlement.

One novel proposal was made: that, in the absence of a German government, negotiations should be directed toward "the preparation of an international statute constituting a new German state and governing the relations of that state with its neighbours and with other parts of the world until it can be replaced by a permanent treaty". A federal system of government for Germany was favoured, and it was emphasized that both central and state governments must be democratic. Frontiers were to be drawn with a view to achieving stability. A section on the German economy suggested an economic commission for Europe, accepted the principle of international control in industrial areas, stressed that German trade must provide equal opportunity for all nations, and argued that reparation deliveries should not be allowed to create a centre of economic depression. Finally, the government expressed its belief in complete demilitarization of Germany, safeguarded by international controls.

As the whole question of a German settlement became overshadowed and impeded by the growing rift between the eastern

[5] The text will be found in G. deT. Glazebrook, "The Settlement of Germany" (*International Journal*, II, Spring, 1947, 132).

and western powers, the interest in the development of Canadian policy turns to the United Nations, so largely the theatre for the play of international relations. From the first the Canadian government had been interested in the budding idea of a new association of the nations. From the time when the Moscow conference of 1943 announced the principle of an association of the nations, the Canadian government studied plans for such an association and developed its views on the form which it felt the association might take. At no time was there any doubt in Ottawa as to the desirability of a successor to the League of Nations. Every Canadian interest pointed to it. Whatever might be the lesson of the thirties, it was not that the idea of a league was wrong, or that collective security was a false approach to the problem of peace. Perhaps the covenant could be improved. Certainly it could be given more reality. But the fundamental interest was to find a road to lasting peace. As one of the smaller powers with essential world interests, Canada could hope for more opportunity to influence the course of affairs through an international organization than through diplomatic channels to other countries individually. Moreover, it was to be based on the group of states which had fought a war to preserve themselves against a domination that would be alien not only because imposed from outside but because its whole conception of the individual was foreign to that held in the democracies. The "peace-loving states" of the Moscow declaration would include, too, all those with which Canada had had the closest relations in the past, and hoped to have in the future.

As in the case of participation in the German settlement, the Canadian government was interested in procedure and structure only as means to the substantive question of function. At the time when the United Nations organization was first under discussion and during the early period of its operation, the government was concerned to find the place for a "middle power" in the association. Recognizing throughout that the great powers, as those carrying the greatest responsibility, must be allowed a correspondingly large voice, the government was not willing to see all the remaining members classed as small powers, subject to the rulings of the four great powers. As the prime minister said to the house of commons in one of the first statements on the subject:

The simple division of the world between great powers and the rest is unreal and even dangerous. The great powers are called by that name simply because they possess great power. The other states of the world possess power—and, therefore, the capacity to use it for the maintenance of peace—in varying degrees ranging from almost zero in the case of the smallest and weakest states up to a military potential not very far behind that of the great powers.

In determining what states should be represented on the Council with the great powers, it is, I believe, necessary to apply the functional idea. . . .[6]

Following the meeting of four of the great powers in Washington in 1944, the Dumbarton Oaks proposals were placed before the general meeting at San Francisco in 1945. A large Canadian delegation played an active, and it was generally thought a useful, part in all aspects of the discussions.[7] Neither then nor later did the Canadian government attempt to solve the problem of the "middle powers" by finding for them a specific constitutional position within the United Nations. Rather it attempted, in particular questions, to adjust the "functional idea" to the charter. Like many other delegations, that of Canada objected to the "veto" provided for the great powers in the security council under the voting formula agreed at Yalta; though it withdrew formal opposition when it became evident that it was a necessary element of the agreement between the great powers on the whole, and when it was promised that the veto would be sparingly used. A practical intervention brought a change in the proposed method for decisions on enforcement. Given the veto, any great power could effectively protect its own freedom of action by blocking a decision on the use of armed forces on behalf of the United Nations. The remaining members, however, were not in such a favourable position. They might not, at the time, even be represented on the security council. To remove—or at least reduce—this anomaly the delegation proposed that any state expected to provide armed forces should participate in the discussions of that question in the council. The idea was incorporated into the charter as article 44.

[6] August 4, 1944. See on this general subject G. deT. Glazebrook, "The Middle Powers in the United Nations System" (*International Organization*, I, June, 1947, 307).

[7] A detailed account is in Department of External Affairs, *Report of the United Nations Conference on International Organization*, Conference series, 1945, no. 2 (Ottawa, 1945).

Even with this modification, the commitments under the charter were considerable, and in certain respects went further than those under the covenant. Circumstances, however, were making for less concern about commitments and more about the solution of particular problems. It has already been suggested that Canada, like the other allies of the second war, came out of it in a mood very different from that of the period which followed the first war. There was a realistic appreciation that preventive action might well be taken at a cost far less than that involved if disputes were allowed to grow into full-scale warfare. For a time there was a comparatively united approach to the problems of the world, which, in sum, added up to the general problem of world peace. As the crack between the eastern and western powers gradually widened into a gulf, the issue before the Canadian government was new, not in kind, but in focus. Instead of the differences in view common to any gatherings of individuals or of states, the government gradually saw itself facing a position in which almost every question of international concern was coloured by a basic political cleavage between east and west. That change did not reduce, it increased, the need for facing responsibilities. Thus the United Nations was at once the mechanism for the collective handling of world problems and the forum for the ever-increasing dispute between one group of powers and another.

It is not intended to attempt here a description of the part played by Canada in the United Nations. The record[8] shows that the Canadian representatives to its various organs expressed views based on continuous study of the various topics arising, formed a part of no voting bloc, and abandoned the formulas too common with Canadian delegates to the League of Nations for more mature attempts at compromise in drafting or by discussion. A brief comparison of the reports of the Canadian delegates to the League with those of the delegates to the United Nations will indicate how far Canada had travelled along the road to nationhood in action.

One of the important developments then, and one not easy to measure—was the growing concern with a great variety of foreign questions, some of them apparently remote from Canadian interests,

[8] The annual reports of the Department of External Affairs on the United Nations show Canadian policy in the general setting. Readers may also consult the official records of the United Nations for detailed accounts.

and all of them in reality close because they all affected the major problems of world order and peace. It was the acceptance of this relationship that, more than anything else, marked the change in Canadian policy after the war. It manifested itself in serious study of, and independent judgment on, the problems that came before the United Nations. Obvious enough to all observers, it still lacked definition as a principle. Furthermore, it awaited an accepted relationship to the corollary: that with interest went a sense of responsibility, and with responsibility commitments. When Canada was elected to the security council for the period 1948-9, the secretary of state for external affairs, in a statement on October 1, 1947, laid down the whole position in unmistakable terms:

Canada's election to the Security Council of the United Nations confronts the Government and people of Canada with new and grave responsibilities. During the years 1948 and 1949, the Government will be faced as never before, with the necessity of making decisions on the major questions affecting the peace and security of the world. Many of these questions will arise from situations having their origins far from our shores. At first glance these might not appear to affect directly the interests of the Canadian people. In so far, however, as these far away events are factors in world security, they are of first importance to the future of this country.

During our tenure of office on the Council we shall be obliged to play our part in trying to settle international disputes many of which are complicated by differences between the Great Powers. One has only to read the front page of any newspaper to-day to realize the magnitude of the job to which we are about to put our hands.

Canada will be one of the eleven states on which will rest the main responsibility for overcoming the obstacles on the road to a just and lasting peace. We shall have to stand up and be counted before the eyes of a hopeful world. . . .

It is now more important than ever that the people of Canada understand the serious obligations and responsibilities which this country accepted when it signed the Charter of the United Nations. Our election to the Security Council brings us face to face with the heaviest of these responsibilities.

No such statement could have been made in the years before the war; no Canadian government would have felt it possible to break so completely the old tradition of caution and of limited liability. It was assumed—and probably rightly—that the Canadian people would not have considered being drawn so far from the cherished belief in physical and diplomatic detachment from the quarrels of the old world. But now the situation had vastly changed, and with that the Canadian view. No longer did the broad seas afford evident safeguards against attacks on Canadian soil. No longer did the peace-loving nations move warily from phrase to phrase, from compromise to compromise. With eyes wide open to the grim possibilities that showed ahead, the democratic states faced a new period of tension almost before the old had gone. For states historically involved in international relations the period between the two great wars had been but one episode in a long series. For Canada it had been the entire background, not of her interest in foreign affairs, but of her participation in them as a principal. Behind that again was for Canada a period of varying degrees of colonial status. Whereas Great Britain had seen the rise and fall of the concert of Europe in its various forms, had herself gone through all stages of isolationism and intervention, Canada had known only one era in international relations before the situation in the late forties. It happened that in that one period little had been done to achieve the ordered society which was said to be its goal, and the challenge of aggression was met only late and on the field of battle.

The answer to the new challenge was as different in Canada as it was in the other western states. Having accepted collective security as a reality the Canadian government now took a leading part in adjusting that principle to the situation as it had developed by the late forties. Not long before Canadian opinion had shied away nervously from any talk of military sanctions. At the beginning of January 1948 the prime minister told an Ottawa audience that,

> So long as Communism remains a menace to the free world, it is vital to the defence of freedom to maintain a preponderance of military strength on the side of freedom, and to ensure that degree of unity among the nations which will ensure that they cannot be defeated and destroyed one by one.

Two months later he spoke in the house of commons on the Brussels Treaty, explaining the government's belief in this type of collective security:

This pact is far more than an alliance of the old kind. It is a partial realization of the idea of collective security by an arrangement made under the Charter of the United Nations. As such, it is a step towards peace, which may well be followed by other similar steps until there is built up an association of all free states which are willing to accept responsibilities of mutual assistance to prevent aggression and preserve peace. . . .

The Canadian Government has been closely following recent developments in the international sphere. The peoples of all free countries may be assured that Canada will play her full part in every movement to give substance to the conception of an effective system of collective security by the development of regional pacts under the Charter of the United Nations.

By the autumn the discussions looking toward a North Atlantic pact were well under way. Speaking on September 21 in Kingston, L. B. Pearson, secretary of state for external affairs, brought together the pieces of the picture:

The Canadian Government has made it clear that it is not only willing, but anxious, to join the other North Atlantic democracies in establishing a regional collective security pact for the North Atlantic. As you know, representatives of the Canadian Government have been participating for over two months now in informal and exploratory discussions in Washington on the problems of security raised in the Vandenberg Resolution. These discussions have taken place between representatives of the United States, the United Kingdom, France, the Benelux countries and Canada. . . .

The Canadian Government has also, since the end of July, had an observer present at the discussions in London of the Military Committee of the Brussels Powers—the United Kingdom, France and Benelux. . . .

The Canadian Government has taken these steps towards the creation of an effective regional security system with, I am sure, the overwhelming support of the people of Canada. The people of Canada have given this support knowing that Canada's participation in such a security system may require that, in an emergency, we share not only our risks but our resources. It would, for instance, be the task of a North Atlantic security system, once it is established, to agree upon a fair allocation of duties among the participating countries, under which each will undertake to do that share of the joint defence and production job that it can do most efficiently. . . .[9]

[9] The three quotations above will be found in *Reference Paper* no. 33, issued by the Department of External Affairs, Oct. 29, 1948.

On Remembrance Day the prime minister, L. S. St. Laurent, denounced in ringing terms the idea of isolationism, and left no doubt that his government was prepared, in the interest of peace, to accept the full obligations involved in the proposed North Atlantic Treaty.

The establishment of international peace and security is the greatest problem we face today. It is Canada's first concern in world affairs. For my part, I believe that the most certain and the most practical approach to security for us is the achievement, as soon as possible, of an alliance of the North Atlantic nations. It is not enough to have right on our side; it is just as important to have the strength to defend the right. The only way to achieve that strength is for us and the other North Atlantic nations to combine our resources. We know only too well where isolationism leads. The last war proved conclusively that isolationism is no guarantee of security. True, one or two small countries were able to maintain their neutrality and yet survive, but we know that was only because of the Allied victory. If the other free nations had not won the war, the few neutral states would soon have come under the Nazi yoke. The choice we face today is a choice between isolationism with its certain weakness, and the hope, through collective action, of preventing another war. I consider it is my duty to make the utmost effort, both within Canada and in our negotiations with the other governments concerned, to have a system of collective security firmly established. We do not want a third world war. Let us all do everything we can to prevent it. . . .

If a third world war should break out, Canada could not be neutral. We are situated right between two great powers, and whether we liked it or not, another world war would be fought at our very gates. It would, moreover, be a conflict not merely between two great powers, but between an atheistic communist world and our democratic Christian civilization.

It is no secret for anyone that the leaders of the Soviet Union aspire to world domination. It is equally clear that they count as much on the weaknesses of the free nations as they do on their own armed strength. By demonstrating to the Soviet Union that the free nations of the world are really taking the measures necessary to defend themselves and to ensure respect for the principles of the Charter, the free nations may well convince the Soviets that it would be impossible for them to win a war if they started one. Now no one is likely to start a war with the prospect of losing it.

What I want particularly to emphasize at this point is that we should build up our strength not for the purpose of waging war, but for the purpose of preventing war. We want to avoid a repetition of the tragedy of a totalitarian power conquering the nations of Europe one by one. It must not become necessary to liberate the nations of Europe a second time. The sufferings of the occupied countries, and the losses of the armies of liberation might well, the next time, be much greater than they were in the last war. The liberation itself would be much more difficult, would take much longer, and would be very much more costly in every way.

Like many of you, I have paid for fire insurance since I first began to own a home. Happily, there has never been a fire in my house, but I feel no regret for having paid the premiums and I shall continue to pay them as long as I own any property. When I ask you to support a North Atlantic Treaty, I am simply asking you to pay an insurance premium which will be far, far less costly than the losses we would face if a new conflagration devastated the world. . . .

Some twenty years earlier a Canadian representative at Geneva had announced the then popular doctrine that Canadians lived in a fire-proof house. It was not Canadians alone who had learned to see the hollowness of that hope. Hardly had the fires of the second war died when the threat of a new one alarmed a world to which peace had become as precarious as it was desirable. As these lines are written the Canadian government, speaking with a new note of firmness and determination, is marching with its old allies of the United Kingdom, Western Europe, and the United States toward a firm agreement for a firm stand against aggression and war.

INDEX